SHONEN JUMP MANGA EDITION

PSYREN

15
SIREN

Story and Art by
Toshiaki Iwashiro

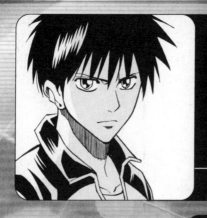

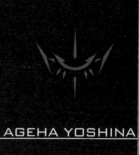

AGEHA YOSHINA

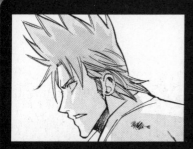

SAKURAKO AMAMIYA

HIRYU ASAGA

OBORO MOCHIZUKI

KABUTO KIRISAKI

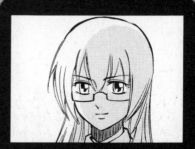

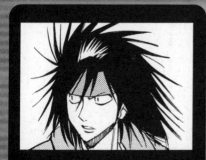

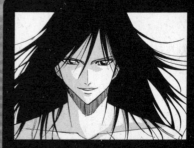

Characters

GRANAR

MATSURI YAGUMO

MIROKU AMAGI

KAGETORA HYODO

Story

THIS IS THE STORY OF A GROUP OF TEENAGERS CAUGHT UP IN A LIFE-OR-DEATH GAME THAT HAS THEM TRAVELING BACK AND FORTH BETWEEN THE PRESENT AND THE FUTURE, IN A DESPERATE BATTLE TO AVERT THE END OF THE WORLD AS THEY KNOW IT.

ON THEIR FIFTH TRIP TO PSYREN, W.I.S.E ATTACKS THE ROOT WITH THEIR SPECIAL FORCES TROUPE, THE SCOURGE. AGEHA AND HIS FRIENDS BATTLE FIERCELY TO PROTECT THEIR COLONY, SLOWLY GAINING THE UPPER HAND. BUT THE TABLES TURN WHEN STAR COMMANDER JUNAS APPEARS. LUCKILY, AGEHA'S FATHER ASUKA SAVES THE DAY, ALONG WITH HIRYU, WHO HAS ALSO SURVIVED IN PSYREN. THE FRIENDS MANAGE TO DRIVE W.I.S.E AWAY, BUT NOT BEFORE MARI, FUBUKI, AND DOZENS OF OTHER ROOT COLONISTS HAVE BEEN TAKEN PRISONER...

VOL. 15
SIREN
CONTENTS

Call.126: Hand in Hand 007

Call.127: The Meaning of Life 027

Call.128: Siren 047

Call.129: The Last Sun 067

Call.130: Fusion 087

Call.131: Turn of the Tide 107

Call.132: Halvsies 127

Call.133: Thanks for Waiting 146

Call.134: Requiem 167

Call.135: Sheep and Wolf 187

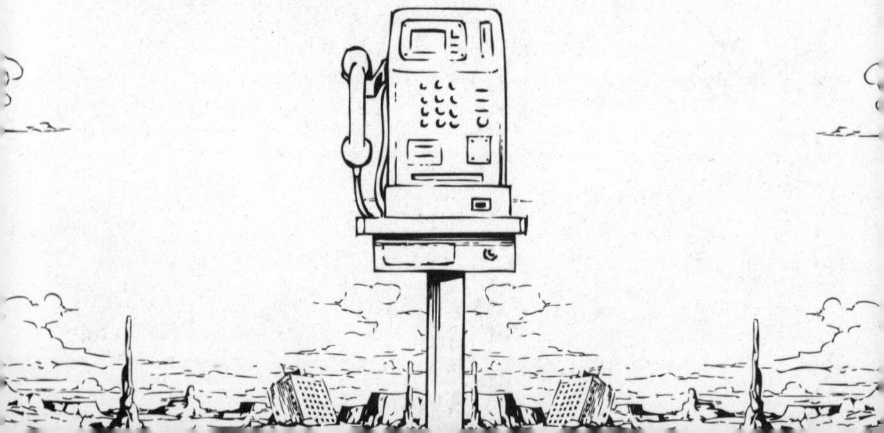

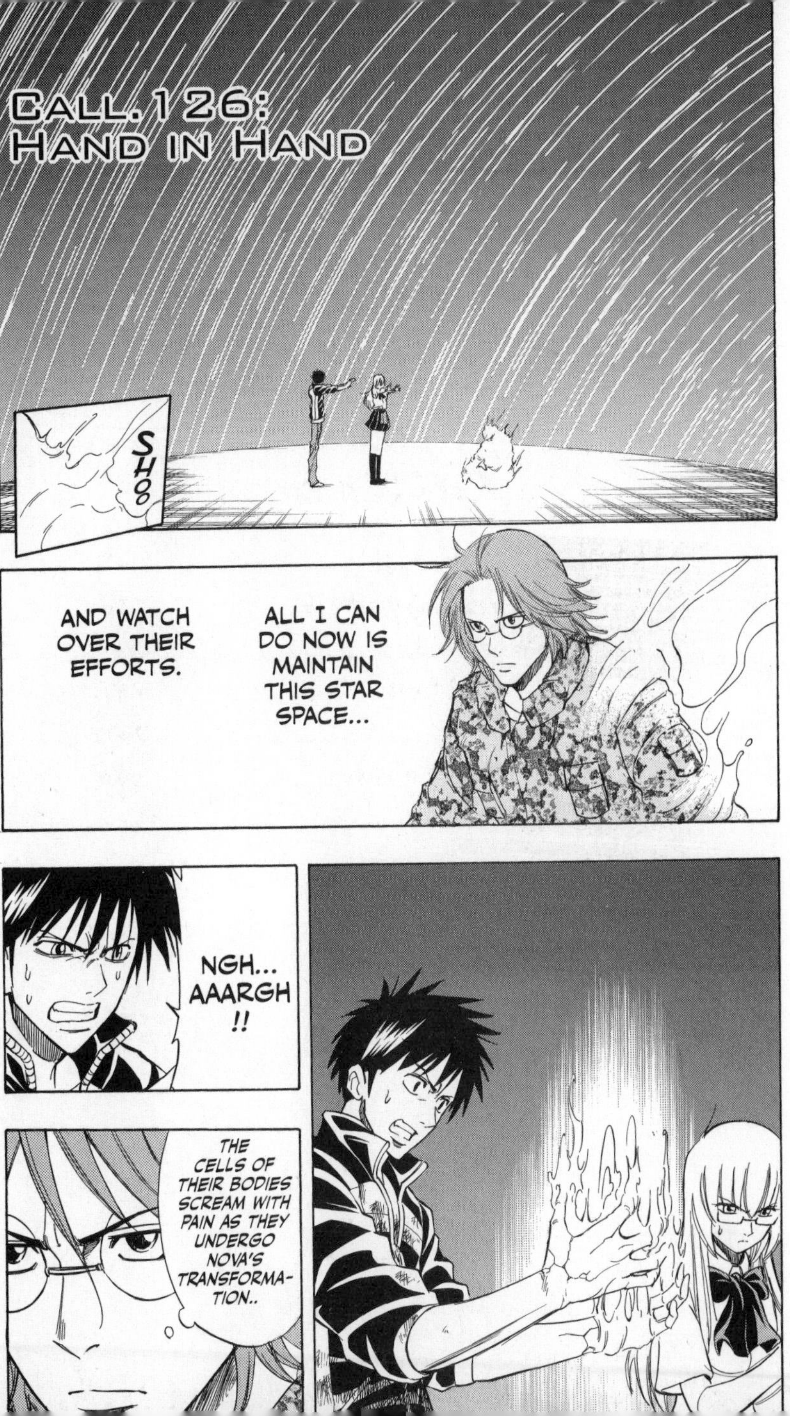
CALL.126:
HAND IN HAND
SHOO
ALL I CAN DO NOW IS MAINTAIN THIS STAR SPACE...
AND WATCH OVER THEIR EFFORTS.
NGH... AAARGH!!
THE CELLS OF THEIR BODIES SCREAM WITH PAIN AS THEY UNDERGO NOVA'S TRANSFORMATION..

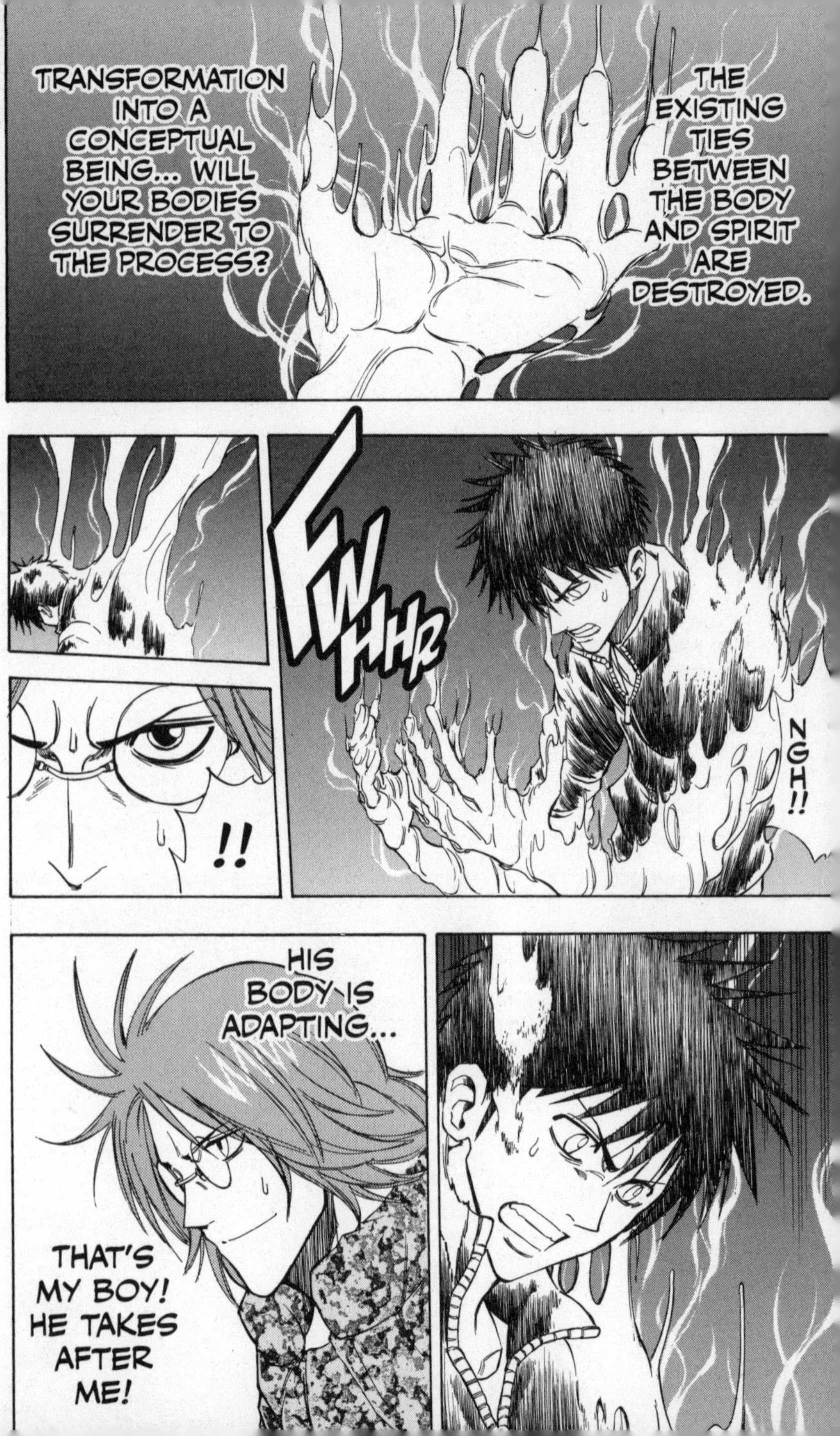
THE EXISTING TIES BETWEEN THE BODY AND SPIRIT ARE DESTROYED.
TRANSFORMATION INTO A CONCEPTUAL BEING... WILL YOUR BODIES SURRENDER TO THE PROCESS?
FWHHR
NGH!!
!!
HIS BODY IS ADAPTING...
THAT'S MY BOY! HE TAKES AFTER ME!

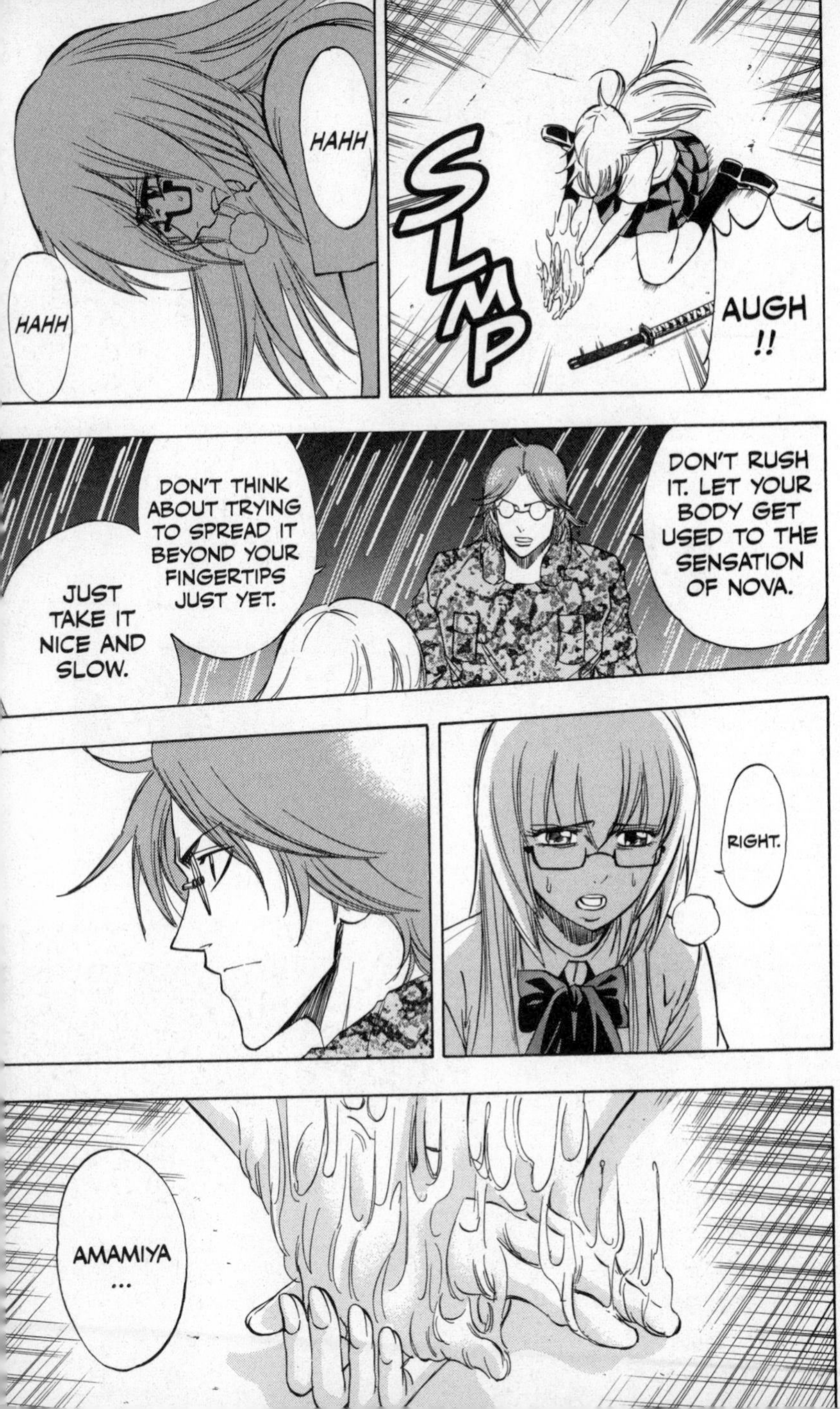
SLMP
AUGH !!
HAHH
HAHH
DON'T RUSH IT. LET YOUR BODY GET USED TO THE SENSATION OF NOVA.
DON'T THINK ABOUT TRYING TO SPREAD IT BEYOND YOUR FINGERTIPS JUST YET.
JUST TAKE IT NICE AND SLOW.
RIGHT.
AMAMIYA ...

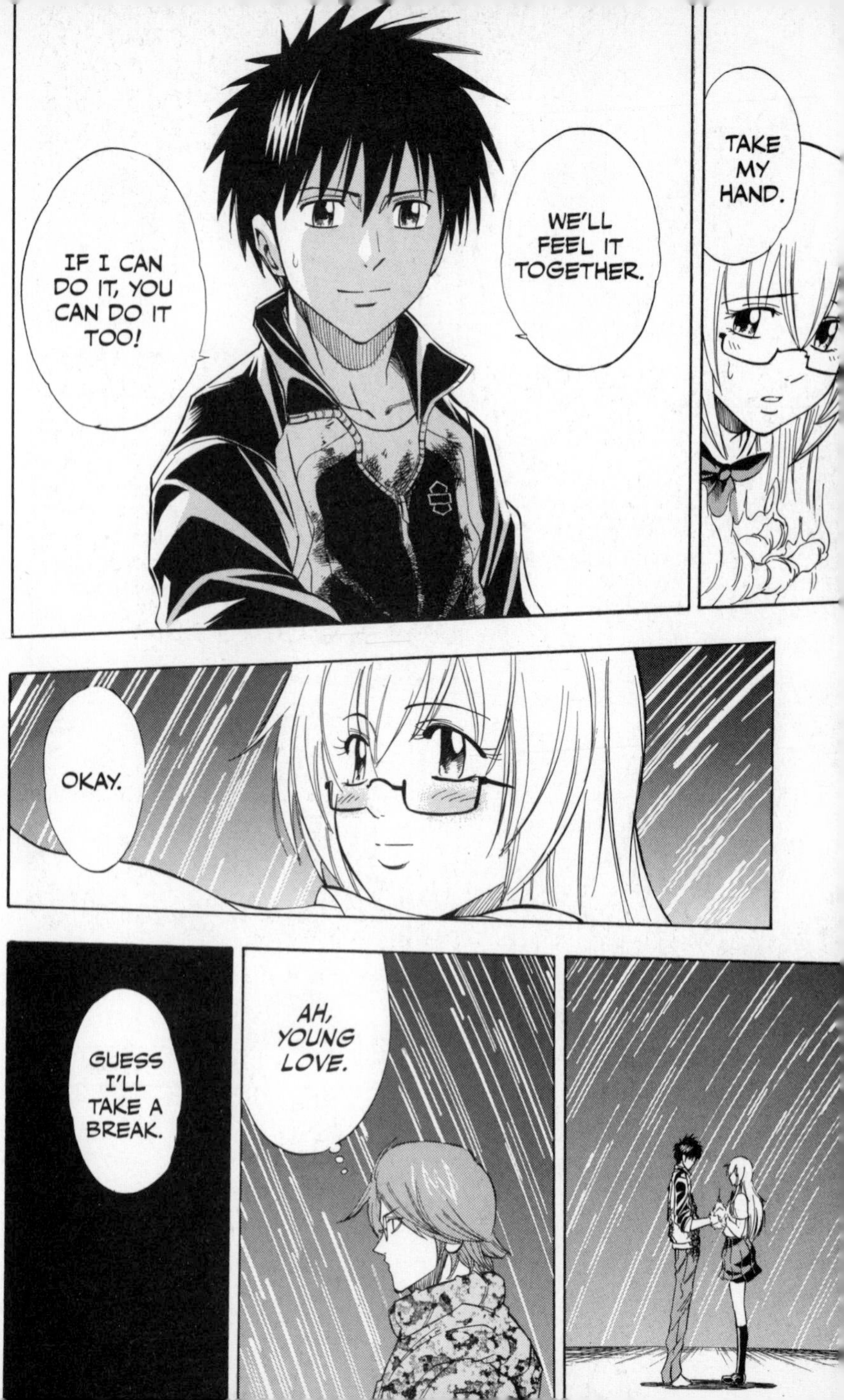
TAKE MY HAND.
WE'LL FEEL IT TOGETHER.
IF I CAN DO IT, YOU CAN DO IT TOO!
OKAY.
AH, YOUNG LOVE.
GUESS I'LL TAKE A BREAK.

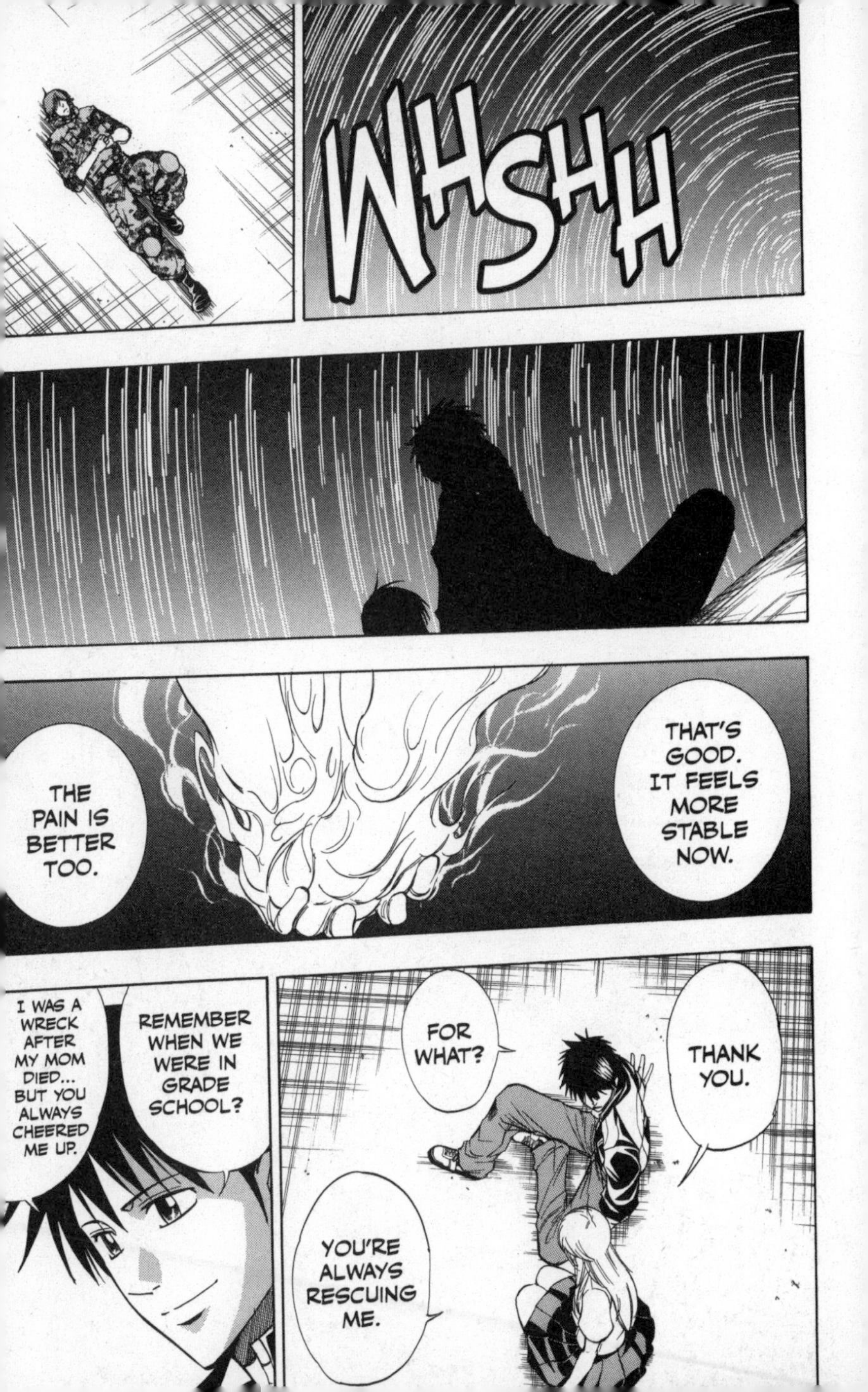
WHSHH
THAT'S GOOD. IT FEELS MORE STABLE NOW.
THE PAIN IS BETTER TOO.
THANK YOU.
FOR WHAT?
YOU'RE ALWAYS RESCUING ME.
REMEMBER WHEN WE WERE IN GRADE SCHOOL?
I WAS A WRECK AFTER MY MOM DIED... BUT YOU ALWAYS CHEERED ME UP.

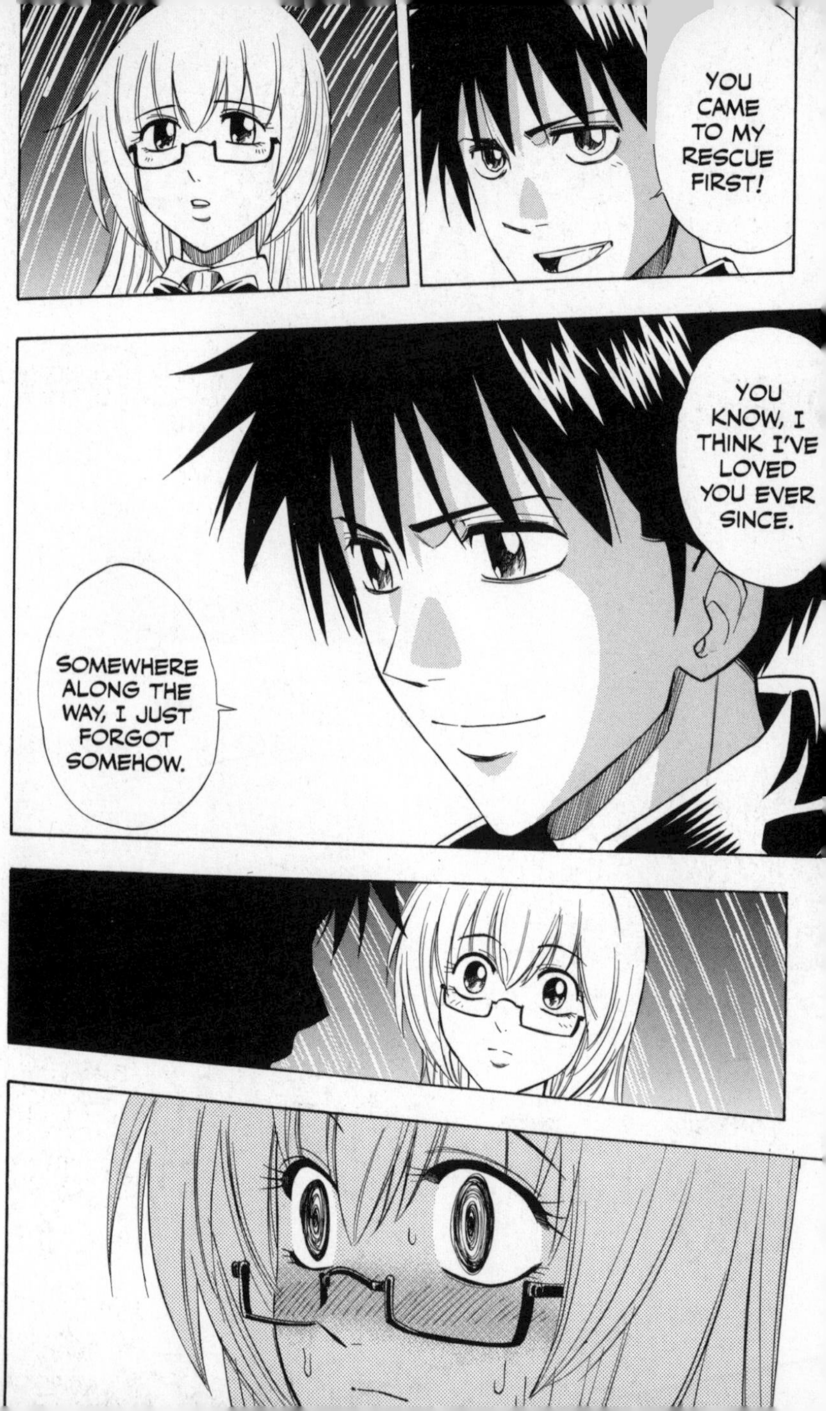
YOU CAME TO MY RESCUE FIRST!
YOU KNOW, I THINK I'VE LOVED YOU EVER SINCE.
SOMEWHERE ALONG THE WAY, I JUST FORGOT SOMEHOW.

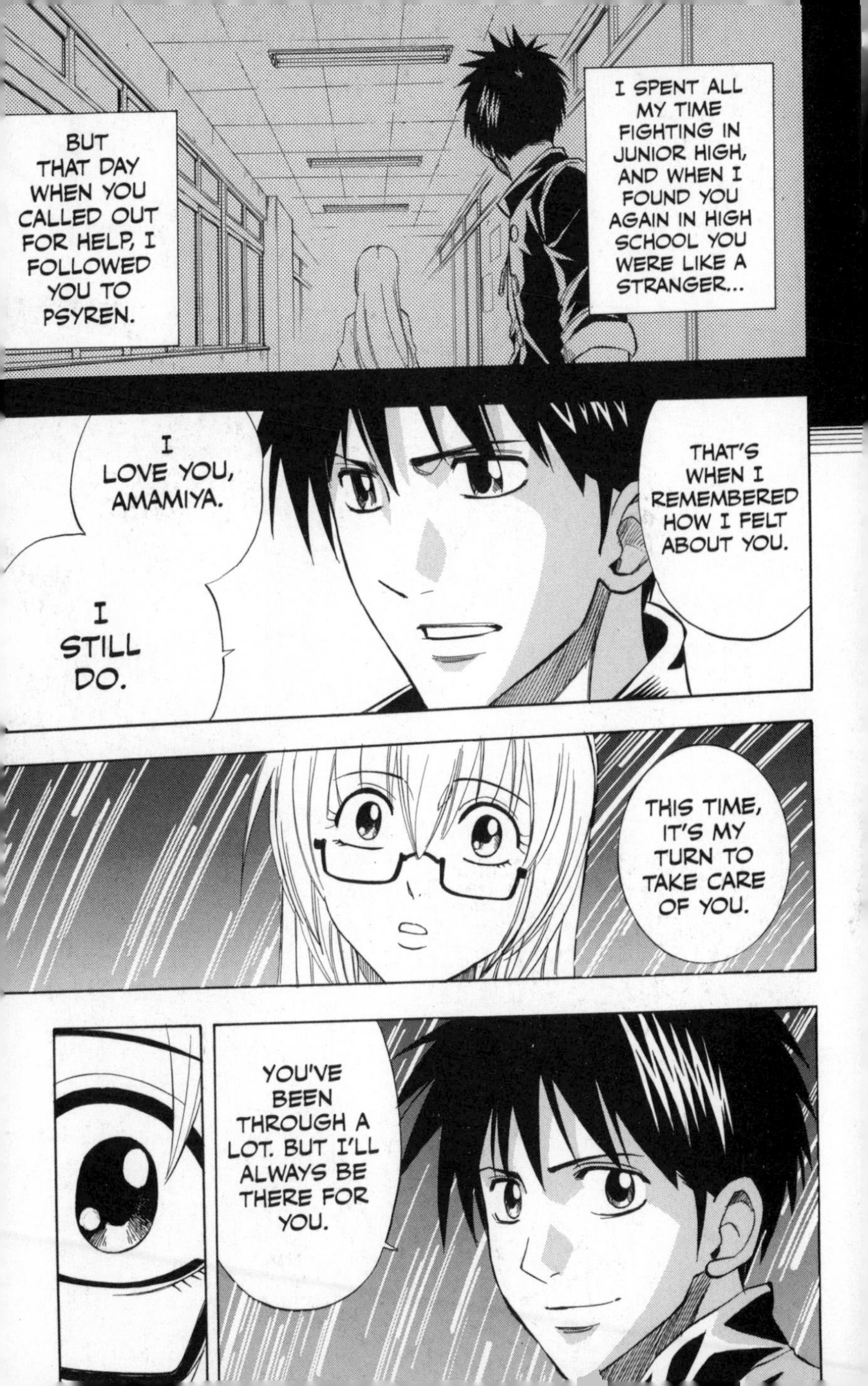
I SPENT ALL MY TIME FIGHTING IN JUNIOR HIGH, AND WHEN I FOUND YOU AGAIN IN HIGH SCHOOL YOU WERE LIKE A STRANGER...
BUT THAT DAY WHEN YOU CALLED OUT FOR HELP, I FOLLOWED YOU TO PSYREN.
THAT'S WHEN I REMEMBERED HOW I FELT ABOUT YOU.
I LOVE YOU, AMAMIYA.
I STILL DO.
THIS TIME, IT'S MY TURN TO TAKE CARE OF YOU.
YOU'VE BEEN THROUGH A LOT. BUT I'LL ALWAYS BE THERE FOR YOU.

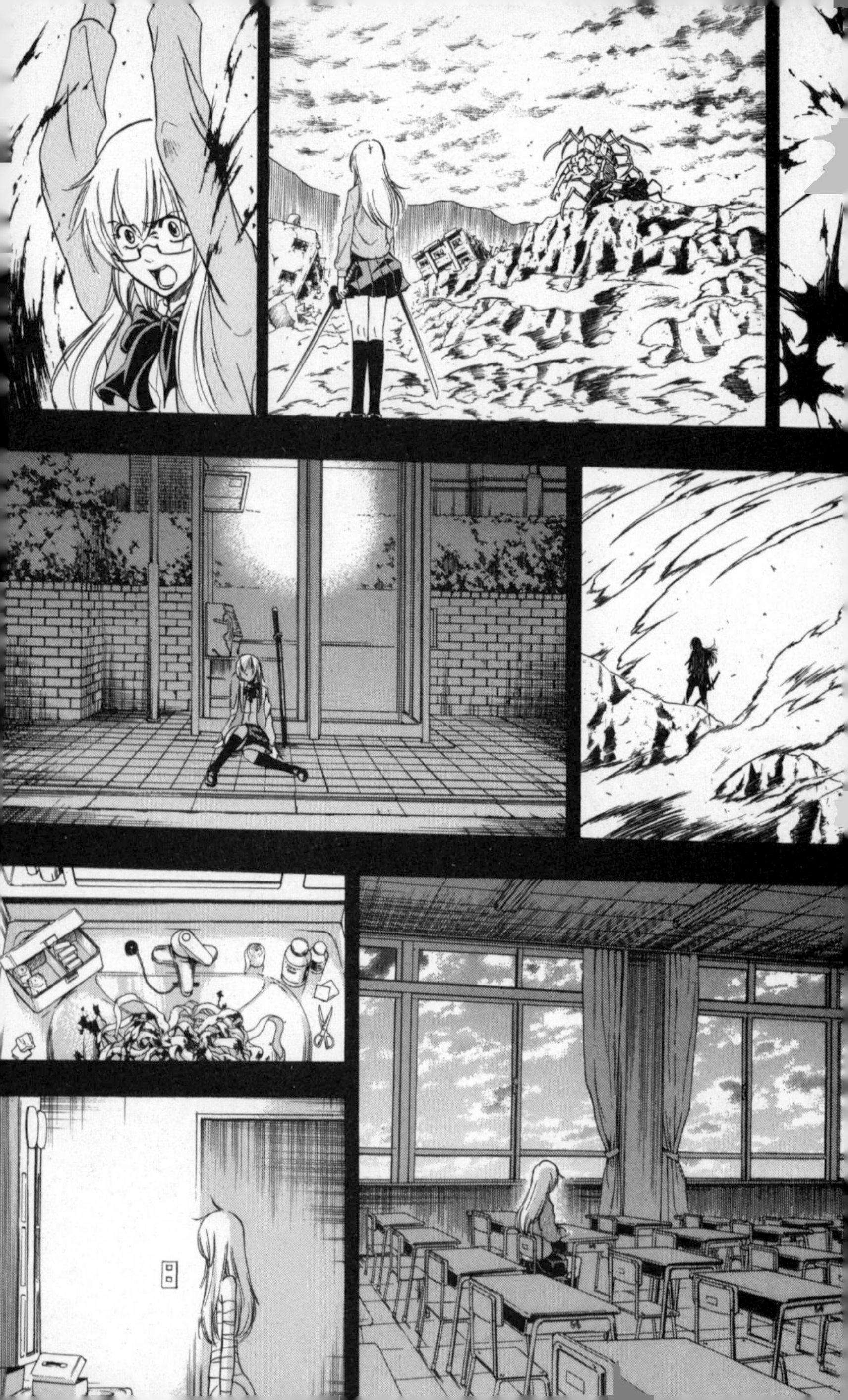

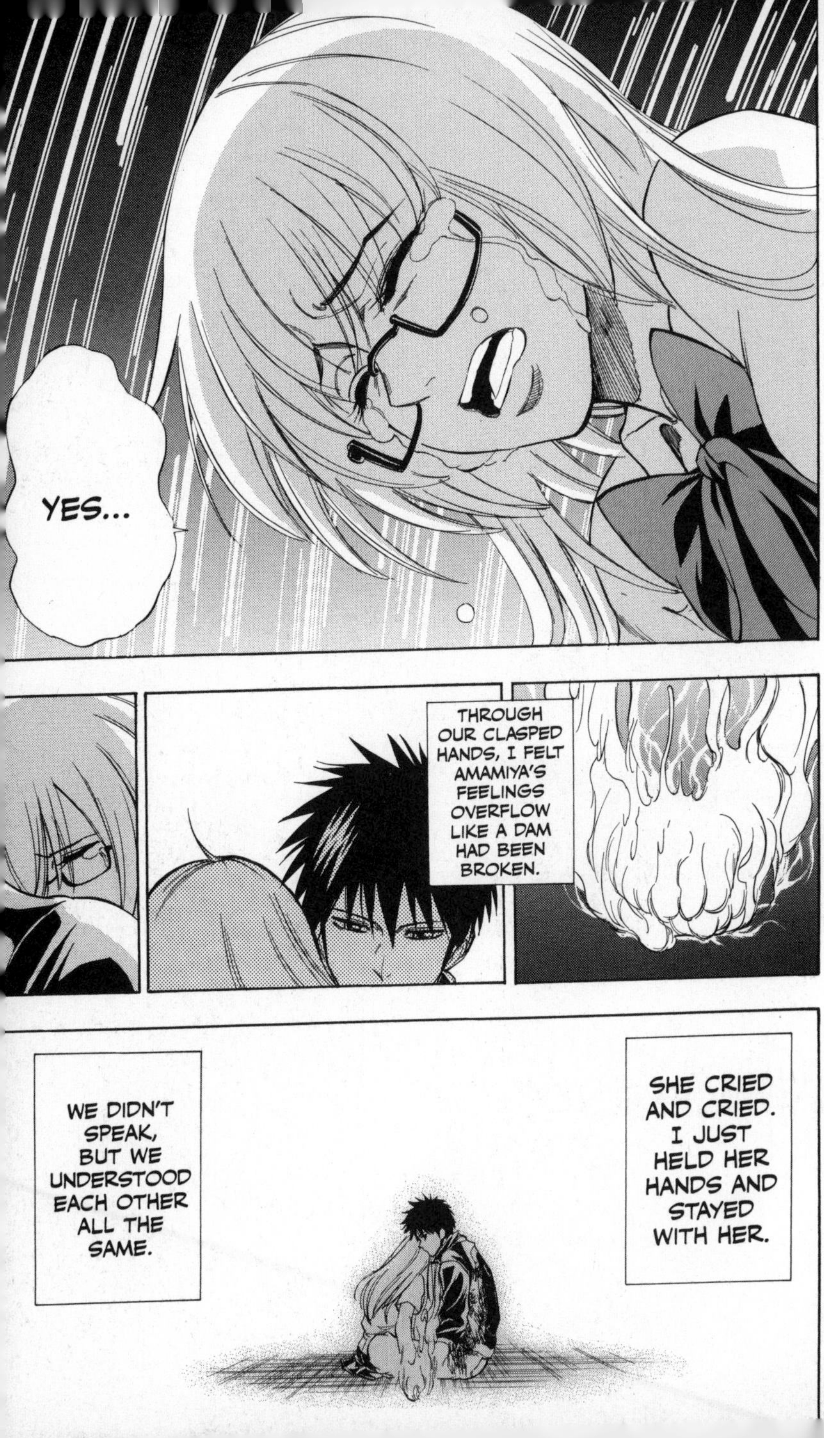
YES...
THROUGH OUR CLASPED HANDS, I FELT AMAMIYA'S FEELINGS OVERFLOW LIKE A DAM HAD BEEN BROKEN.
SHE CRIED AND CRIED. I JUST HELD HER HANDS AND STAYED WITH HER.
WE DIDN'T SPEAK, BUT WE UNDERSTOOD EACH OTHER ALL THE SAME.

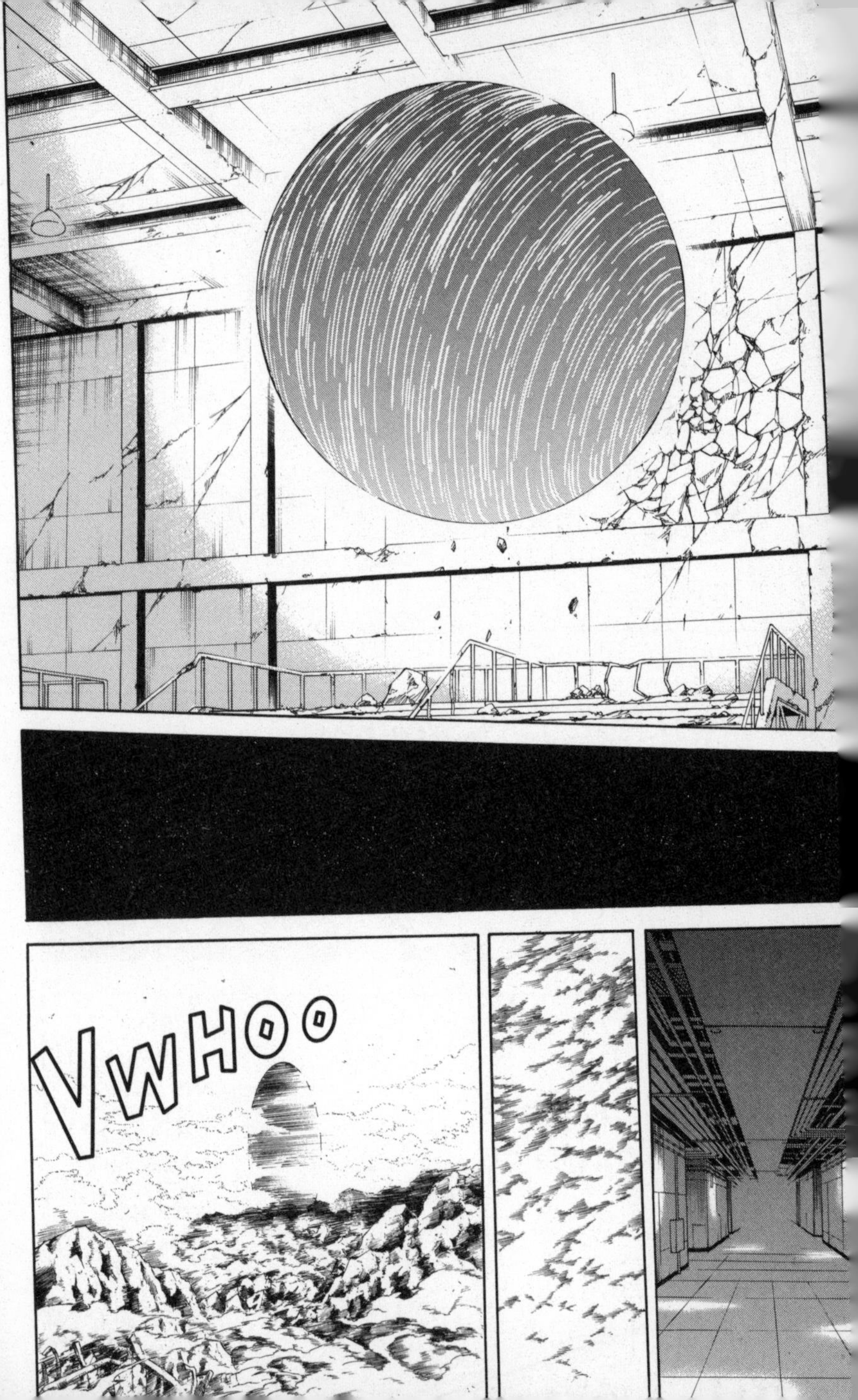
VWHOO

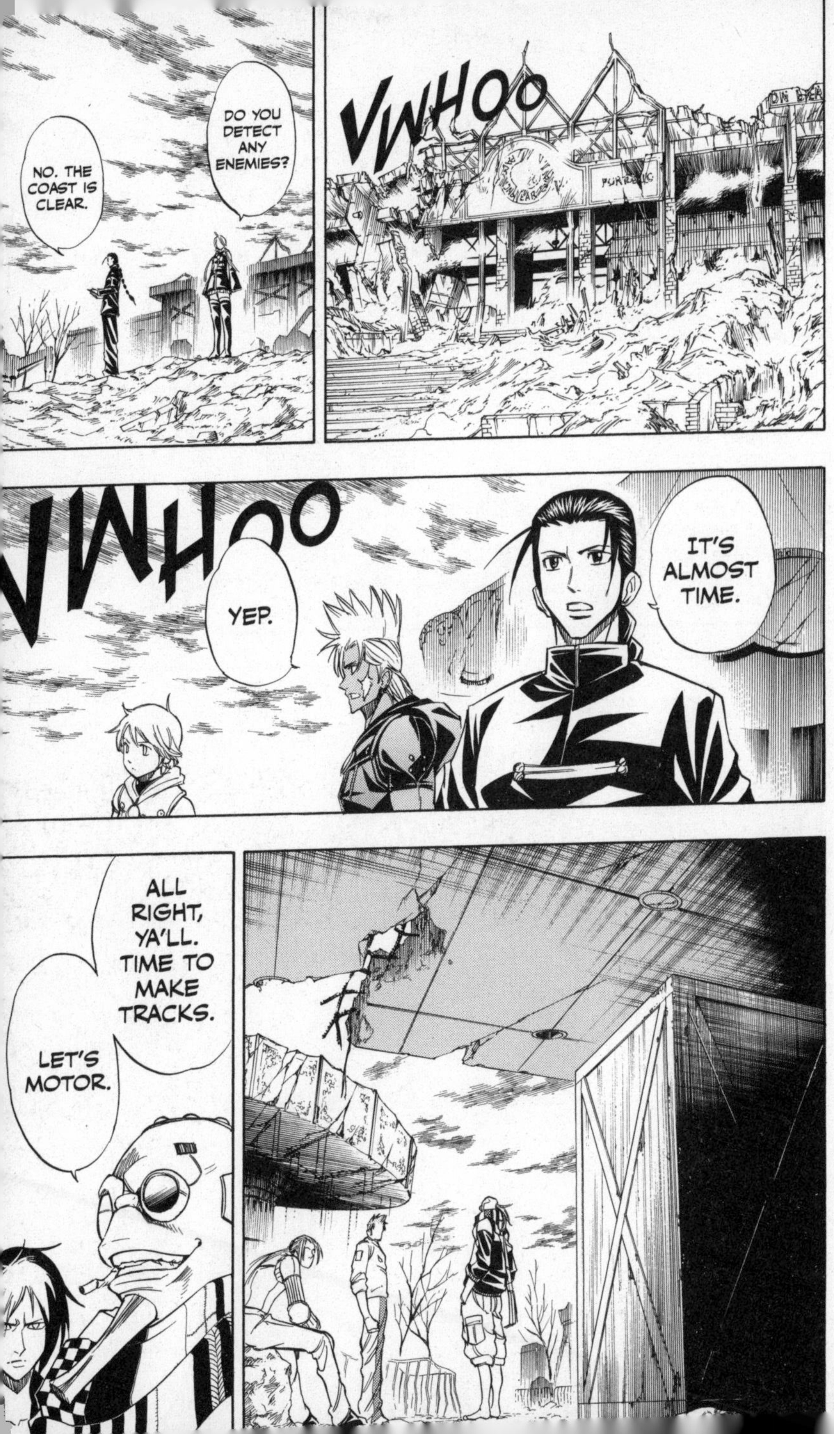
VWHOO
DO YOU DETECT ANY ENEMIES?
NO. THE COAST IS CLEAR.
IT'S ALMOST TIME.
YEP.
VWHOO
ALL RIGHT, YA'LL. TIME TO MAKE TRACKS.
LET'S MOTOR.

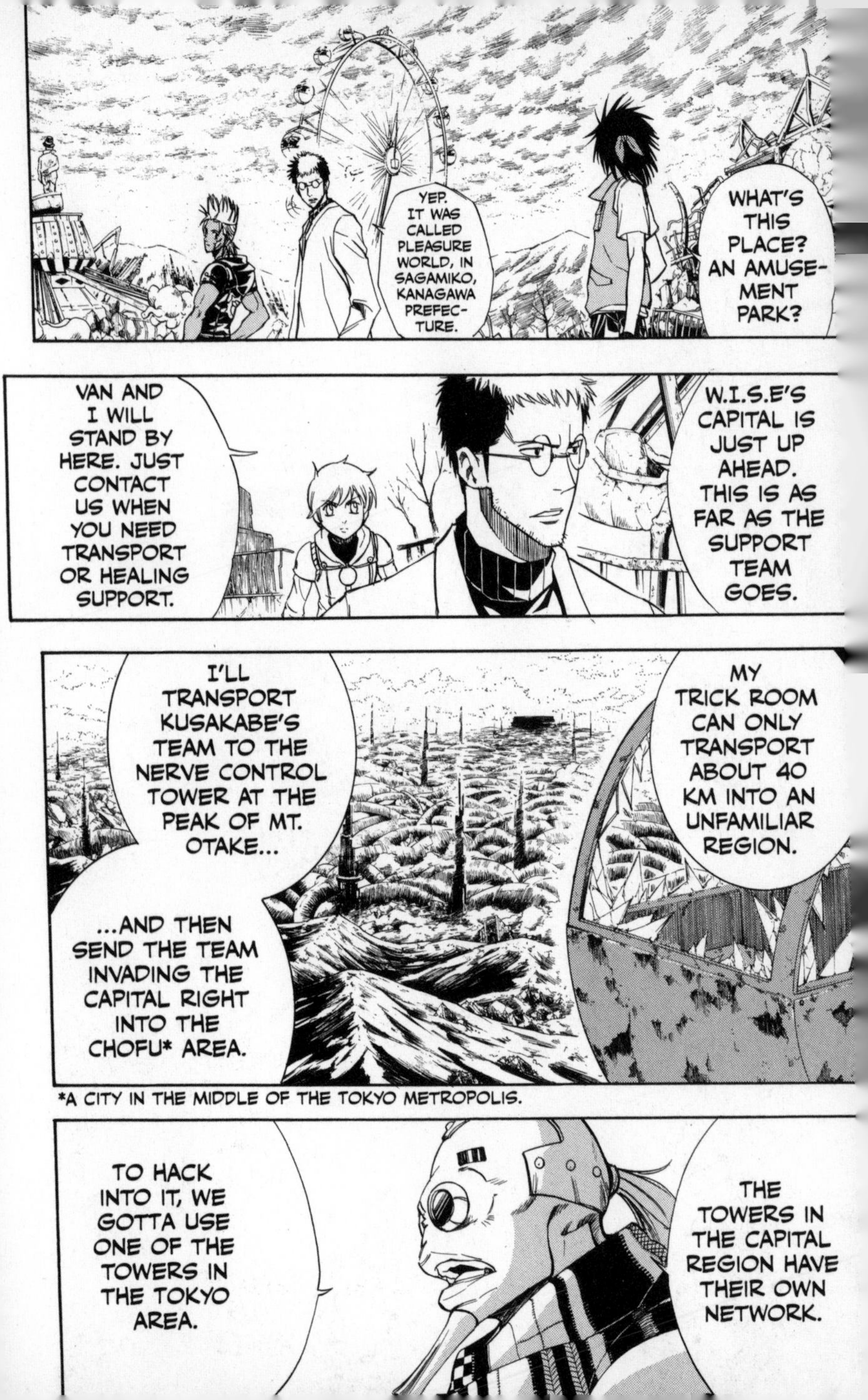
WHAT'S THIS PLACE? AN AMUSEMENT PARK?
YEP. IT WAS CALLED PLEASURE WORLD, IN SAGAMIKO, KANAGAWA PREFECTURE.
W.I.S.E'S CAPITAL IS JUST UP AHEAD. THIS IS AS FAR AS THE SUPPORT TEAM GOES.
VAN AND I WILL STAND BY HERE. JUST CONTACT US WHEN YOU NEED TRANSPORT OR HEALING SUPPORT.
MY TRICK ROOM CAN ONLY TRANSPORT ABOUT 40 KM INTO AN UNFAMILIAR REGION.
I'LL TRANSPORT KUSAKABE'S TEAM TO THE NERVE CONTROL TOWER AT THE PEAK OF MT. OTAKE...
...AND THEN SEND THE TEAM INVADING THE CAPITAL RIGHT INTO THE CHOFU* AREA.
THE TOWERS IN THE CAPITAL REGION HAVE THEIR OWN NETWORK.
TO HACK INTO IT, WE GOTTA USE ONE OF THE TOWERS IN THE TOKYO AREA.

*A CITY IN THE MIDDLE OF THE TOKYO METROPOLIS.

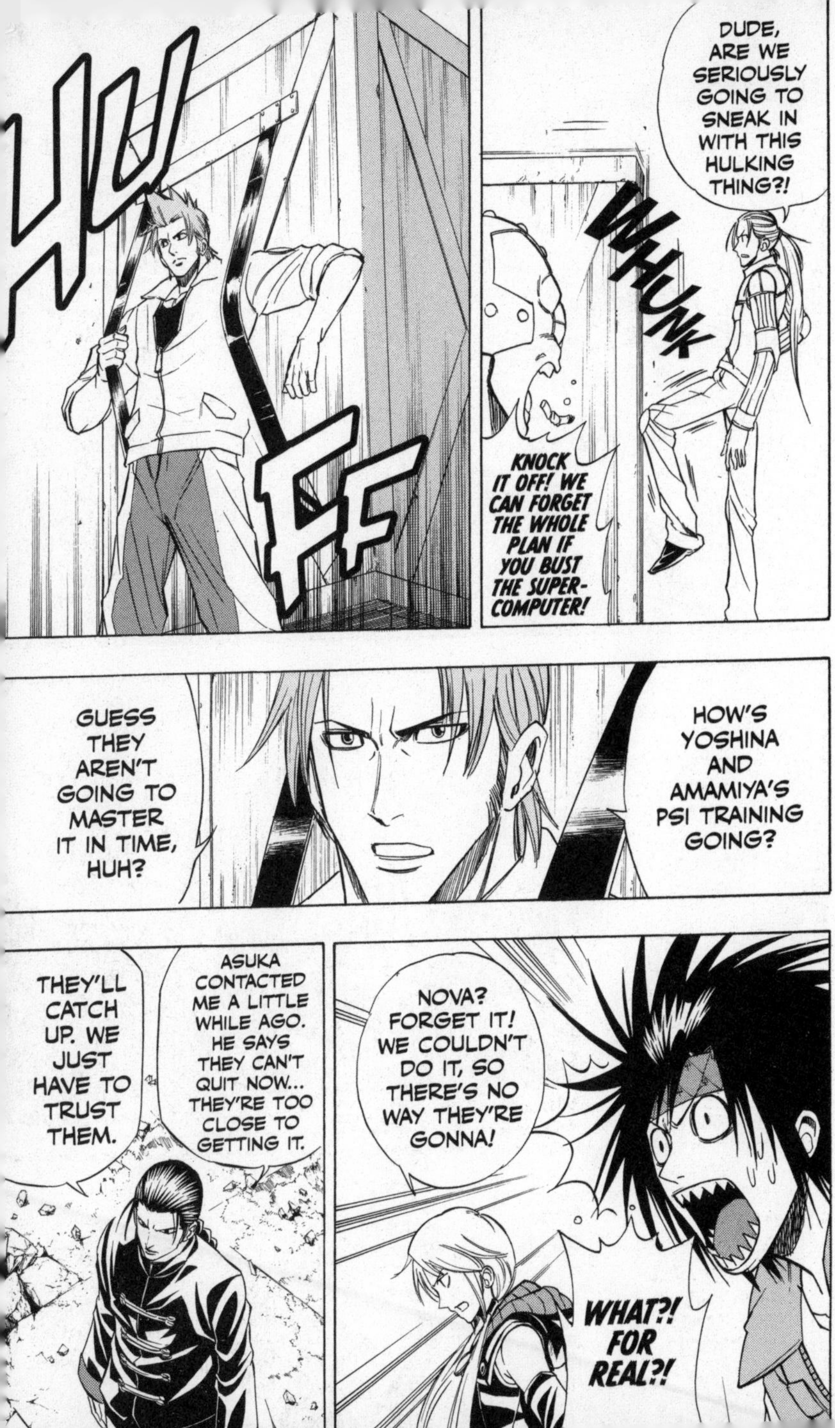
DUDE, ARE WE SERIOUSLY GOING TO SNEAK IN WITH THIS HULKING THING?!
WHUNK
KNOCK IT OFF! WE CAN FORGET THE WHOLE PLAN IF YOU BUST THE SUPER-COMPUTER!
HU
FF
HOW'S YOSHINA AND AMAMIYA'S PSI TRAINING GOING?
GUESS THEY AREN'T GOING TO MASTER IT IN TIME, HUH?
NOVA? FORGET IT! WE COULDN'T DO IT, SO THERE'S NO WAY THEY'RE GONNA!
WHAT?! FOR REAL?!
ASUKA CONTACTED ME A LITTLE WHILE AGO. HE SAYS THEY CAN'T QUIT NOW... THEY'RE TOO CLOSE TO GETTING IT.
THEY'LL CATCH UP. WE JUST HAVE TO TRUST THEM.

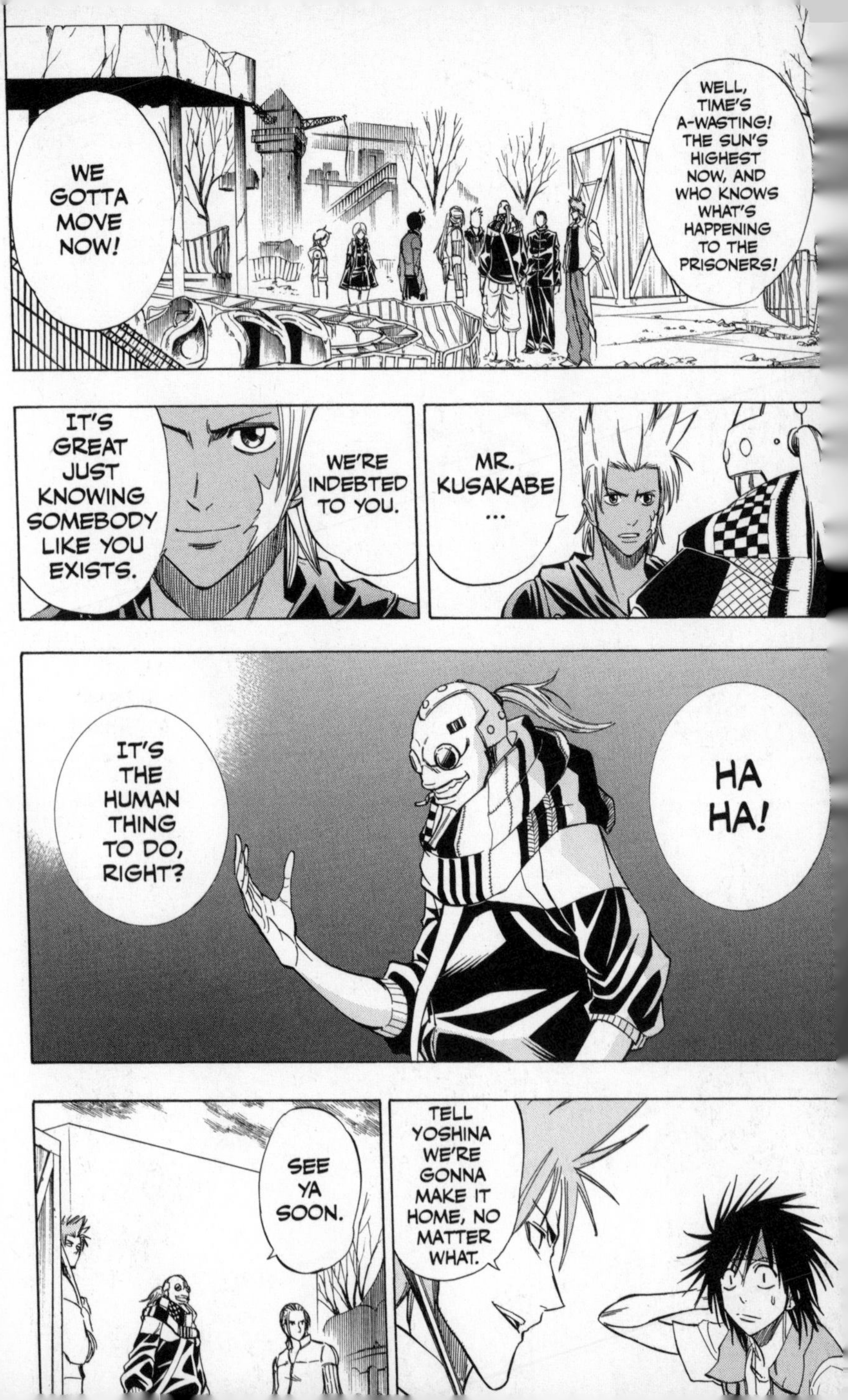
WELL, TIME'S A-WASTING! THE SUN'S HIGHEST NOW, AND WHO KNOWS WHAT'S HAPPENING TO THE PRISONERS!
WE GOTTA MOVE NOW!
MR. KUSAKABE ...
WE'RE INDEBTED TO YOU.
IT'S GREAT JUST KNOWING SOMEBODY LIKE YOU EXISTS.
HA HA!
IT'S THE HUMAN THING TO DO, RIGHT?
TELL YOSHINA WE'RE GONNA MAKE IT HOME, NO MATTER WHAT.
SEE YA SOON.

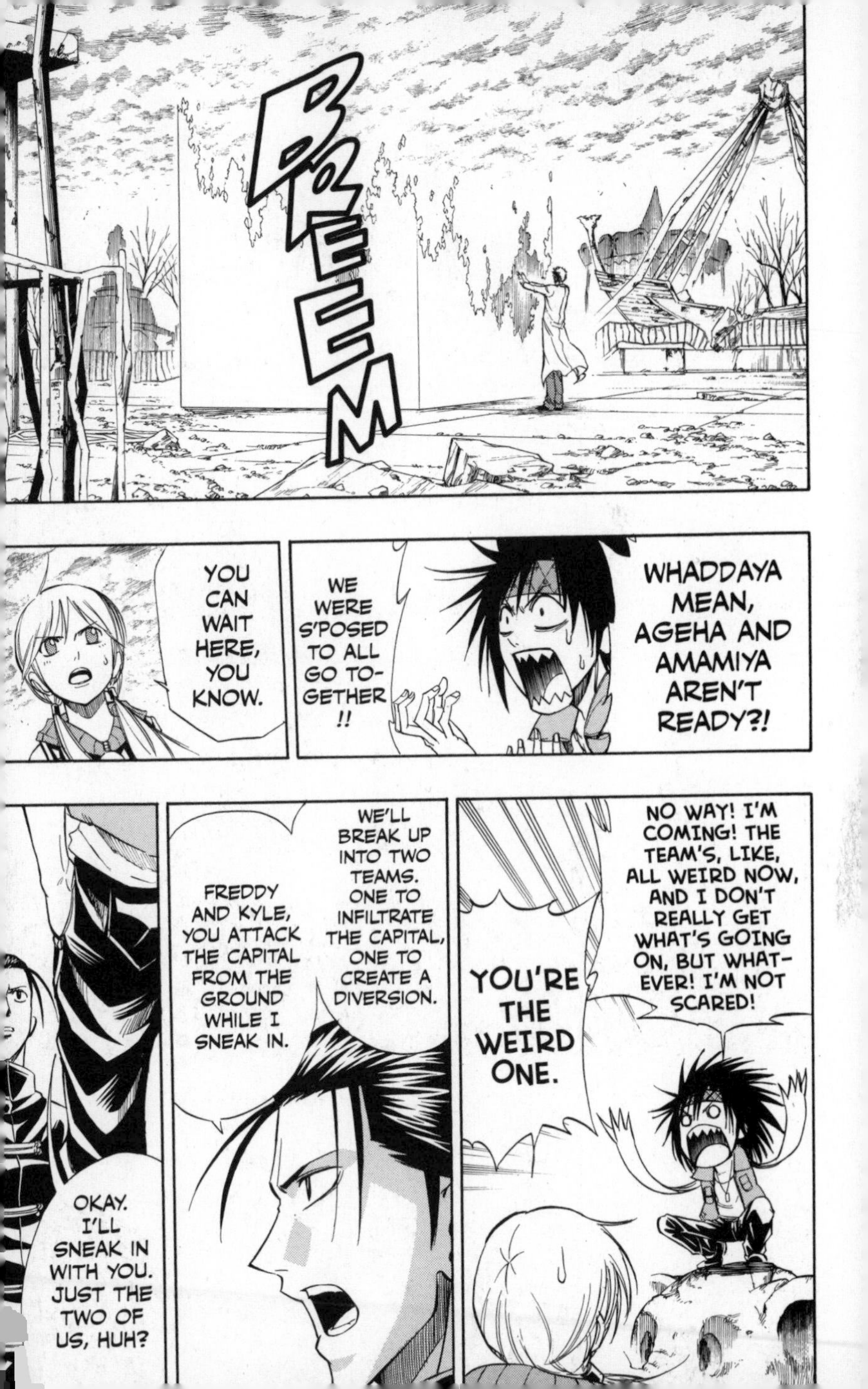
BREEM
WHADDAYA MEAN, AGEHA AND AMAMIYA AREN'T READY?!
WE WERE S'POSED TO ALL GO TO-GETHER !!
YOU CAN WAIT HERE, YOU KNOW.
NO WAY! I'M COMING! THE TEAM'S, LIKE, ALL WEIRD NOW, AND I DON'T REALLY GET WHAT'S GOING ON, BUT WHAT-EVER! I'M NOT SCARED!
YOU'RE THE WEIRD ONE.
WE'LL BREAK UP INTO TWO TEAMS. ONE TO INFILTRATE THE CAPITAL, ONE TO CREATE A DIVERSION.
FREDDY AND KYLE, YOU ATTACK THE CAPITAL FROM THE GROUND WHILE I SNEAK IN.
OKAY. I'LL SNEAK IN WITH YOU. JUST THE TWO OF US, HUH?

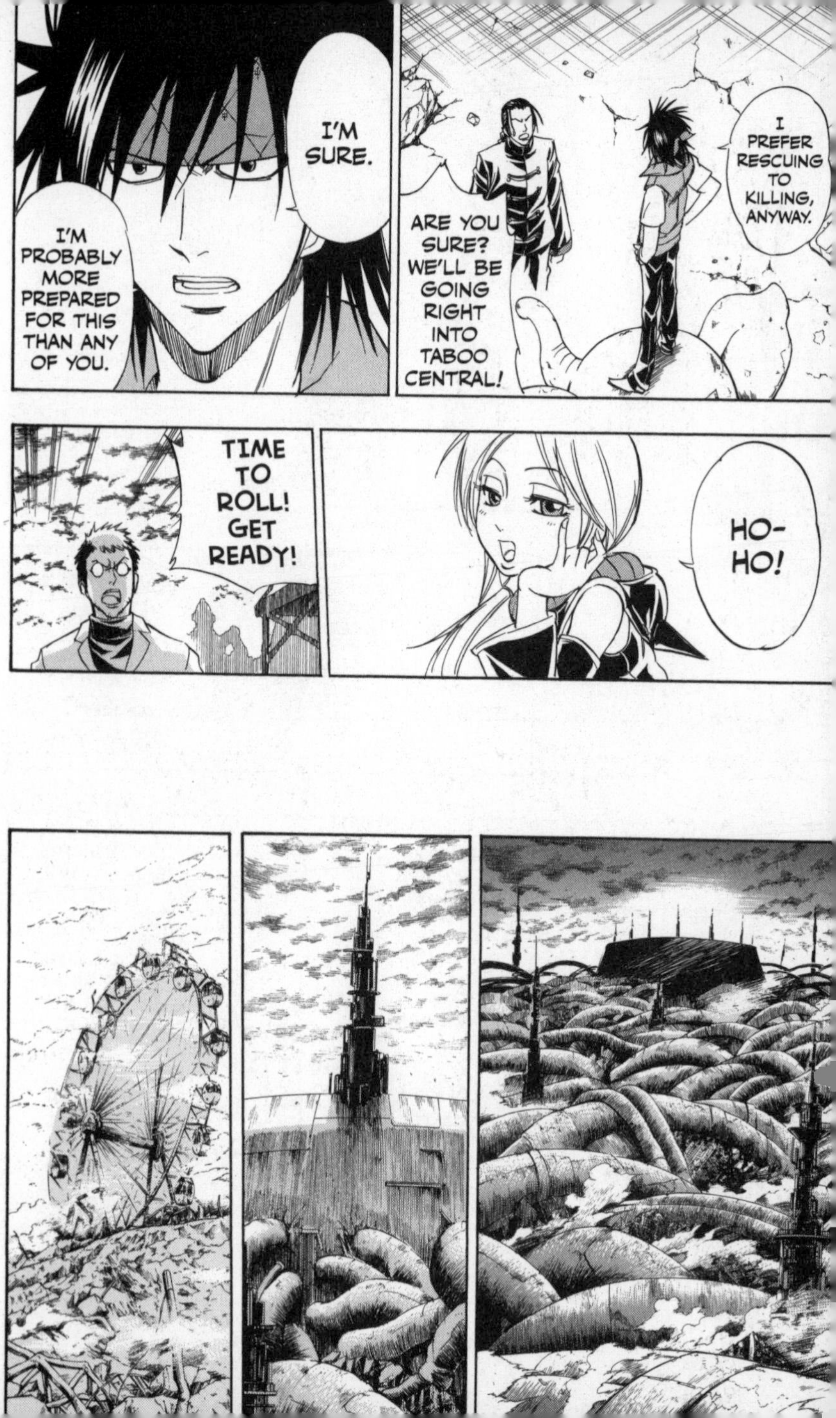
I PREFER RESCUING TO KILLING, ANYWAY.
ARE YOU SURE? WE'LL BE GOING RIGHT INTO TABOO CENTRAL!
I'M SURE.
I'M PROBABLY MORE PREPARED FOR THIS THAN ANY OF YOU.
HO-HO!
TIME TO ROLL! GET READY!

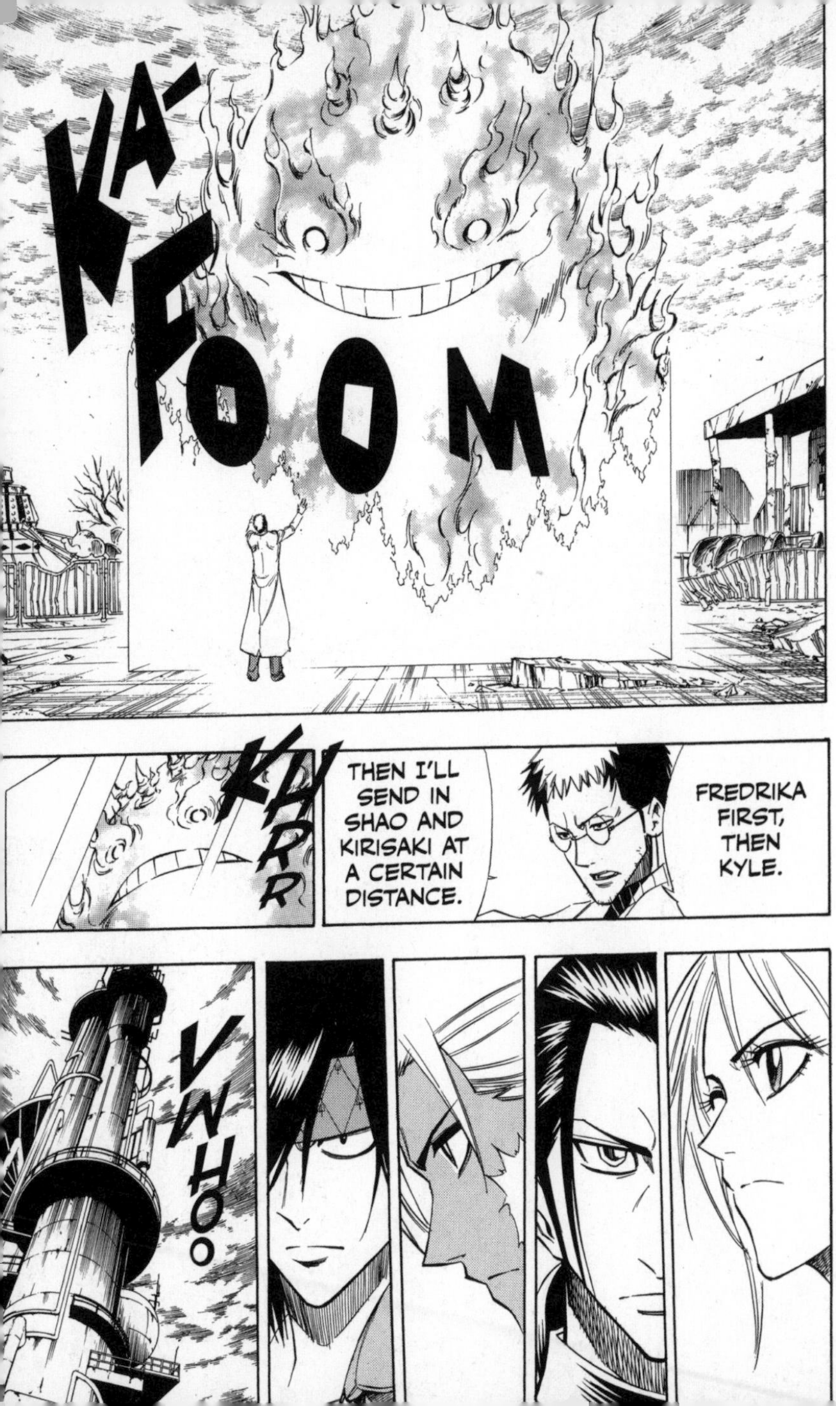
KA-FOOM
FREDRIKA FIRST, THEN KYLE.
THEN I'LL SEND IN SHAO AND KIRISAKI AT A CERTAIN DISTANCE.
KHRRR
VWHOOO

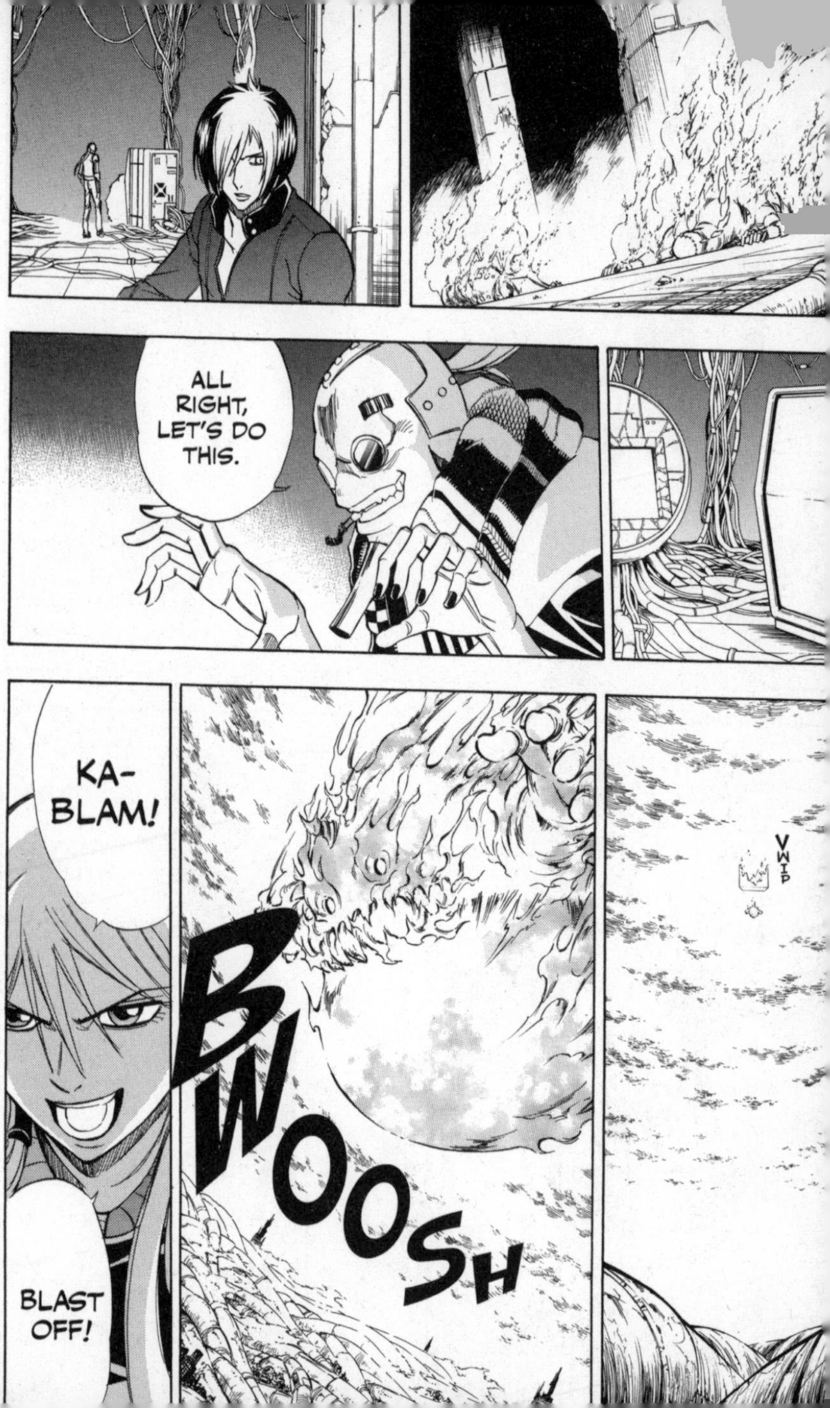
ALL RIGHT, LET'S DO THIS.
VWIP
BWOOSH
KA-BLAM!
BLAST OFF!

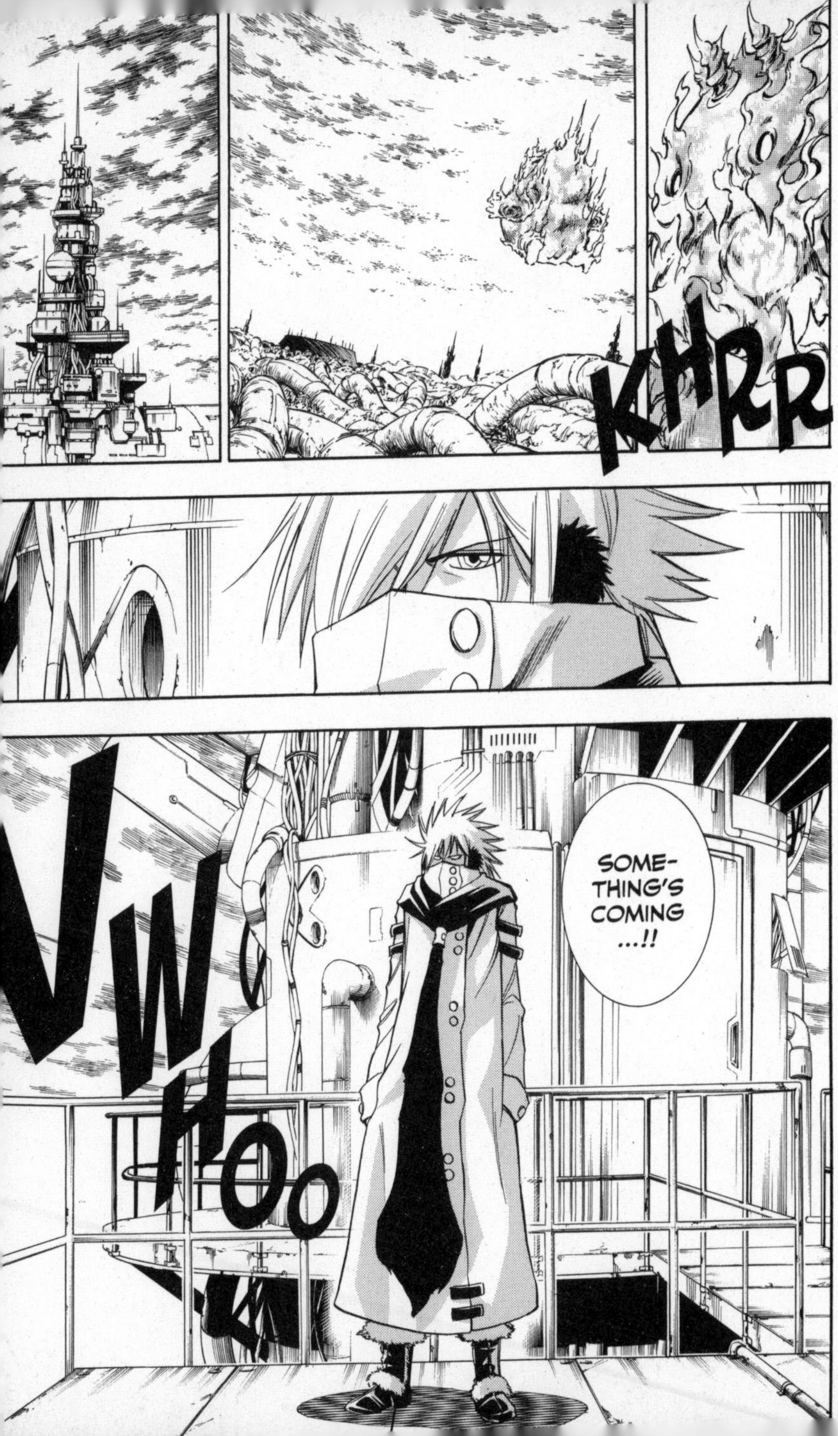
KHRR
SOME-THING'S COMING ...!!
VWHOO

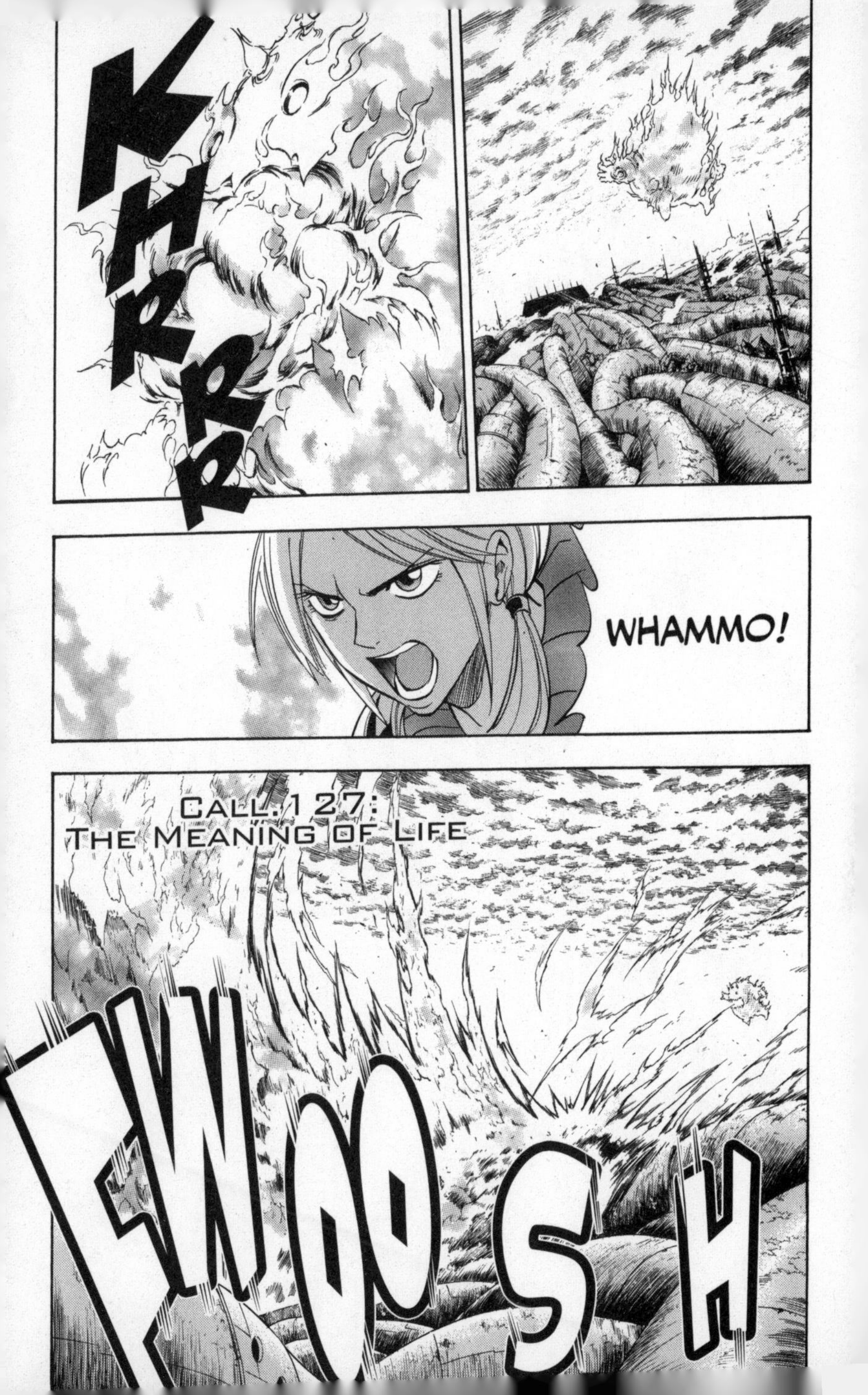
KHRRR
WHAMMO!
CALL 127:
THE MEANING OF LIFE
FWOOSH

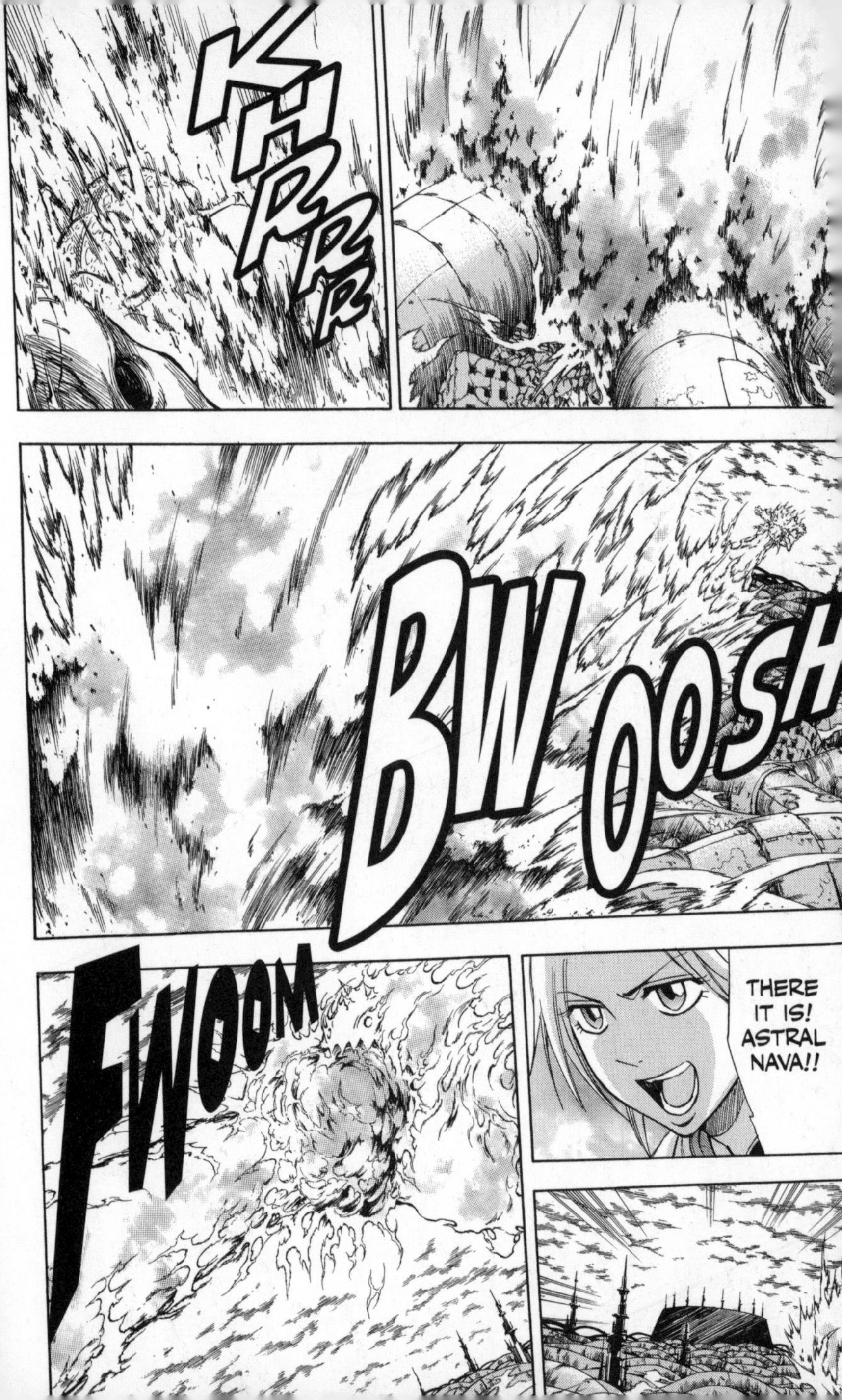
KHRRR
BWOOSH
THERE IT IS! ASTRAL NAVA!!
FWOOM

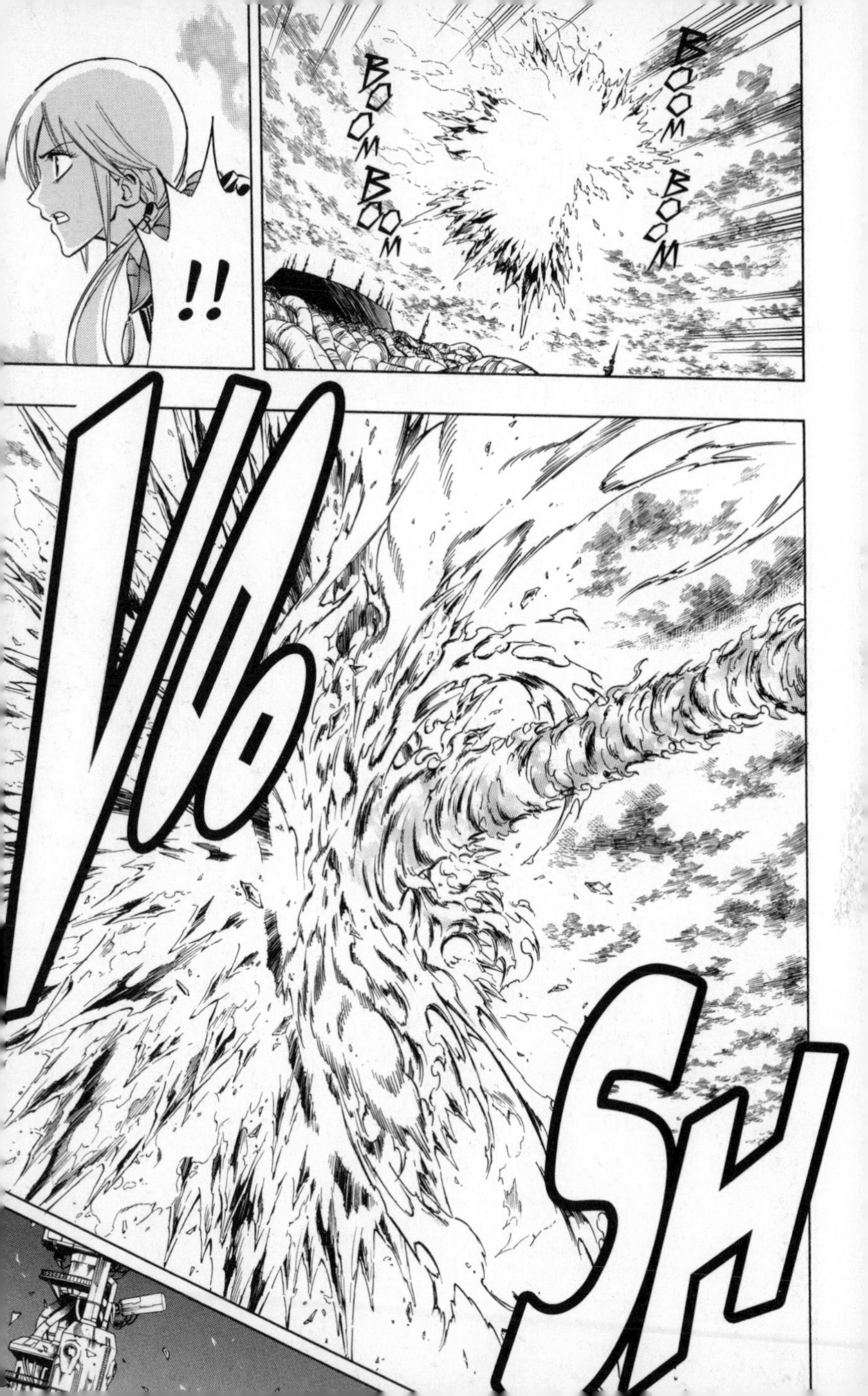
BOOM BOOM
BOOM BOOM
!!
VWO
SH

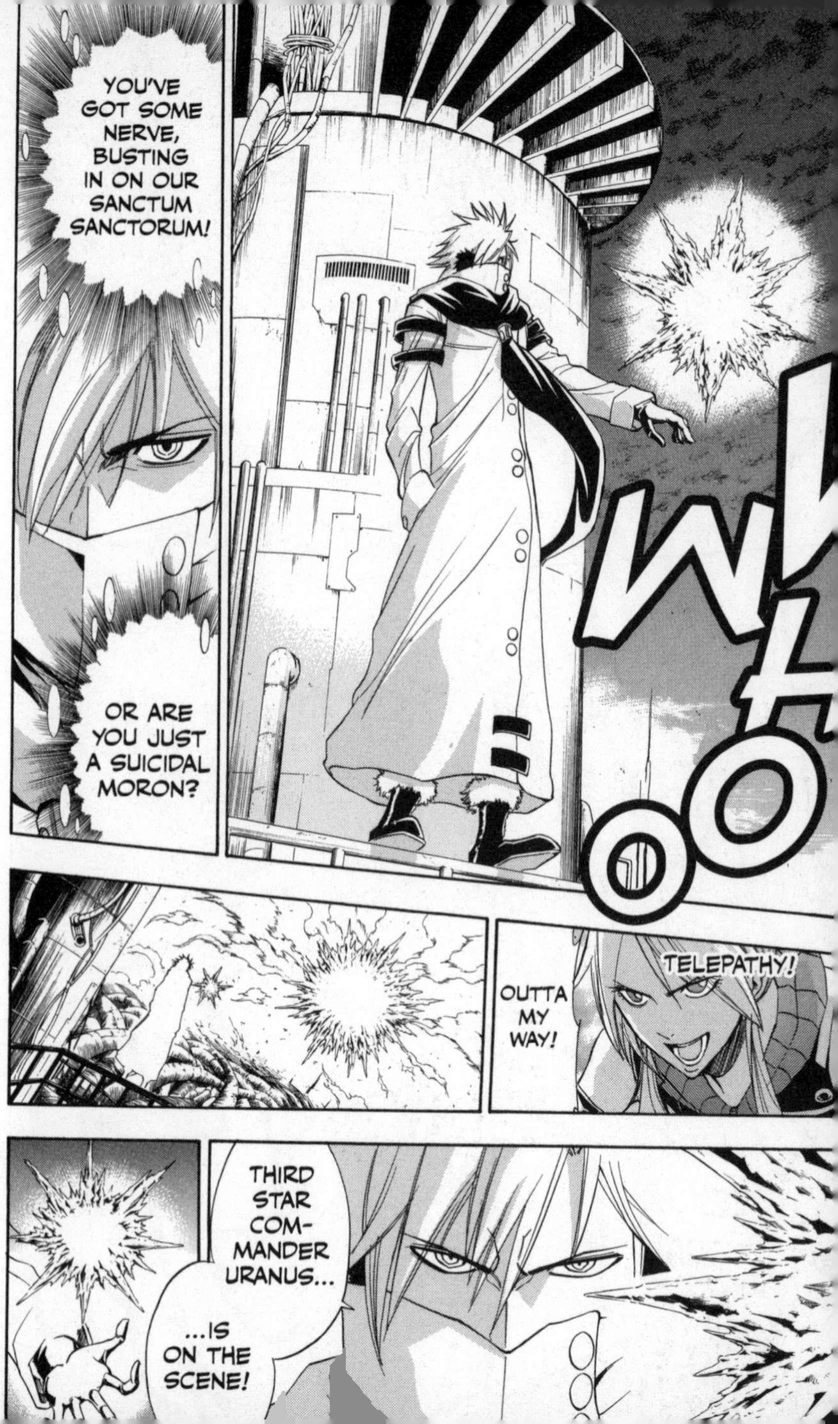
YOU'VE GOT SOME NERVE, BUSTING IN ON OUR SANCTUM SANCTORUM!
OR ARE YOU JUST A SUICIDAL MORON?
TELEPATHY!
OUTTA MY WAY!
THIRD STAR COM-MANDER URANUS...
...IS ON THE SCENE!

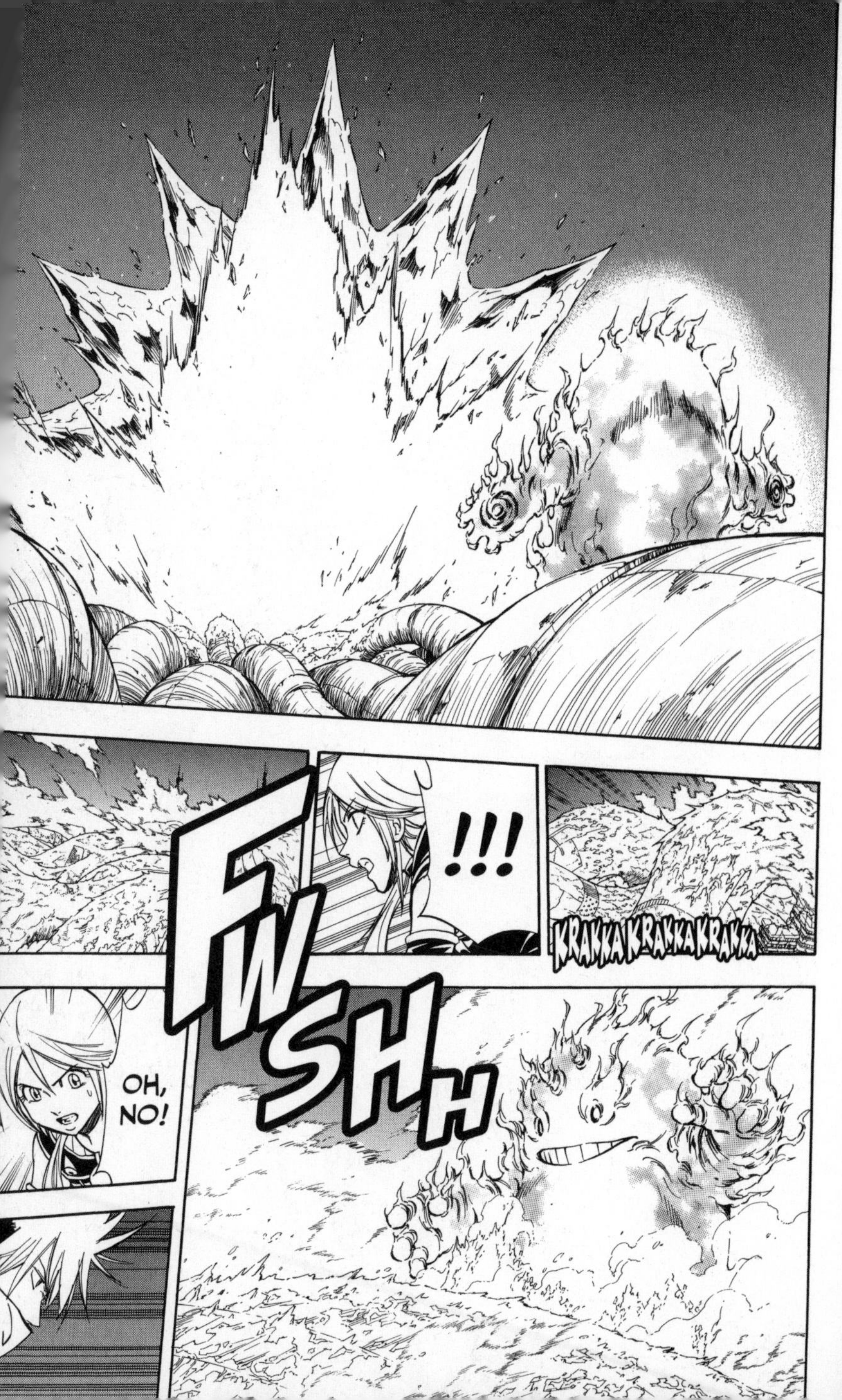
KRAKKA KRAKKA KRAKKA
!!!
FWSHH
OH, NO!

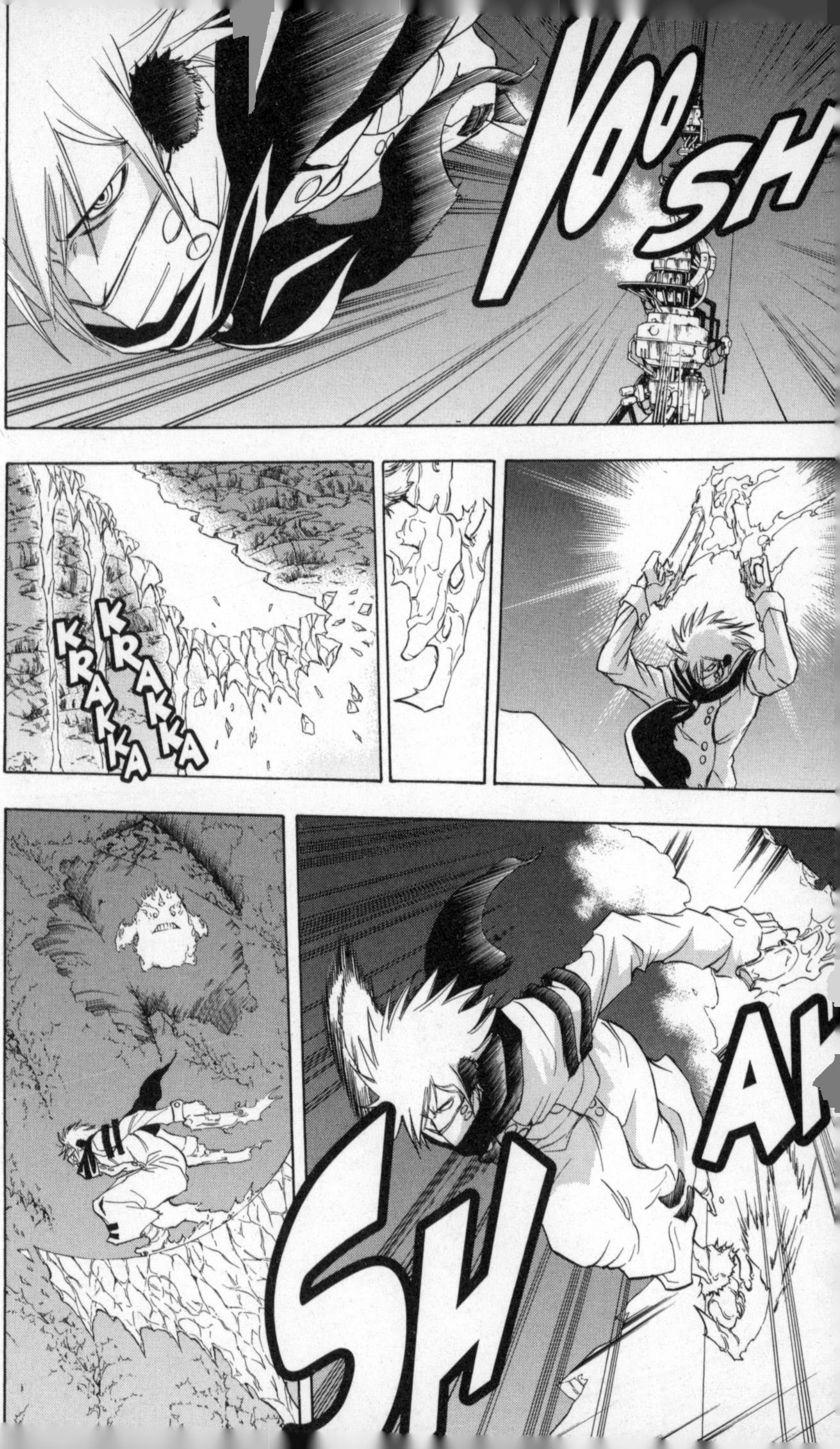
VOOOSH
KRAKKA
KRAKKA
SH
AK

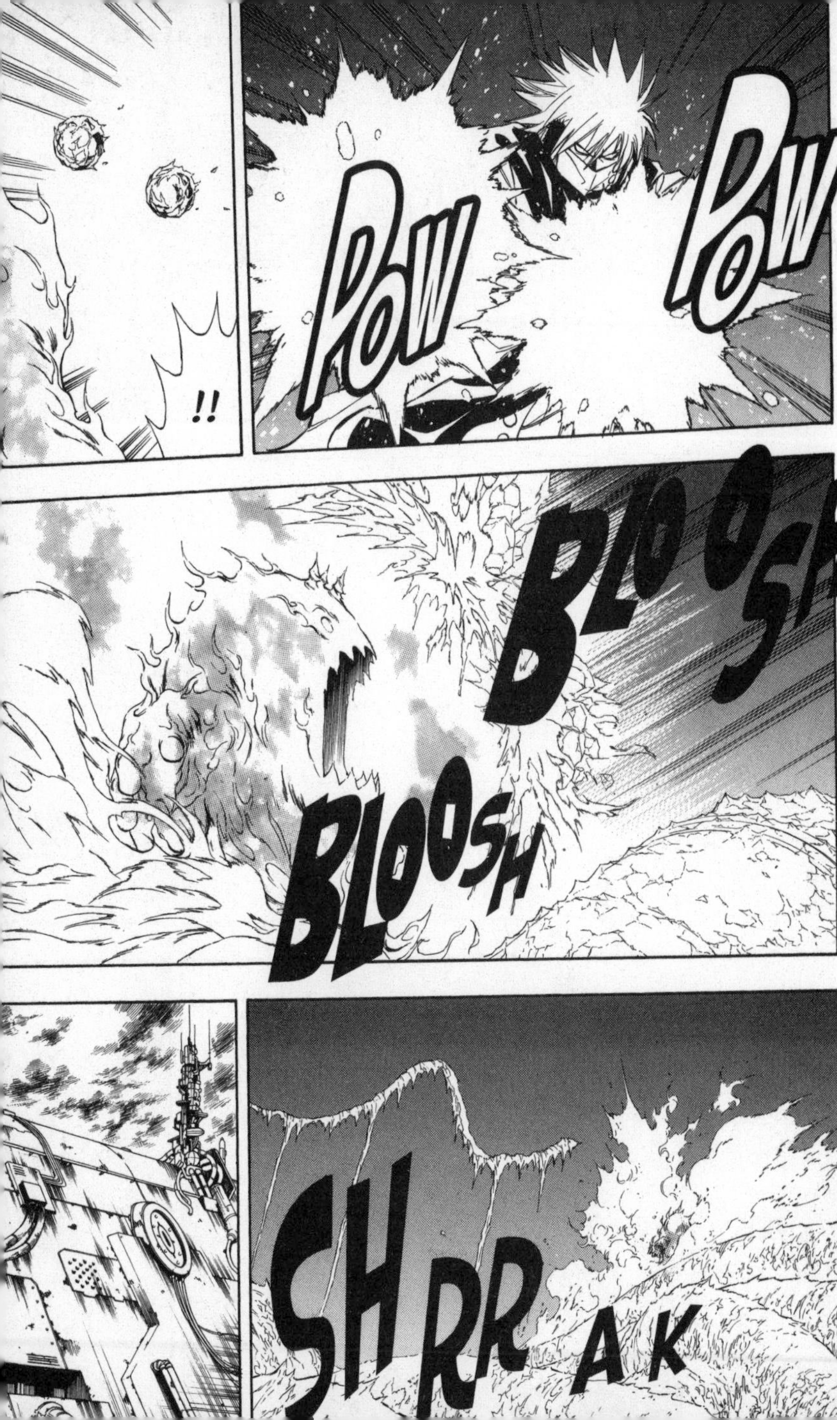
POW
POW
!!
BLOOSH
BLOOSH
SHRRAK

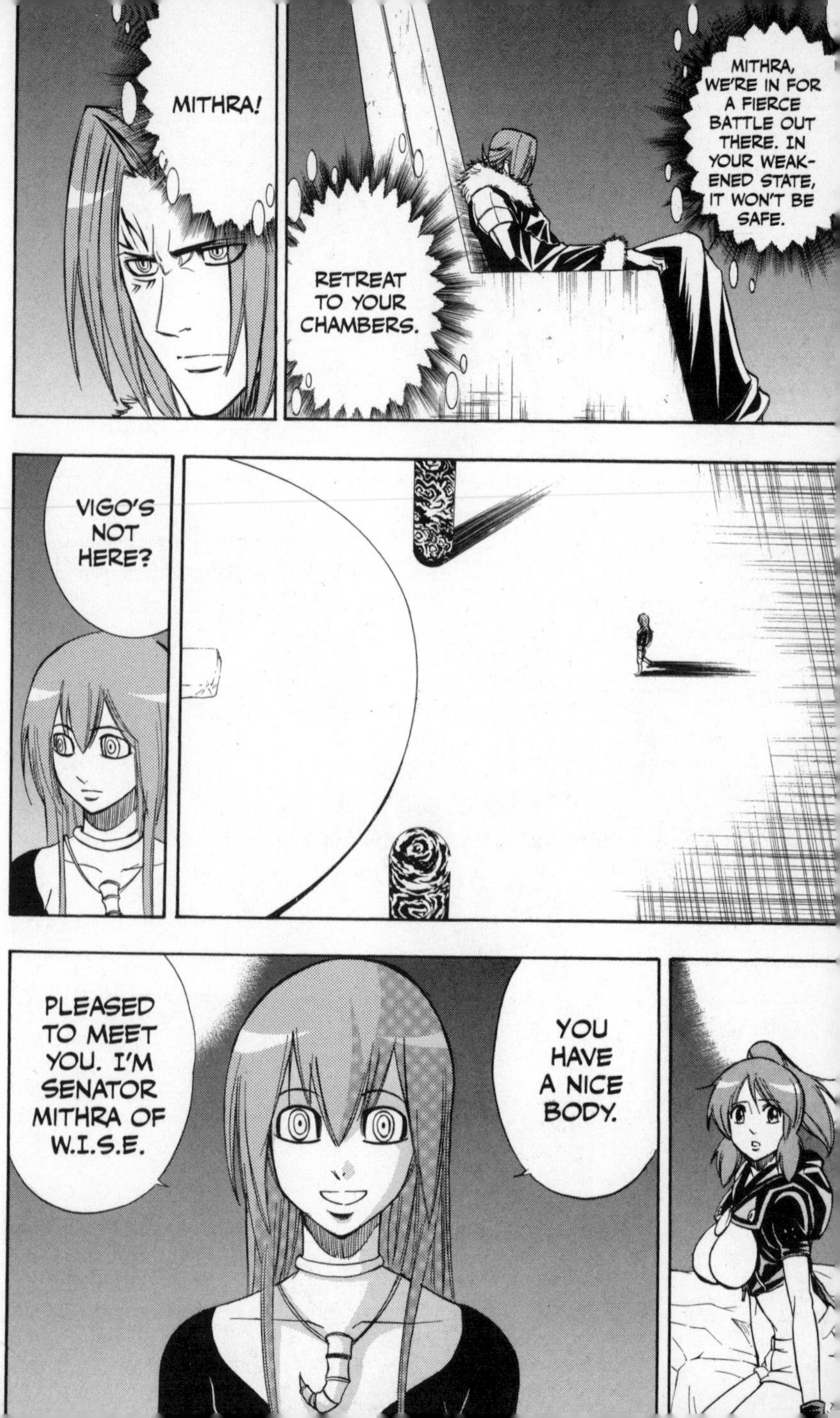
MITHRA, WE'RE IN FOR A FIERCE BATTLE OUT THERE. IN YOUR WEAKENED STATE, IT WON'T BE SAFE.
RETREAT TO YOUR CHAMBERS.
MITHRA!
VIGO'S NOT HERE?
YOU HAVE A NICE BODY.
PLEASED TO MEET YOU. I'M SENATOR MITHRA OF W.I.S.E.

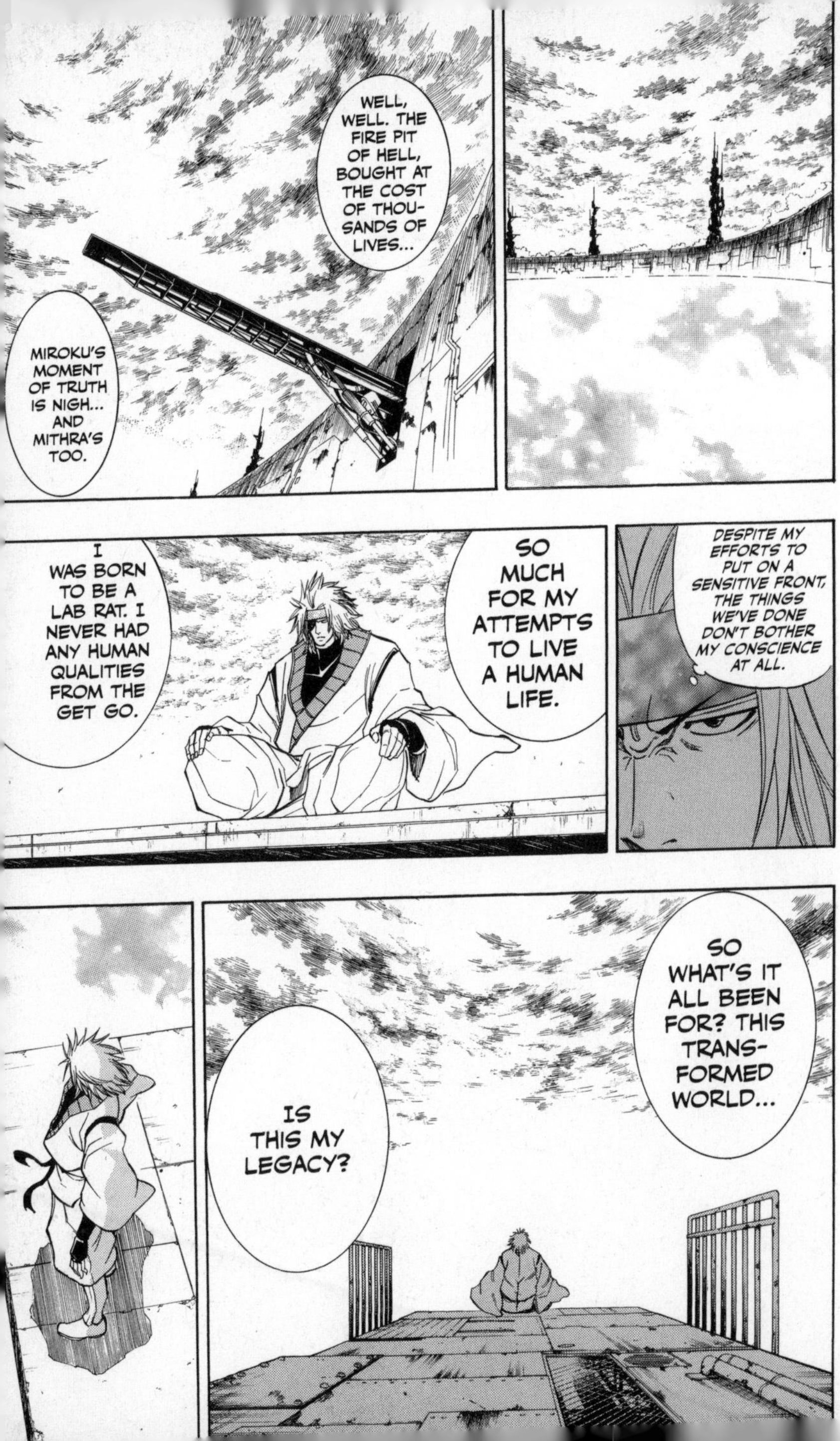
WELL, WELL. THE FIRE PIT OF HELL, BOUGHT AT THE COST OF THOU-SANDS OF LIVES...
MIROKU'S MOMENT OF TRUTH IS NIGH... AND MITHRA'S TOO.
DESPITE MY EFFORTS TO PUT ON A SENSITIVE FRONT, THE THINGS WE'VE DONE DON'T BOTHER MY CONSCIENCE AT ALL.
SO MUCH FOR MY ATTEMPTS TO LIVE A HUMAN LIFE.
I WAS BORN TO BE A LAB RAT. I NEVER HAD ANY HUMAN QUALITIES FROM THE GET GO.
SO WHAT'S IT ALL BEEN FOR? THIS TRANS-FORMED WORLD...
IS THIS MY LEGACY?

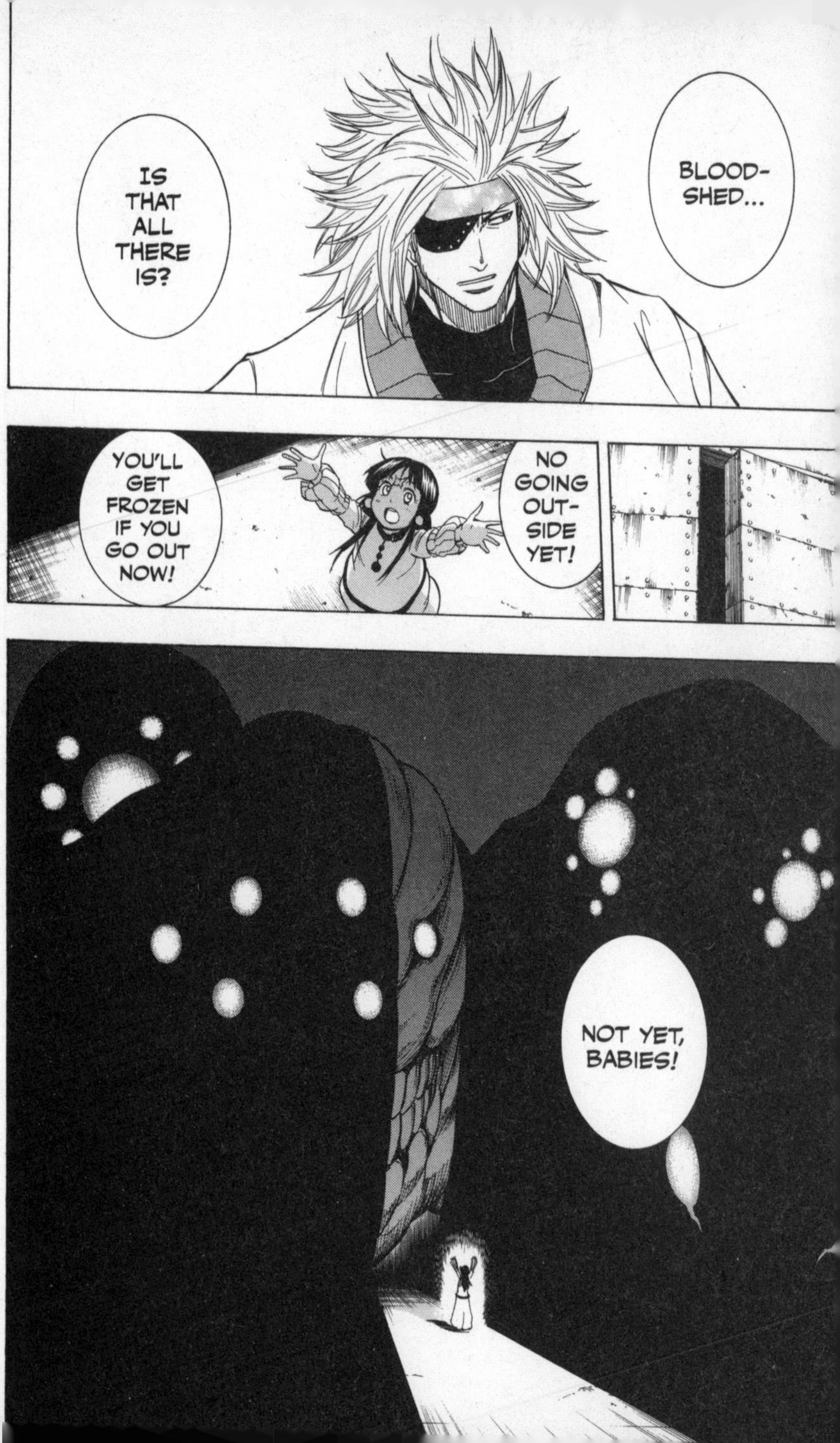
BLOOD-SHED...
IS THAT ALL THERE IS?
NO GOING OUT-SIDE YET!
YOU'LL GET FROZEN IF YOU GO OUT NOW!
NOT YET, BABIES!

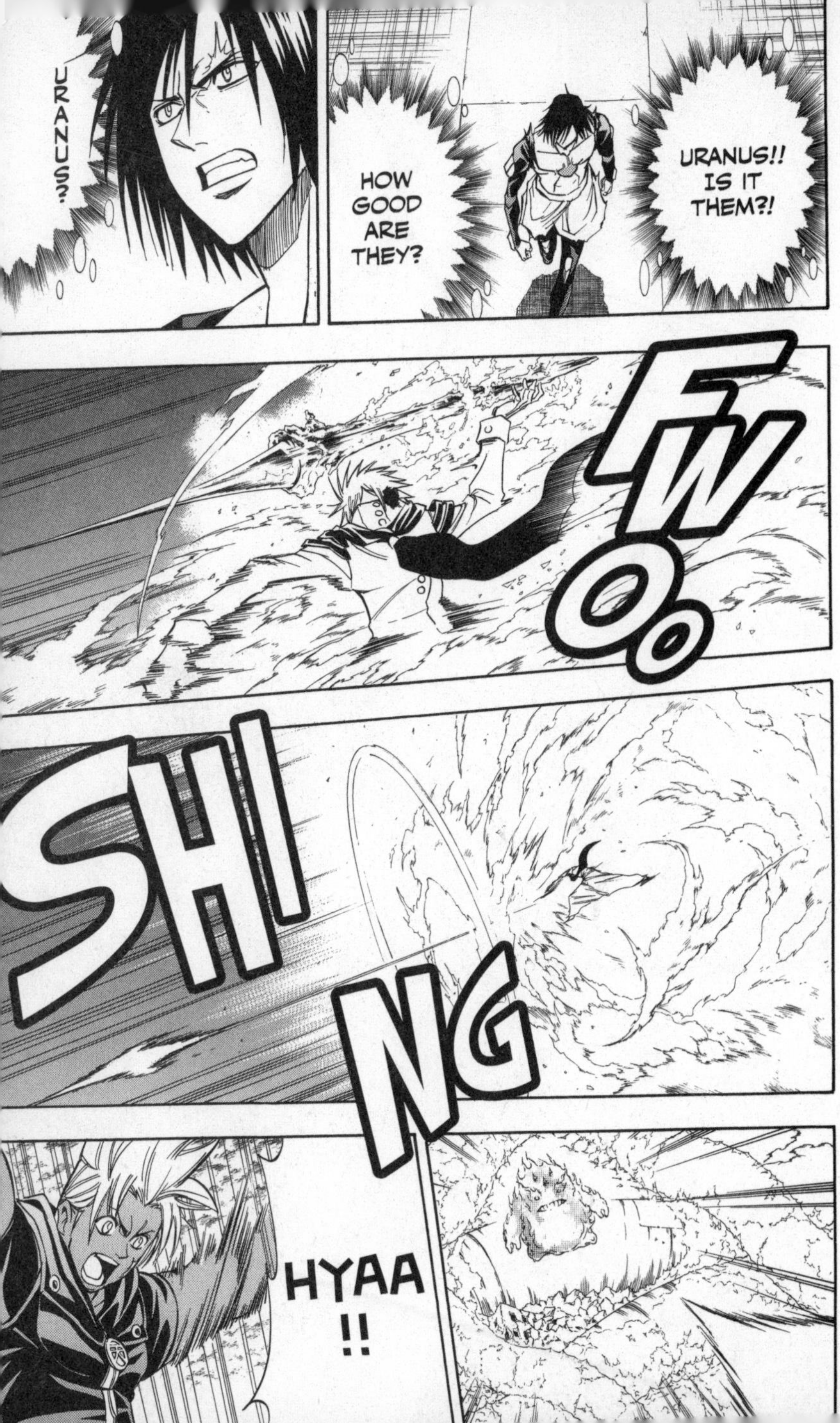
URANUS!! IS IT THEM?!
HOW GOOD ARE THEY?
URANUS?
FWOO
SHING
HYAA !!

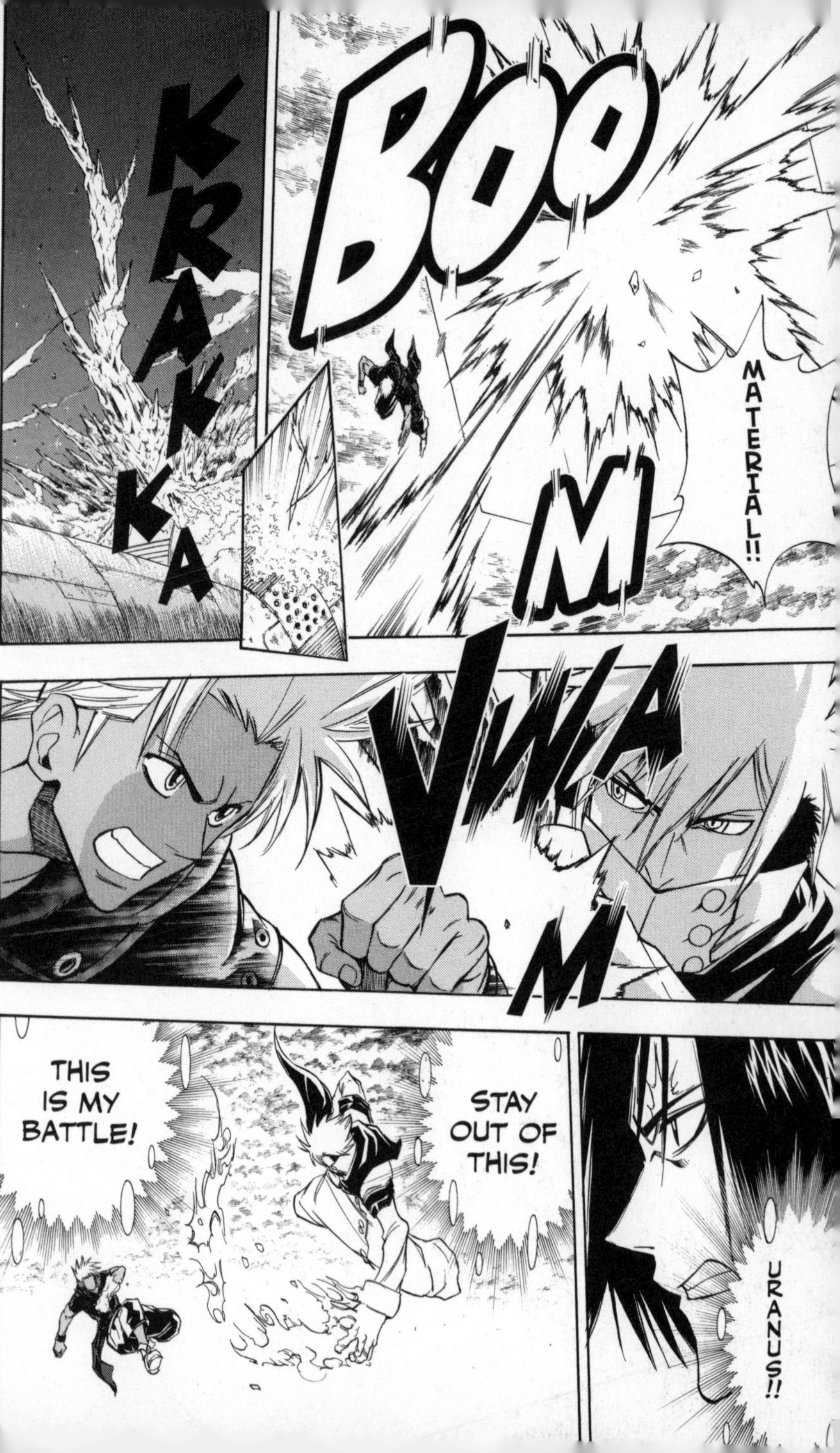
BOOM
MATERIAL!!
KRAKKA
VWAMM
URANUS!!
STAY OUT OF THIS!
THIS IS MY BATTLE!

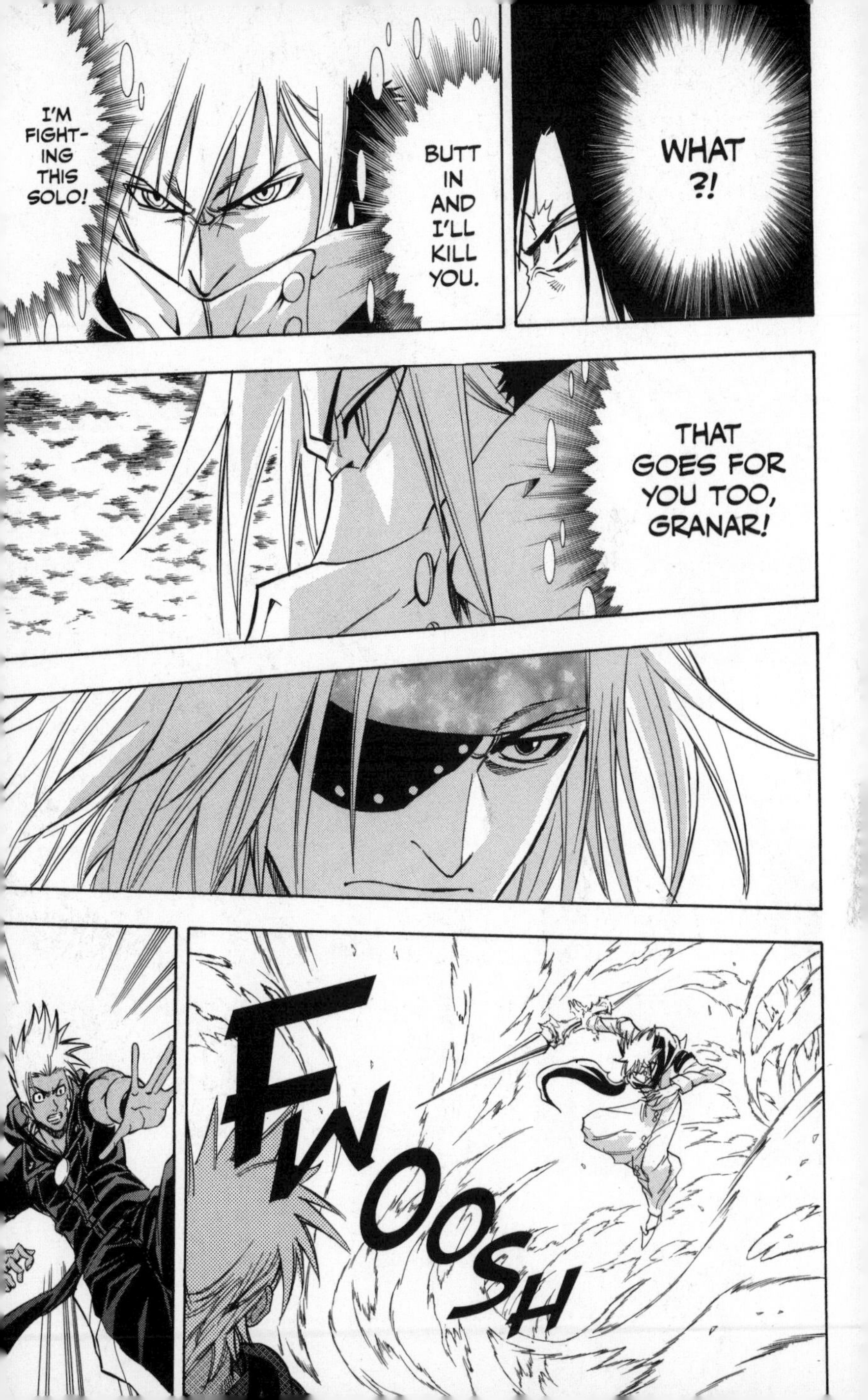
WHAT ?!
BUTT IN AND I'LL KILL YOU.
I'M FIGHTING THIS SOLO!
THAT GOES FOR YOU TOO, GRANAR!
FWOOSH

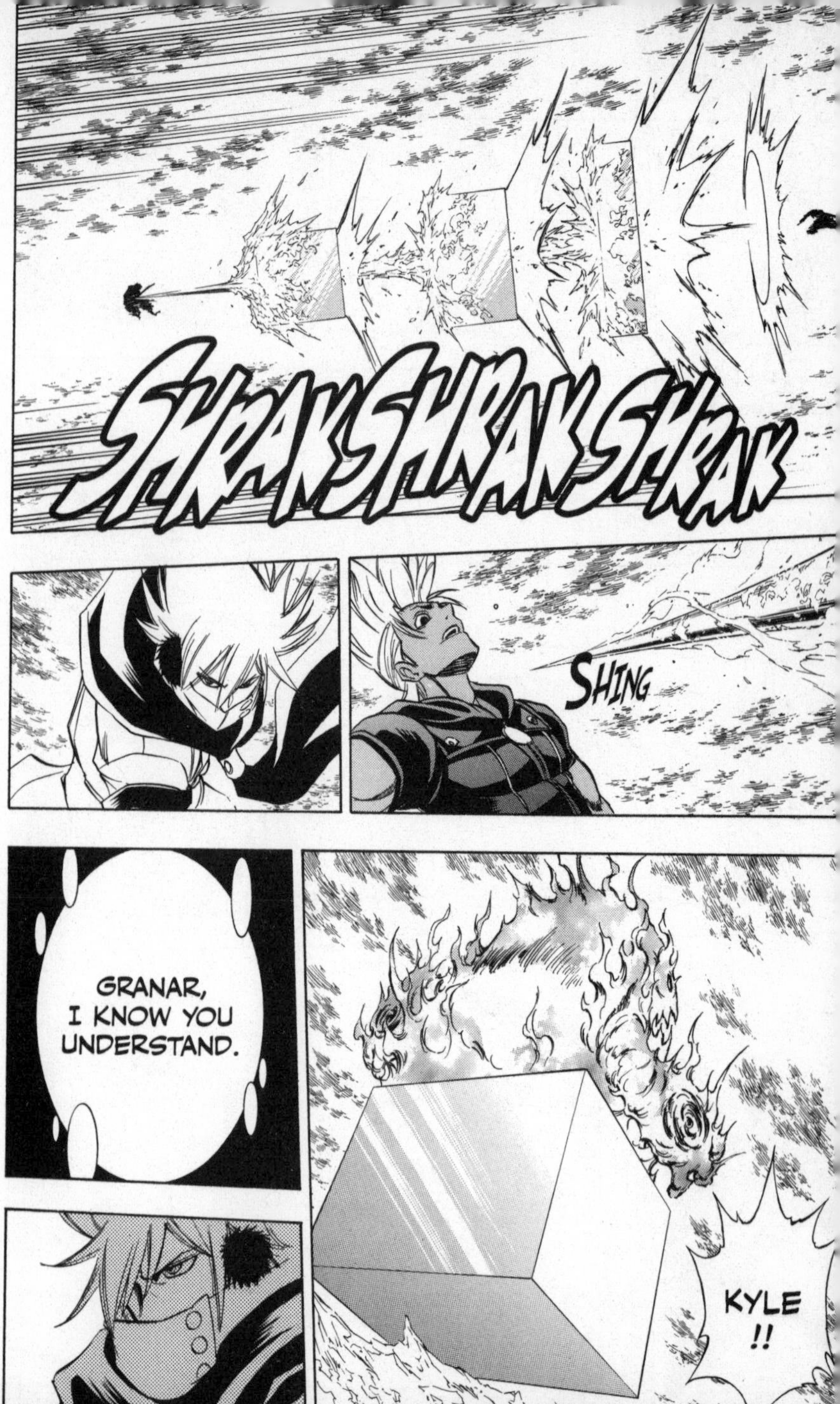
SHRAK SHRAK SHRAK
SHING
KYLE !!
GRANAR, I KNOW YOU UNDERSTAND.

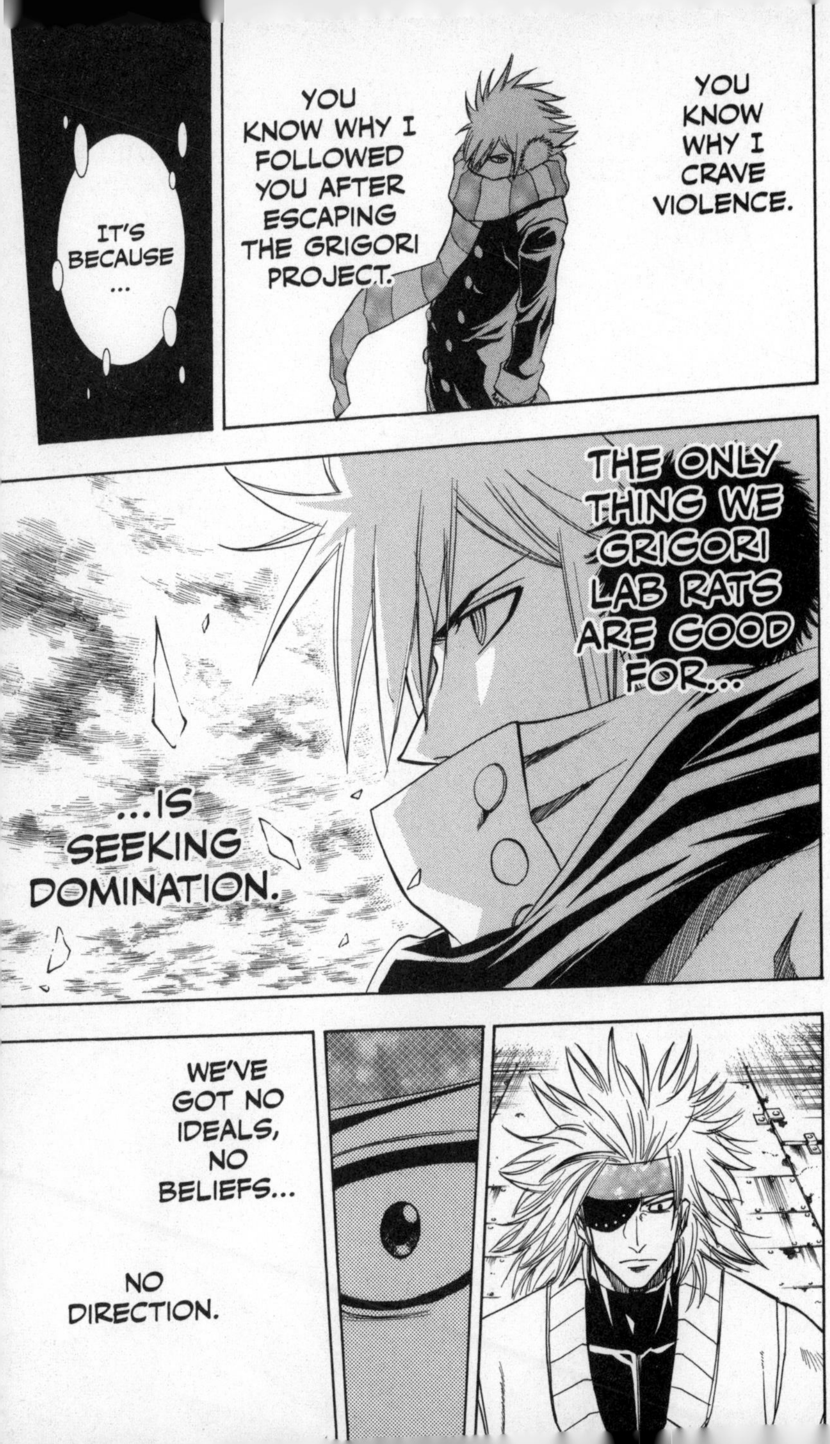
YOU KNOW WHY I CRAVE VIOLENCE.
YOU KNOW WHY I FOLLOWED YOU AFTER ESCAPING THE GRIGORI PROJECT.
IT'S BECAUSE ...
THE ONLY THING WE GRIGORI LAB RATS ARE GOOD FOR...
...IS SEEKING DOMINATION.
WE'VE GOT NO IDEALS, NO BELIEFS...
NO DIRECTION.

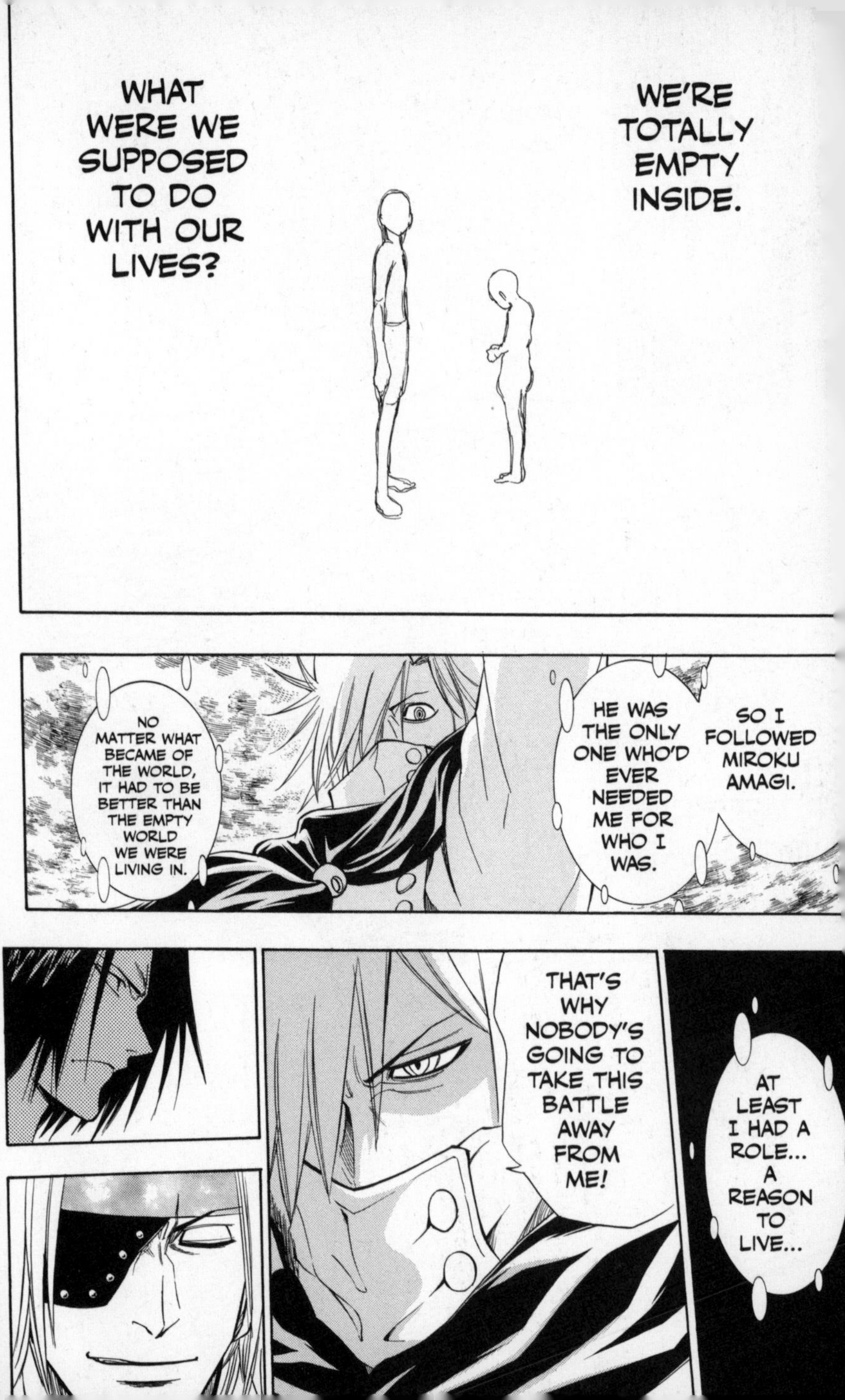
WE'RE TOTALLY EMPTY INSIDE.
WHAT WERE WE SUPPOSED TO DO WITH OUR LIVES?
SO I FOLLOWED MIROKU AMAGI.
HE WAS THE ONLY ONE WHO'D EVER NEEDED ME FOR WHO I WAS.
NO MATTER WHAT BECAME OF THE WORLD, IT HAD TO BE BETTER THAN THE EMPTY WORLD WE WERE LIVING IN.
AT LEAST I HAD A ROLE... A REASON TO LIVE...
THAT'S WHY NOBODY'S GOING TO TAKE THIS BATTLE AWAY FROM ME!

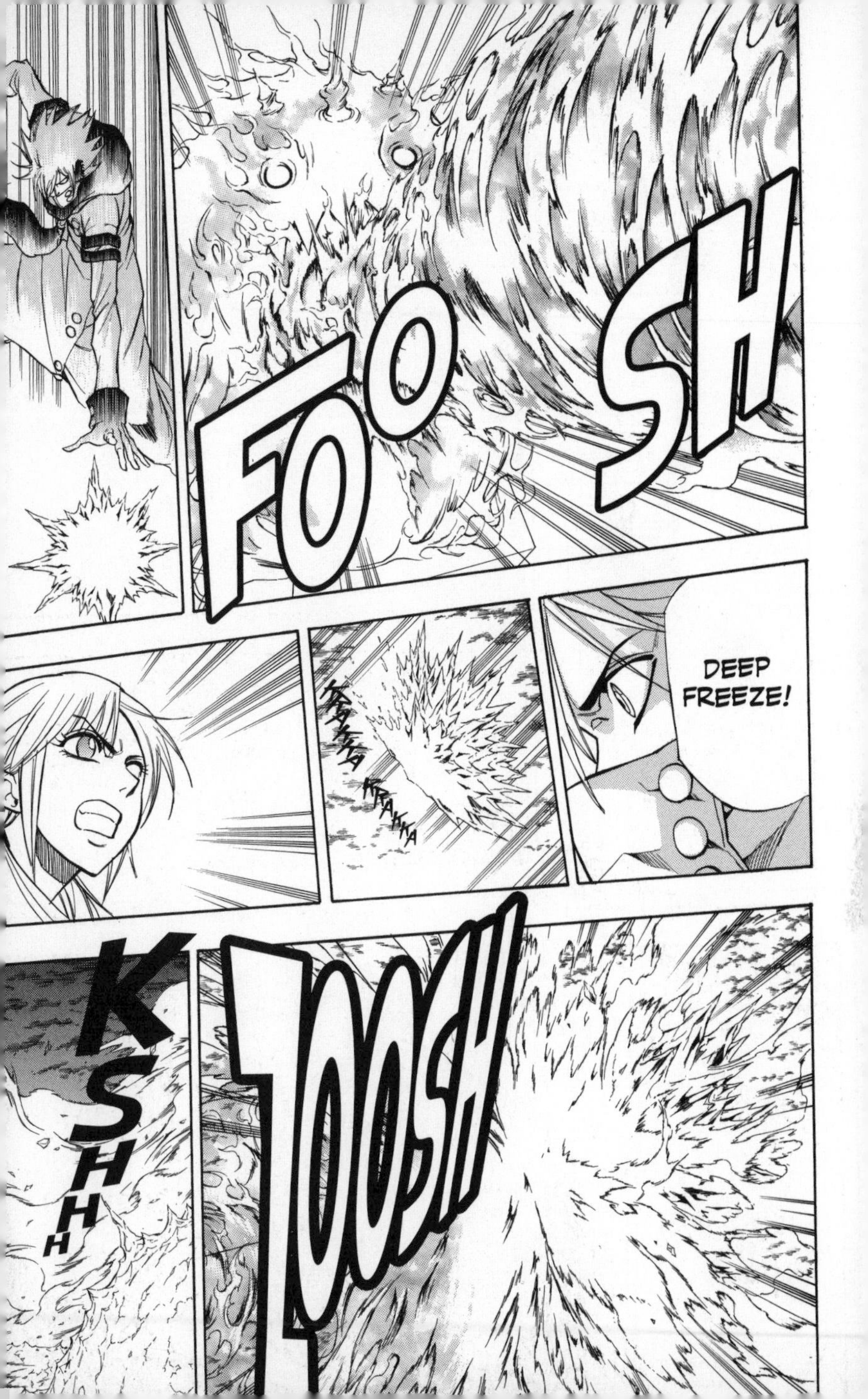
FOOSH
DEEP FREEZE!
KRAKKA
KRAKKA
TOOSH
KSHHHH

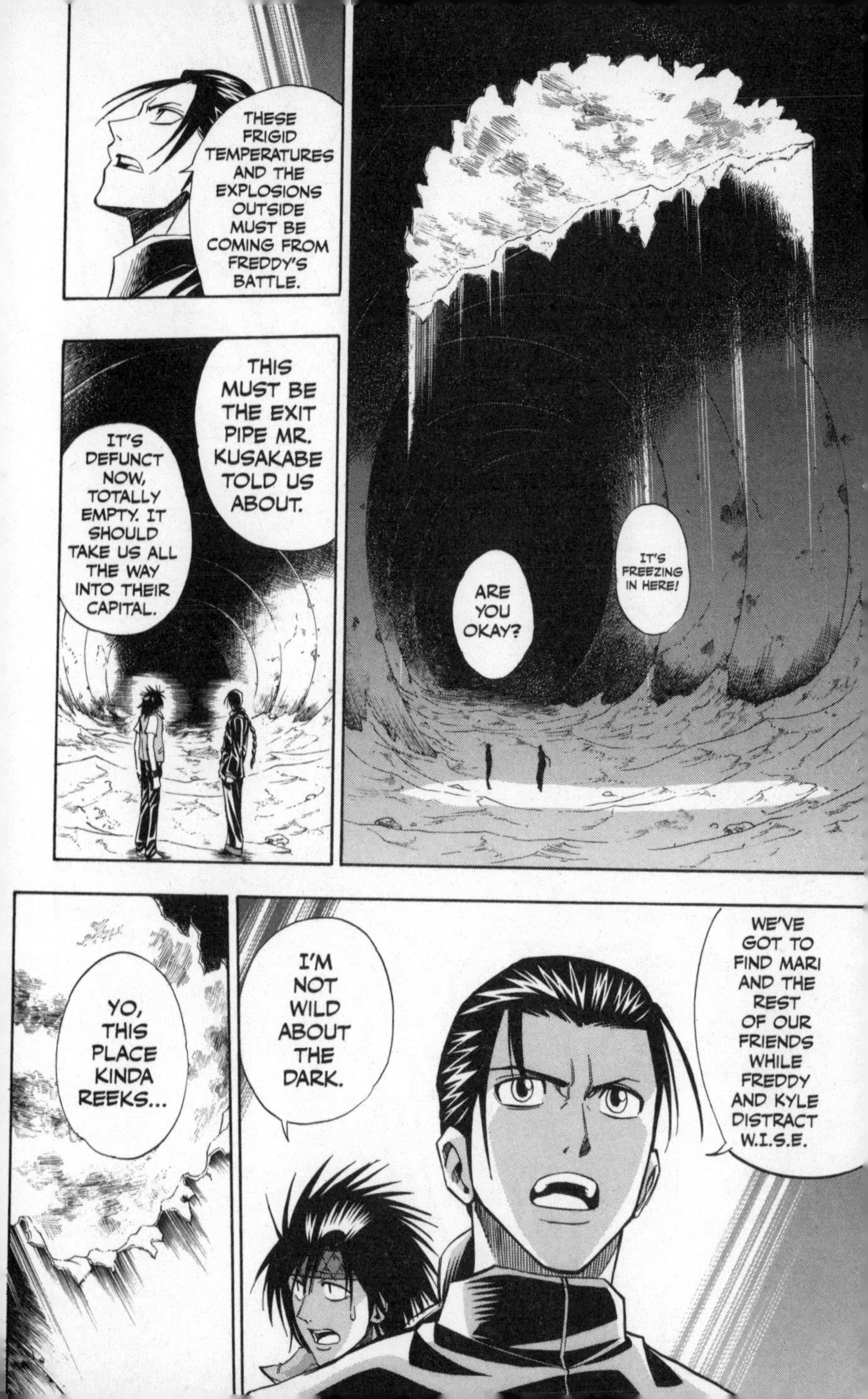
IT'S FREEZING IN HERE!
ARE YOU OKAY?
THESE FRIGID TEMPERATURES AND THE EXPLOSIONS OUTSIDE MUST BE COMING FROM FREDDY'S BATTLE.
THIS MUST BE THE EXIT PIPE MR. KUSAKABE TOLD US ABOUT.
IT'S DEFUNCT NOW, TOTALLY EMPTY. IT SHOULD TAKE US ALL THE WAY INTO THEIR CAPITAL.
WE'VE GOT TO FIND MARI AND THE REST OF OUR FRIENDS WHILE FREDDY AND KYLE DISTRACT W.I.S.E.
I'M NOT WILD ABOUT THE DARK.
YO, THIS PLACE KINDA REEKS...

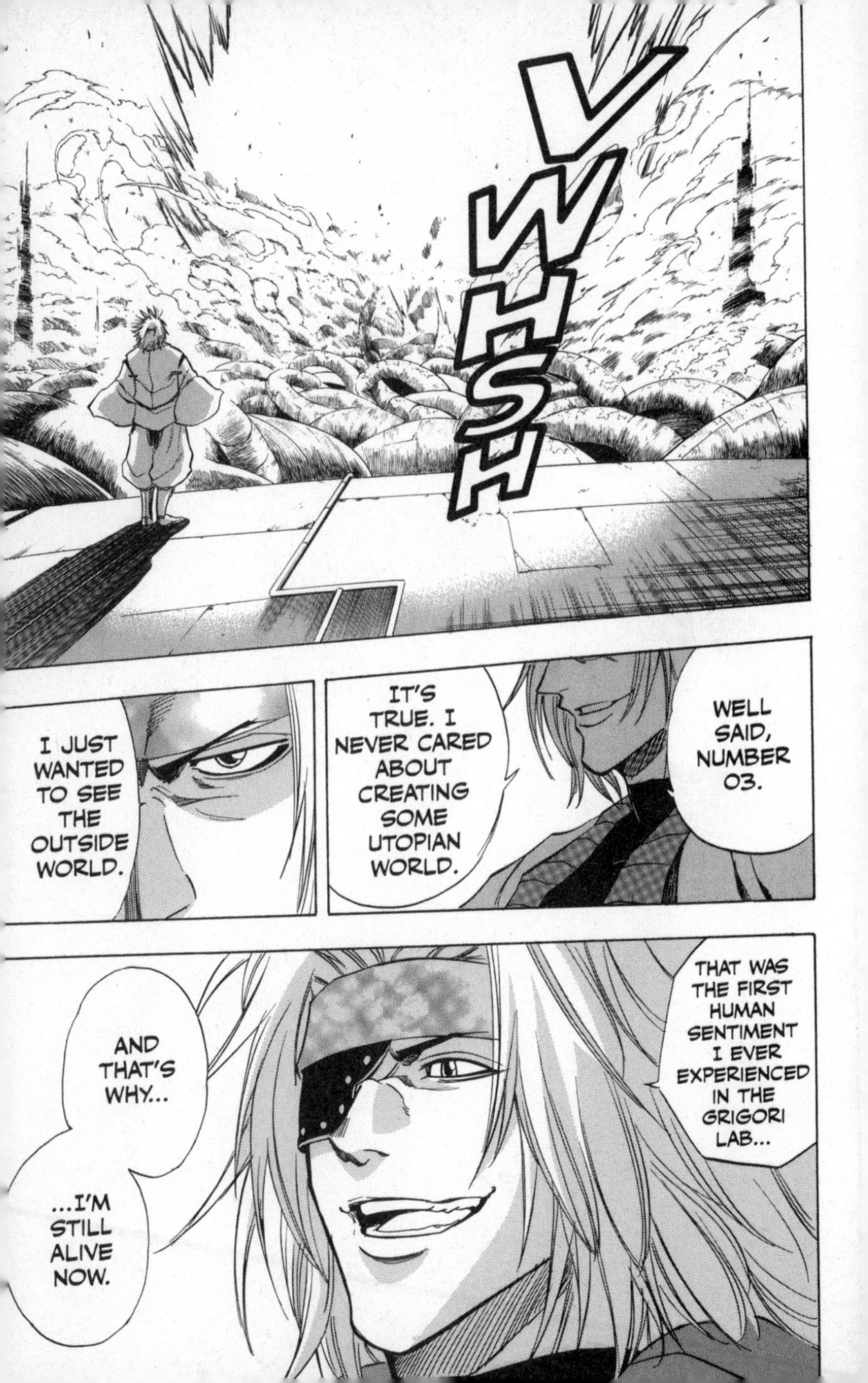
VWHSH
WELL SAID, NUMBER 03.
IT'S TRUE. I NEVER CARED ABOUT CREATING SOME UTOPIAN WORLD.
I JUST WANTED TO SEE THE OUTSIDE WORLD.
THAT WAS THE FIRST HUMAN SENTIMENT I EVER EXPERIENCED IN THE GRIGORI LAB...
AND THAT'S WHY...
...I'M STILL ALIVE NOW.

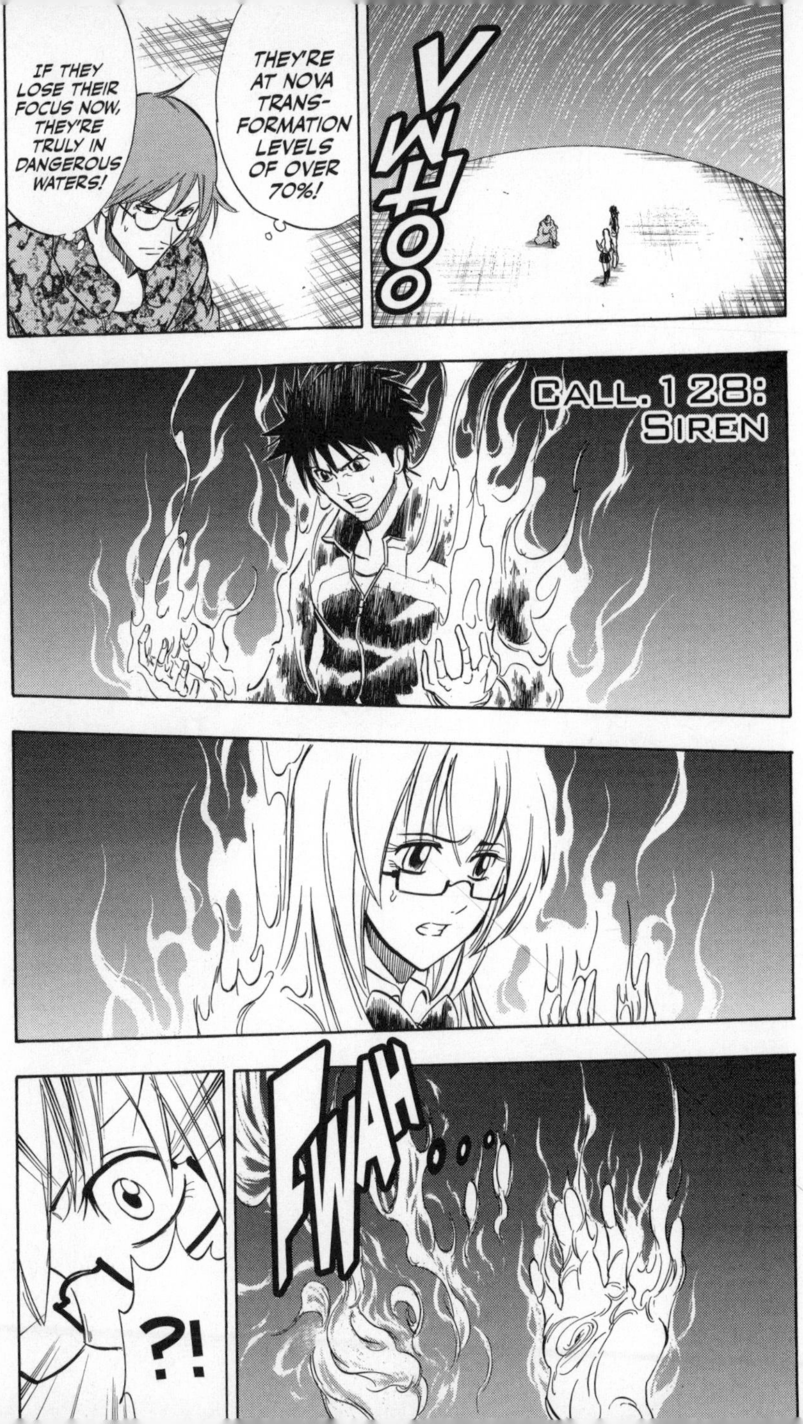
VWHOO
THEY'RE AT NOVA TRANS-FORMATION LEVELS OF OVER 70%!
IF THEY LOSE THEIR FOCUS NOW, THEY'RE TRULY IN DANGEROUS WATERS!
CALL. 128: SIREN
FWAH...
?!

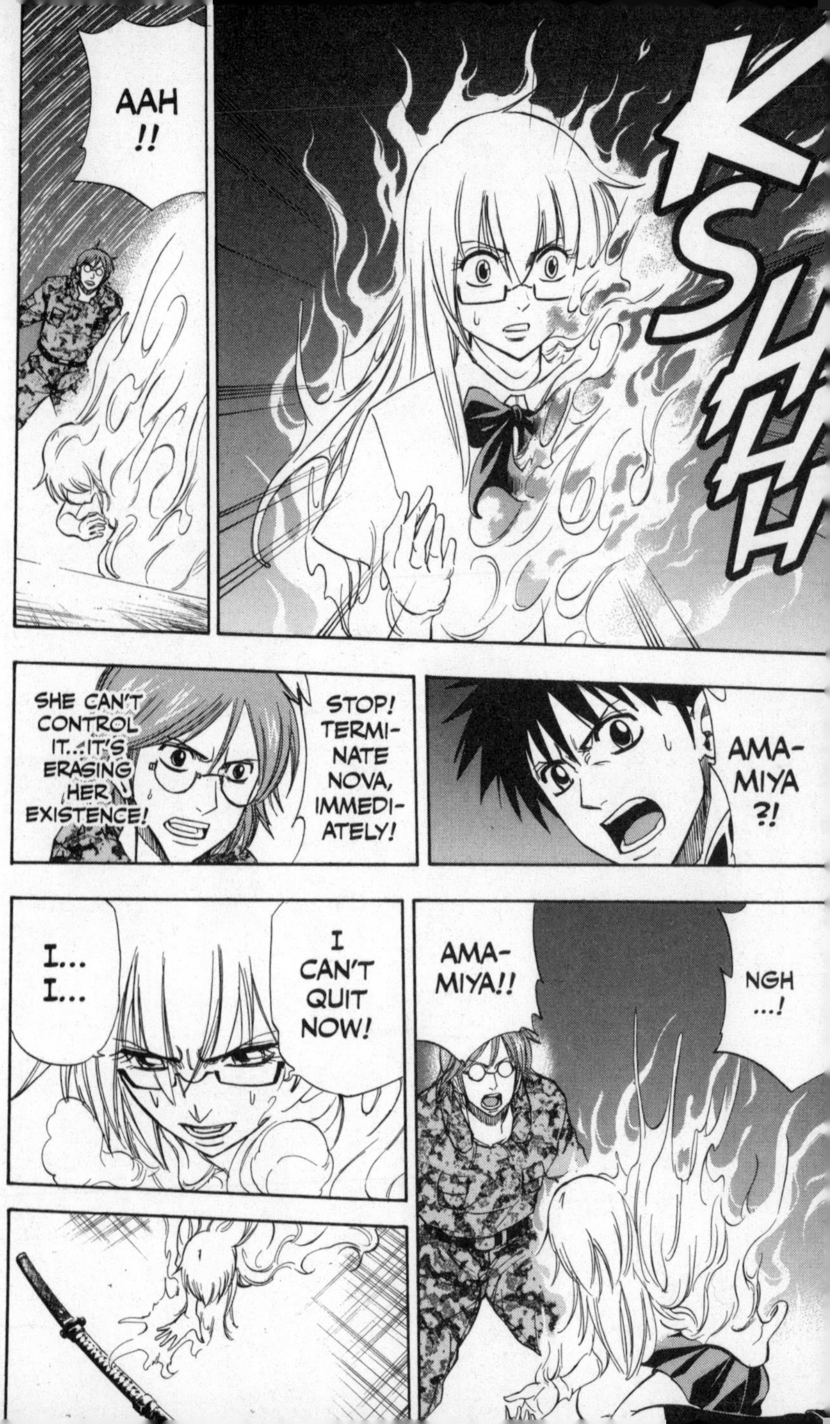
KSHHH
AAH !!
AMA-MIYA ?!
STOP! TERMI-NATE NOVA, IMMEDI-ATELY!
SHE CAN'T CONTROL IT... IT'S ERASING HER EXISTENCE!
NGH ...!
AMA-MIYA!!
I CAN'T QUIT NOW!
I... I...

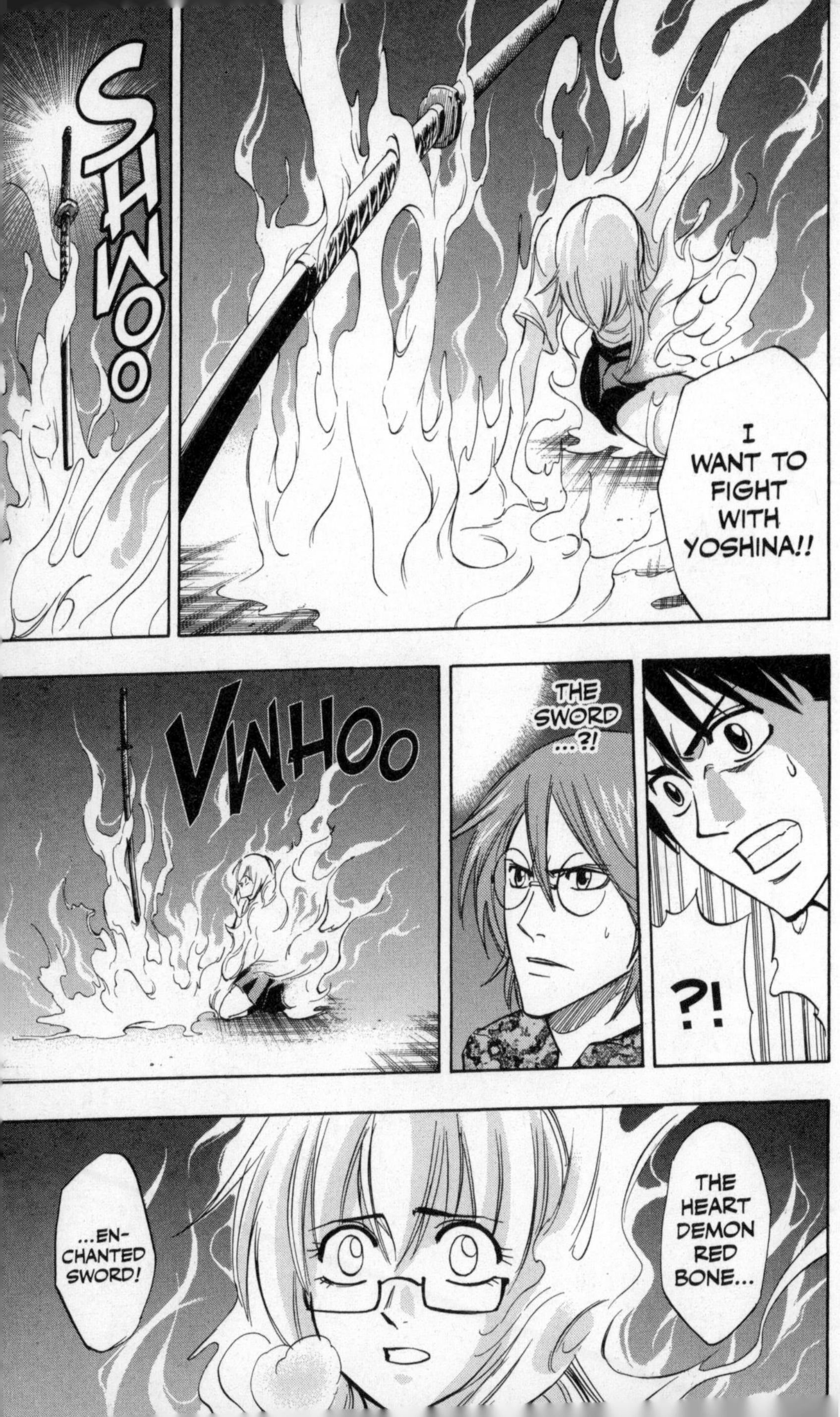
I WANT TO FIGHT WITH YOSHINA!!
SHWOO
?!
THE SWORD ...?!
VWHOO
THE HEART DEMON RED BONE...
...EN-CHANTED SWORD!

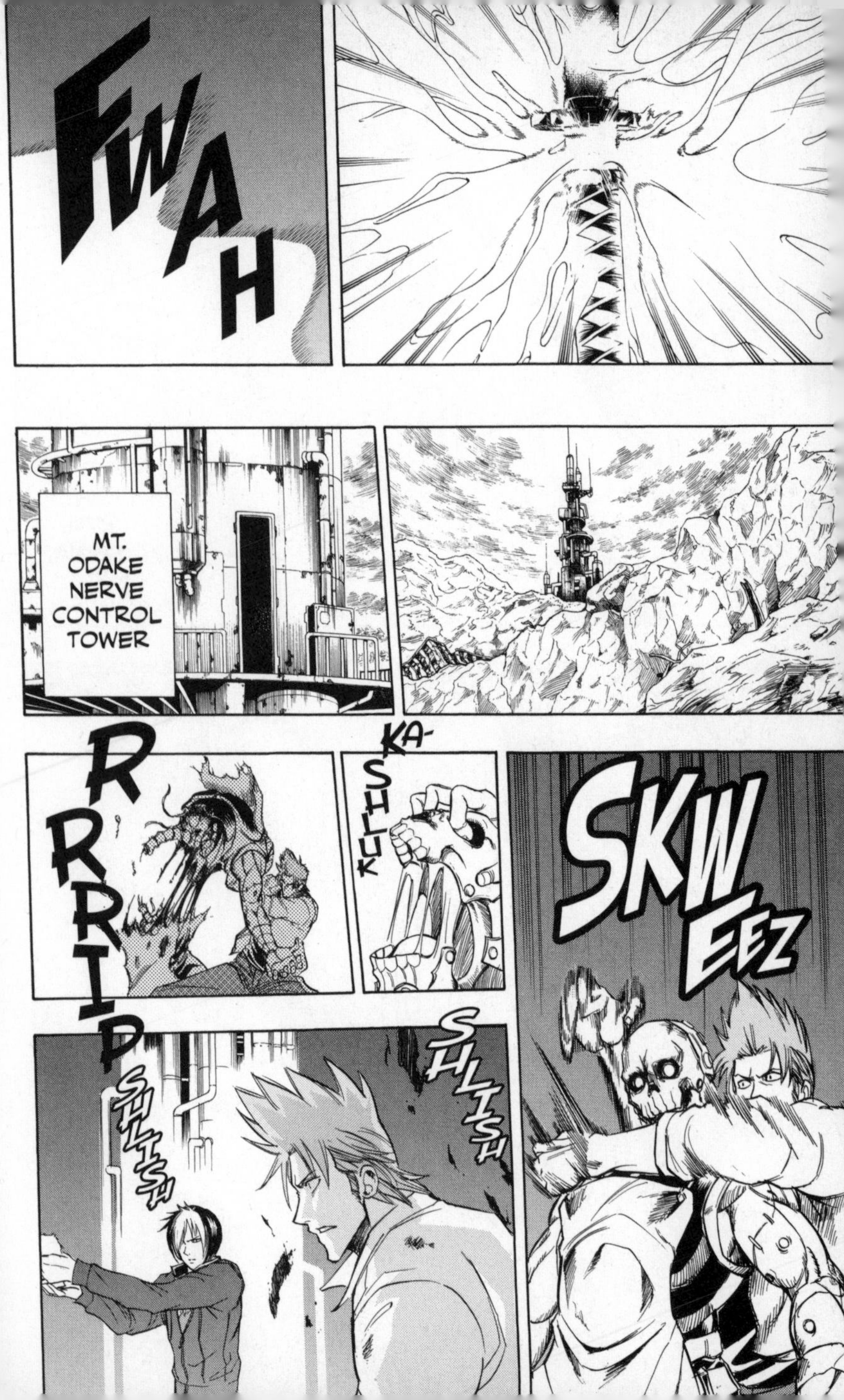
FWAH
MT. ODAKE NERVE CONTROL TOWER
SKWEEZ
KA-SHLUK
RRRIP
SHLISH
SHLISH

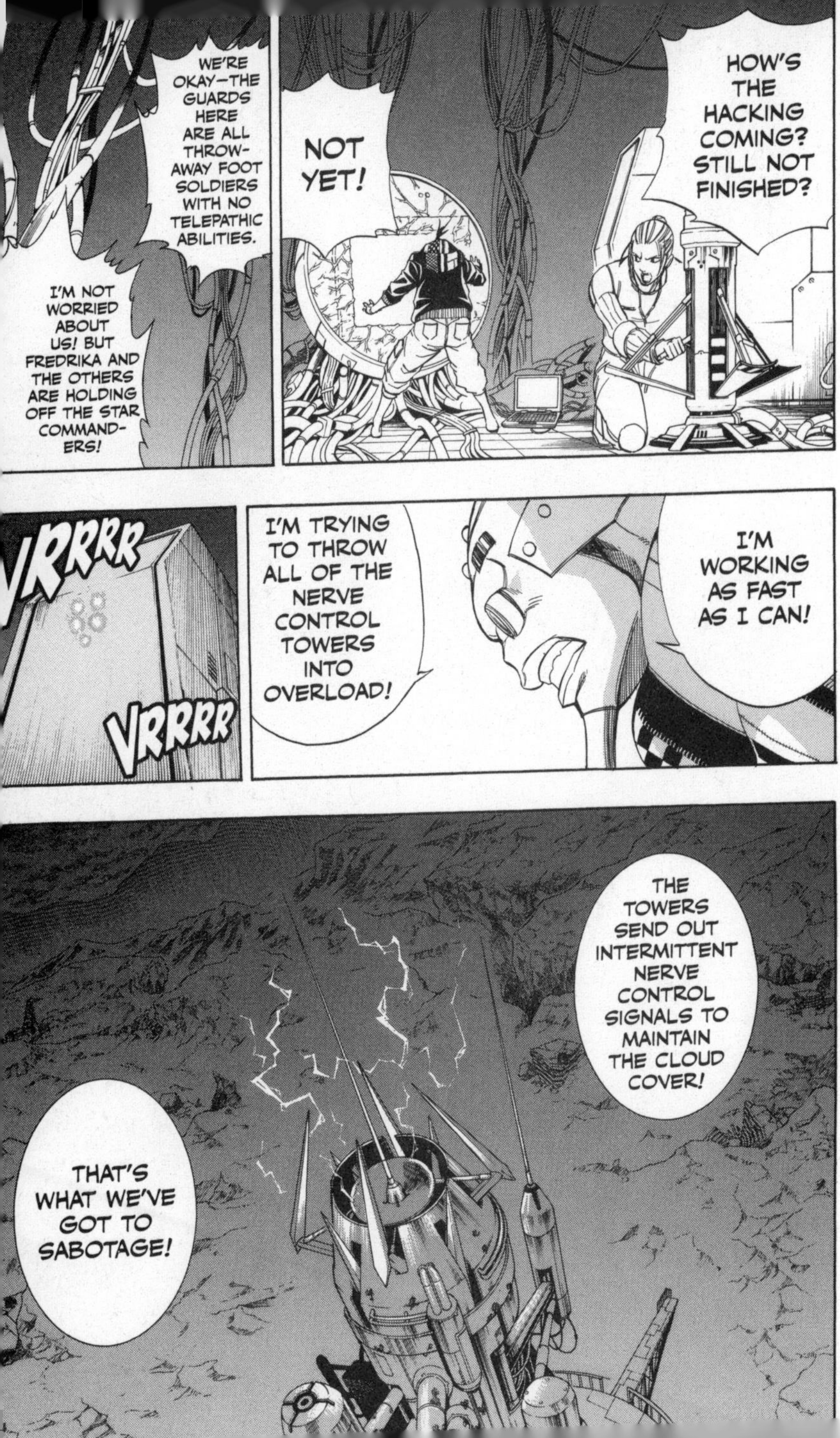
HOW'S THE HACKING COMING? STILL NOT FINISHED?
NOT YET!
WE'RE OKAY—THE GUARDS HERE ARE ALL THROW-AWAY FOOT SOLDIERS WITH NO TELEPATHIC ABILITIES.
I'M NOT WORRIED ABOUT US! BUT FREDRIKA AND THE OTHERS ARE HOLDING OFF THE STAR COMMANDERS!
I'M WORKING AS FAST AS I CAN!
I'M TRYING TO THROW ALL OF THE NERVE CONTROL TOWERS INTO OVERLOAD!
VRRRR
VRRRR
THE TOWERS SEND OUT INTERMITTENT NERVE CONTROL SIGNALS TO MAINTAIN THE CLOUD COVER!
THAT'S WHAT WE'VE GOT TO SABOTAGE!

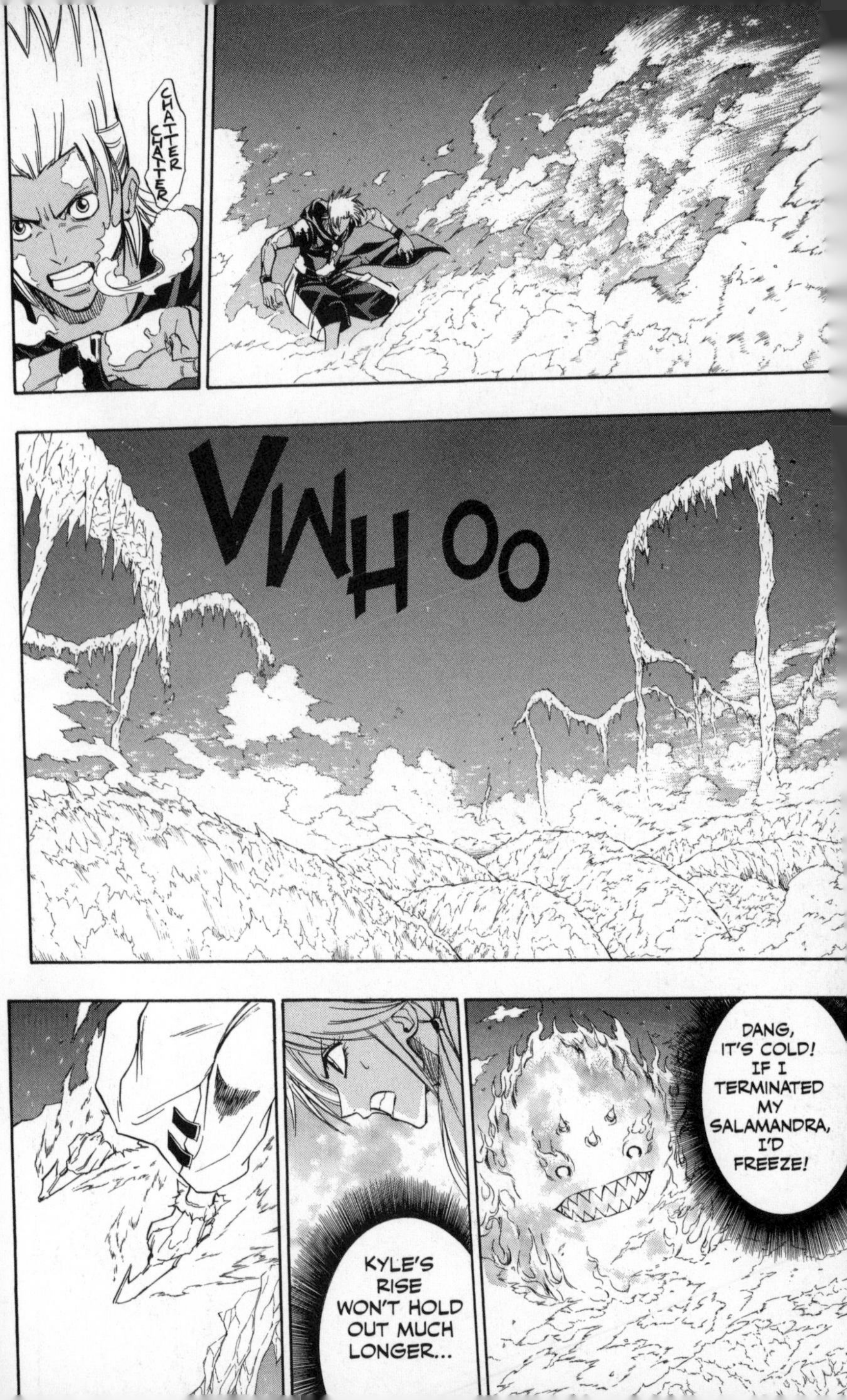
CHATTER CHATTER
VWHOO
DANG, IT'S COLD! IF I TERMINATED MY SALAMANDRA, I'D FREEZE!
KYLE'S RISE WON'T HOLD OUT MUCH LONGER...

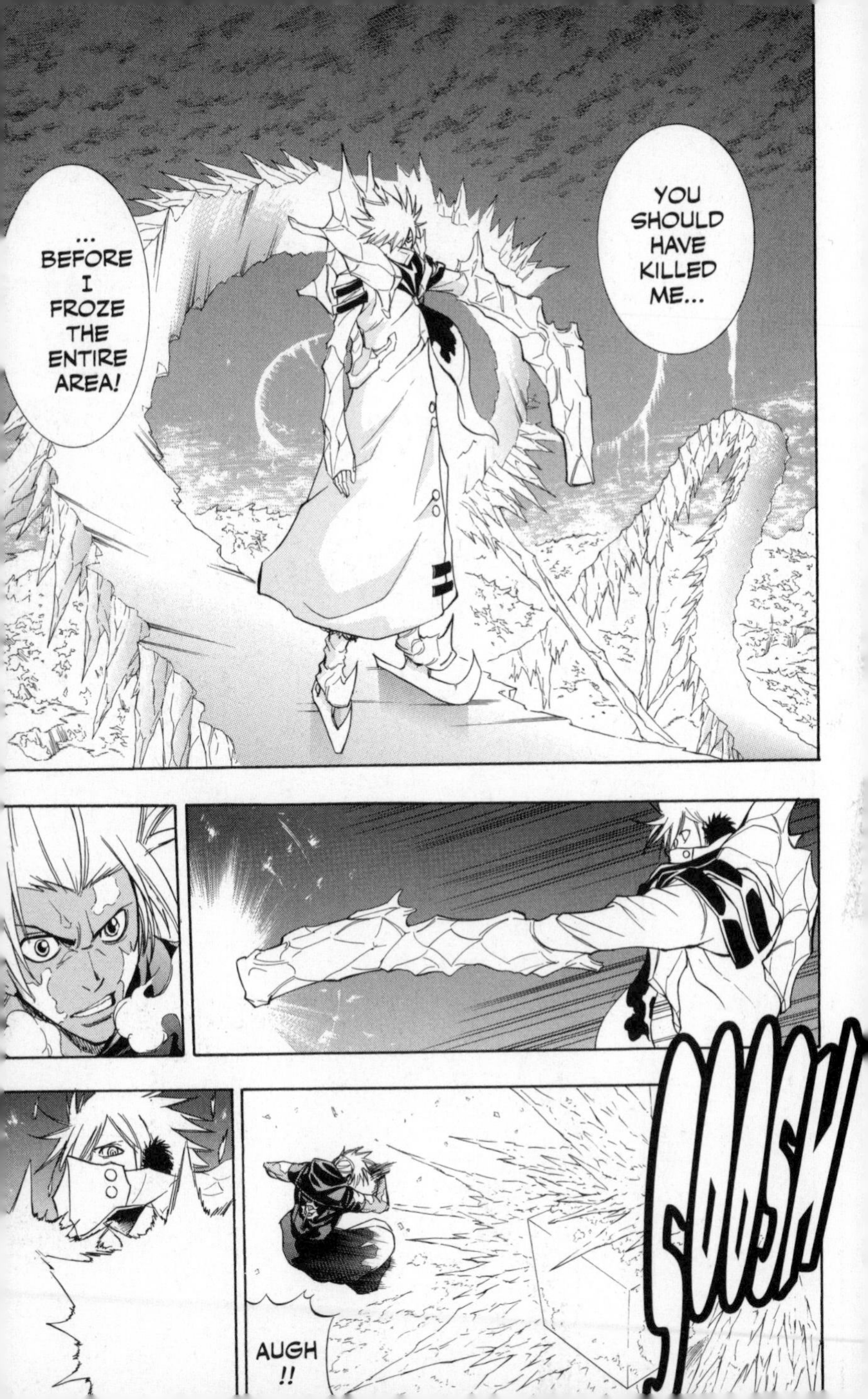
YOU SHOULD HAVE KILLED ME...
... BEFORE I FROZE THE ENTIRE AREA!
AUGH !!

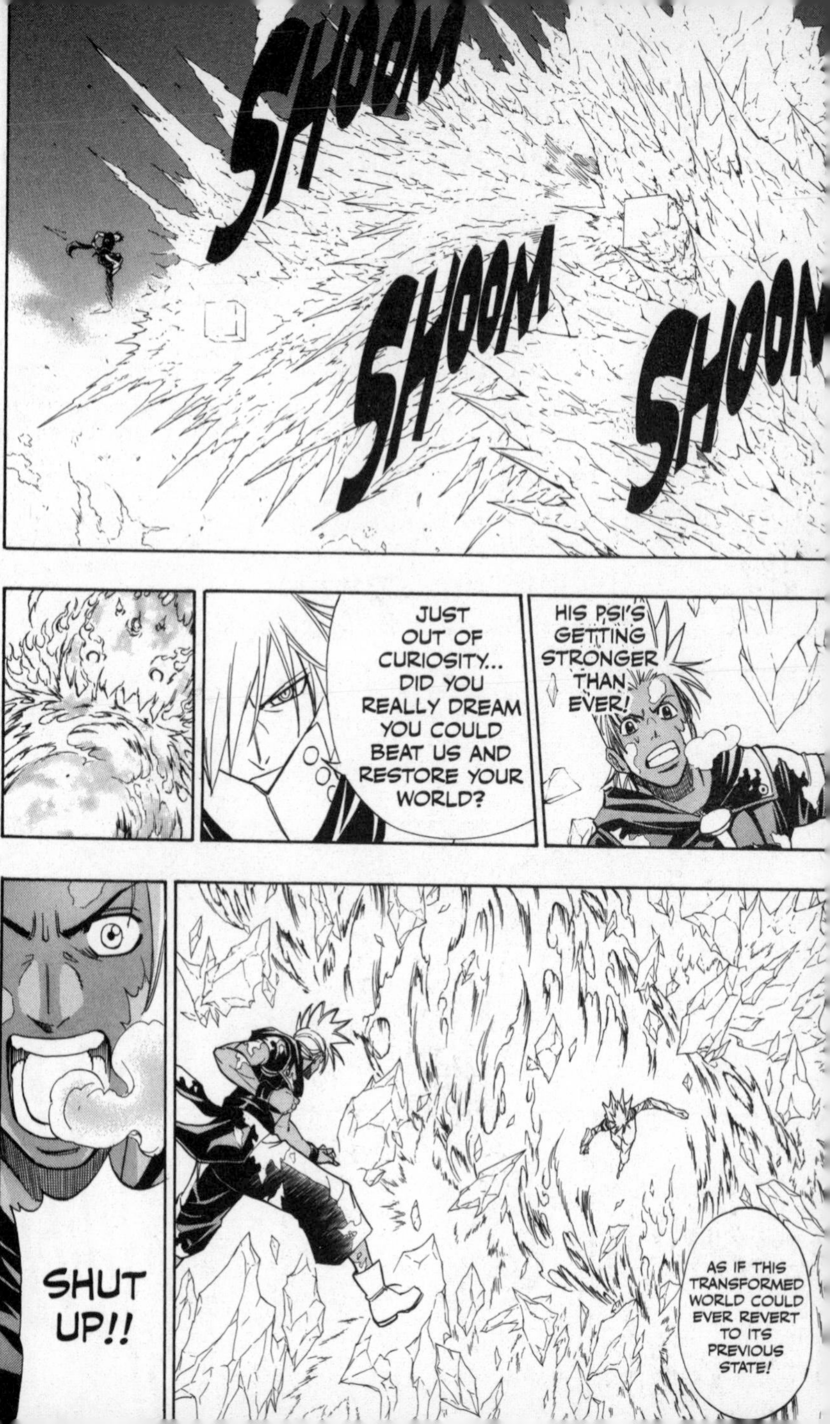
SHOOM
SHOOM
SHOOM
HIS PSI'S GETTING STRONGER THAN EVER!
JUST OUT OF CURIOSITY... DID YOU REALLY DREAM YOU COULD BEAT US AND RESTORE YOUR WORLD?
AS IF THIS TRANSFORMED WORLD COULD EVER REVERT TO ITS PREVIOUS STATE!
SHUT UP!!

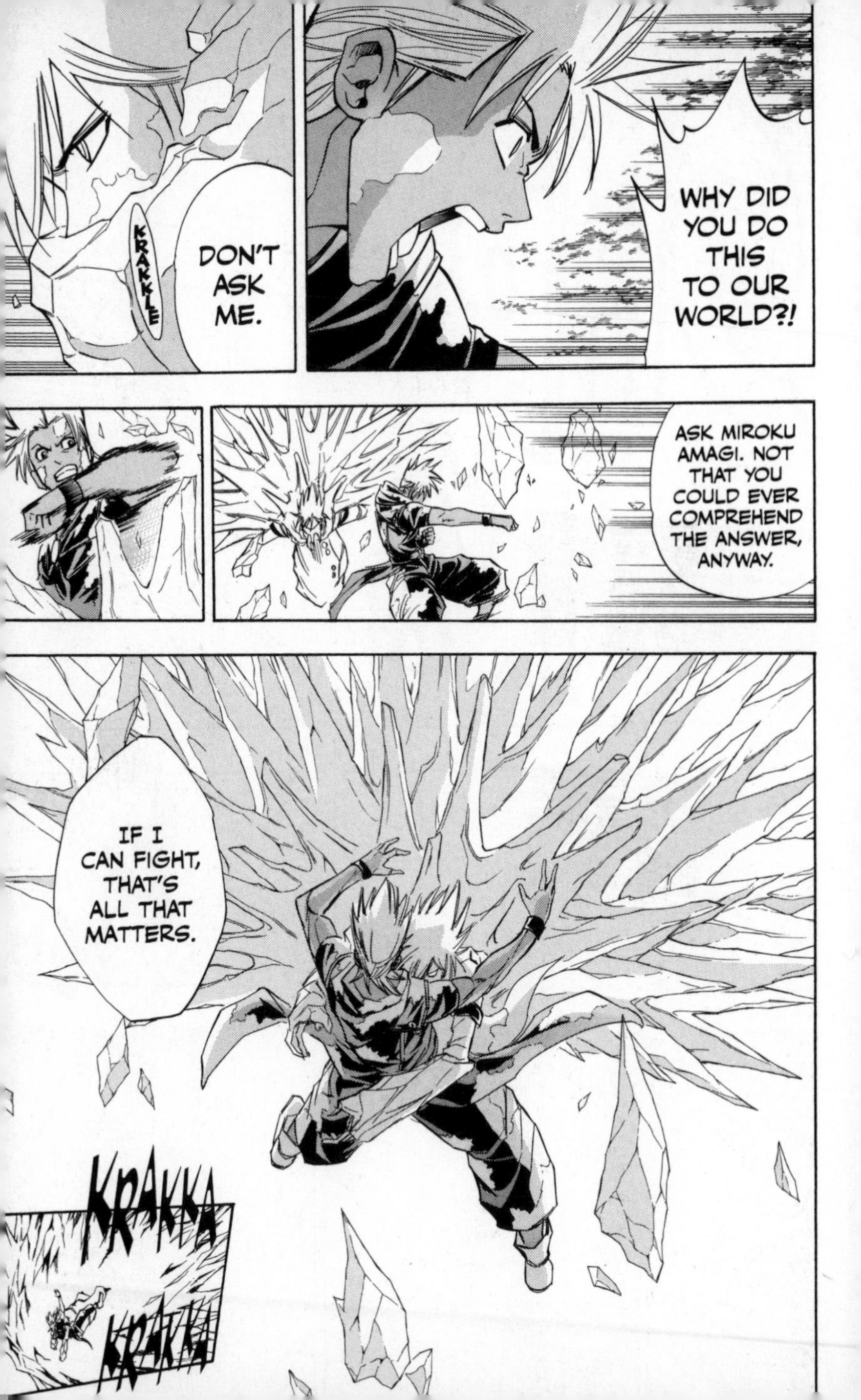
WHY DID YOU DO THIS TO OUR WORLD?!
DON'T ASK ME.
KRAKKLE
ASK MIROKU AMAGI. NOT THAT YOU COULD EVER COMPREHEND THE ANSWER, ANYWAY.
IF I CAN FIGHT, THAT'S ALL THAT MATTERS.
KRAKKA
KRAKKA

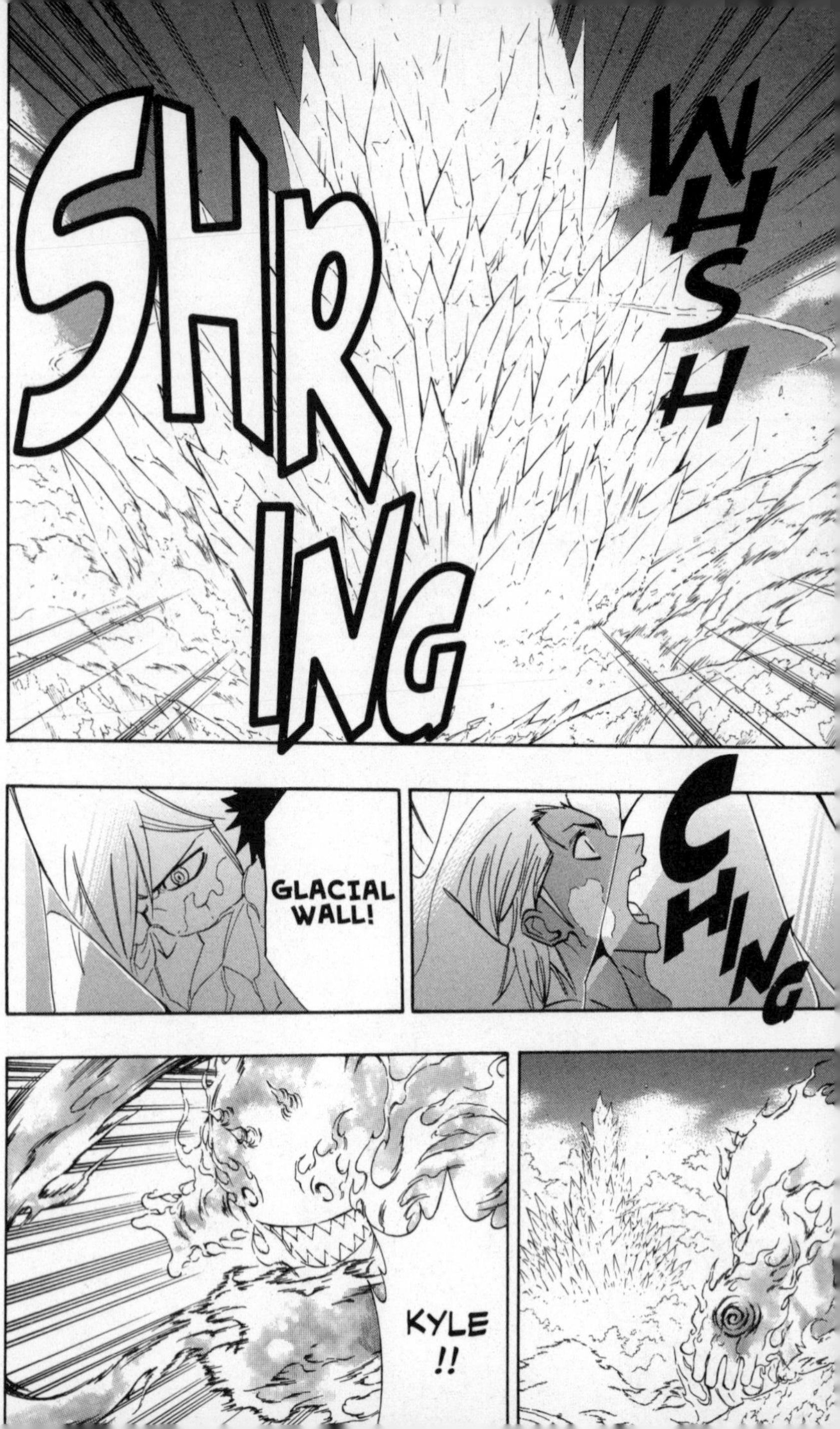
WHSH
SHRING
CHING
GLACIAL WALL!
KYLE!!

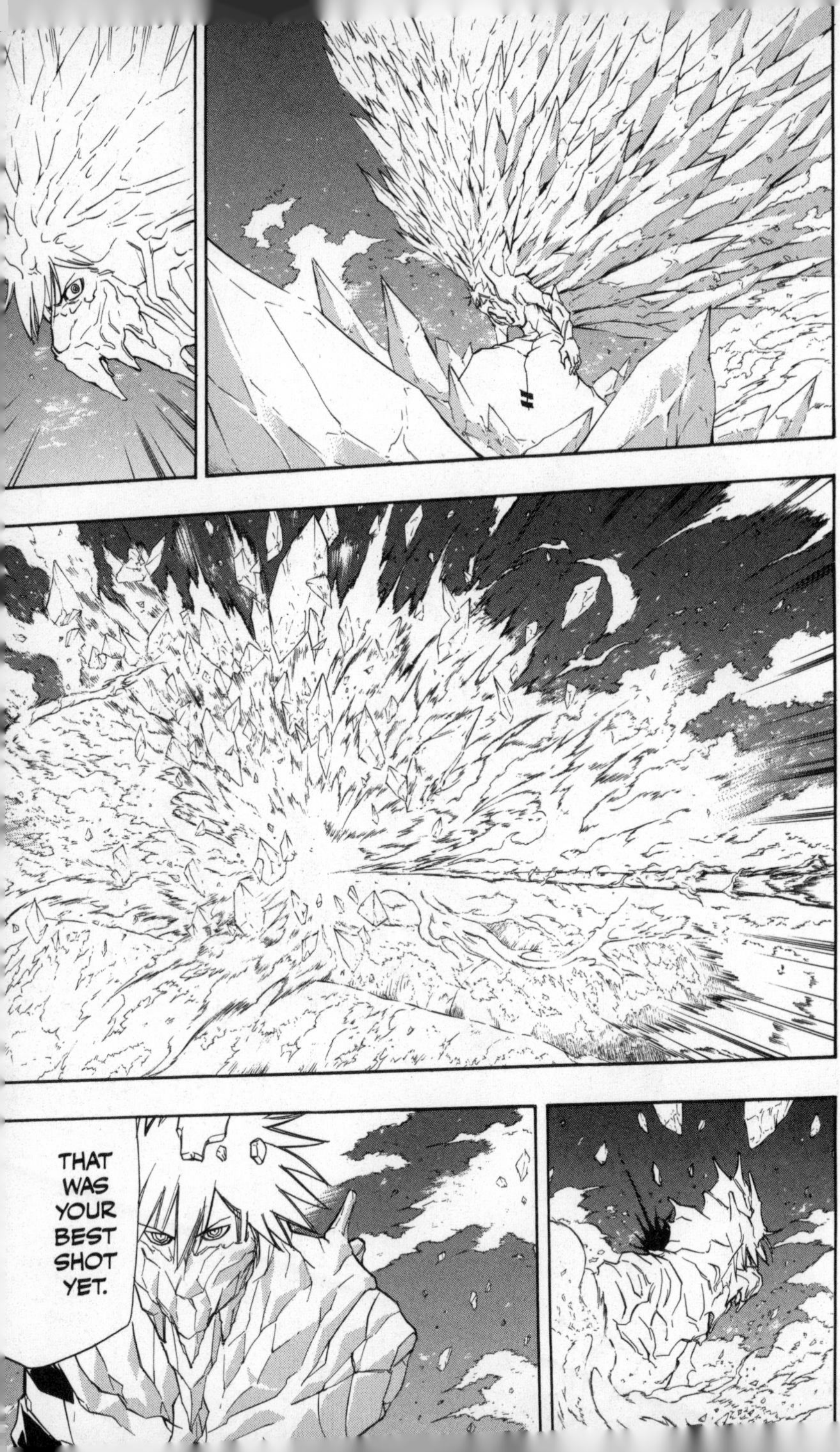
THAT WAS YOUR BEST SHOT YET.

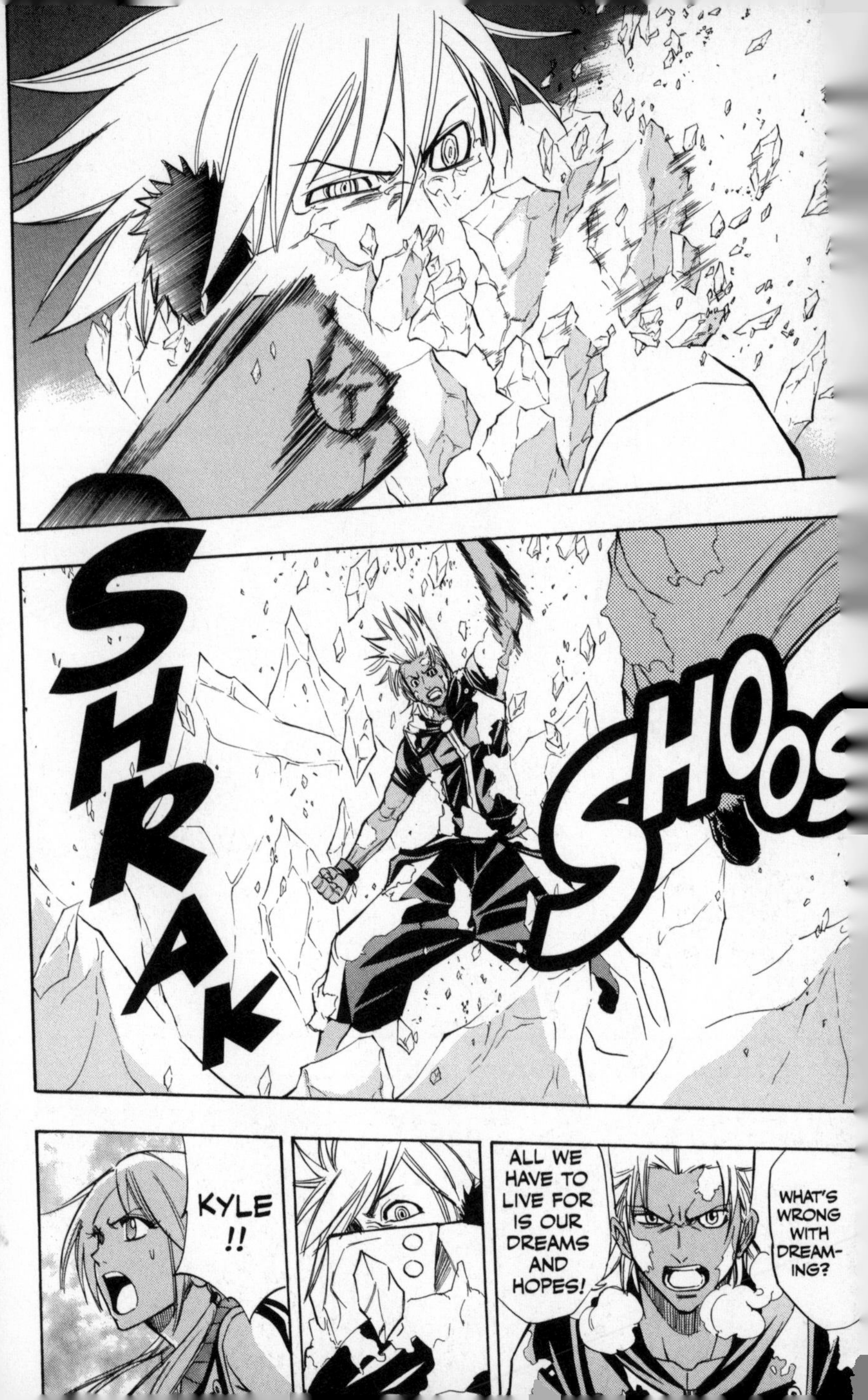
SHOOS
SHRAK
WHAT'S WRONG WITH DREAMING?
ALL WE HAVE TO LIVE FOR IS OUR DREAMS AND HOPES!
KYLE !!

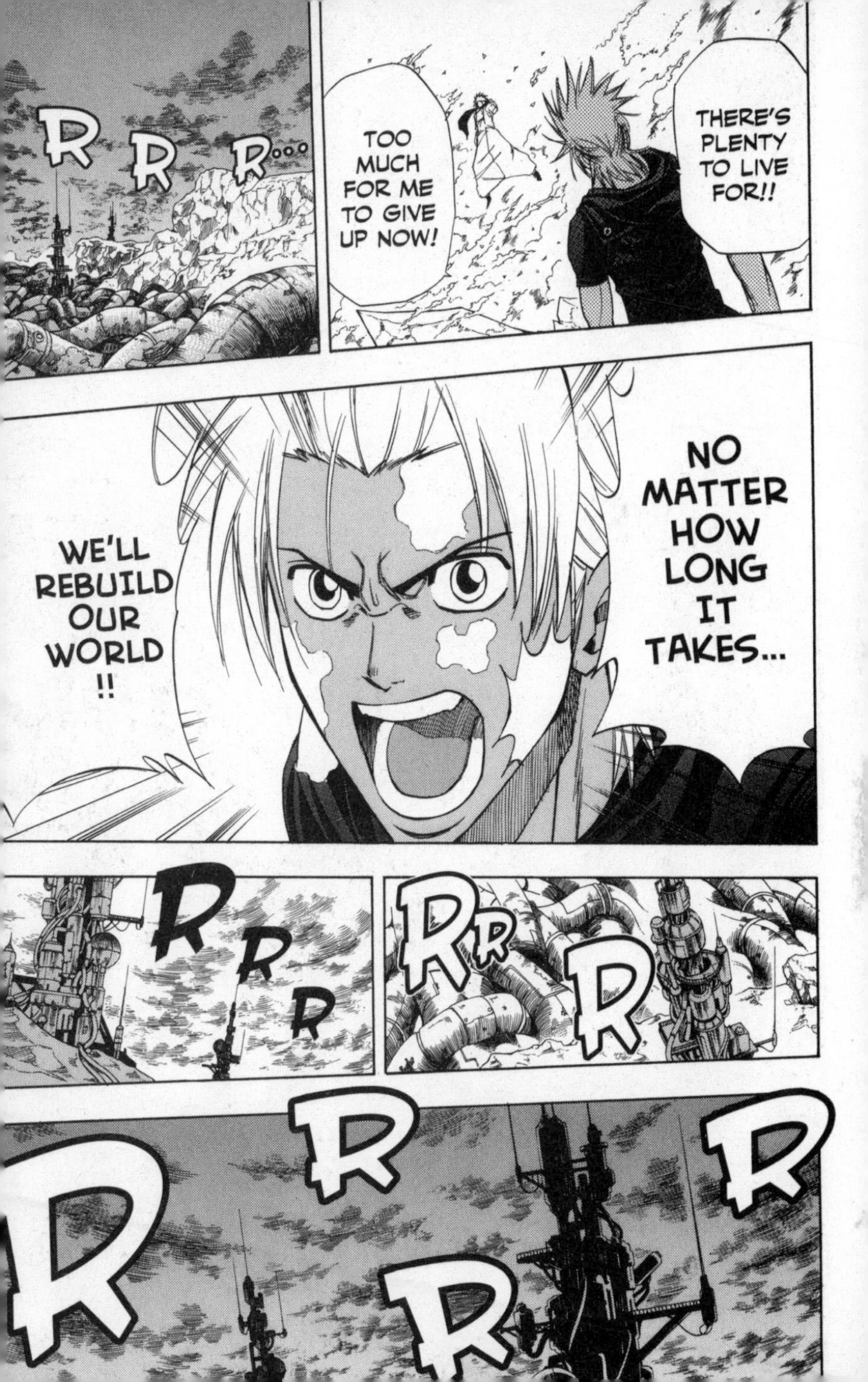
THERE'S PLENTY TO LIVE FOR!!
TOO MUCH FOR ME TO GIVE UP NOW!
R R R...
NO MATTER HOW LONG IT TAKES...
WE'LL REBUILD OUR WORLD!!
RR R
R R R
R R R R

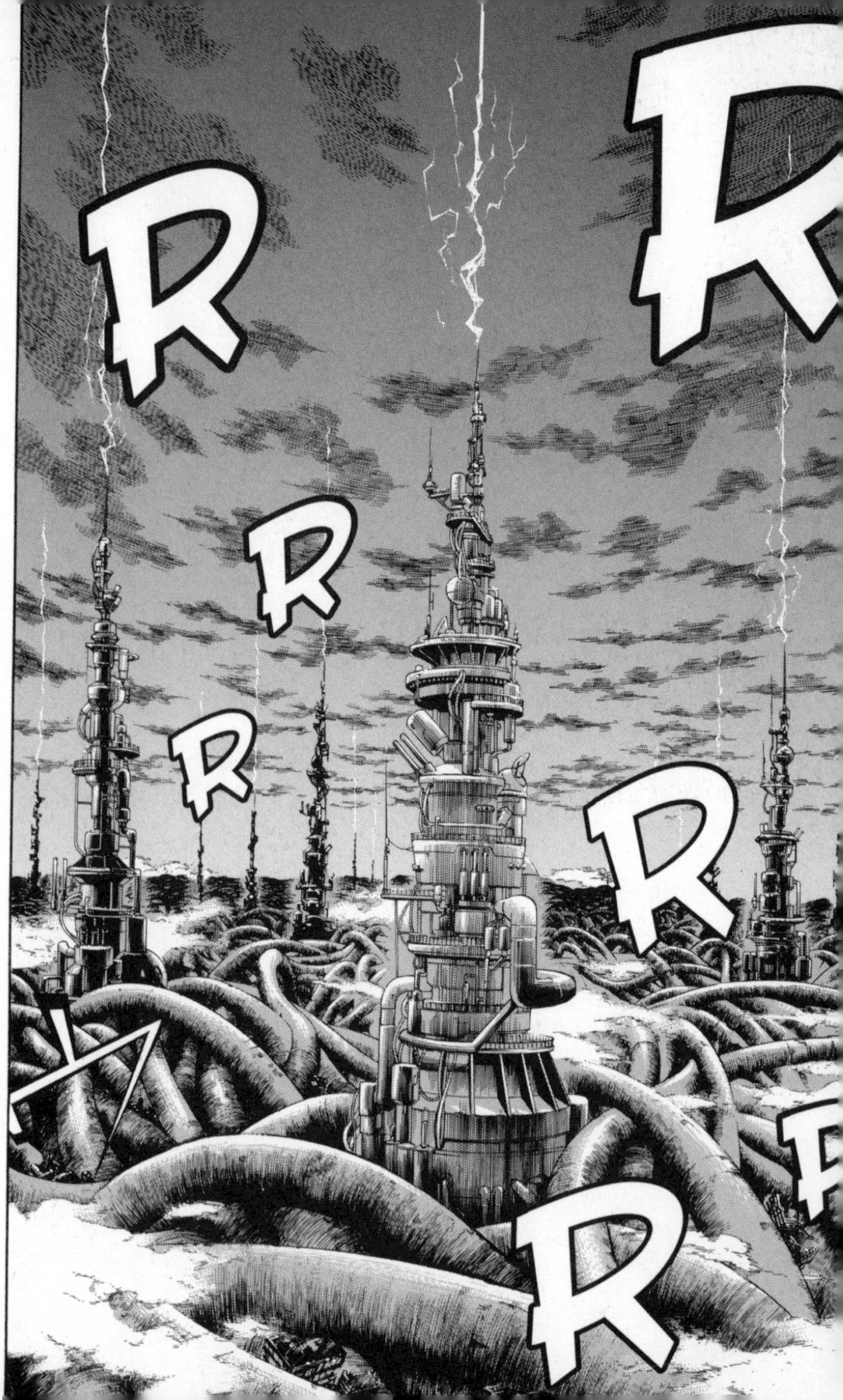
RRRRRRR

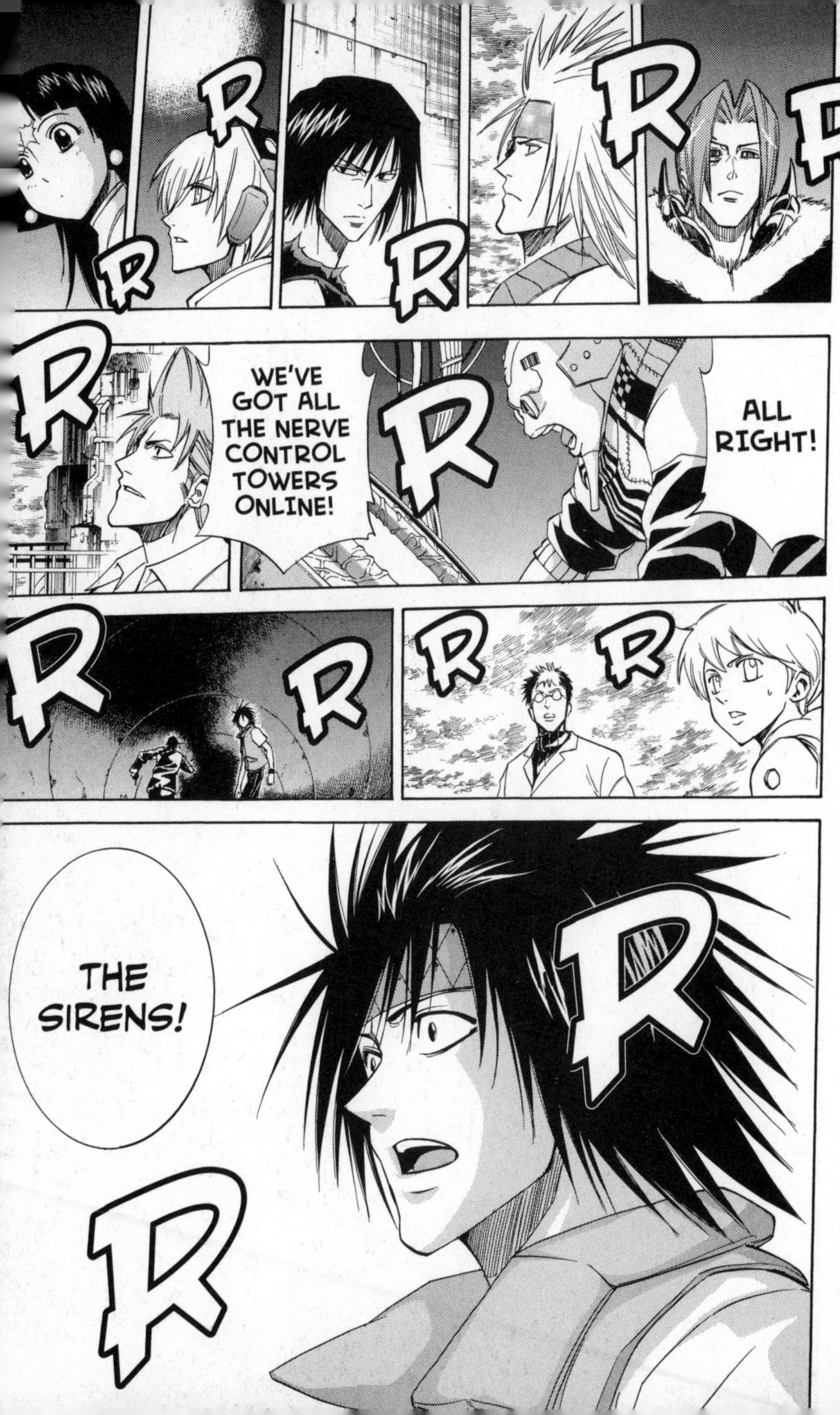
R
R
R
R
R
R
ALL RIGHT!
R
WE'VE GOT ALL THE NERVE CONTROL TOWERS ONLINE!
R
R
R
R
R
R
THE SIRENS!
R
R

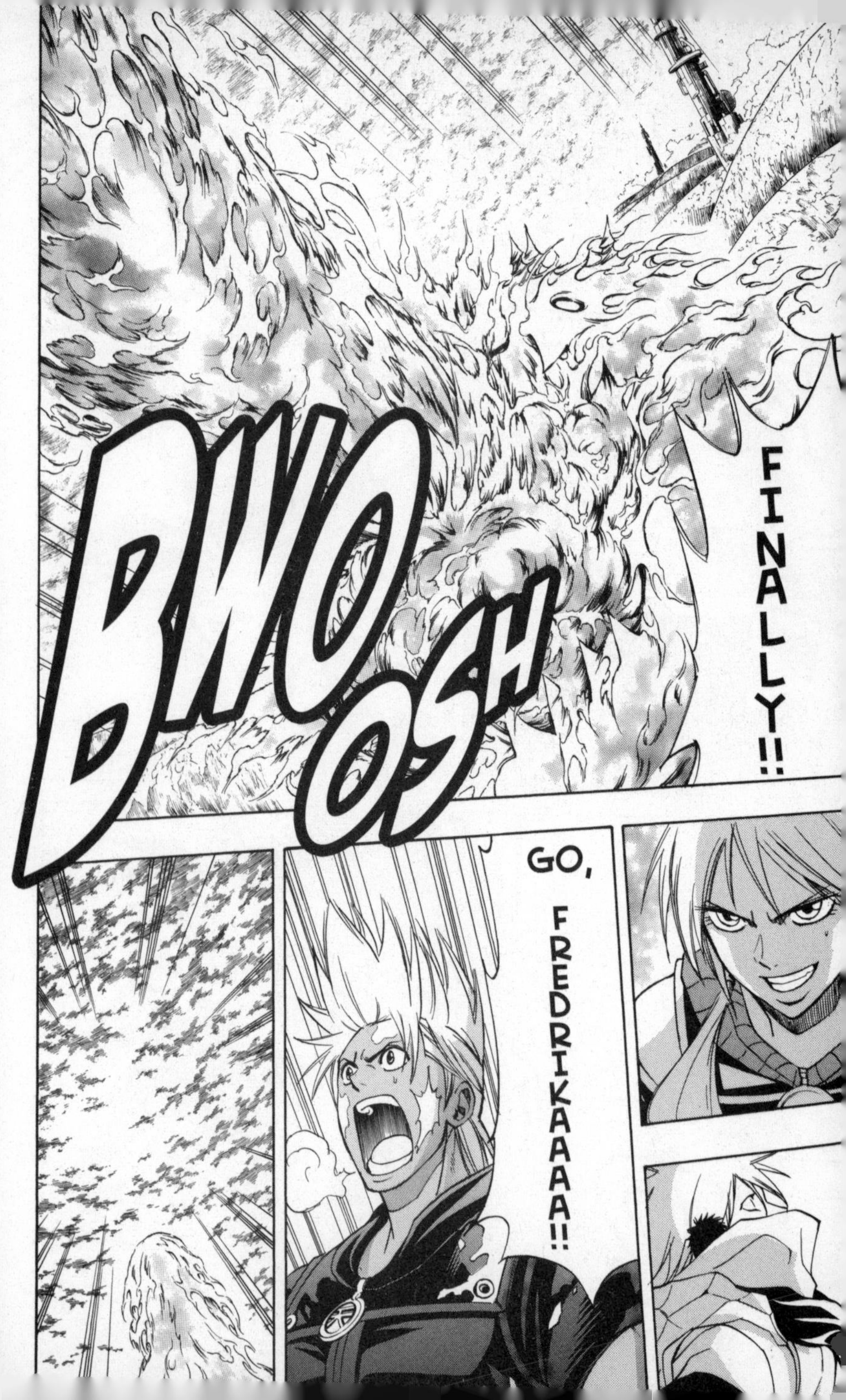
FINALLY!!
BWOOSH
GO, FREDRIKAAAA!!

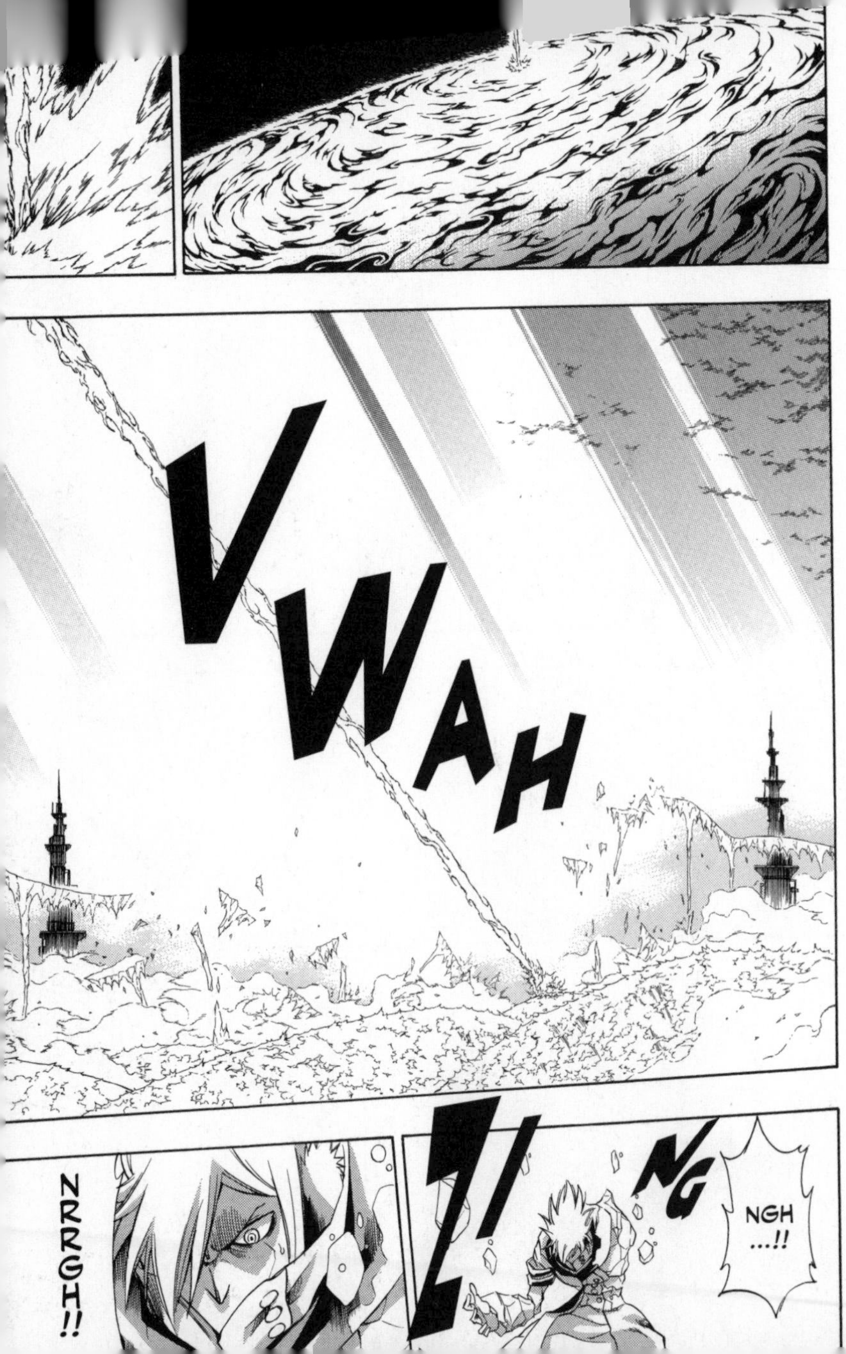
VWAH
ZING
NGH ...!!
NRRGH!!

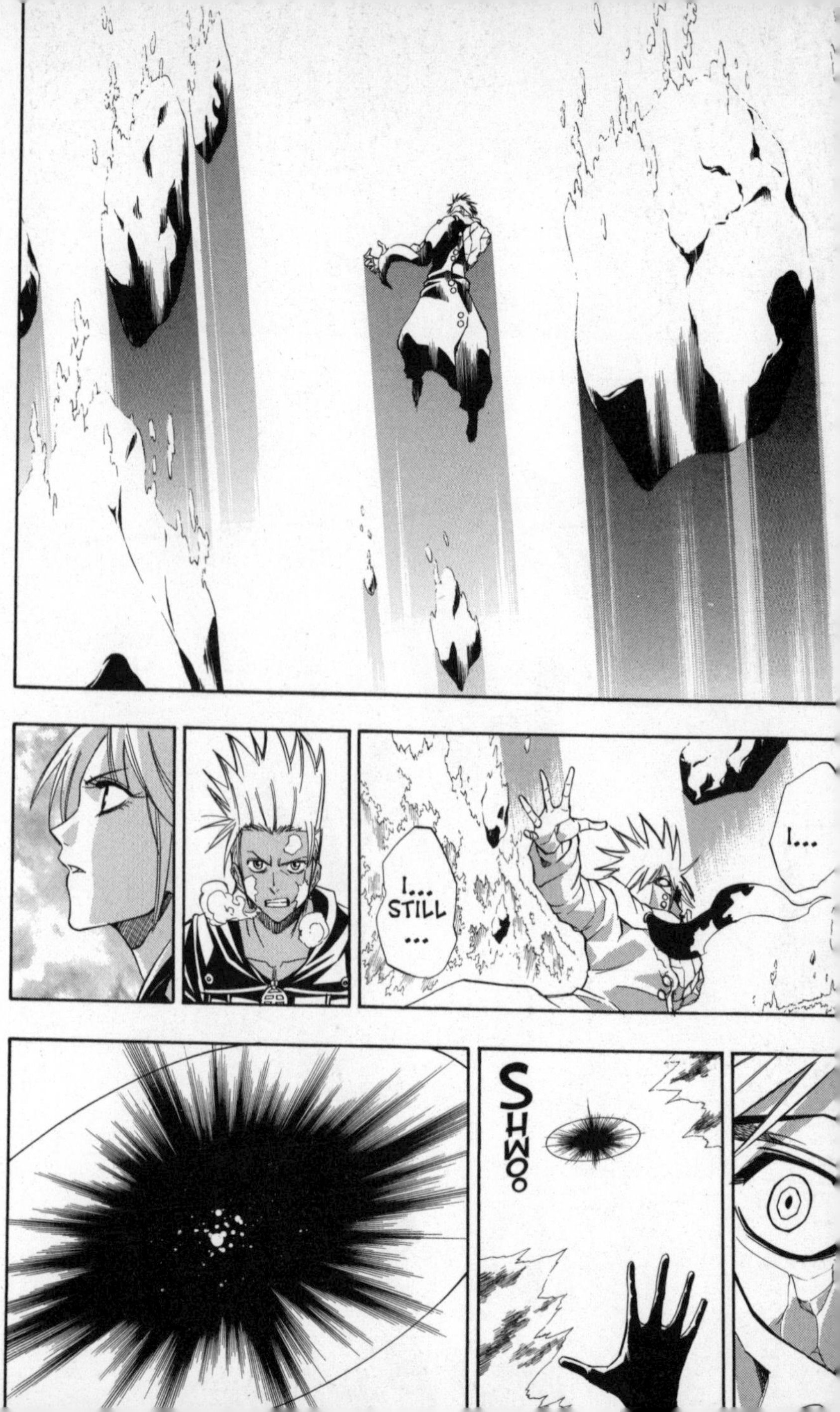
I...
I... STILL ...
SHWOO

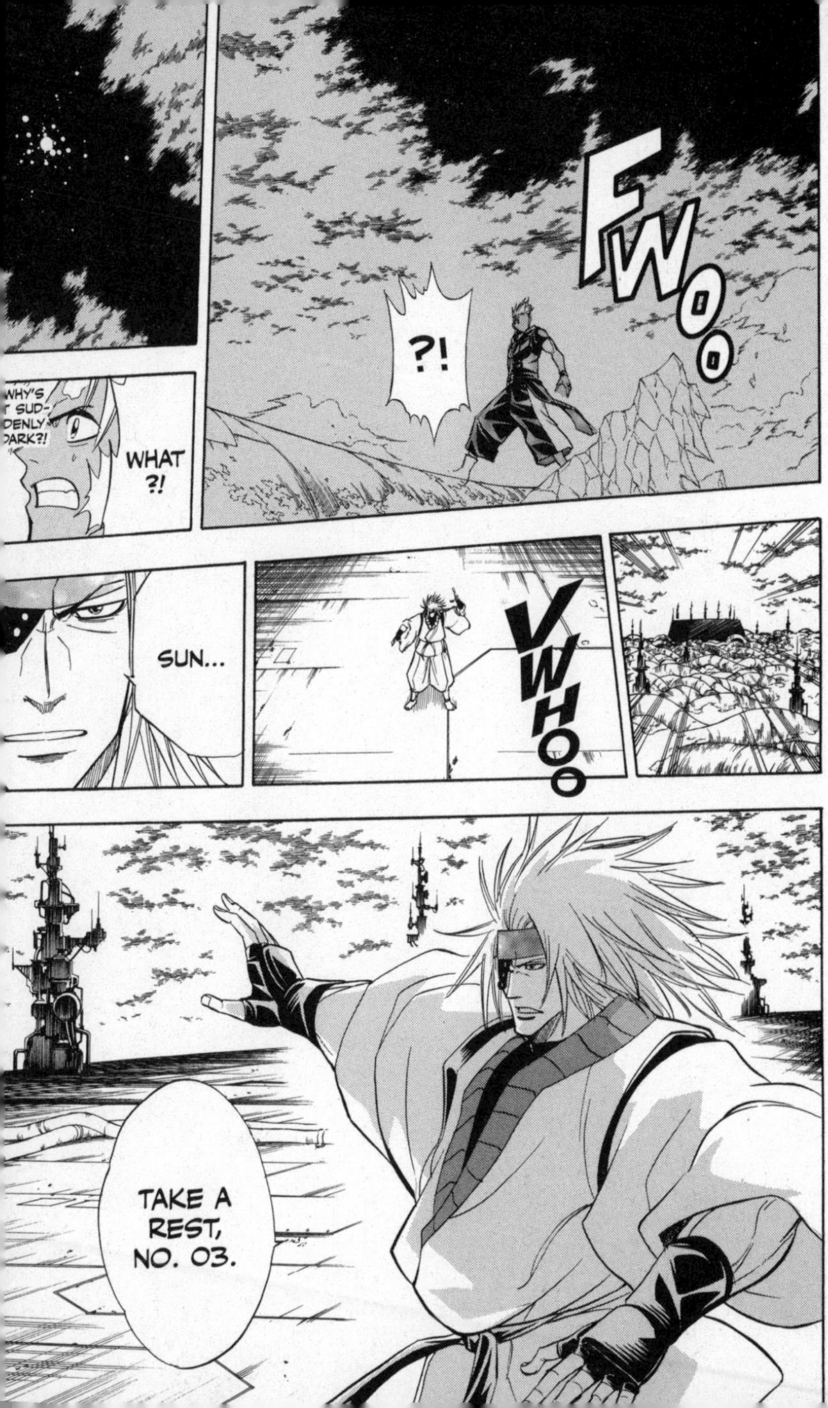
FWOOO
?!
WHAT ?!
WHY'S T SUD-DENLY DARK?!
VWHOOO
SUN...
TAKE A REST, NO. 03.

Mutters and mumblings...

MY ASSISTANTS GAVE ME A BIRTHDAY PRESENT.
IT'S A SUPER REALISTIC FIGURINE OF THE JOKER
BAD GUY FROM *THE DARK KNIGHT* MOVIE.

IT'S SO VISUALLY AMAZING, IT LOOKS LIKE IT MIGHT
COME TO LIFE!

THANK YOU, EVERYONE. I'LL DISPLAY IT PROMINENTLY!

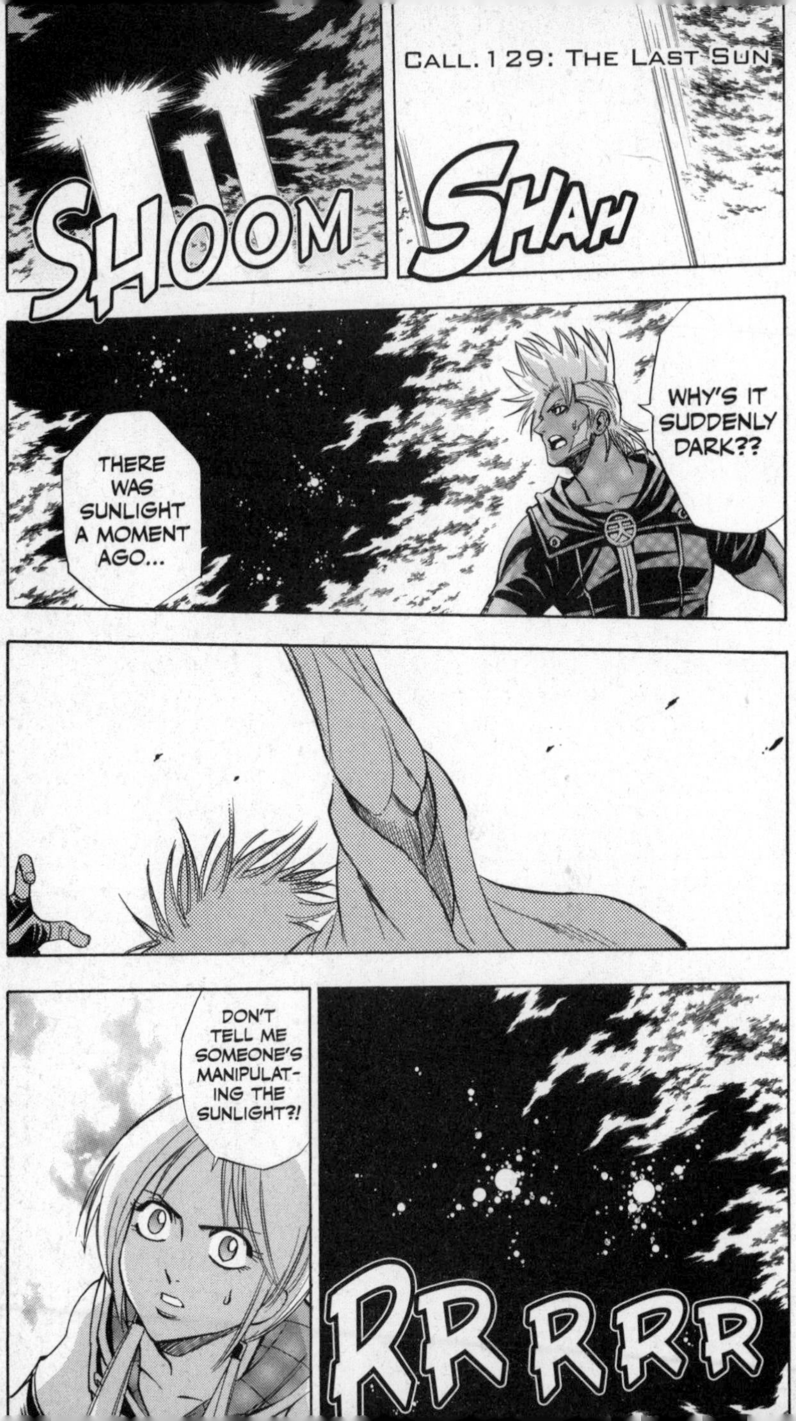
CALL. 129: THE LAST SUN
SHAH
SHOOM
WHY'S IT SUDDENLY DARK??
THERE WAS SUNLIGHT A MOMENT AGO...
RRRRR
DON'T TELL ME SOMEONE'S MANIPULATING THE SUNLIGHT?!

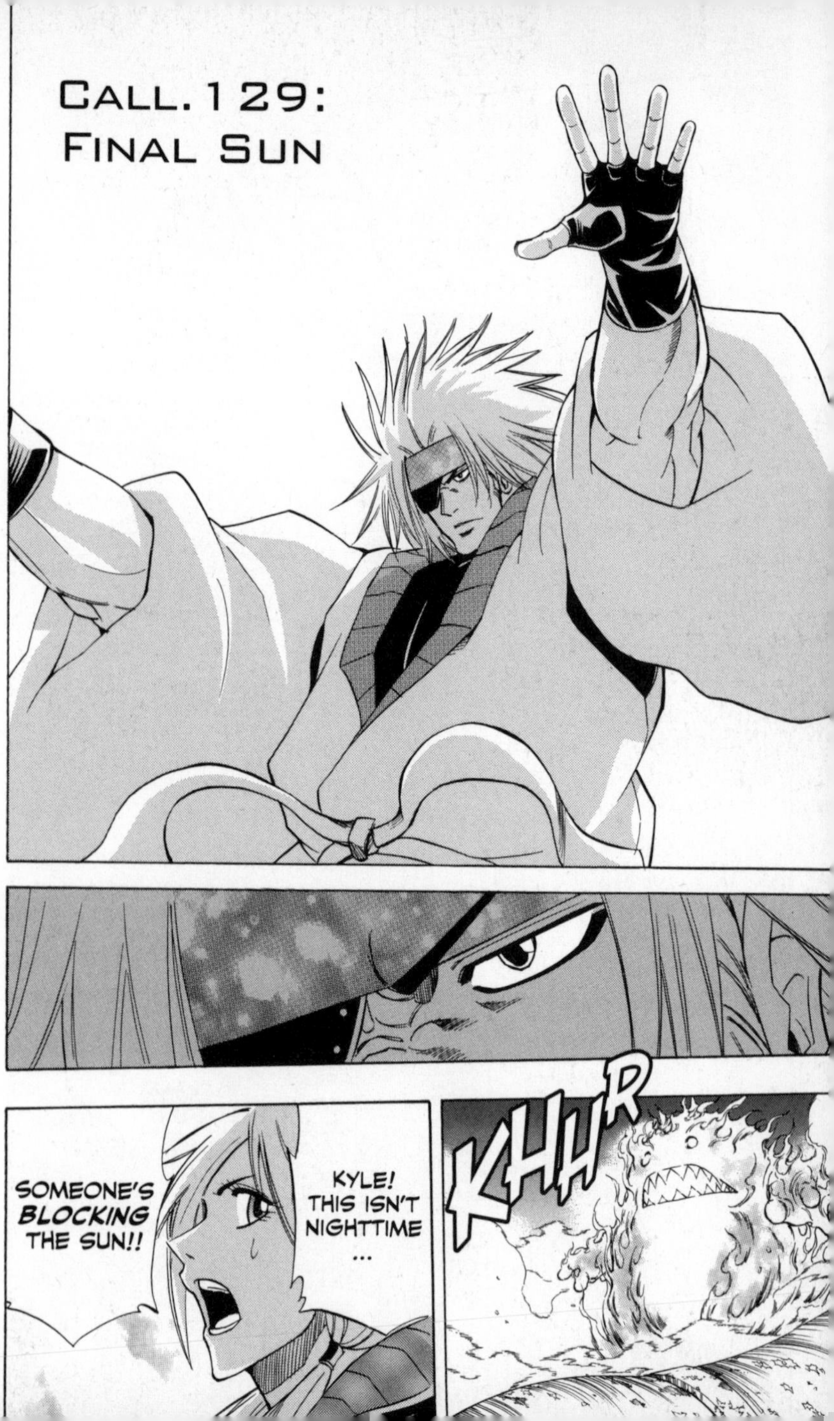
Call. 129:
Final Sun
KHHR
Kyle! This isn't nighttime...
Someone's blocking the sun!!

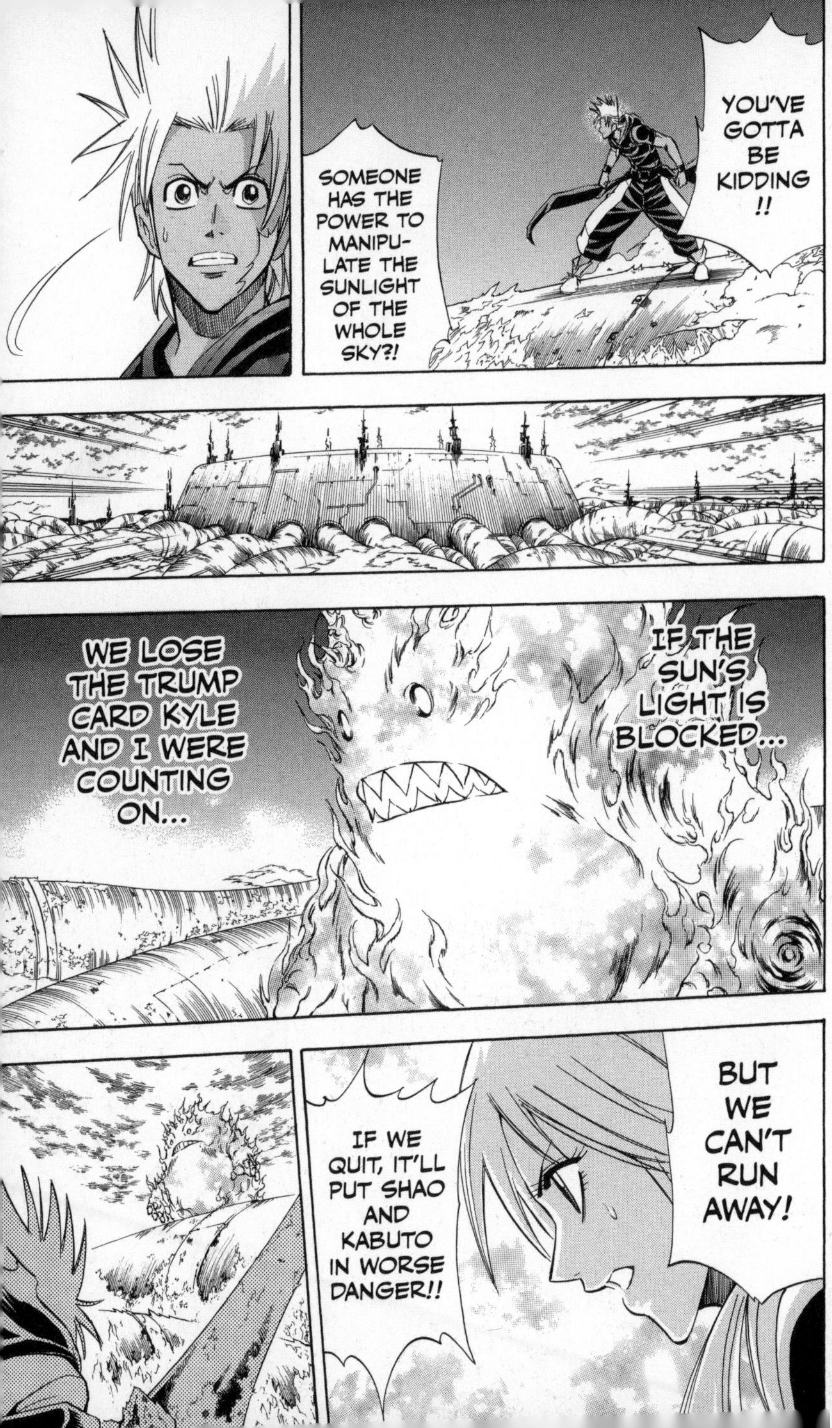
YOU'VE GOTTA BE KIDDING!!
SOMEONE HAS THE POWER TO MANIPU-LATE THE SUNLIGHT OF THE WHOLE SKY?!
IF THE SUN'S LIGHT IS BLOCKED...
WE LOSE THE TRUMP CARD KYLE AND I WERE COUNTING ON...
BUT WE CAN'T RUN AWAY!
IF WE QUIT, IT'LL PUT SHAO AND KABUTO IN WORSE DANGER!!

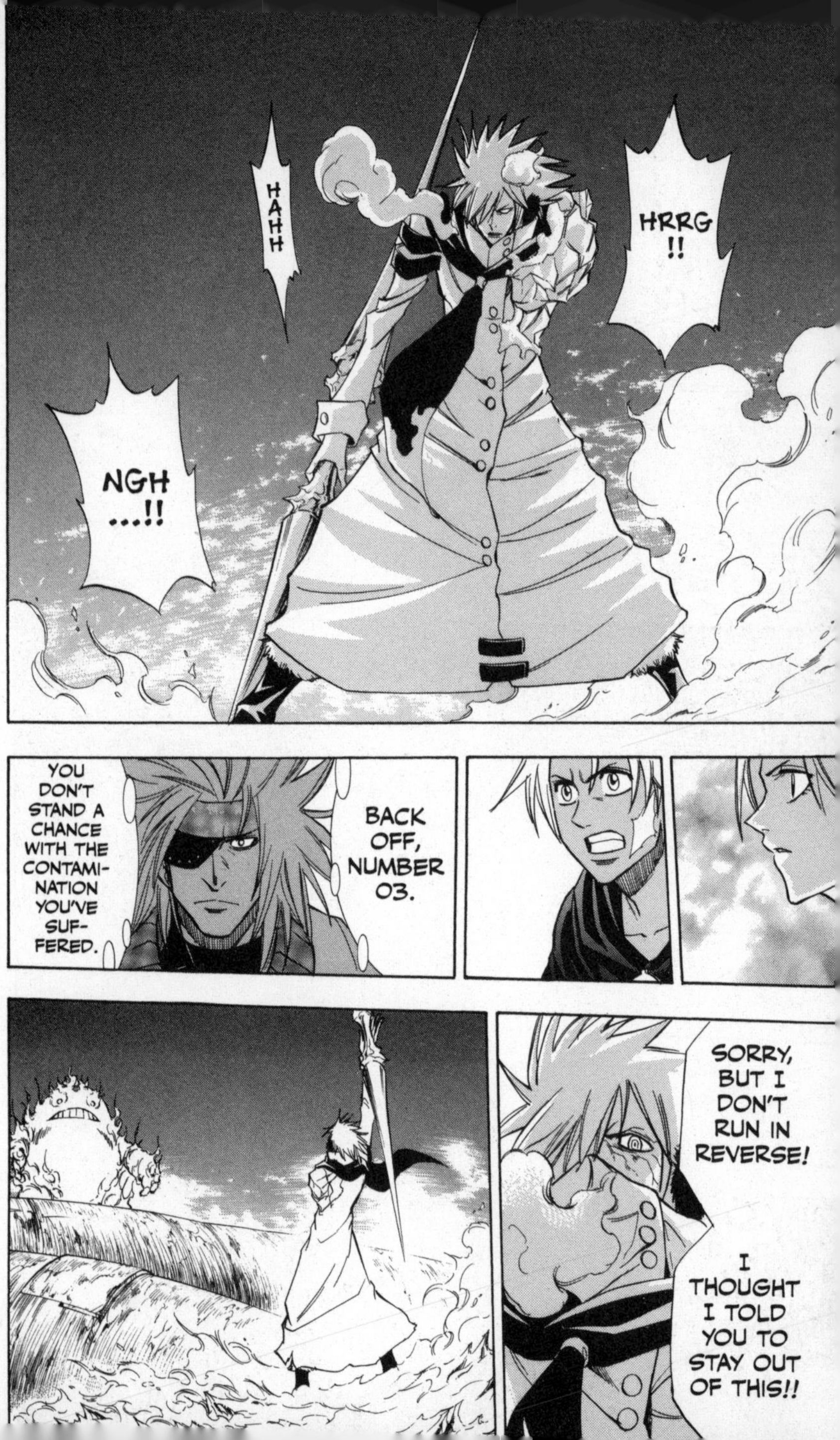
HRRG!!
HAHH
NGH...!!
BACK OFF, NUMBER 03.
YOU DON'T STAND A CHANCE WITH THE CONTAMINATION YOU'VE SUFFERED.
SORRY, BUT I DON'T RUN IN REVERSE!
I THOUGHT I TOLD YOU TO STAY OUT OF THIS!!

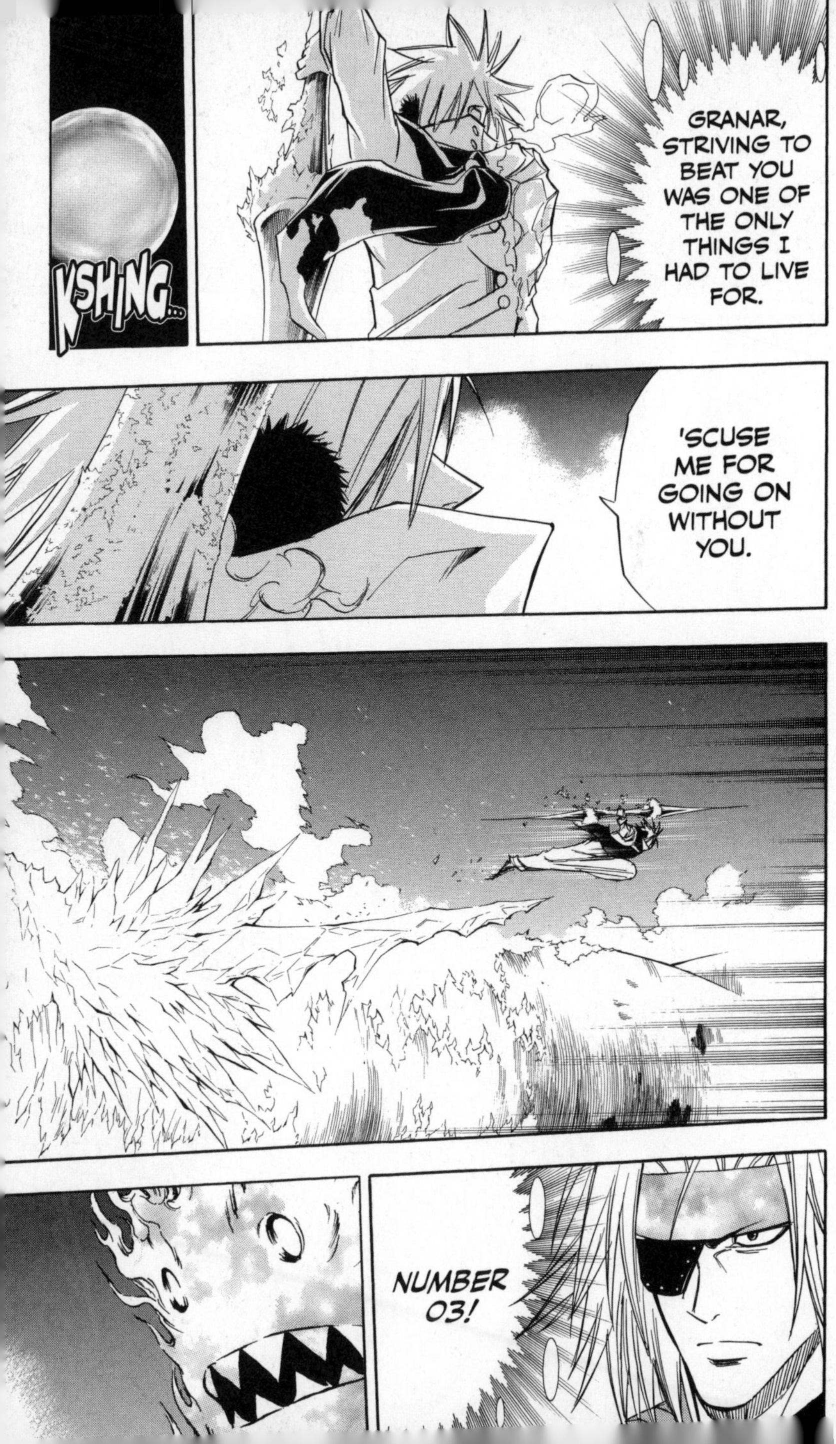
GRANAR, STRIVING TO BEAT YOU WAS ONE OF THE ONLY THINGS I HAD TO LIVE FOR.
KSHING...
'SCUSE ME FOR GOING ON WITHOUT YOU.
NUMBER 03!

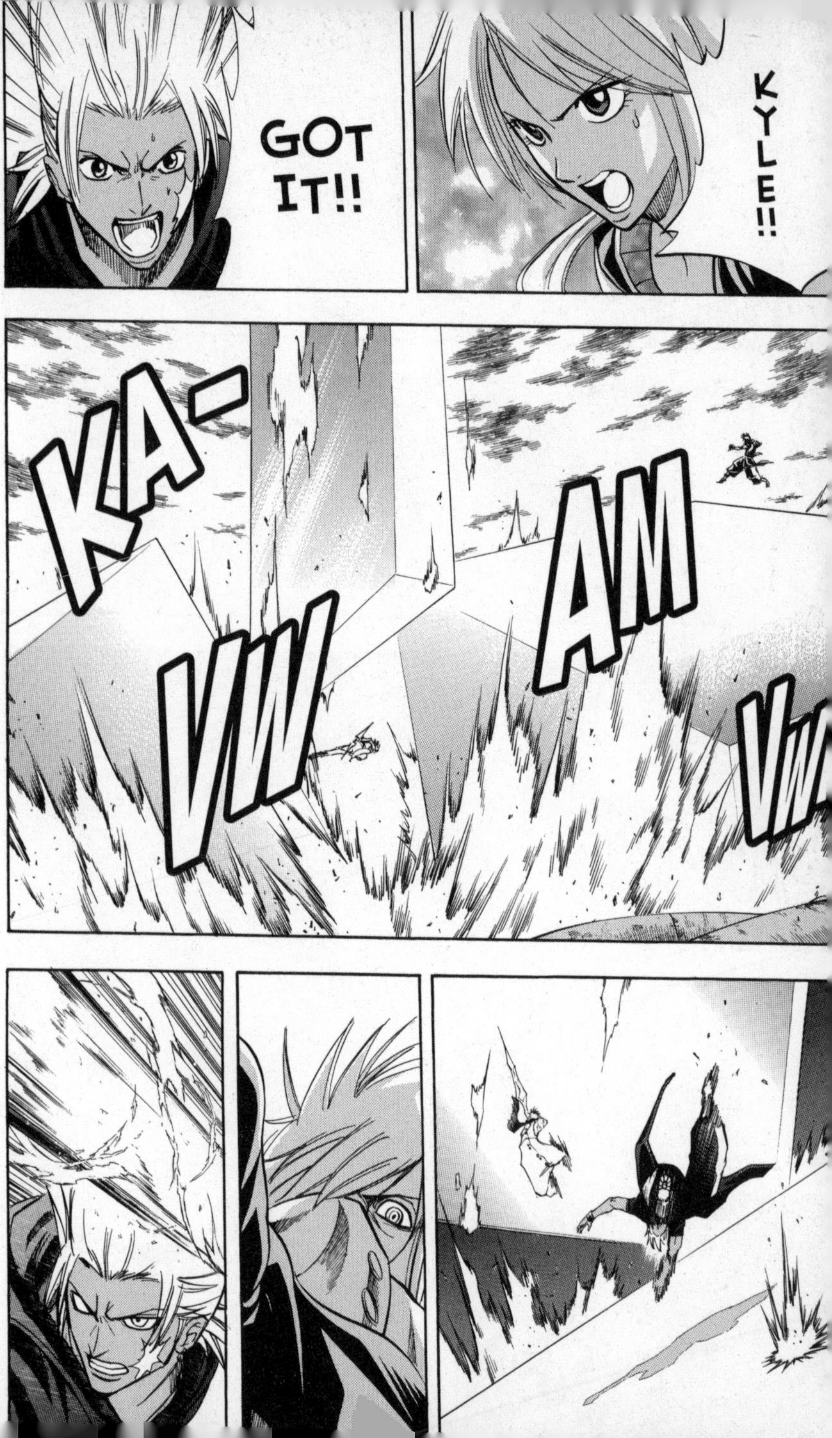
KYLE!!
GOT IT!!
KA-
VVV
AM
VVV

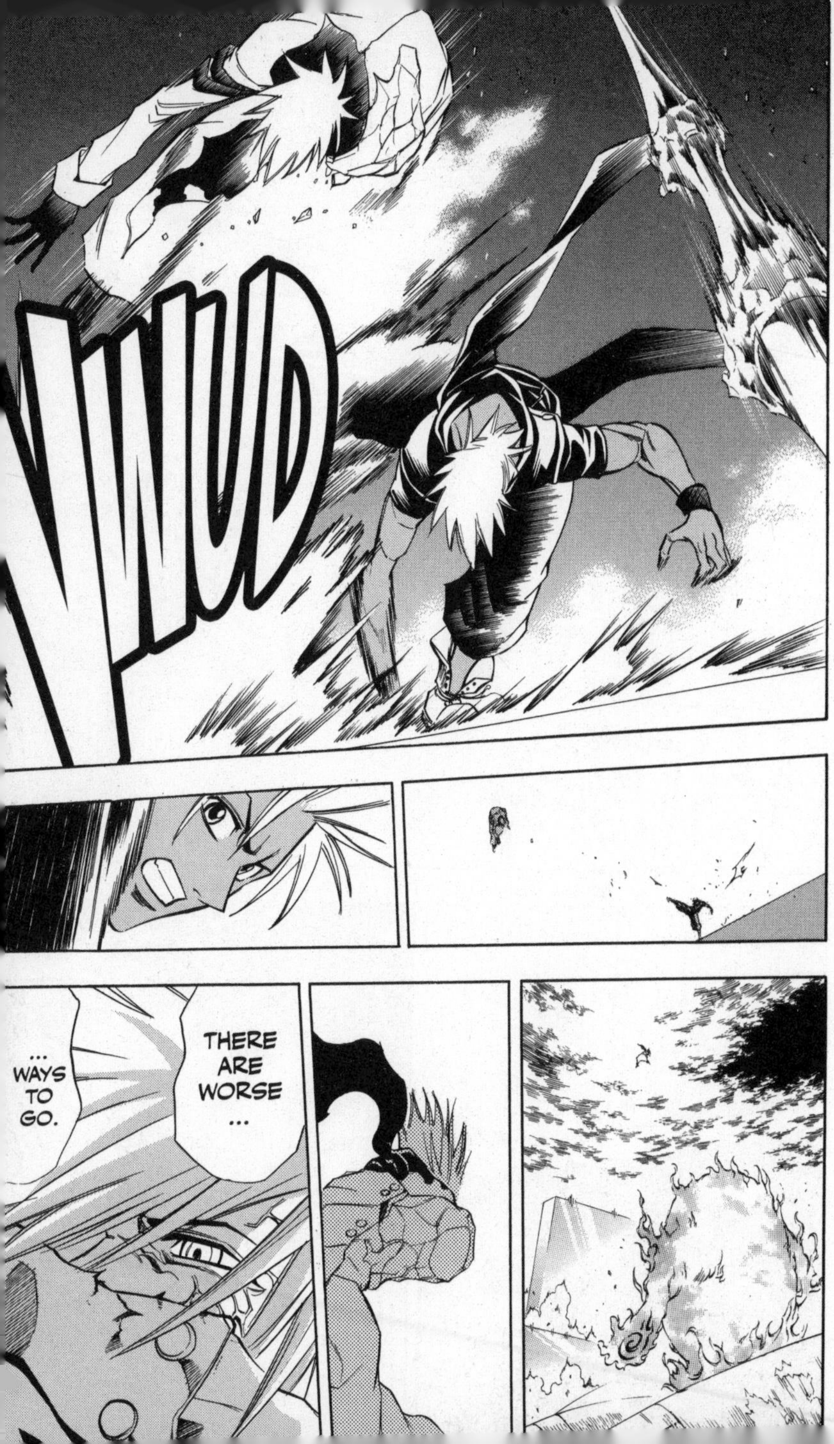
VWUD
THERE ARE WORSE ...
... WAYS TO GO.

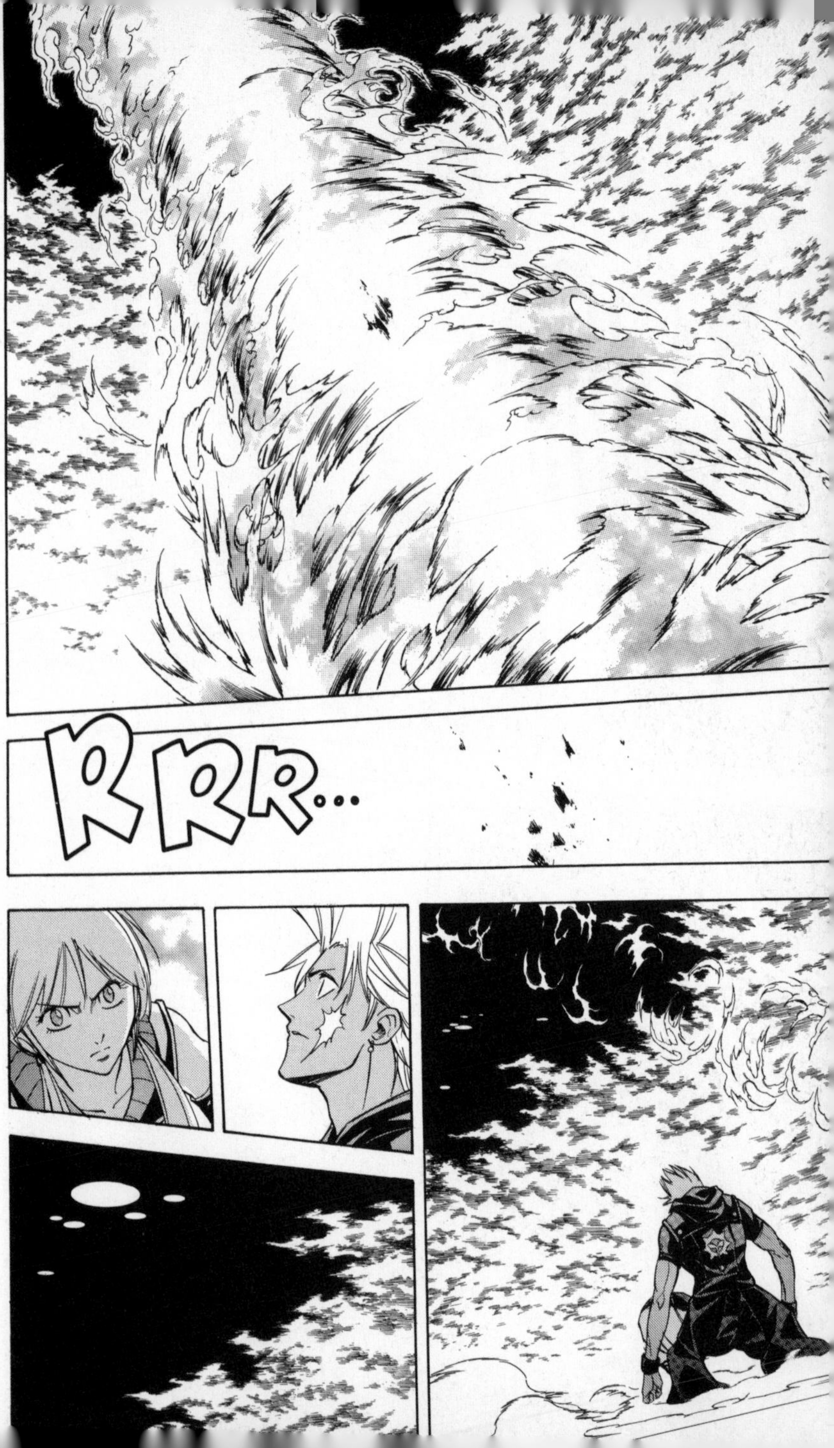
RRR...

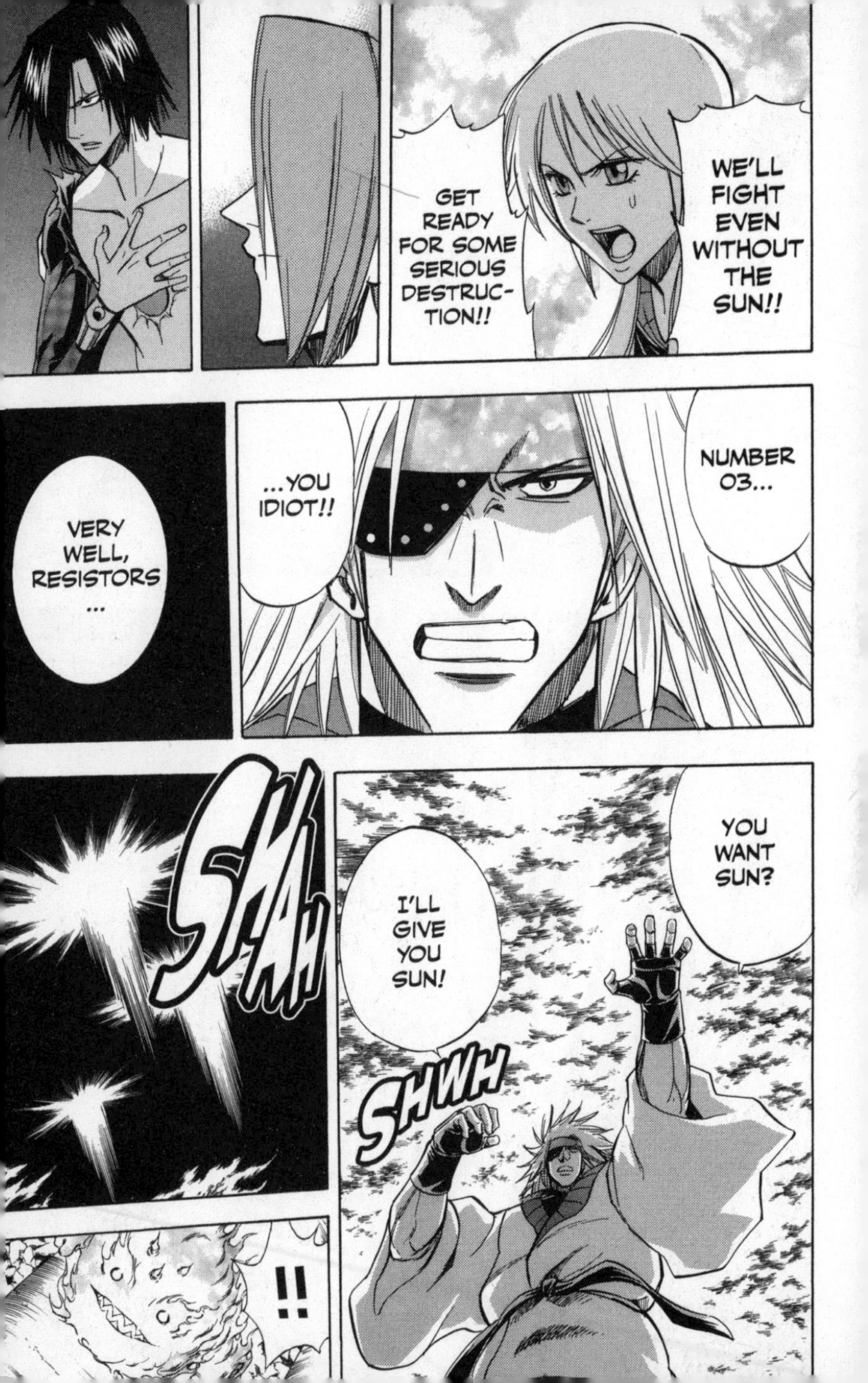
WE'LL FIGHT EVEN WITHOUT THE SUN!!
GET READY FOR SOME SERIOUS DESTRUC-TION!!
NUMBER 03...
...YOU IDIOT!!
VERY WELL, RESISTORS ...
YOU WANT SUN?
I'LL GIVE YOU SUN!
SHWH
!!

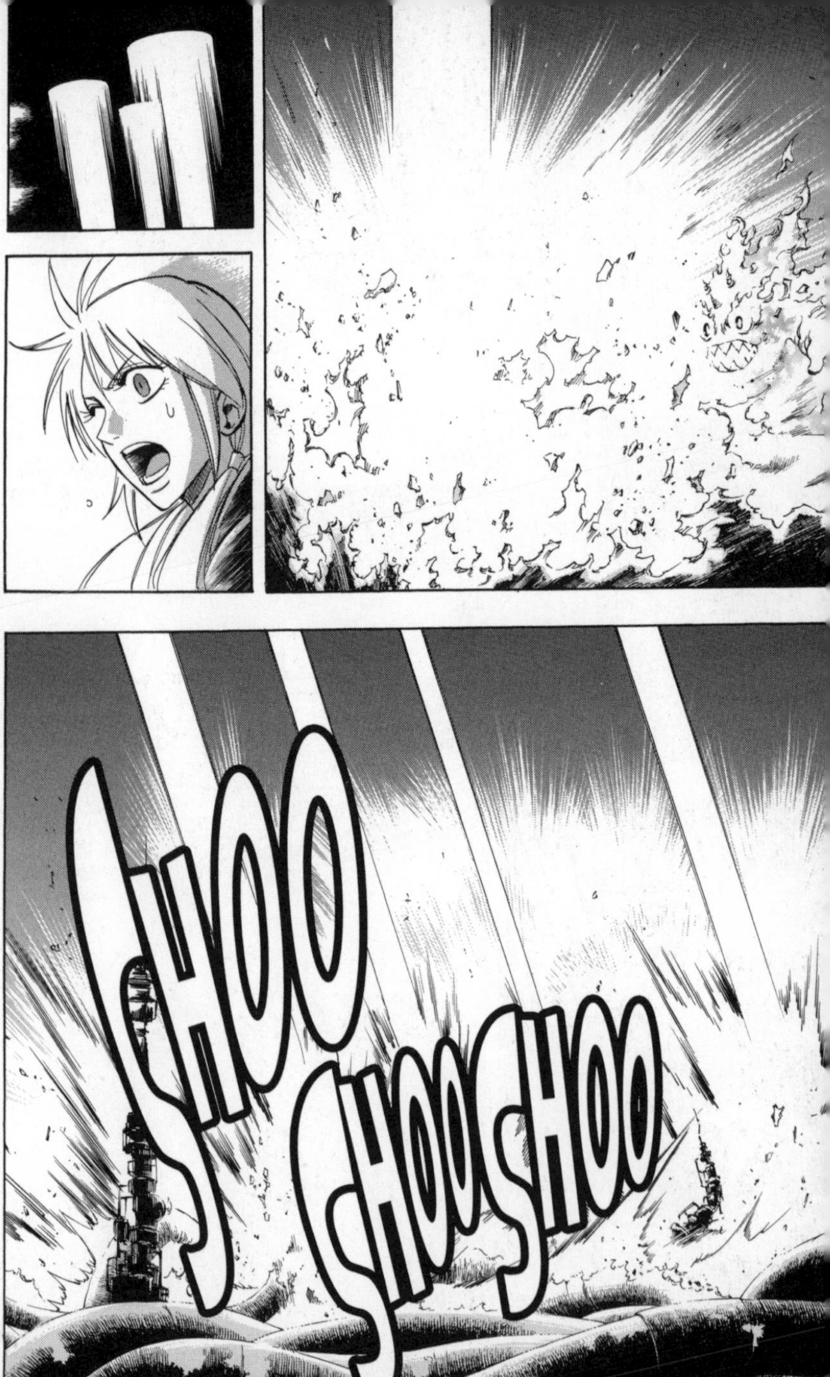
SHOO
SHOOSHOO

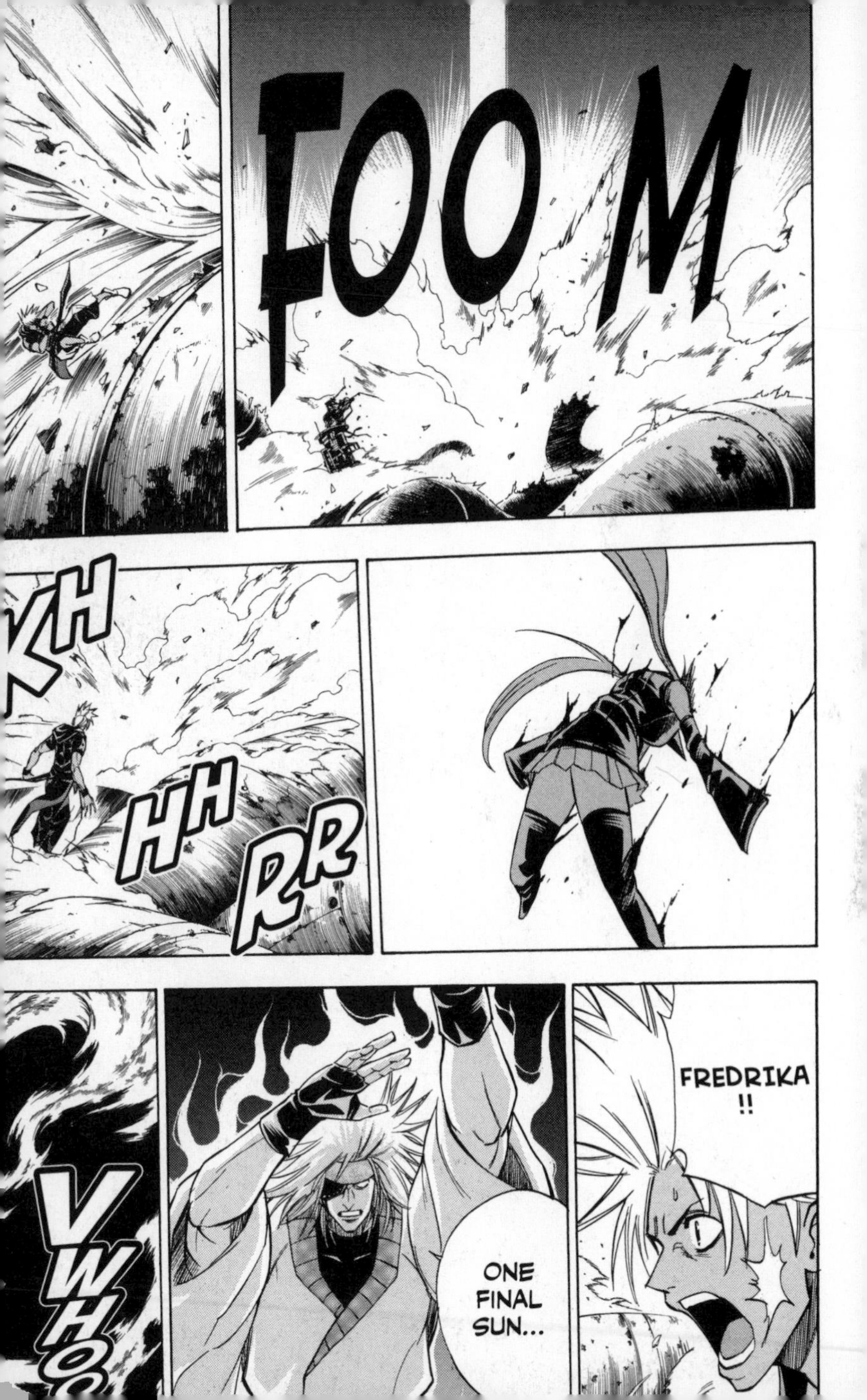
FOOM
KHHHRR
FREDRIKA !!
ONE FINAL SUN...
VWHO

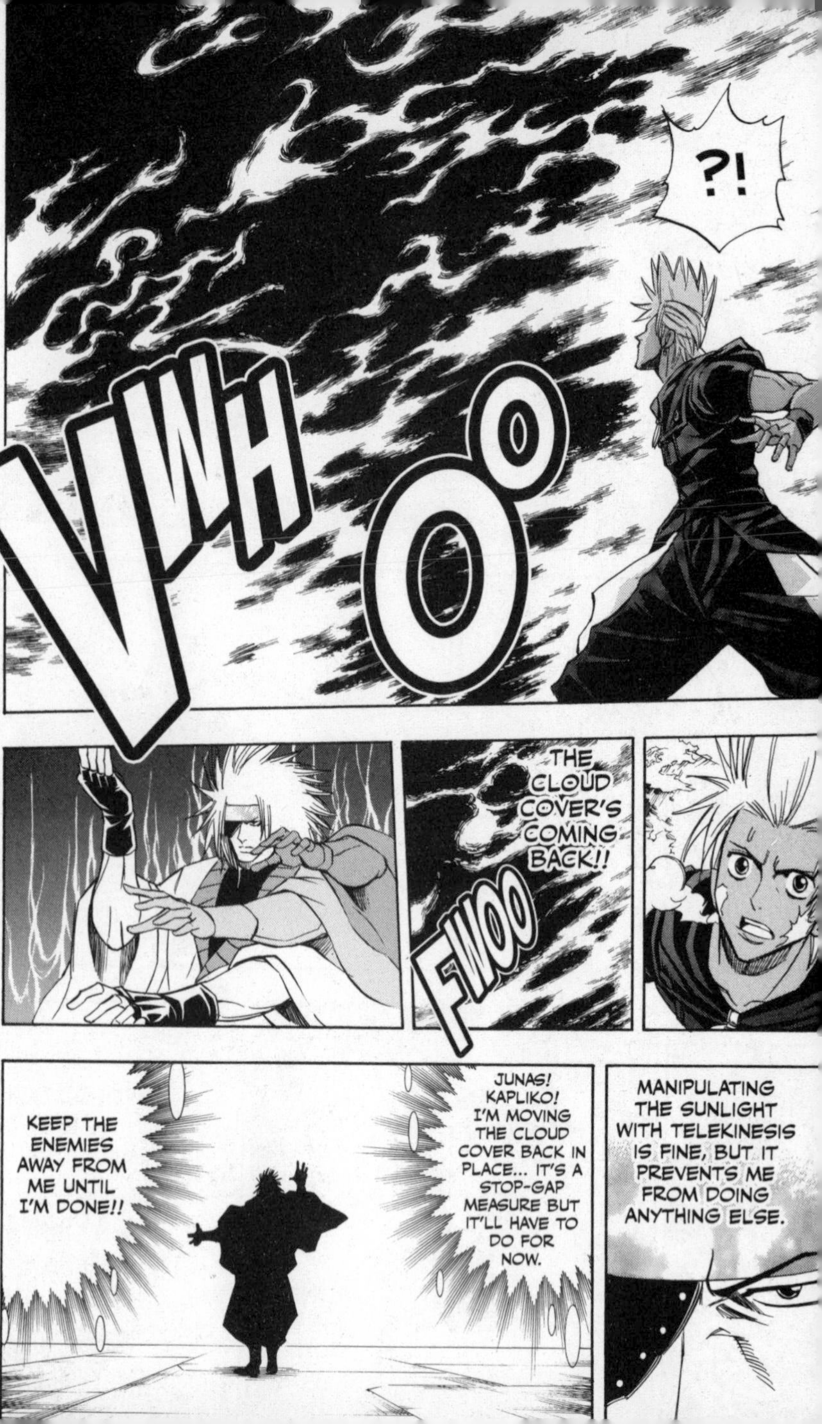
?!
VWHOOO
THE CLOUD COVER'S COMING BACK!!
FWOO
MANIPULATING THE SUNLIGHT WITH TELEKINESIS IS FINE, BUT IT PREVENTS ME FROM DOING ANYTHING ELSE.
JUNAS! KAPLIKO! I'M MOVING THE CLOUD COVER BACK IN PLACE... IT'S A STOP-GAP MEASURE BUT IT'LL HAVE TO DO FOR NOW.
KEEP THE ENEMIES AWAY FROM ME UNTIL I'M DONE!!

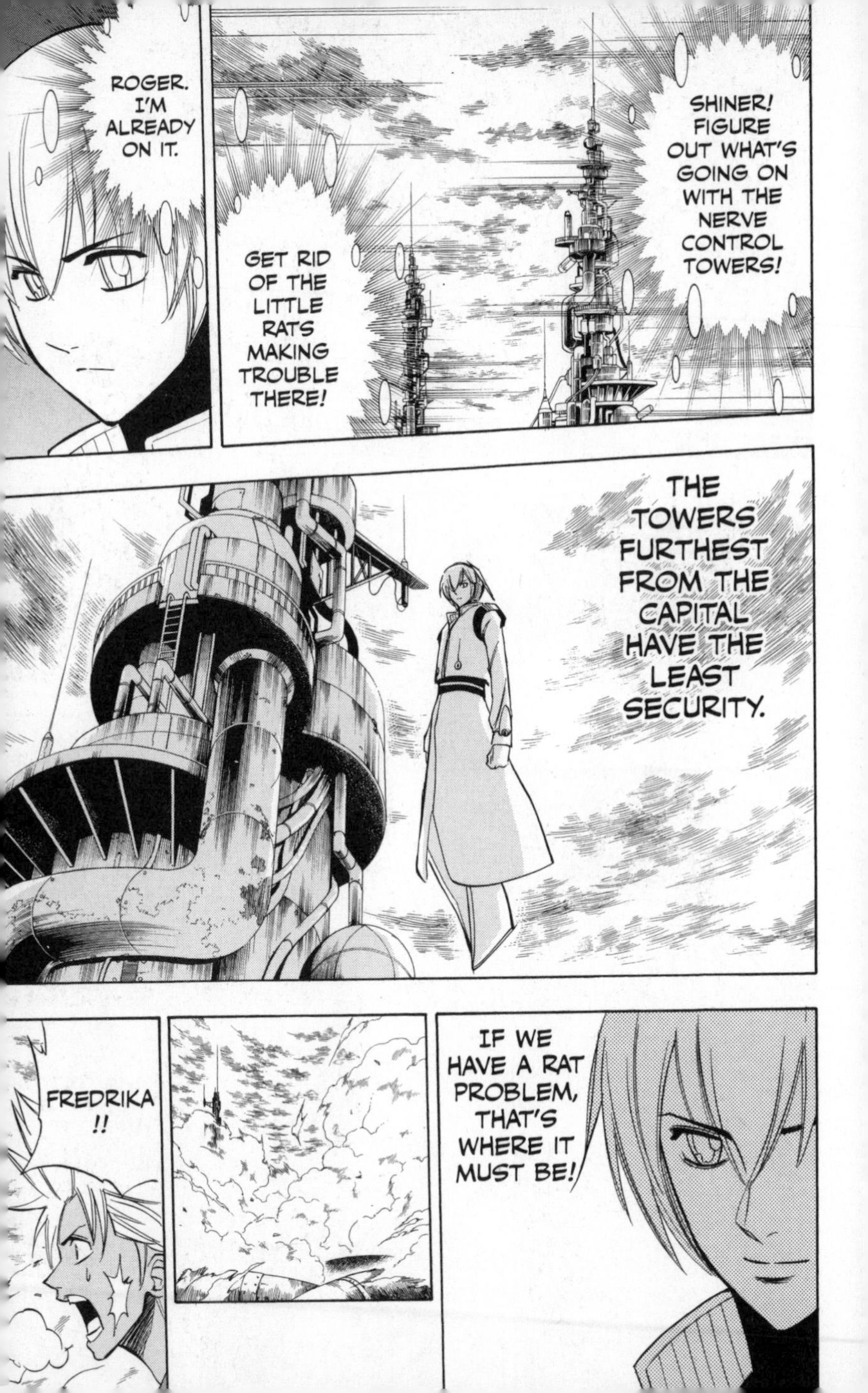
SHINER! FIGURE OUT WHAT'S GOING ON WITH THE NERVE CONTROL TOWERS!
GET RID OF THE LITTLE RATS MAKING TROUBLE THERE!
ROGER. I'M ALREADY ON IT.
THE TOWERS FURTHEST FROM THE CAPITAL HAVE THE LEAST SECURITY.
IF WE HAVE A RAT PROBLEM, THAT'S WHERE IT MUST BE!
FREDRIKA !!

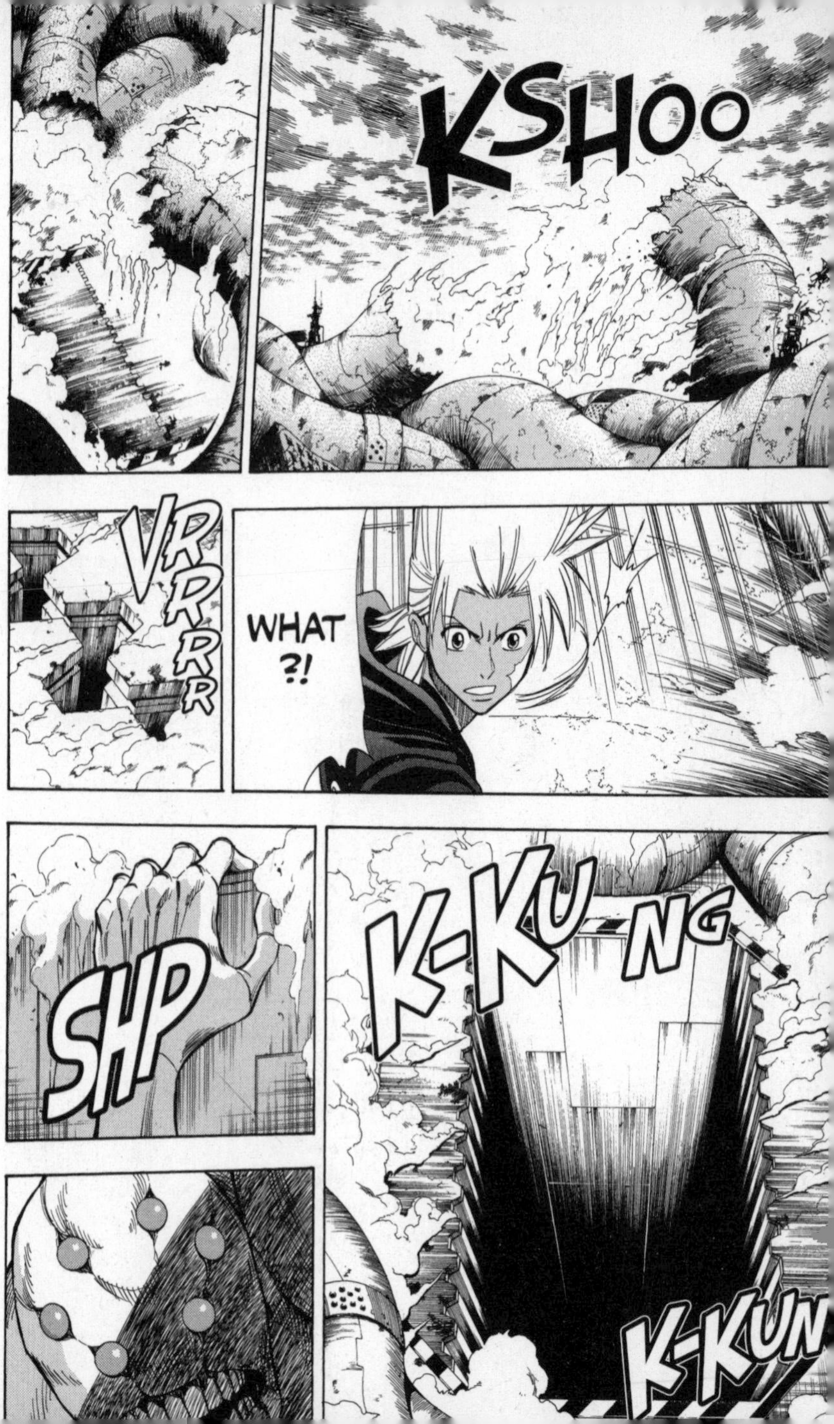
KSHOO
WHAT ?!
VRRRR
K-KUNG
K-KUN
SHP

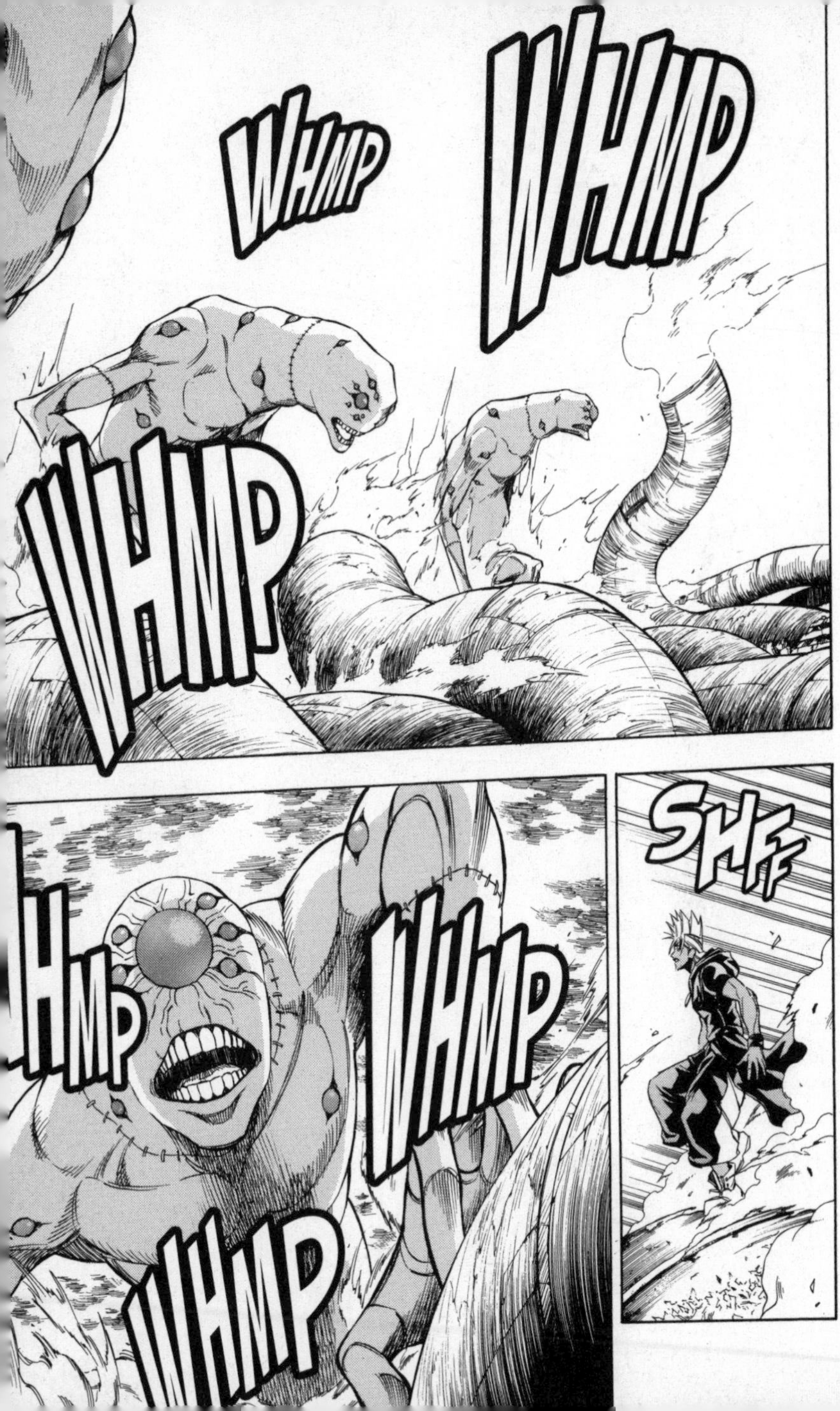
WHMP
WHMP
WHMP
SHFF
WHMP
WHMP

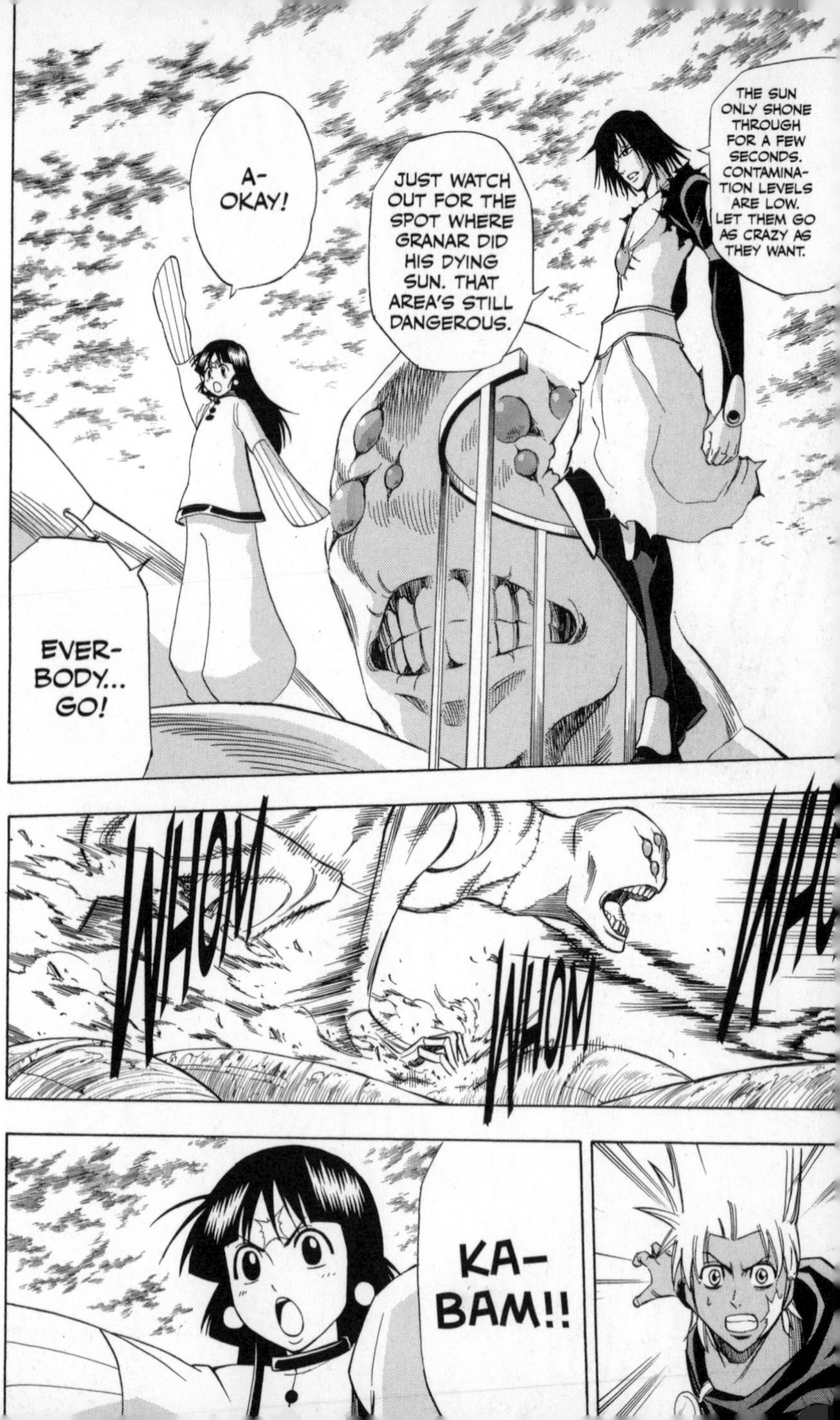
THE SUN ONLY SHONE THROUGH FOR A FEW SECONDS. CONTAMINATION LEVELS ARE LOW. LET THEM GO AS CRAZY AS THEY WANT.
JUST WATCH OUT FOR THE SPOT WHERE GRANAR DID HIS DYING SUN. THAT AREA'S STILL DANGEROUS.
A-OKAY!
EVERBODY... GO!
WHO
WHOM
WHOM
KA-BAM!!

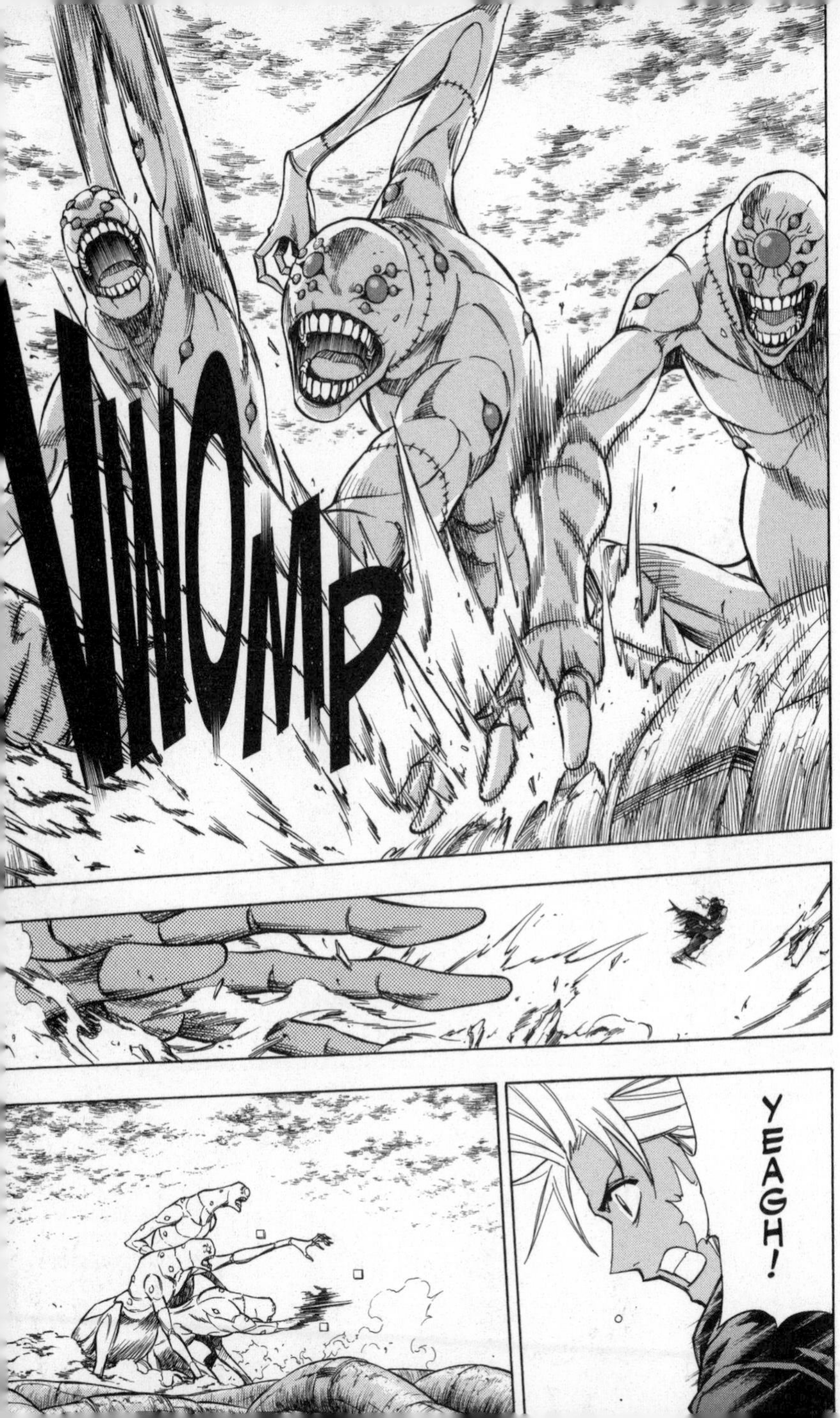
WHOMP
YEAGH!

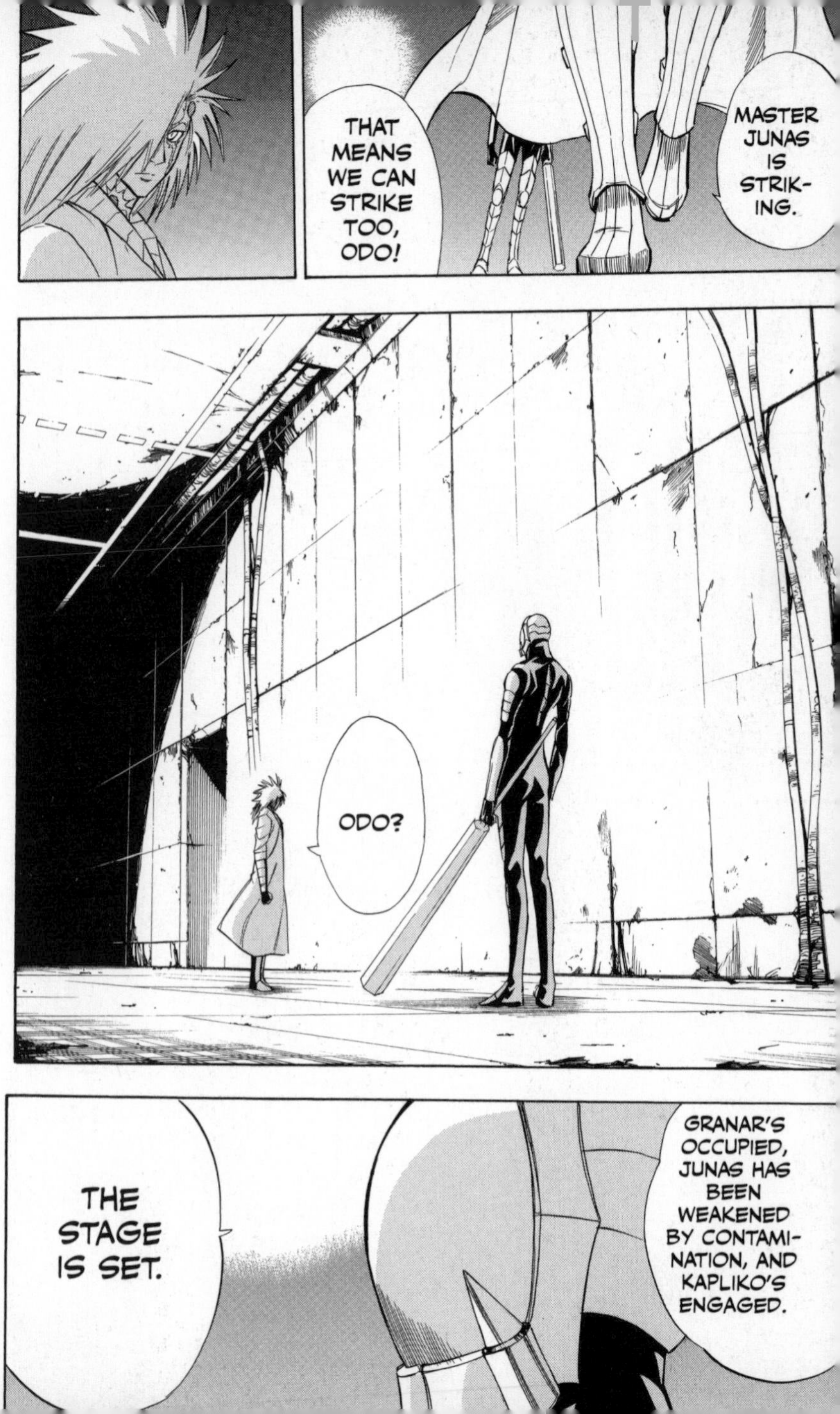
MASTER JUNAS IS STRIKING.
THAT MEANS WE CAN STRIKE TOO, ODO!
ODO?
GRANAR'S OCCUPIED, JUNAS HAS BEEN WEAKENED BY CONTAMINATION, AND KAPLIKO'S ENGAGED.
THE STAGE IS SET.

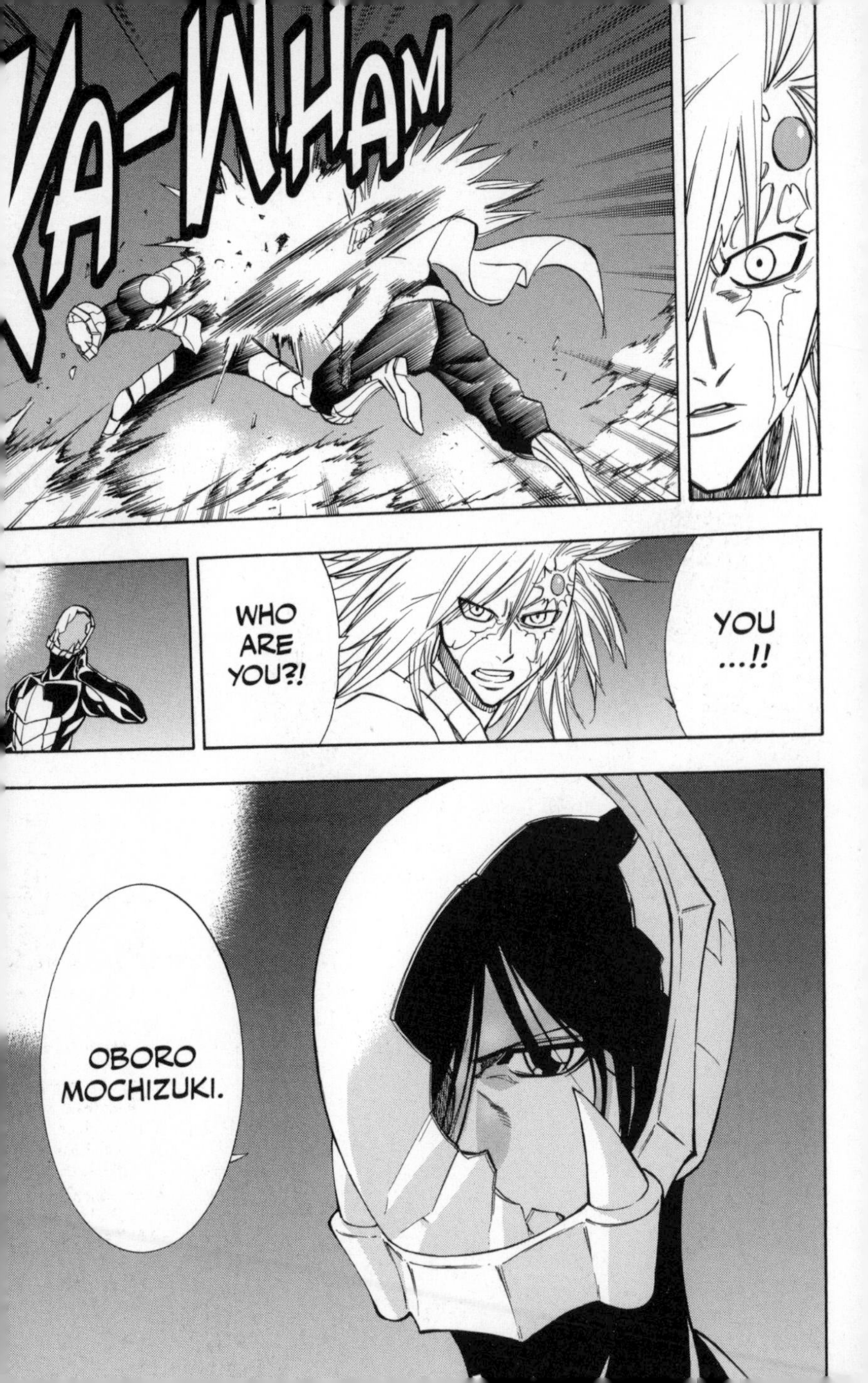
A-WHAM
YOU ...!!
WHO ARE YOU?!
OBORO MOCHIZUKI.

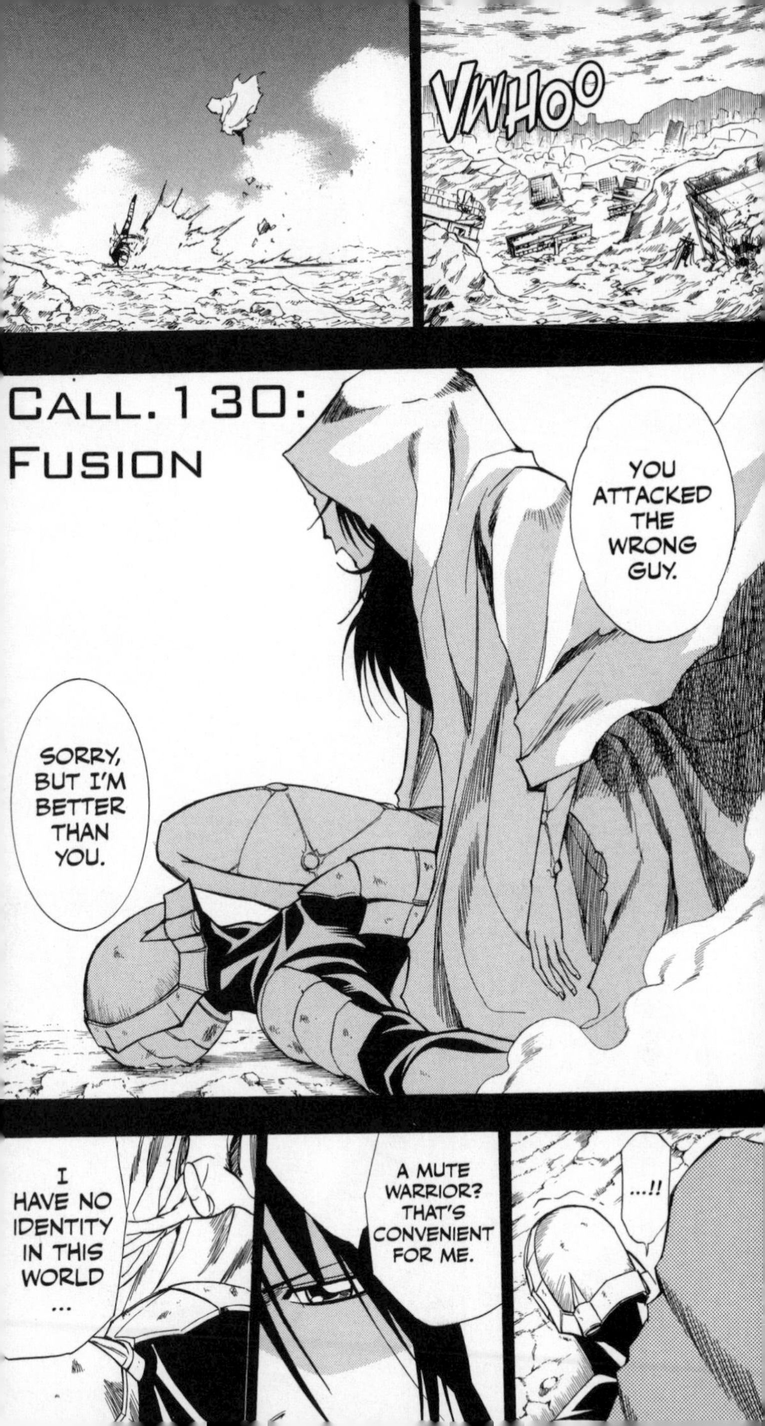
VWHOO
CALL. 130: FUSION
YOU ATTACKED THE WRONG GUY.
SORRY, BUT I'M BETTER THAN YOU.
...!!
A MUTE WARRIOR? THAT'S CONVENIENT FOR ME.
I HAVE NO IDENTITY IN THIS WORLD ...

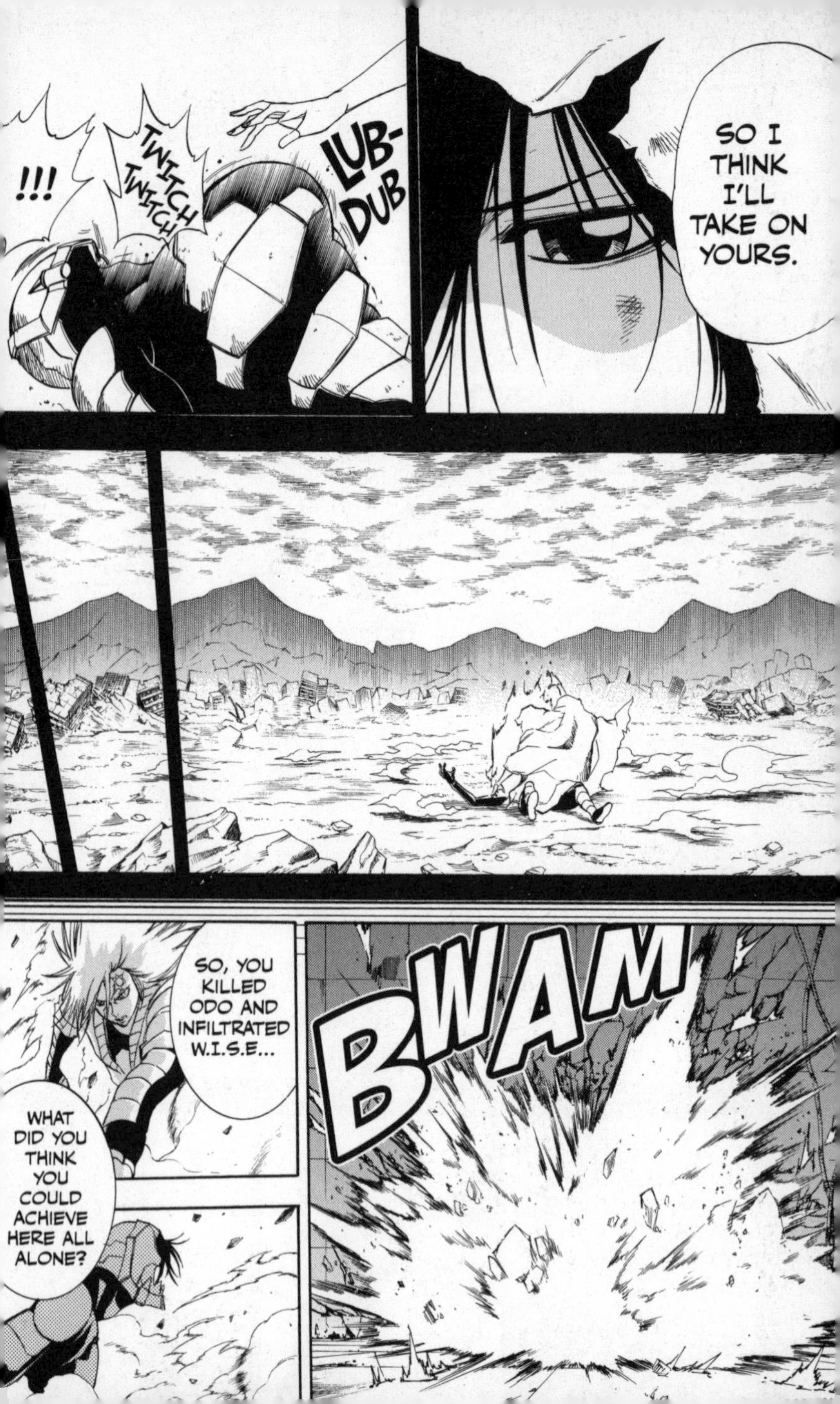
SO I THINK I'LL TAKE ON YOURS.
LUB-DUB
TWITCH TWITCH
!!!
BWAM
SO, YOU KILLED ODO AND INFILTRATED W.I.S.E...
WHAT DID YOU THINK YOU COULD ACHIEVE HERE ALL ALONE?

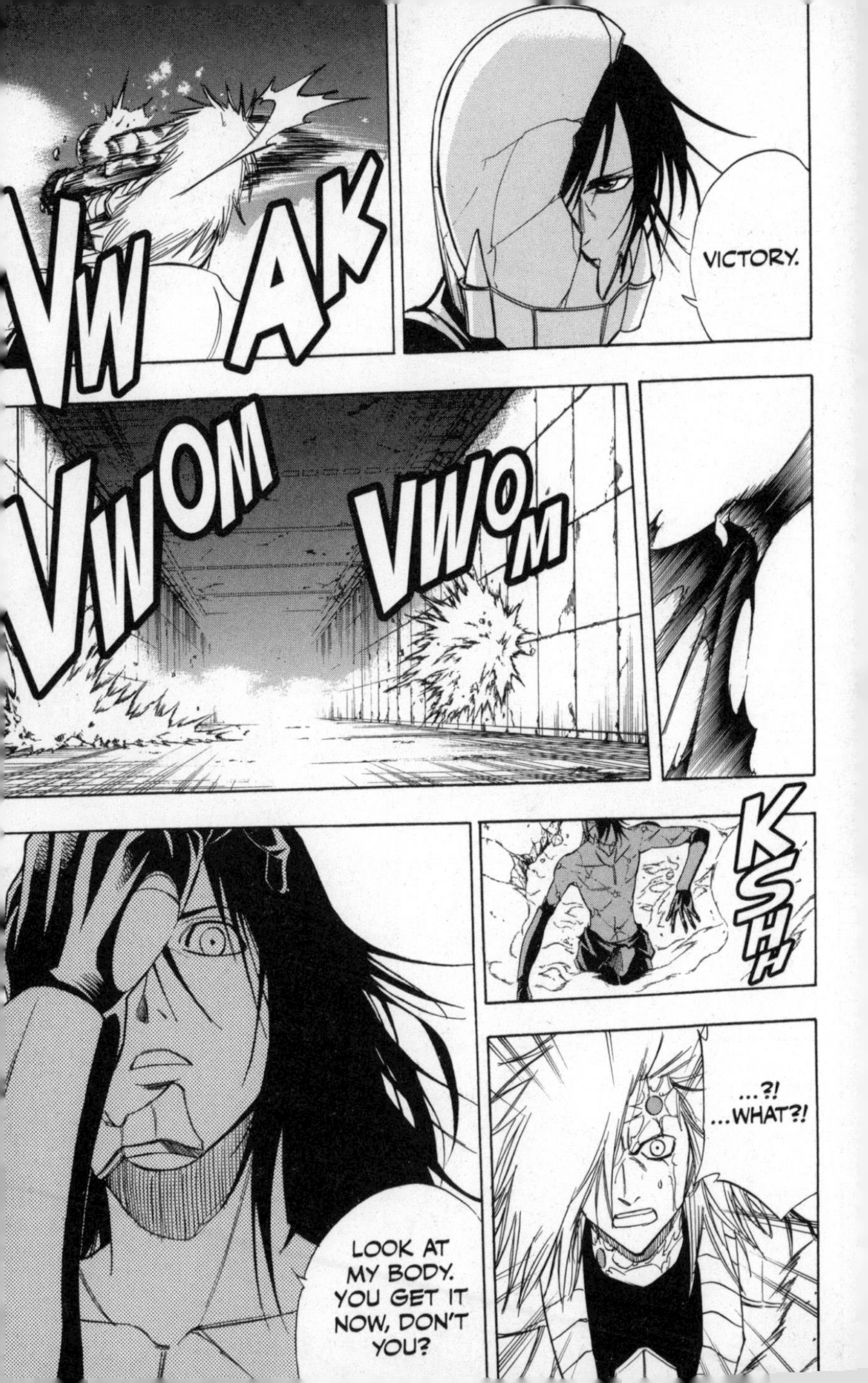
VICTORY.
VWAK
VWOM
VWOM
KSHH
...?!
...WHAT?!
LOOK AT MY BODY. YOU GET IT NOW, DON'T YOU?

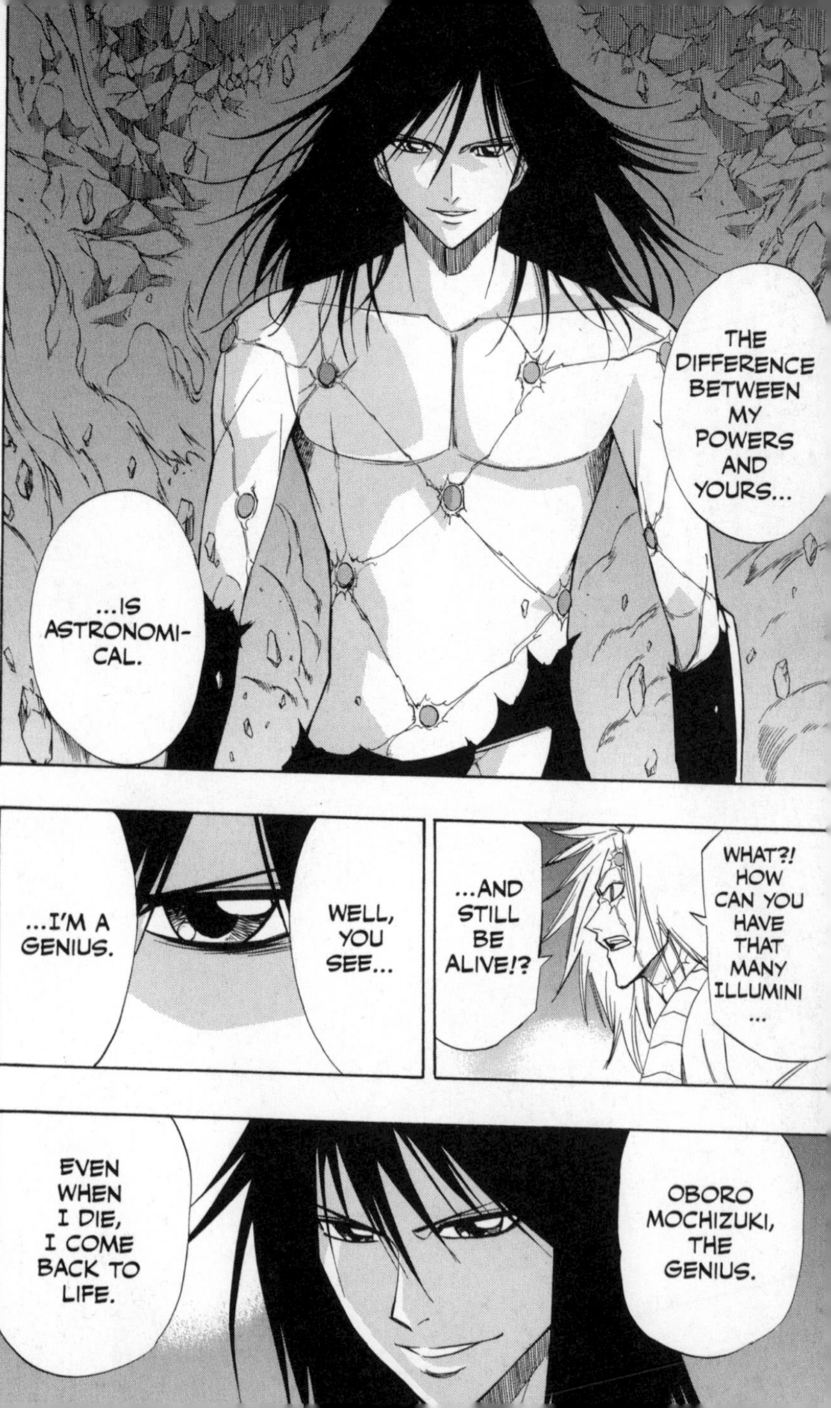
THE DIFFERENCE BETWEEN MY POWERS AND YOURS...
...IS ASTRONOMI-CAL.
WHAT?! HOW CAN YOU HAVE THAT MANY ILLUMINI ...
...AND STILL BE ALIVE!?
WELL, YOU SEE...
...I'M A GENIUS.
OBORO MOCHIZUKI, THE GENIUS.
EVEN WHEN I DIE, I COME BACK TO LIFE.

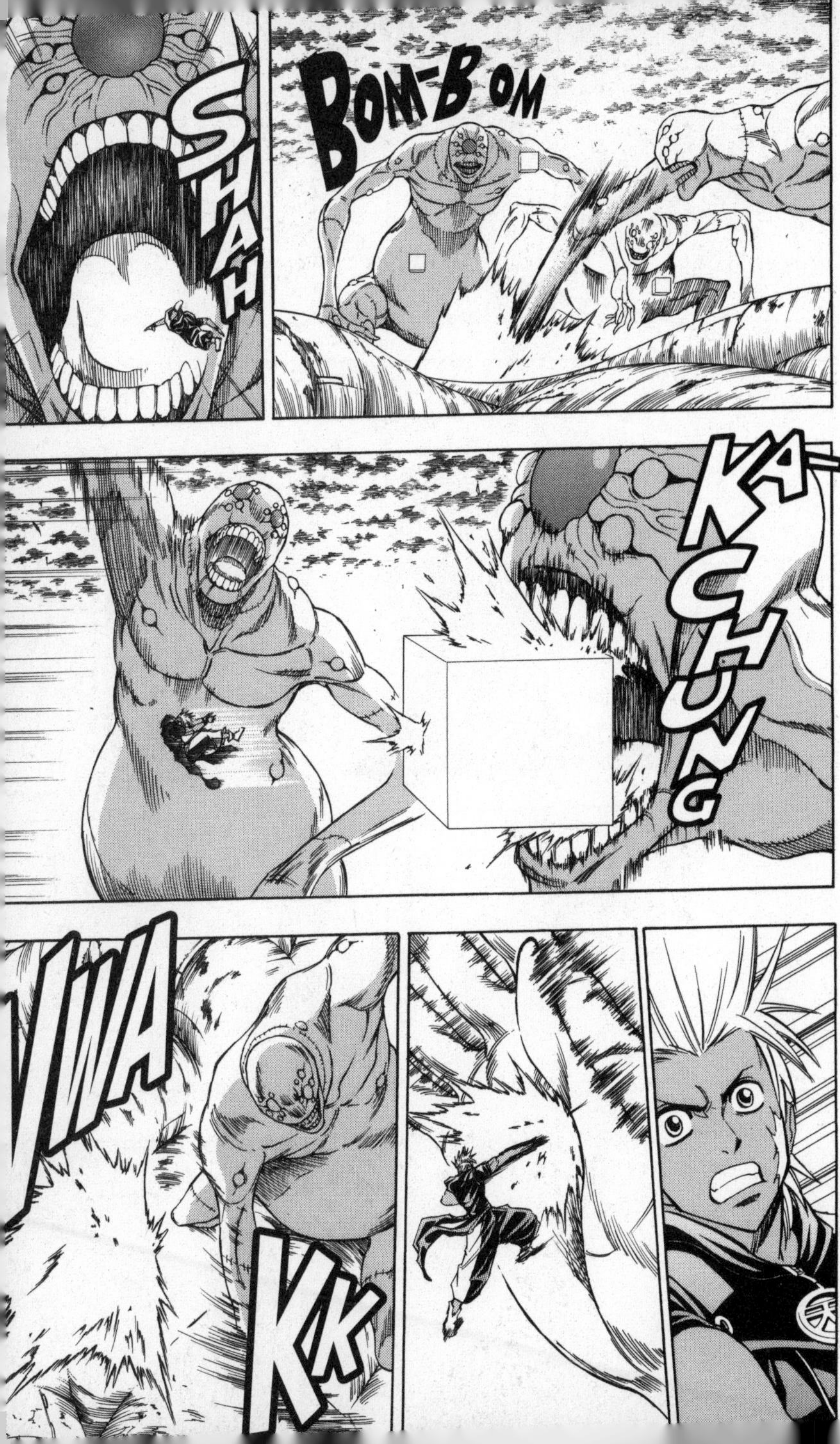
BOM-BOM
SHAHH
KA-CHUNG
KK

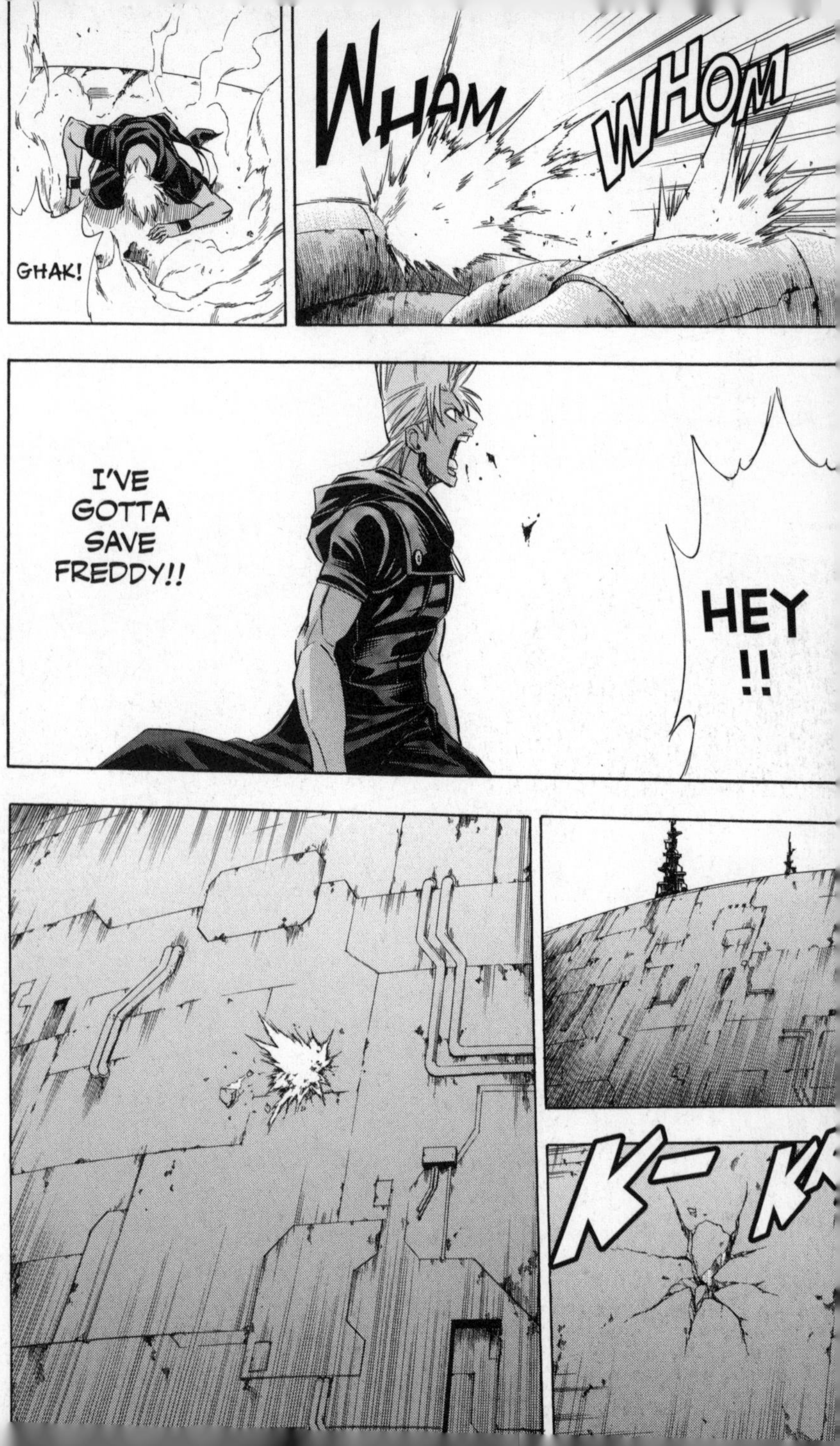

WHAM
WHOM
GHAK!
HEY!!
I'VE GOTTA SAVE FREDDY!!
K- KA

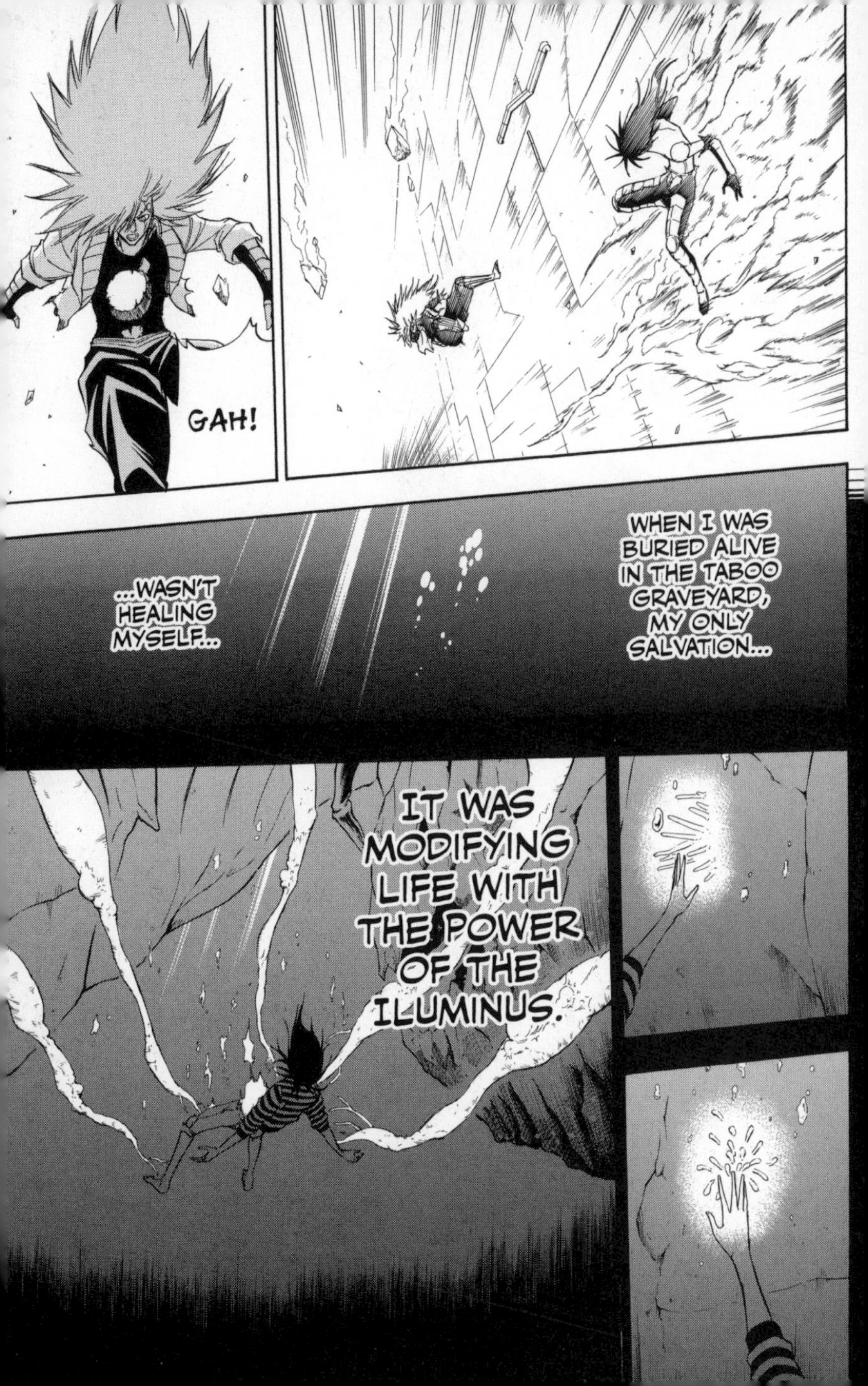
GAH!
WHEN I WAS BURIED ALIVE IN THE TABOO GRAVEYARD, MY ONLY SALVATION...
...WASN'T HEALING MYSELF...
IT WAS MODIFYING LIFE WITH THE POWER OF THE ILUMINUS.

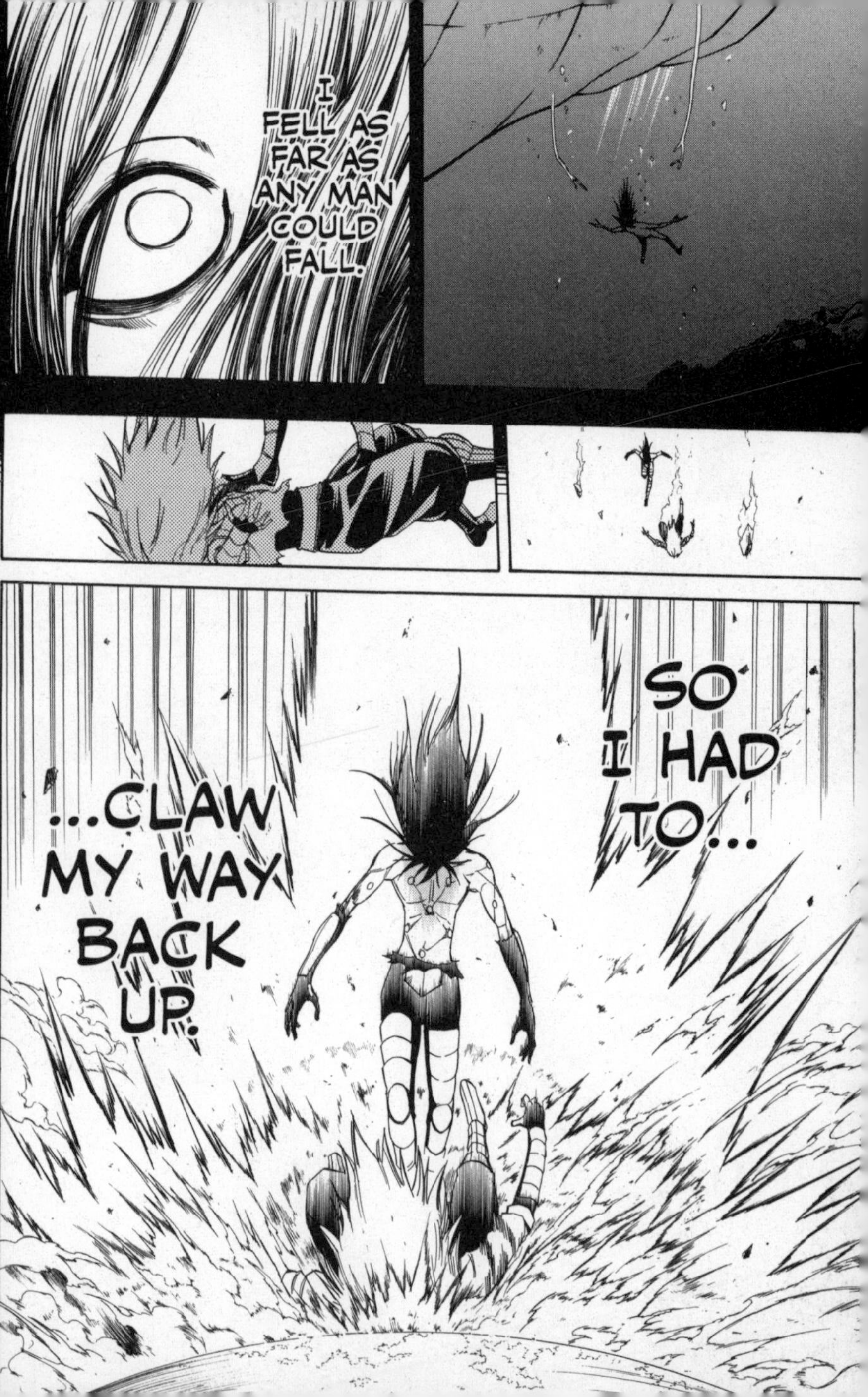
I FELL AS FAR AS ANY MAN COULD FALL.
SO I HAD TO...
...CLAW MY WAY BACK UP.

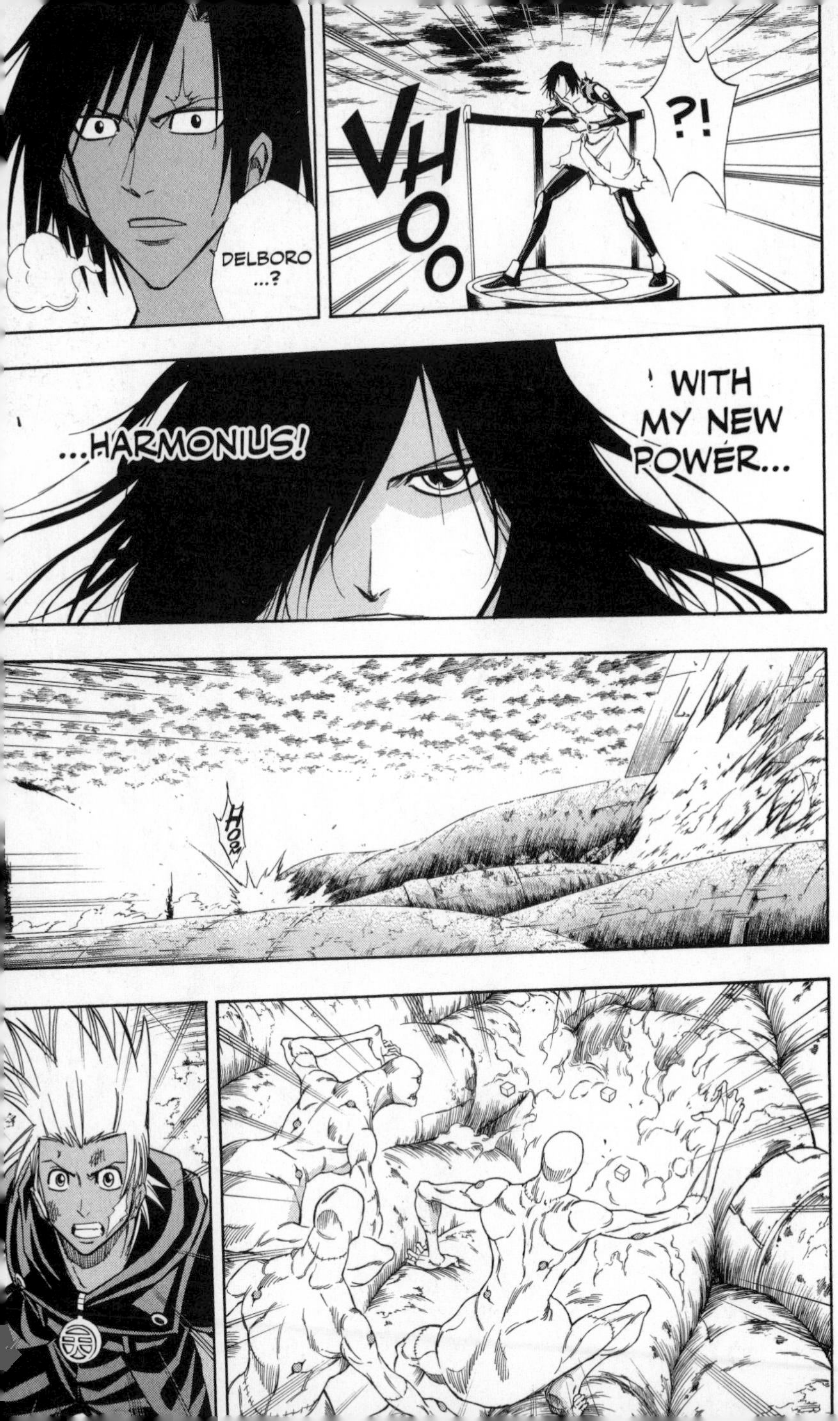
?!
VHOOO
DELBORO ...?
WITH MY NEW POWER...
...HARMONIUS!
HOO

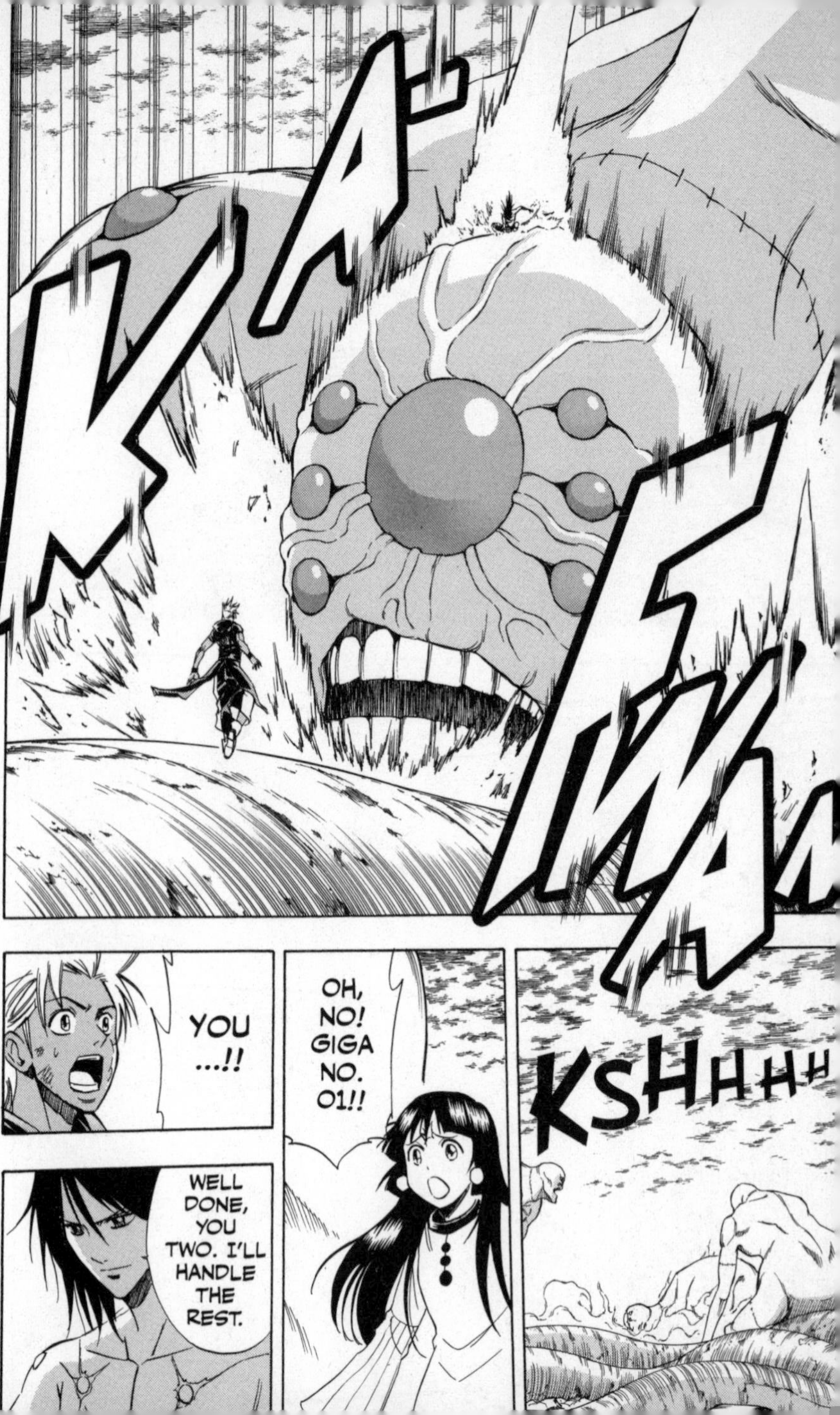
KSHHHH
OH, NO! GIGA NO. 01!!
YOU ...!!
WELL DONE, YOU TWO. I'LL HANDLE THE REST.

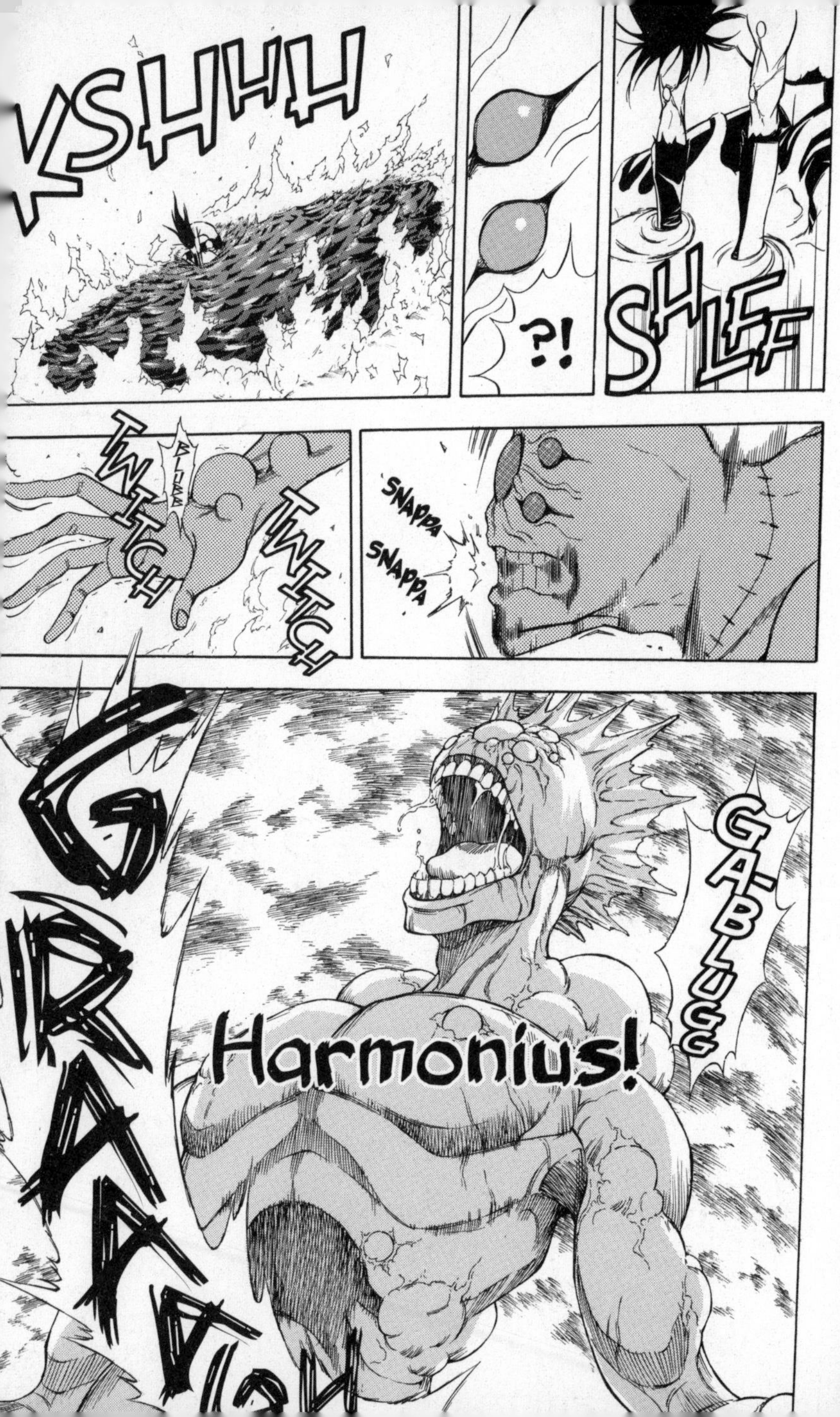
SHLEFF
?!
KSHHH
SNAPPA
SNAPPA
TWITCH
BLUBB
TWITCH
GABLUGG
Harmonius!
GRAAA

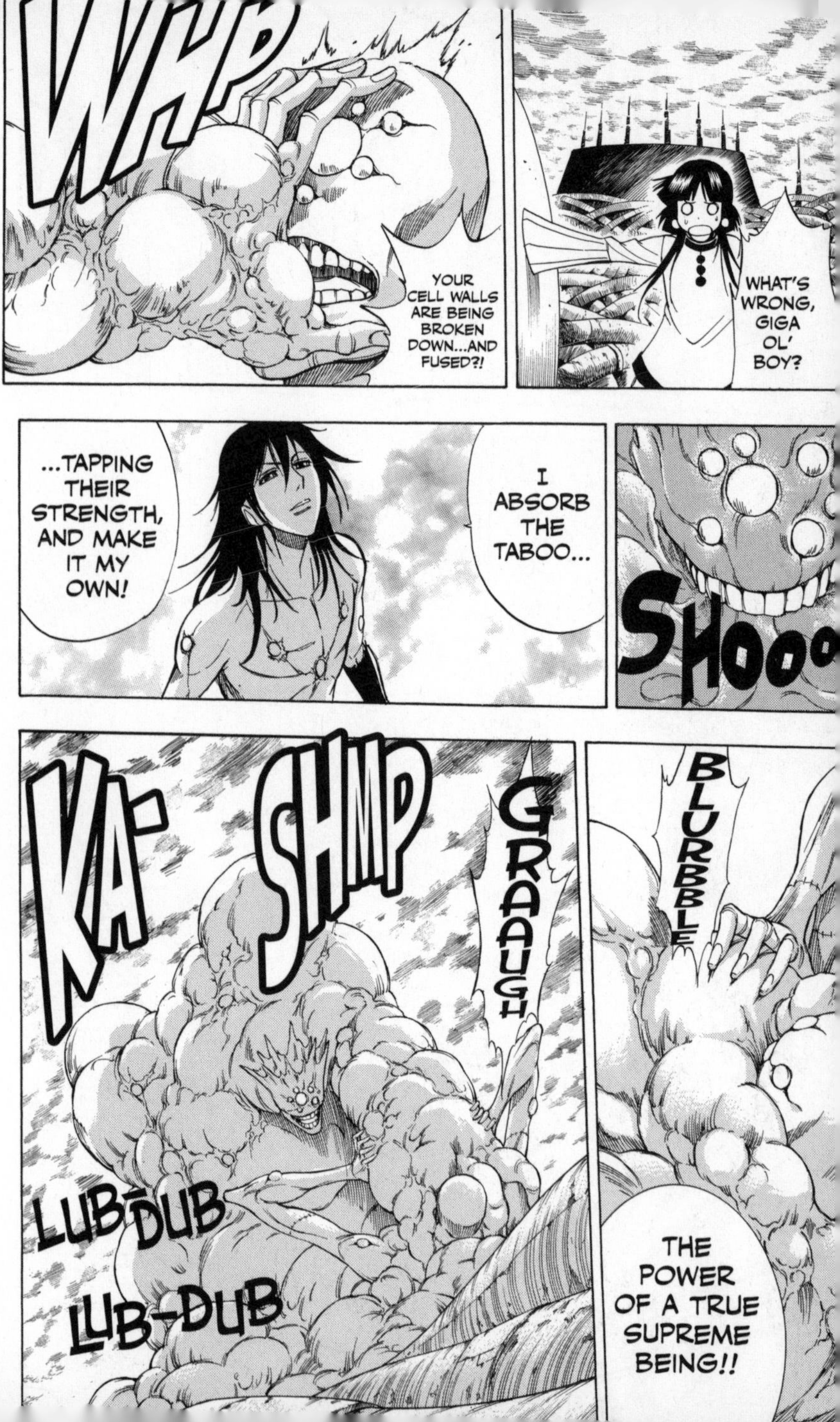
WHAT'S WRONG, GIGA OL' BOY?
WHP
YOUR CELL WALLS ARE BEING BROKEN DOWN...AND FUSED?!
SHOOO
I ABSORB THE TABOO...
...TAPPING THEIR STRENGTH, AND MAKE IT MY OWN!
BLURBBLE
THE POWER OF A TRUE SUPREME BEING!!
GRAAUGH
KA-SHMP
LUB-DUB
LUB-DUB

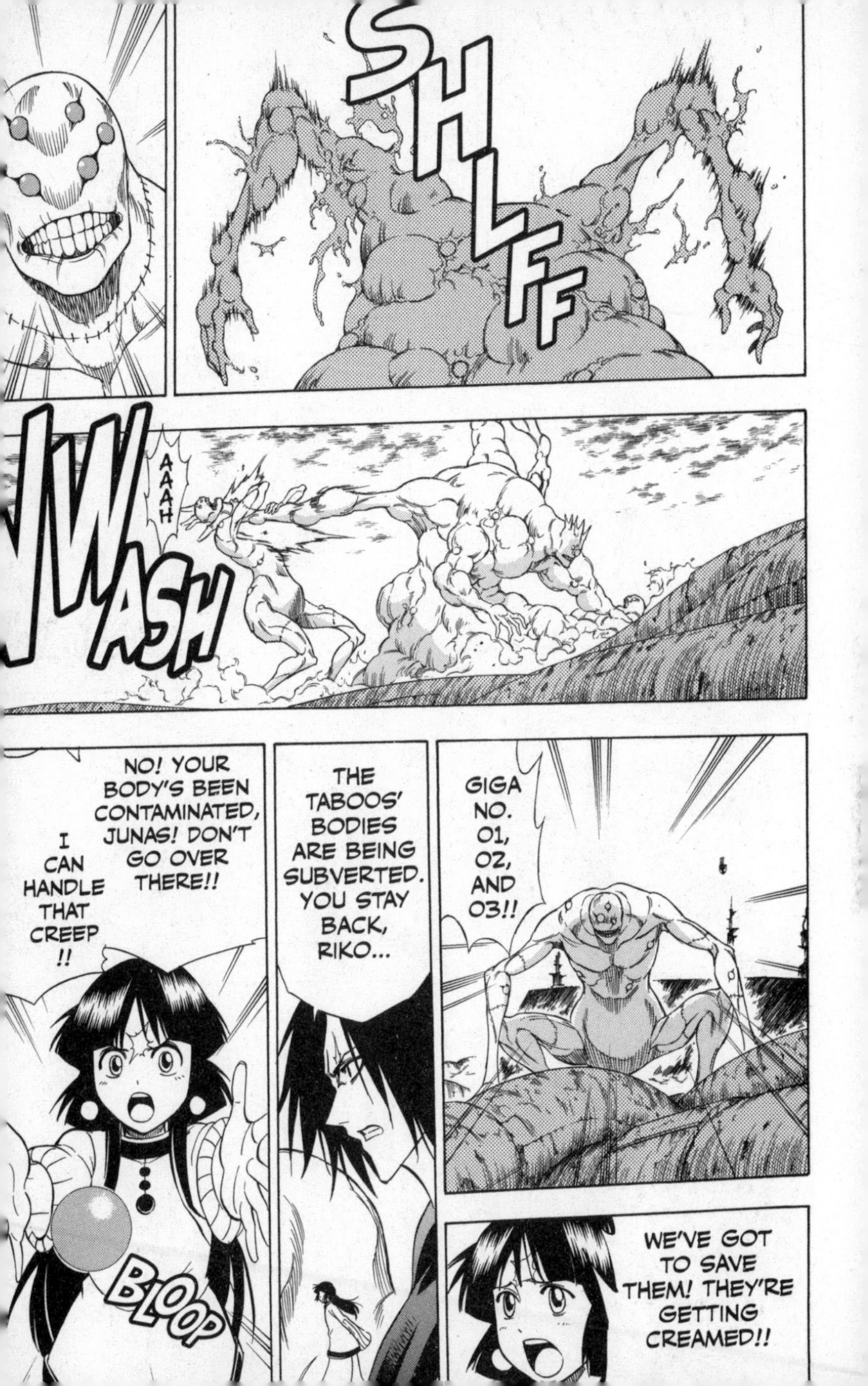
SHLFF
AAAH
WASH
GIGA NO. 01, 02, AND 03!!
WE'VE GOT TO SAVE THEM! THEY'RE GETTING CREAMED!!
THE TABOOS' BODIES ARE BEING SUBVERTED. YOU STAY BACK, RIKO...
NO! YOUR BODY'S BEEN CONTAMINATED, JUNAS! DON'T GO OVER THERE!!
I CAN HANDLE THAT CREEP!!
BLOOP

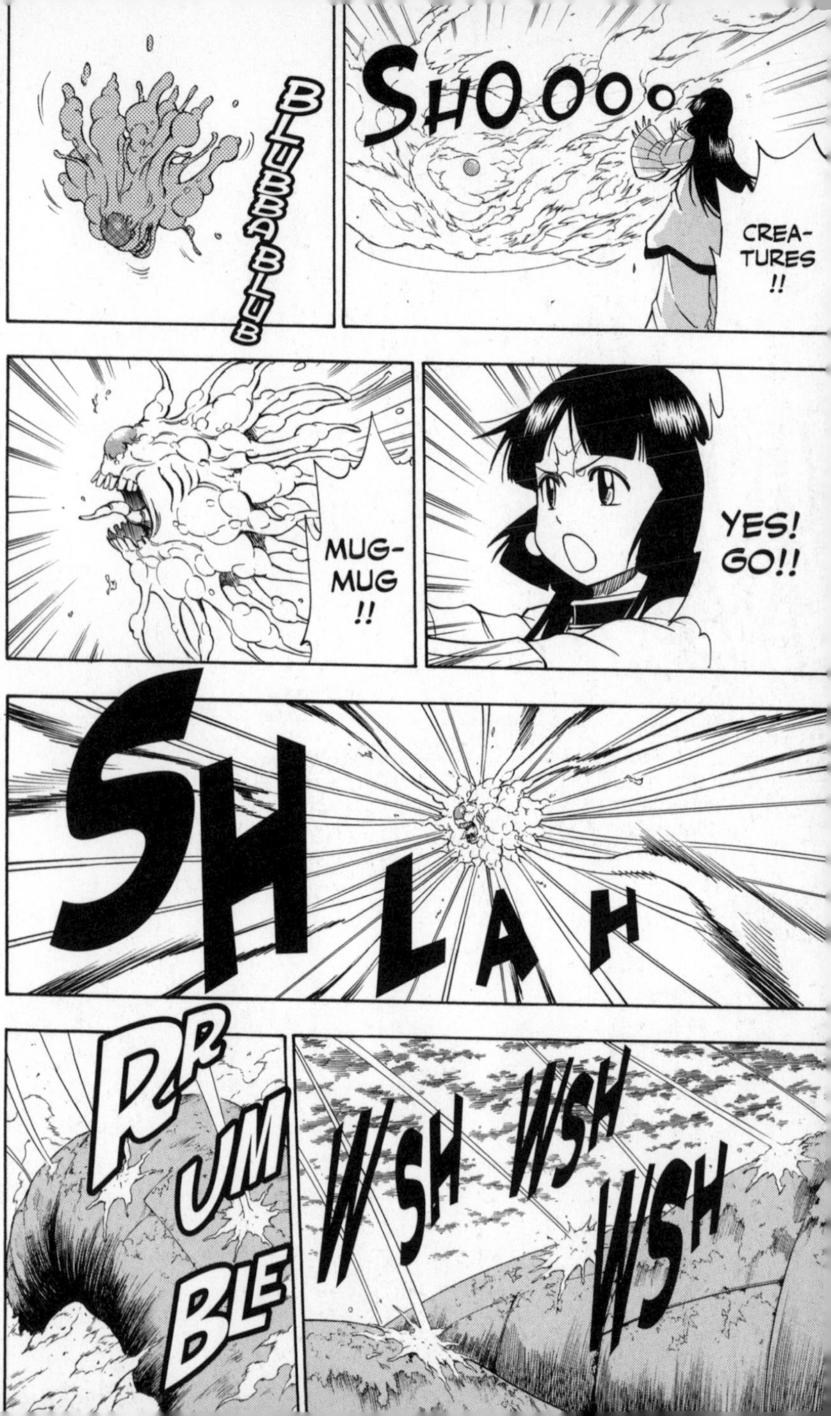
CREA-TURES !!
SHOOOO
BLUBBABLUB
YES! GO!!
MUG-MUG !!
SHLAH
WSH WSH WSH WSH
PRUMBLE

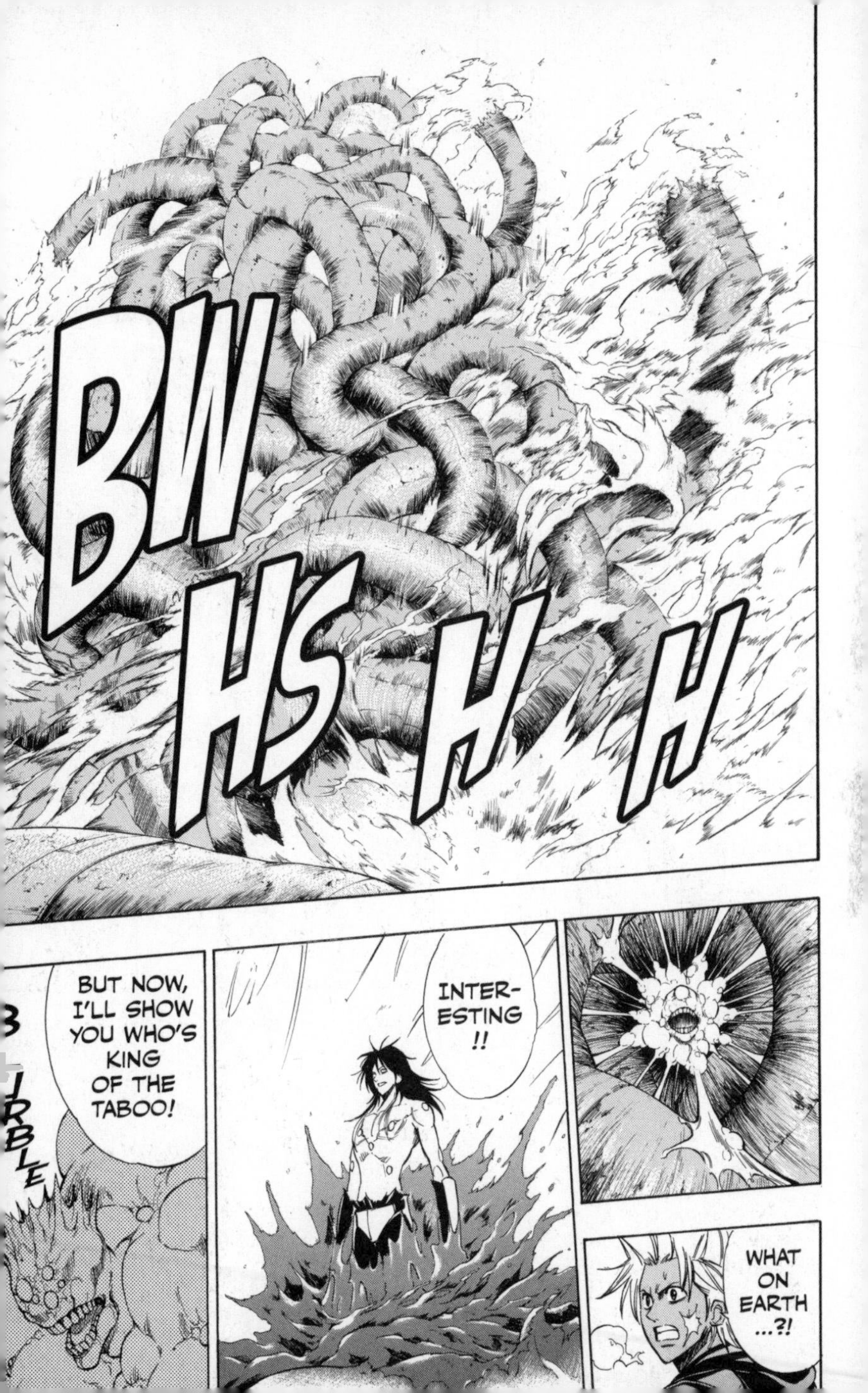
BWHSHH
WHAT ON EARTH ...?!
INTERESTING!!
BUT NOW, I'LL SHOW YOU WHO'S KING OF THE TABOO!

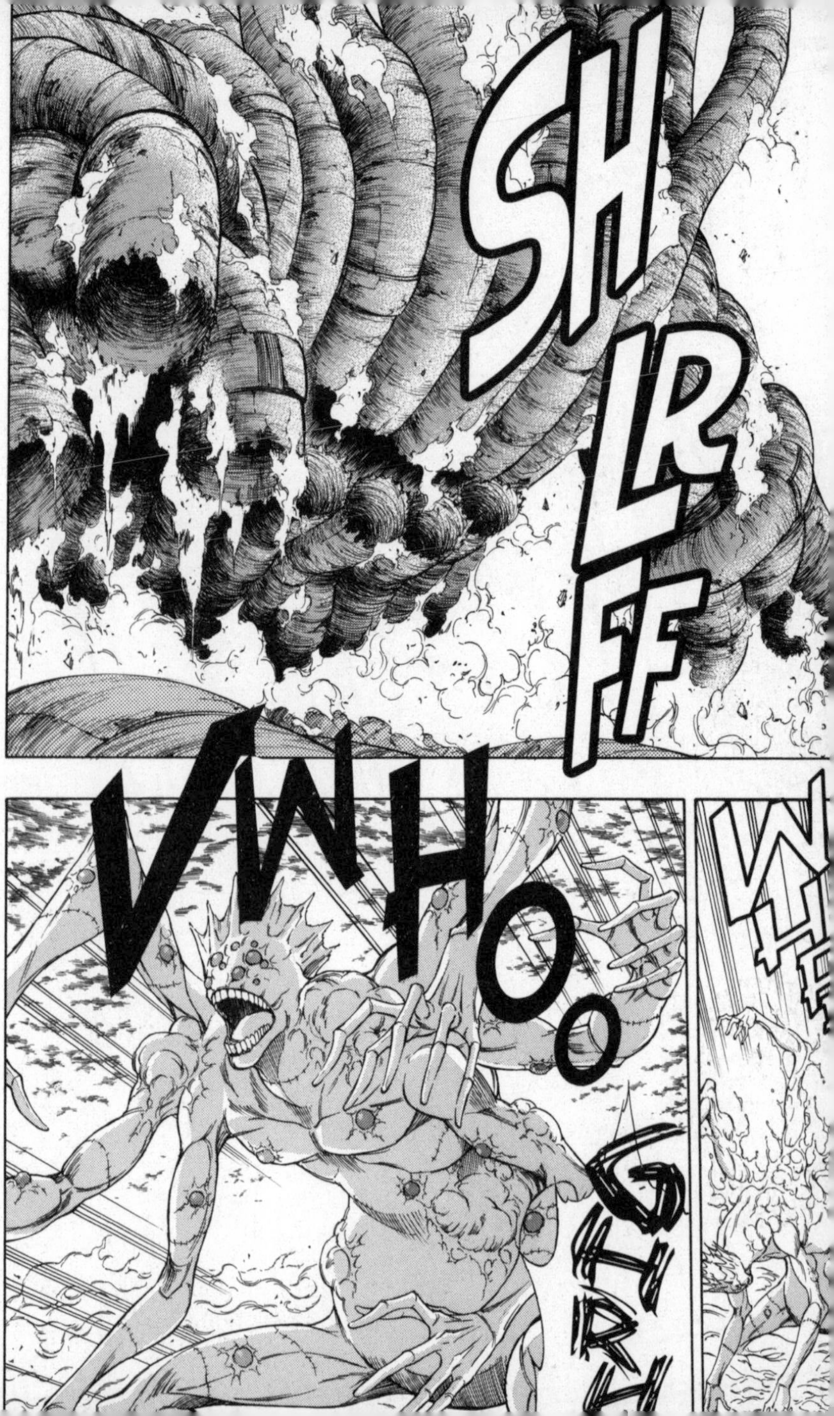
SHLRFF
WHF
VWHOO
GHRH

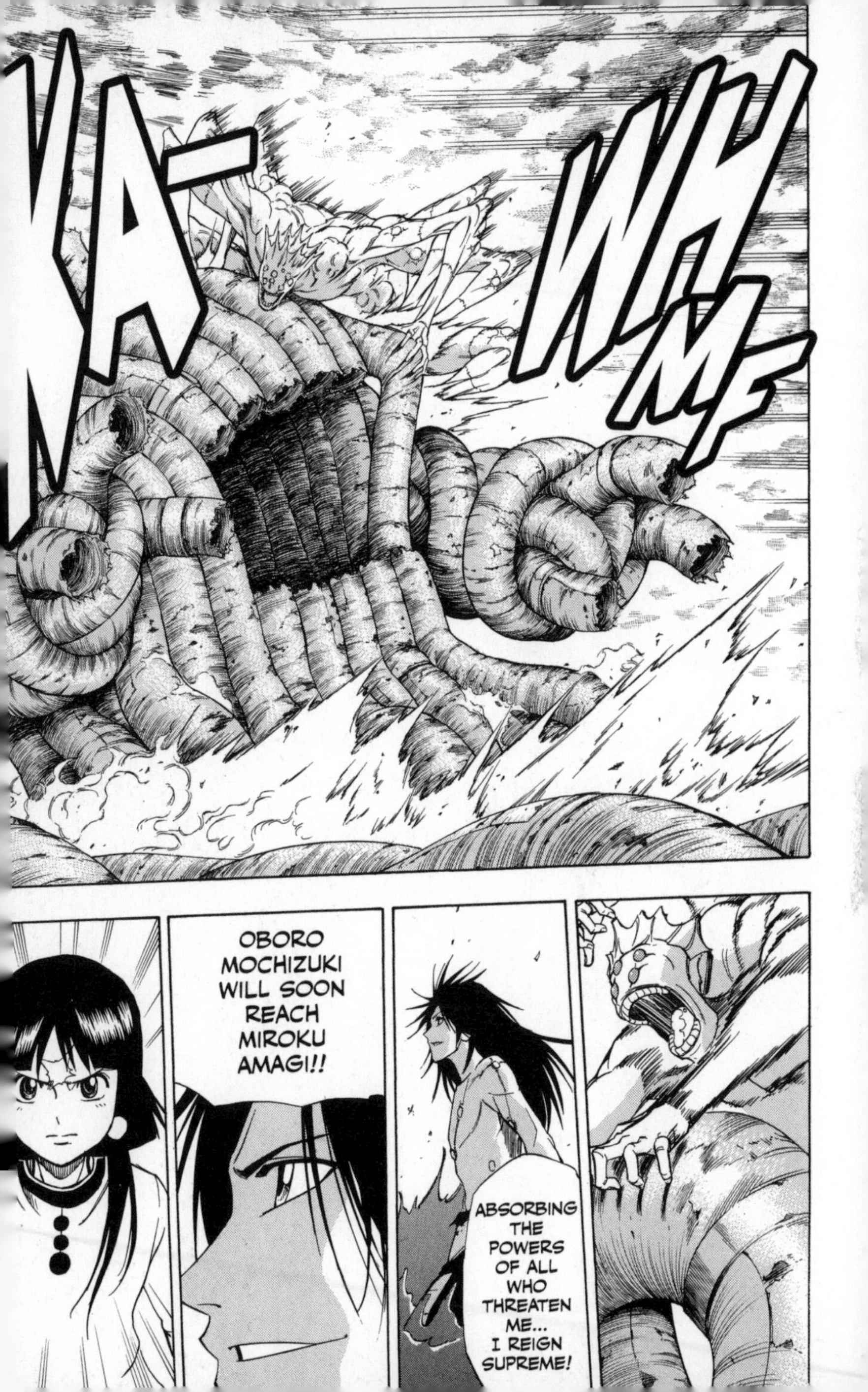
KA-WHMF
ABSORBING THE POWERS OF ALL WHO THREATEN ME... I REIGN SUPREME!
OBORO MOCHIZUKI WILL SOON REACH MIROKU AMAGI!!

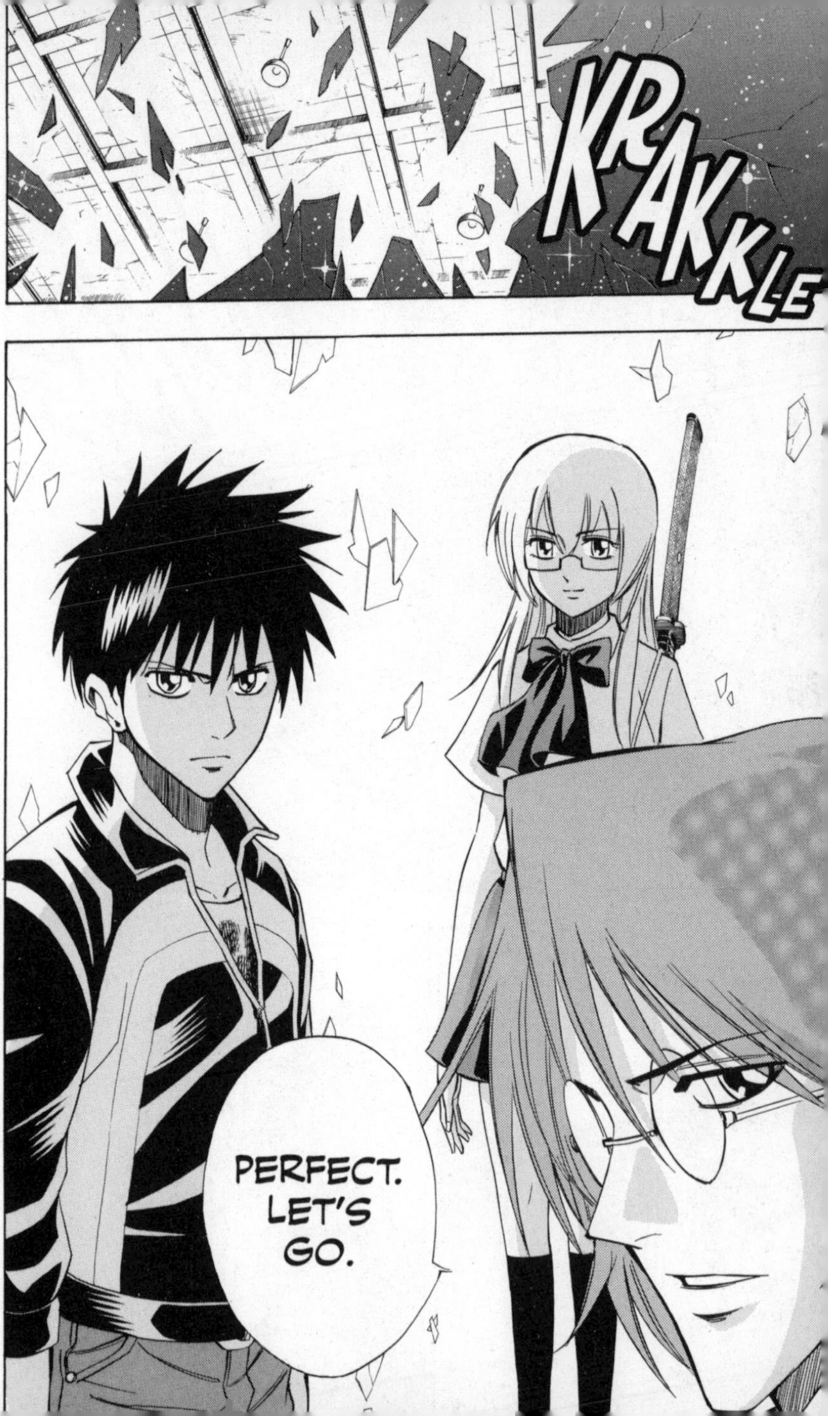
KRAKKLE
PERFECT. LET'S GO.

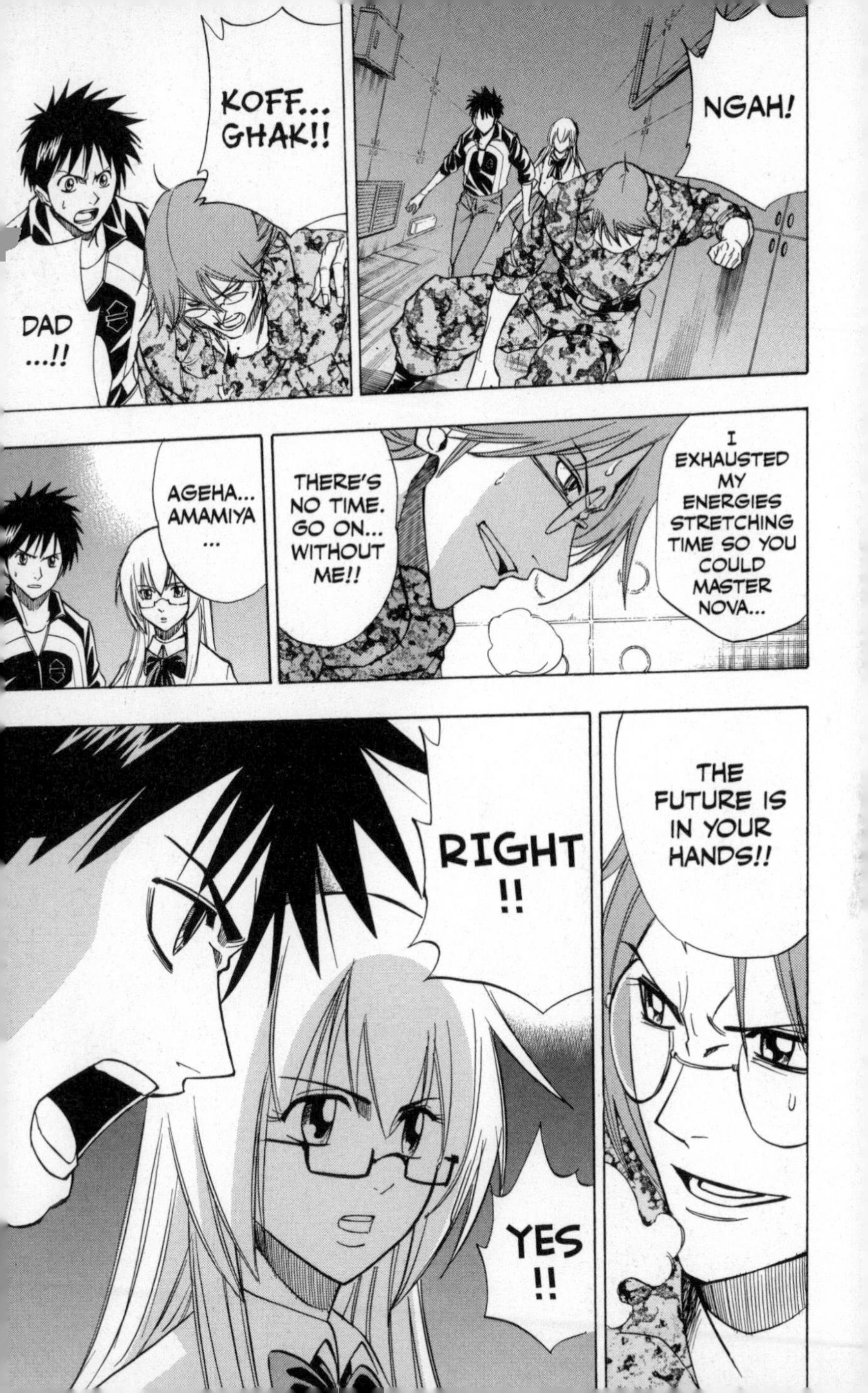
NGAH!
KOFF... GHAK!!
DAD ...!!
I EXHAUSTED MY ENERGIES STRETCHING TIME SO YOU COULD MASTER NOVA...
THERE'S NO TIME. GO ON... WITHOUT ME!!
AGEHA... AMAMIYA ...
THE FUTURE IS IN YOUR HANDS!!
RIGHT !!
YES !!

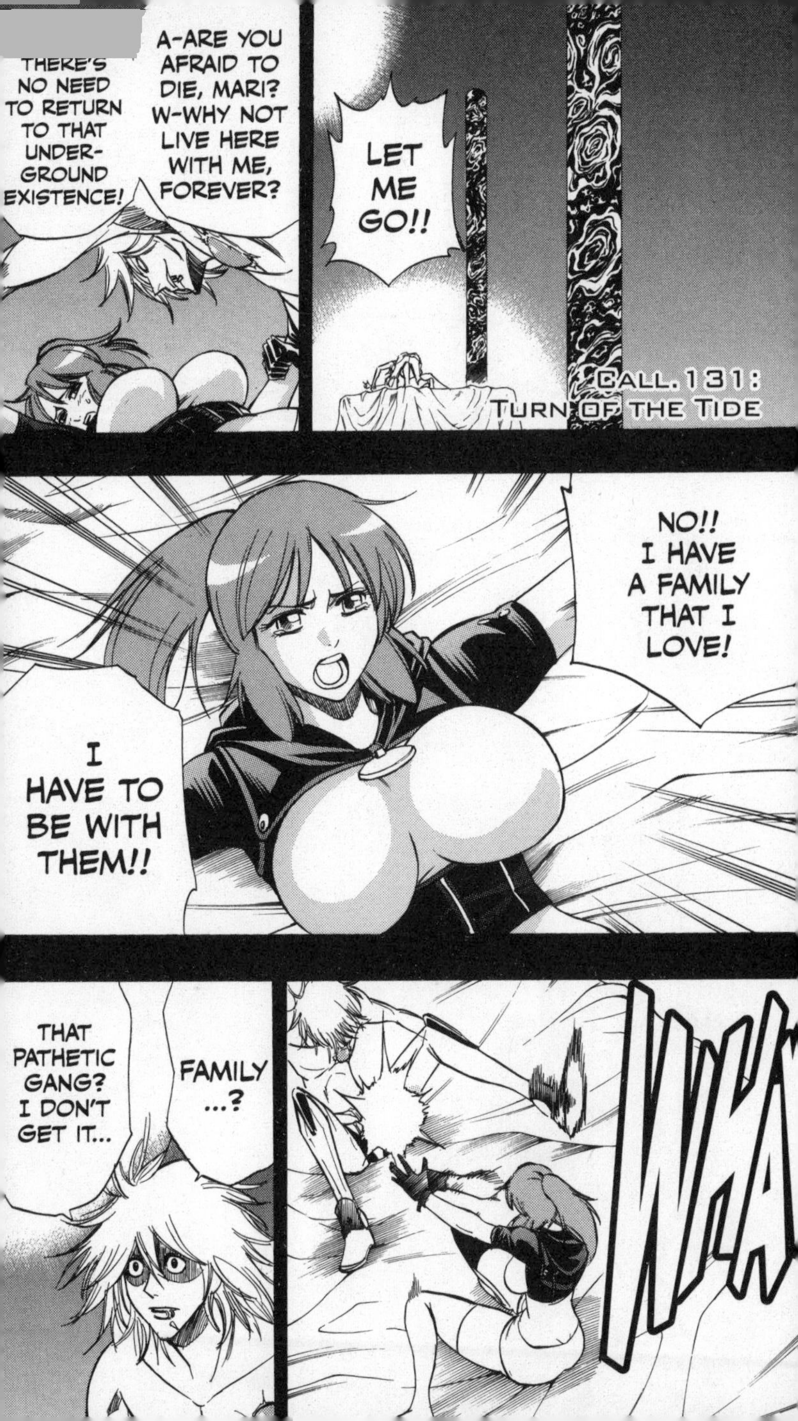
LET ME GO!!
CALL. 131: TURN OF THE TIDE
A-ARE YOU AFRAID TO DIE, MARI? W-WHY NOT LIVE HERE WITH ME, FOREVER?
THERE'S NO NEED TO RETURN TO THAT UNDER-GROUND EXISTENCE!
NO!! I HAVE A FAMILY THAT I LOVE!
I HAVE TO BE WITH THEM!!
WHA
FAMILY ...?
THAT PATHETIC GANG? I DON'T GET IT...

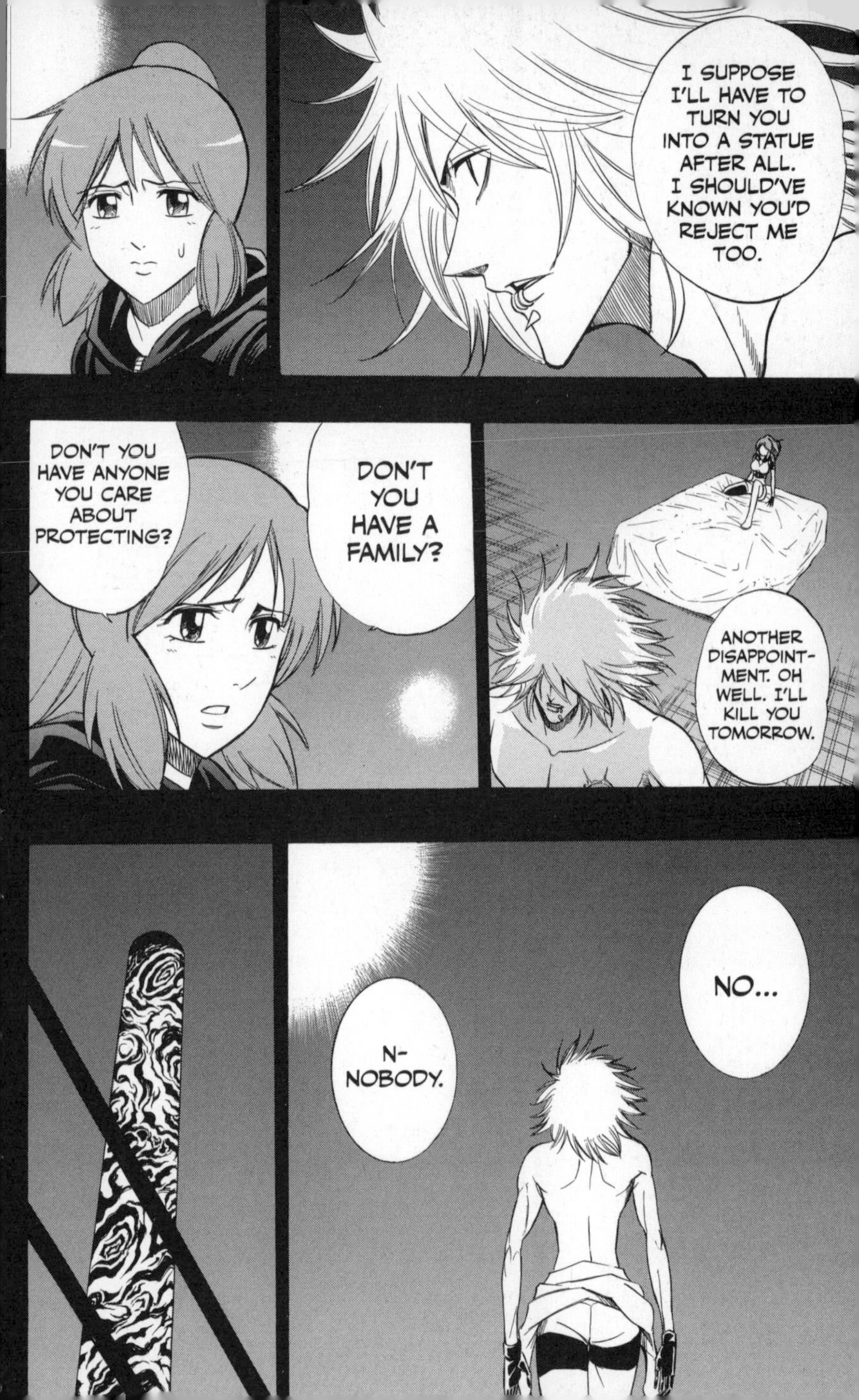
I SUPPOSE I'LL HAVE TO TURN YOU INTO A STATUE AFTER ALL. I SHOULD'VE KNOWN YOU'D REJECT ME TOO.
ANOTHER DISAPPOINTMENT. OH WELL. I'LL KILL YOU TOMORROW.
DON'T YOU HAVE A FAMILY?
DON'T YOU HAVE ANYONE YOU CARE ABOUT PROTECTING?
NO...
N- NOBODY.

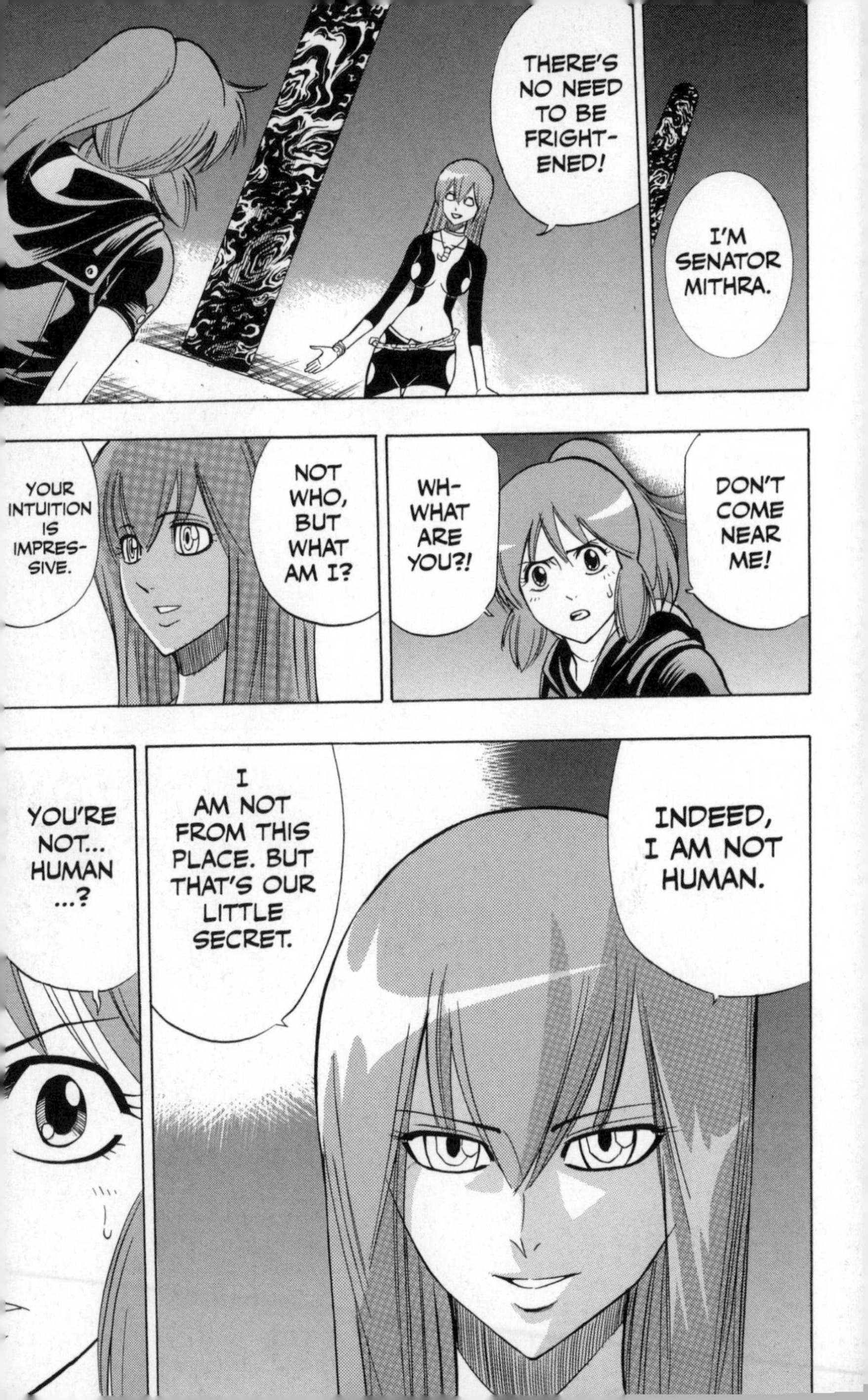
I'M SENATOR MITHRA.
THERE'S NO NEED TO BE FRIGHTENED!
DON'T COME NEAR ME!
WH-WHAT ARE YOU?!
NOT WHO, BUT WHAT AM I?
YOUR INTUITION IS IMPRESSIVE.
INDEED, I AM NOT HUMAN.
I AM NOT FROM THIS PLACE. BUT THAT'S OUR LITTLE SECRET.
YOU'RE NOT... HUMAN ...?

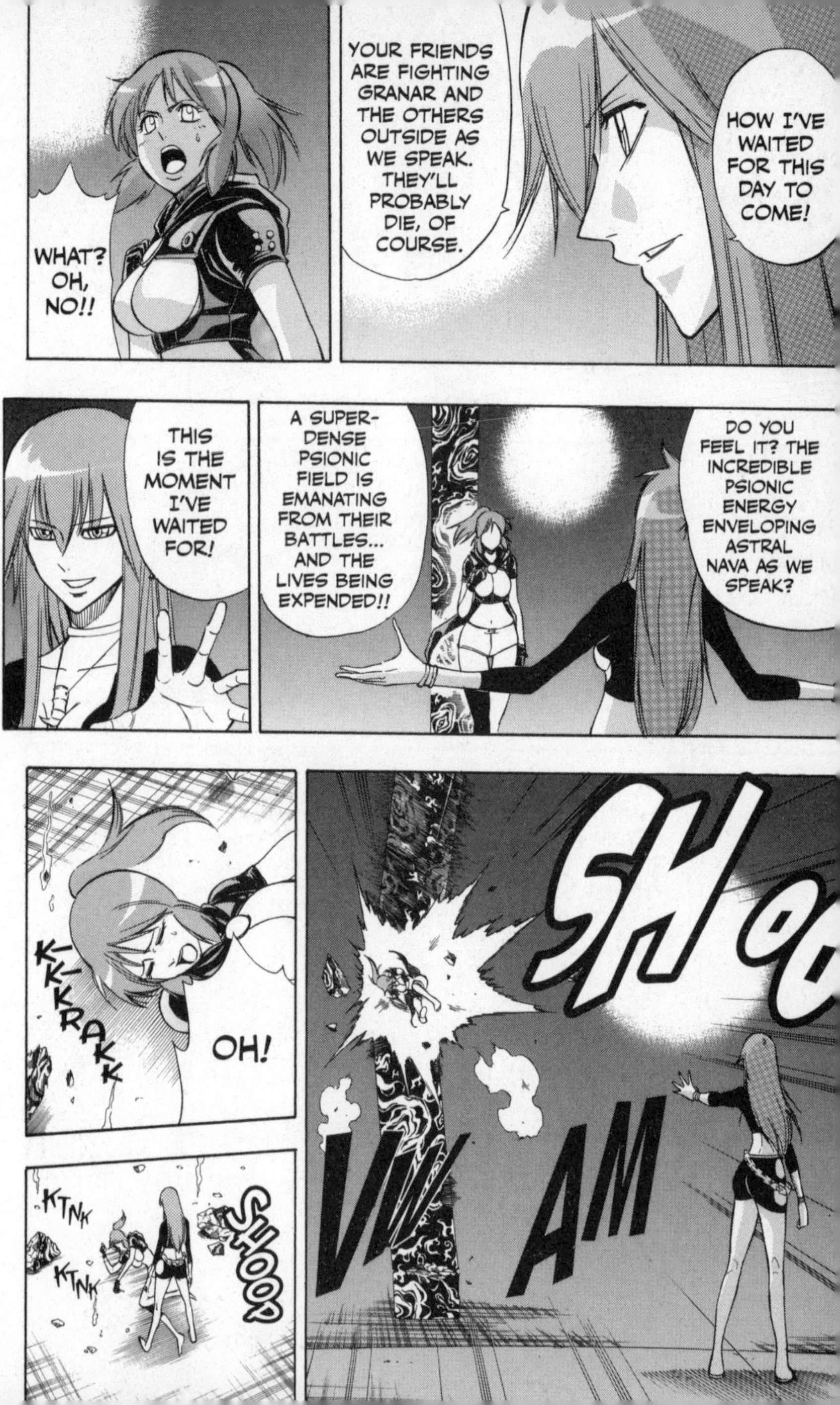
HOW I'VE WAITED FOR THIS DAY TO COME!
YOUR FRIENDS ARE FIGHTING GRANAR AND THE OTHERS OUTSIDE AS WE SPEAK. THEY'LL PROBABLY DIE, OF COURSE.
WHAT? OH, NO!!
DO YOU FEEL IT? THE INCREDIBLE PSIONIC ENERGY ENVELOPING ASTRAL NAVA AS WE SPEAK?
A SUPER-DENSE PSIONIC FIELD IS EMANATING FROM THEIR BATTLES... AND THE LIVES BEING EXPENDED!!
THIS IS THE MOMENT I'VE WAITED FOR!
SHOO
VWAM
KKKRAKK
OH!
KTNK
KTNK
SHOOP

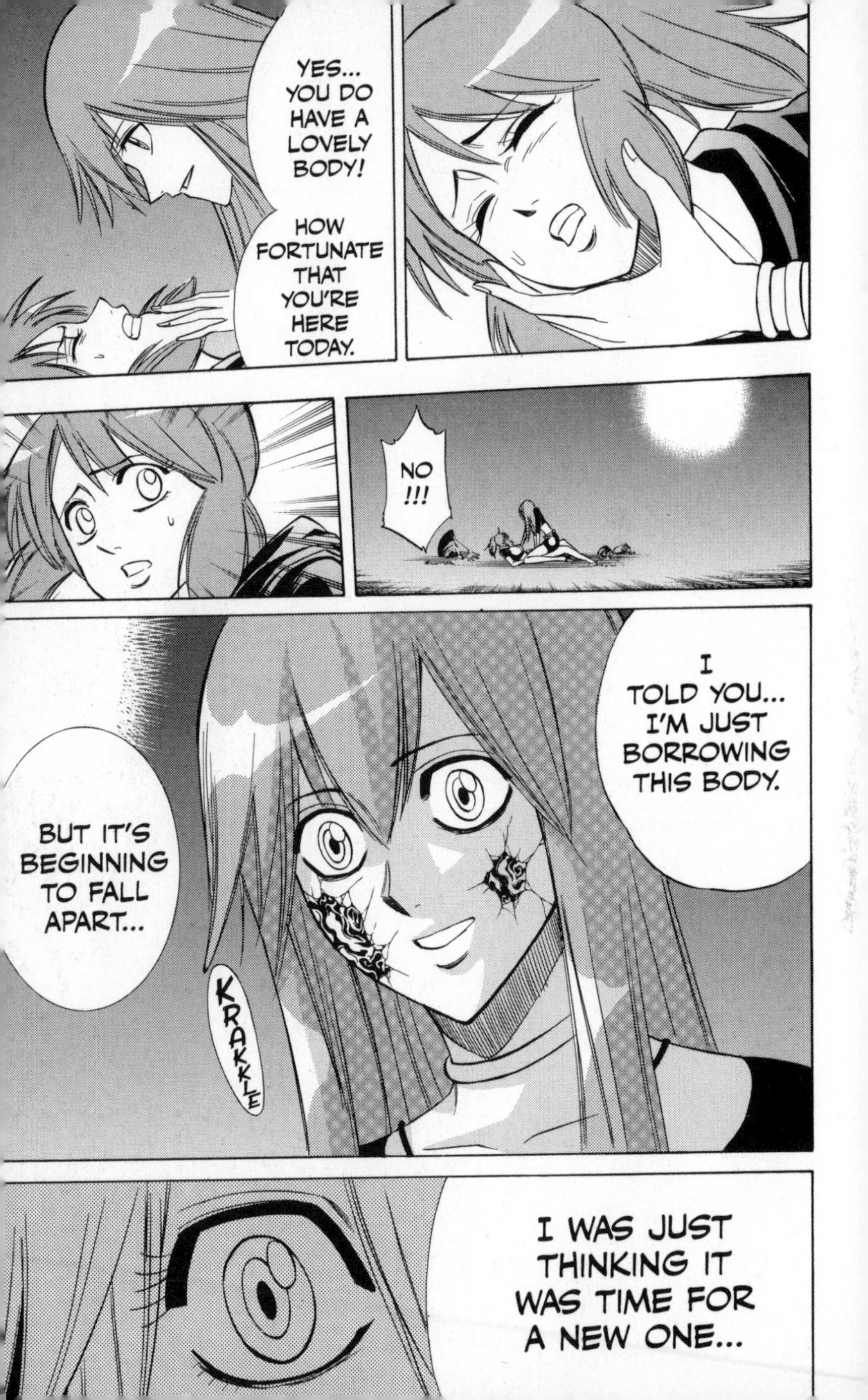
YES... YOU DO HAVE A LOVELY BODY!
HOW FORTUNATE THAT YOU'RE HERE TODAY.
NO !!!
I TOLD YOU... I'M JUST BORROWING THIS BODY.
KRAKKLE
BUT IT'S BEGINNING TO FALL APART...
I WAS JUST THINKING IT WAS TIME FOR A NEW ONE...

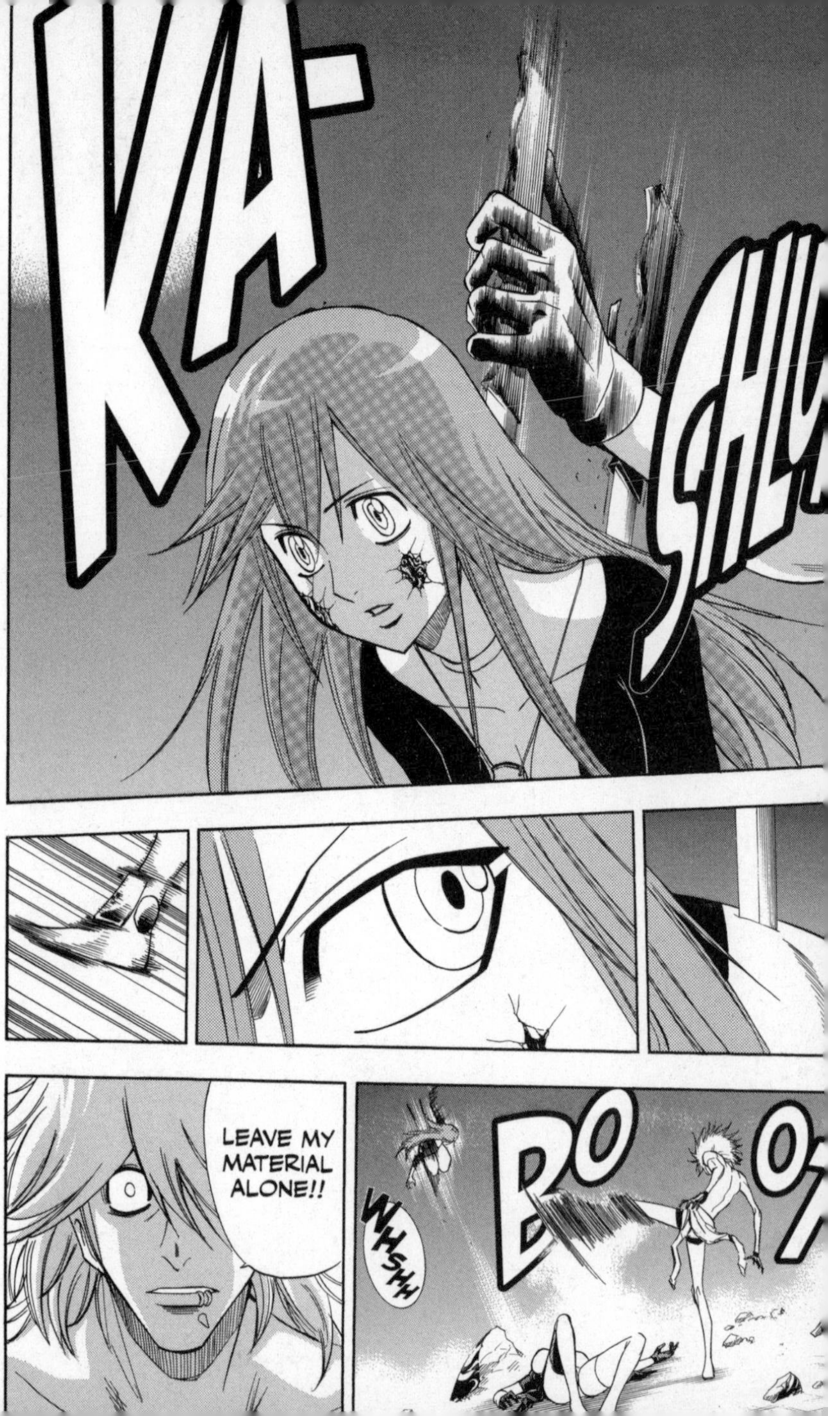
KA-
WHSHH
LEAVE MY MATERIAL ALONE!!

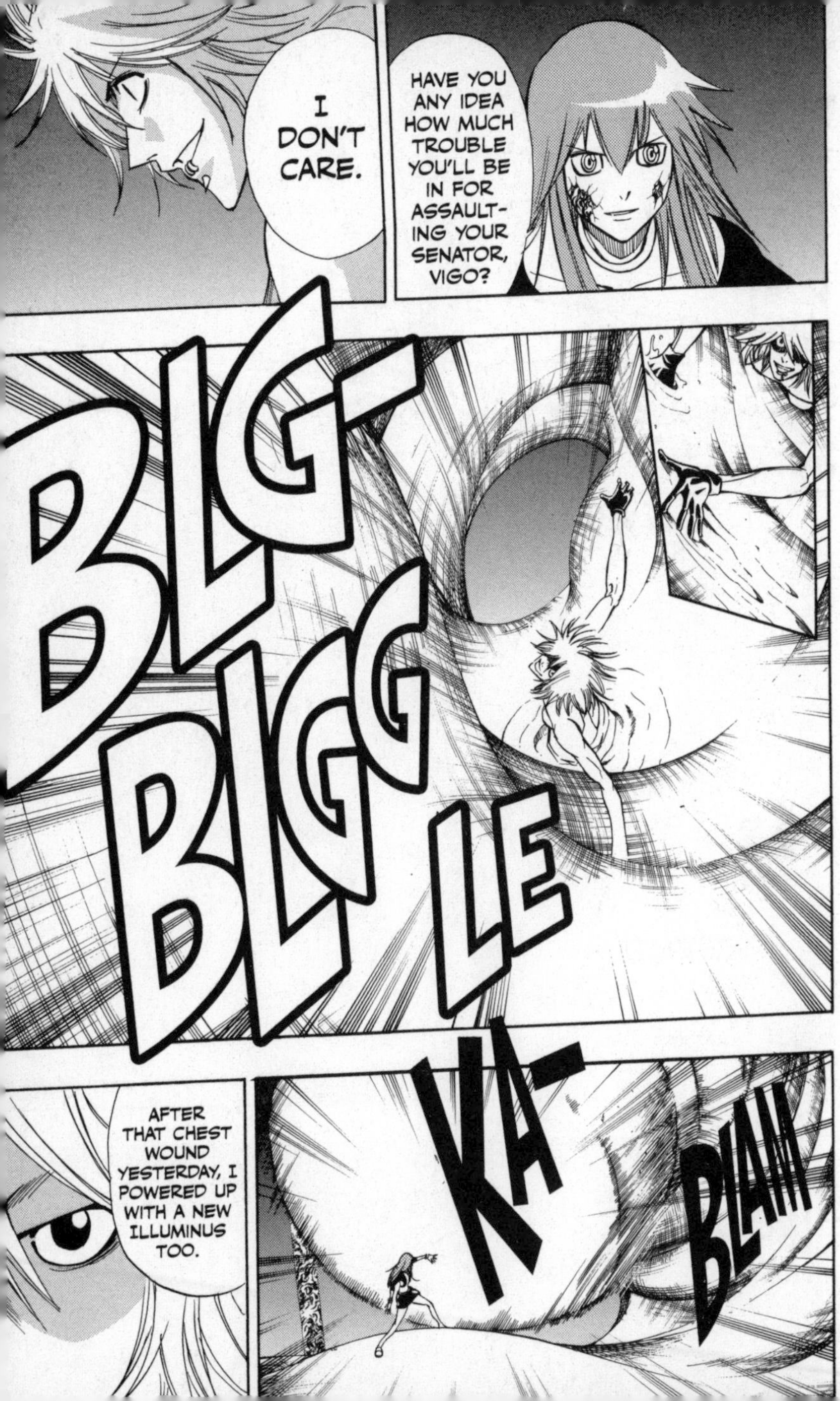
HAVE YOU ANY IDEA HOW MUCH TROUBLE YOU'LL BE IN FOR ASSAULTING YOUR SENATOR, VIGO?
I DON'T CARE.
BIG-
BIGGLE
KA-
BLAM
AFTER THAT CHEST WOUND YESTERDAY, I POWERED UP WITH A NEW ILLUMINUS TOO.

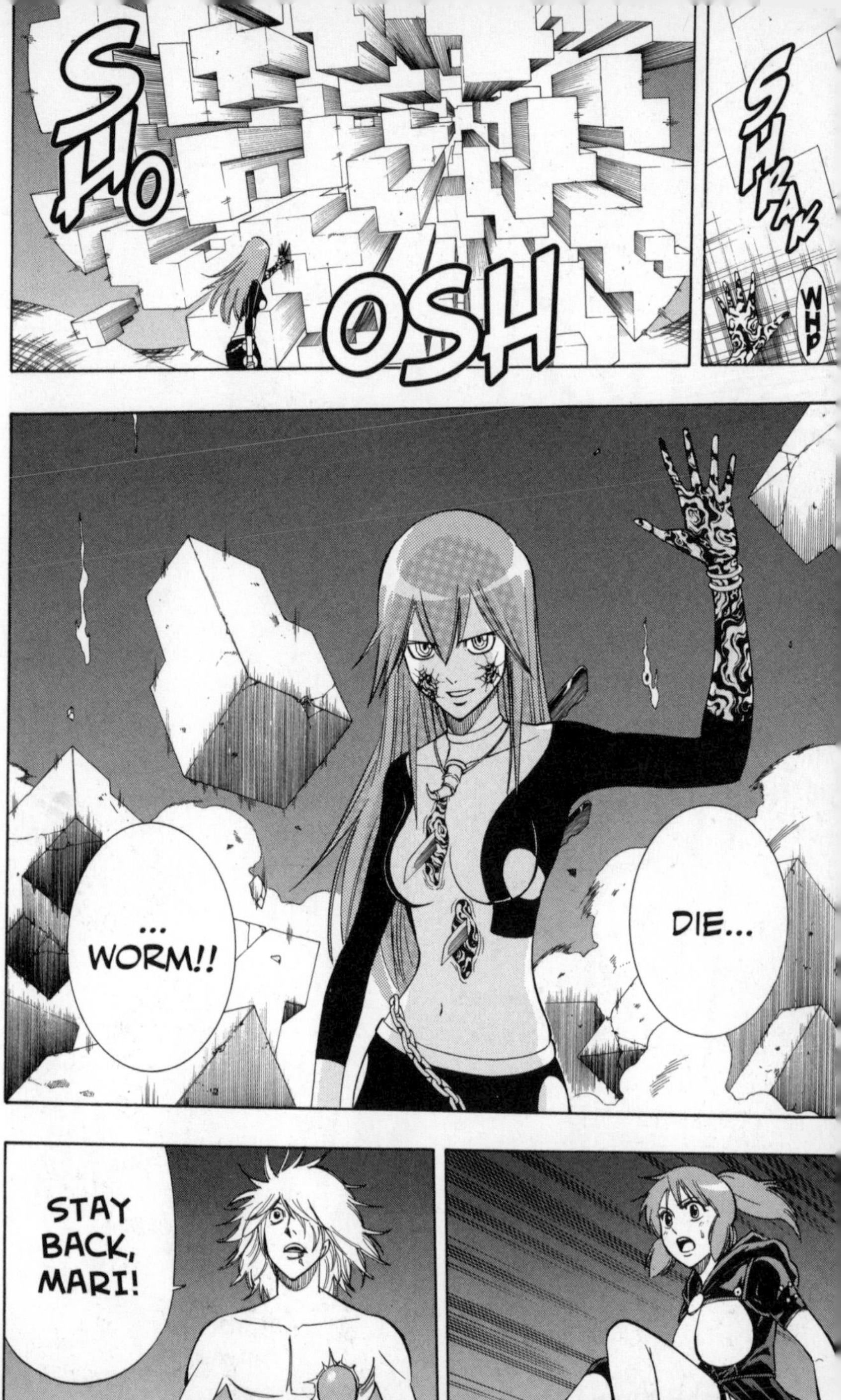
SHRAK
WHP
SHO
OSH
DIE...
...WORM!!
STAY BACK, MARI!

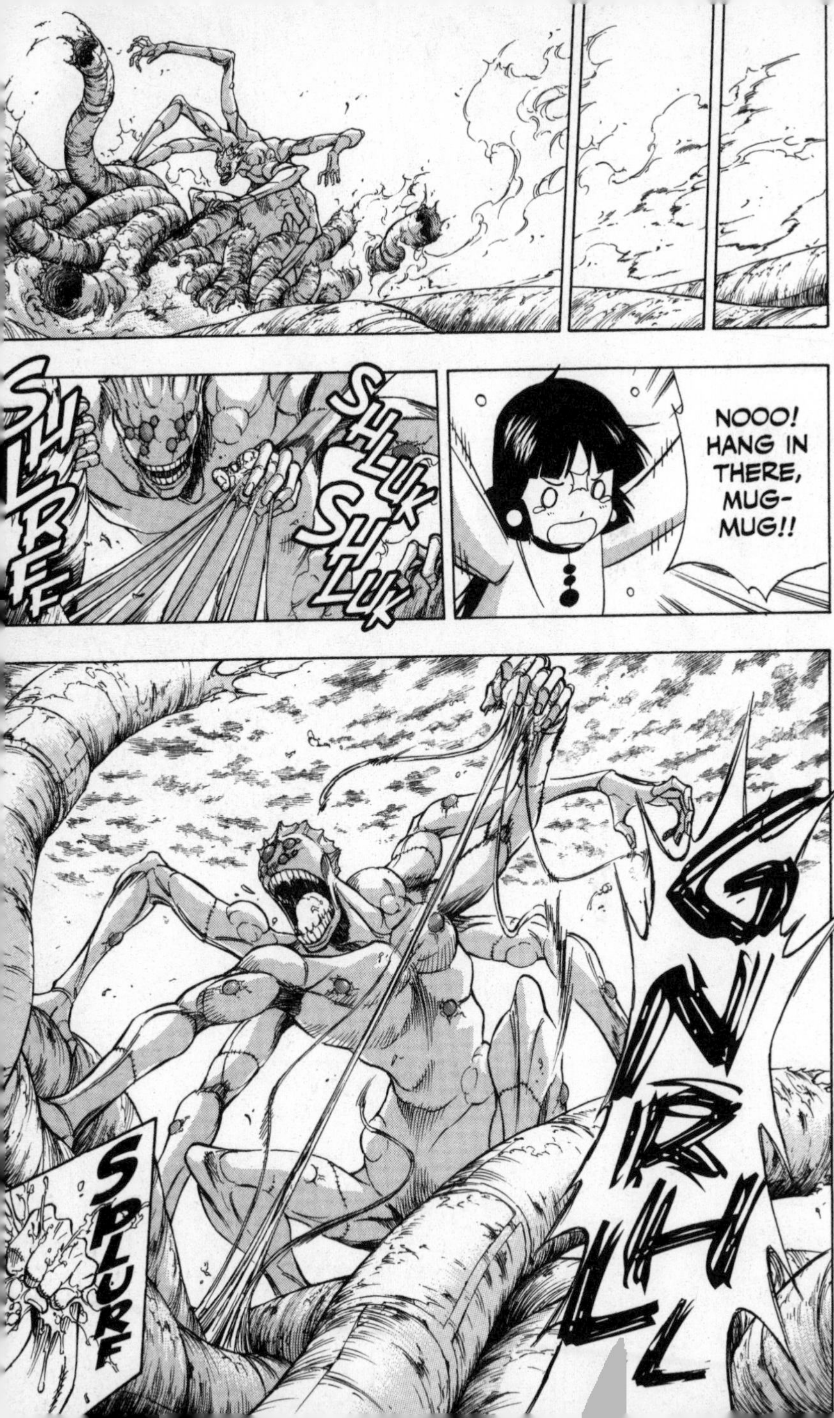
NOOO! HANG IN THERE, MUG-MUG!!
SHLUK SHLUK
SHLREFF
GNRHLL
SPLURF

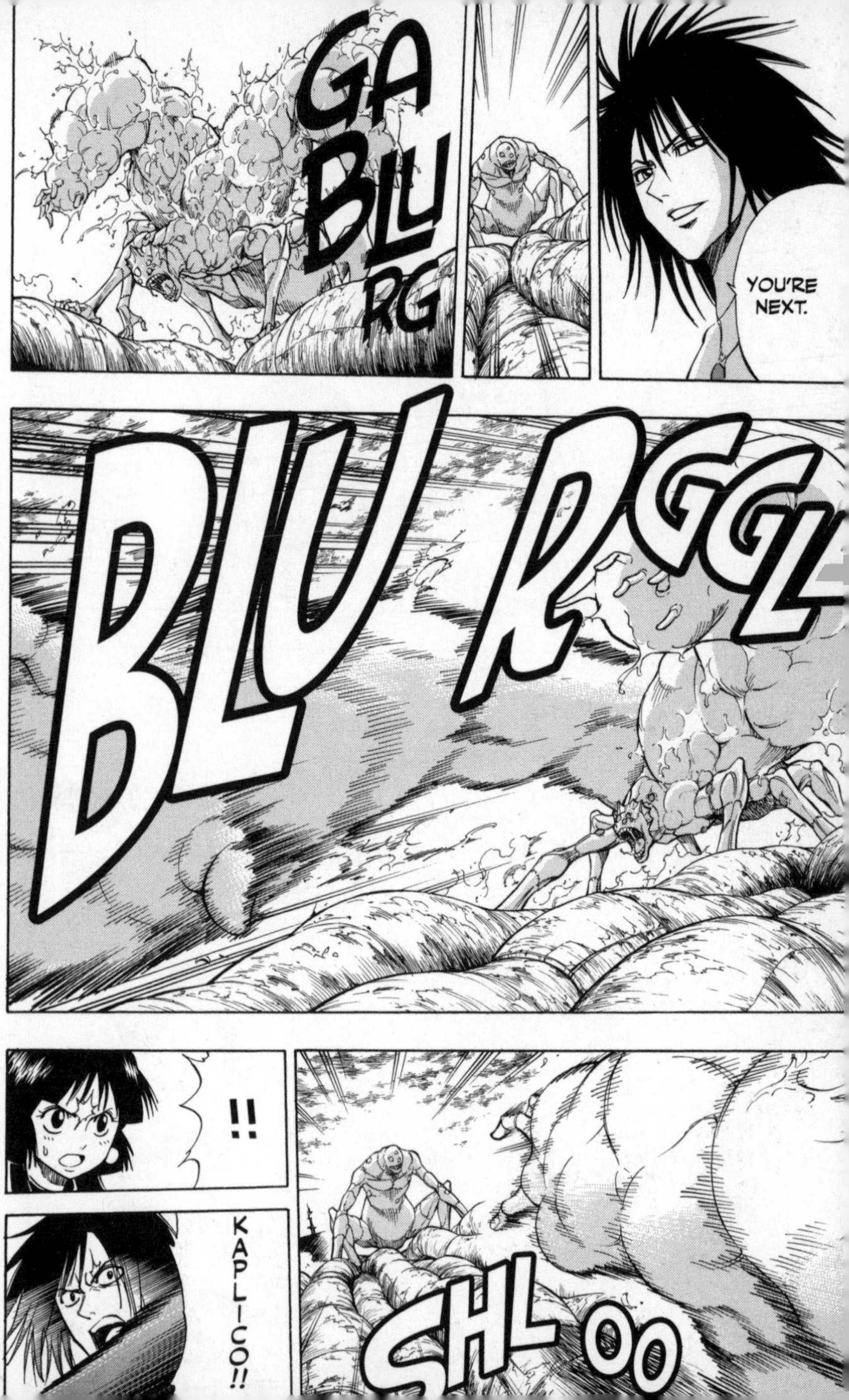
YOU'RE NEXT.
GABLURG
BLURGGL
!!
SHLOO
KAPLICO!!

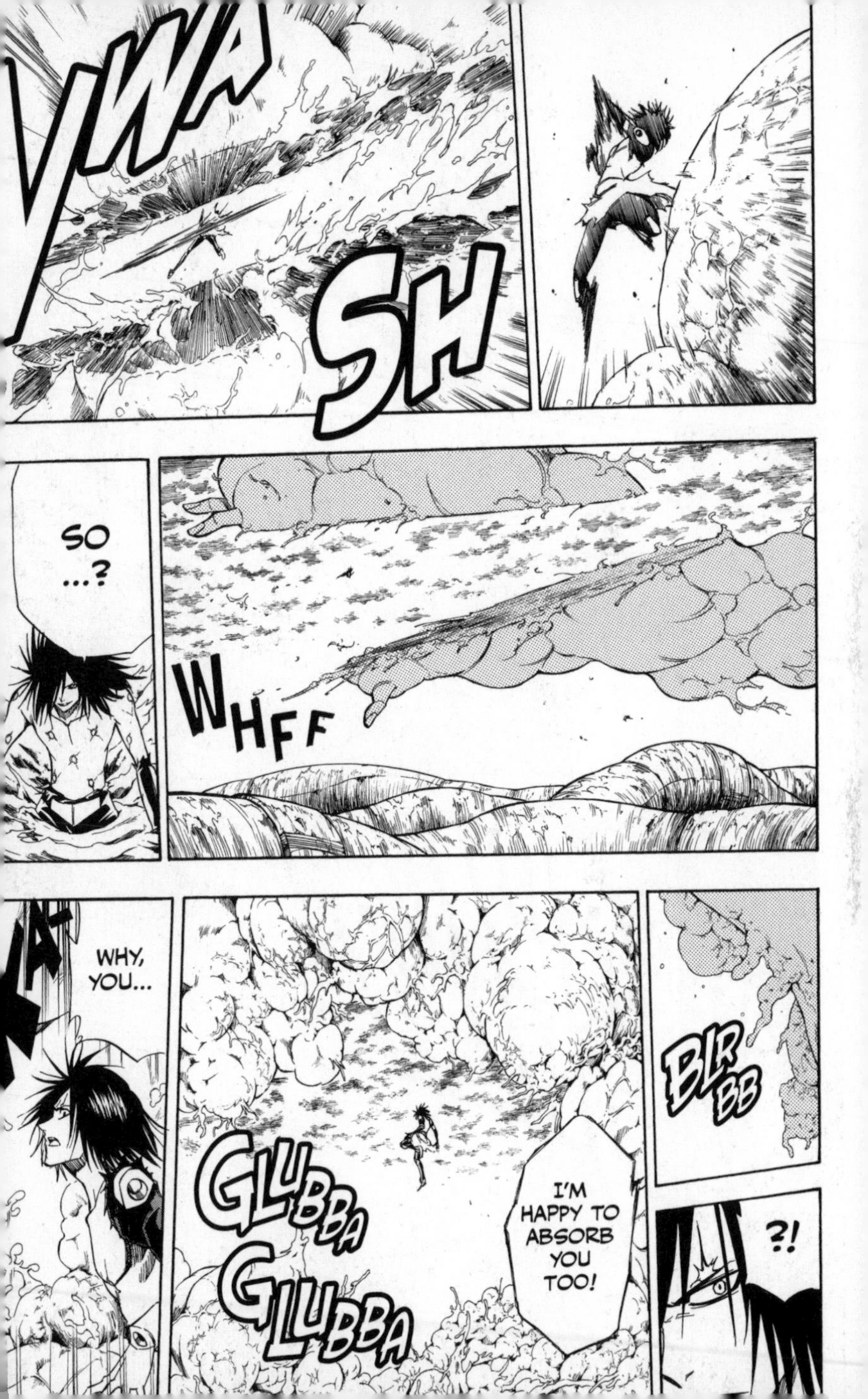
VWA
SH
WHFF
SO ...?
BLRBB
?!
GLUBBA GLUBBA
I'M HAPPY TO ABSORB YOU TOO!
WHY, YOU...

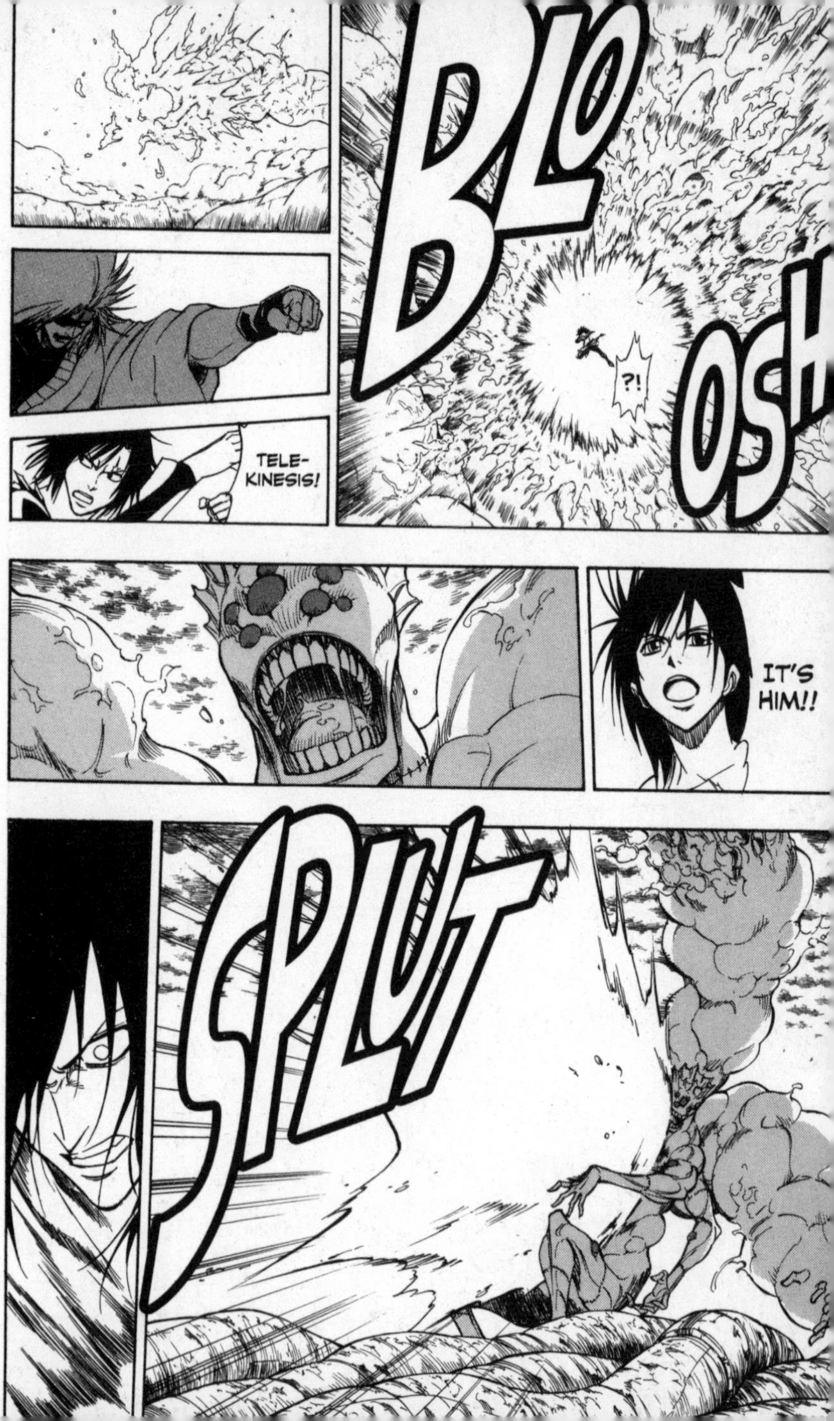
BLOOSH
?!
TELE-KINESIS!
IT'S HIM!!
SPLUT

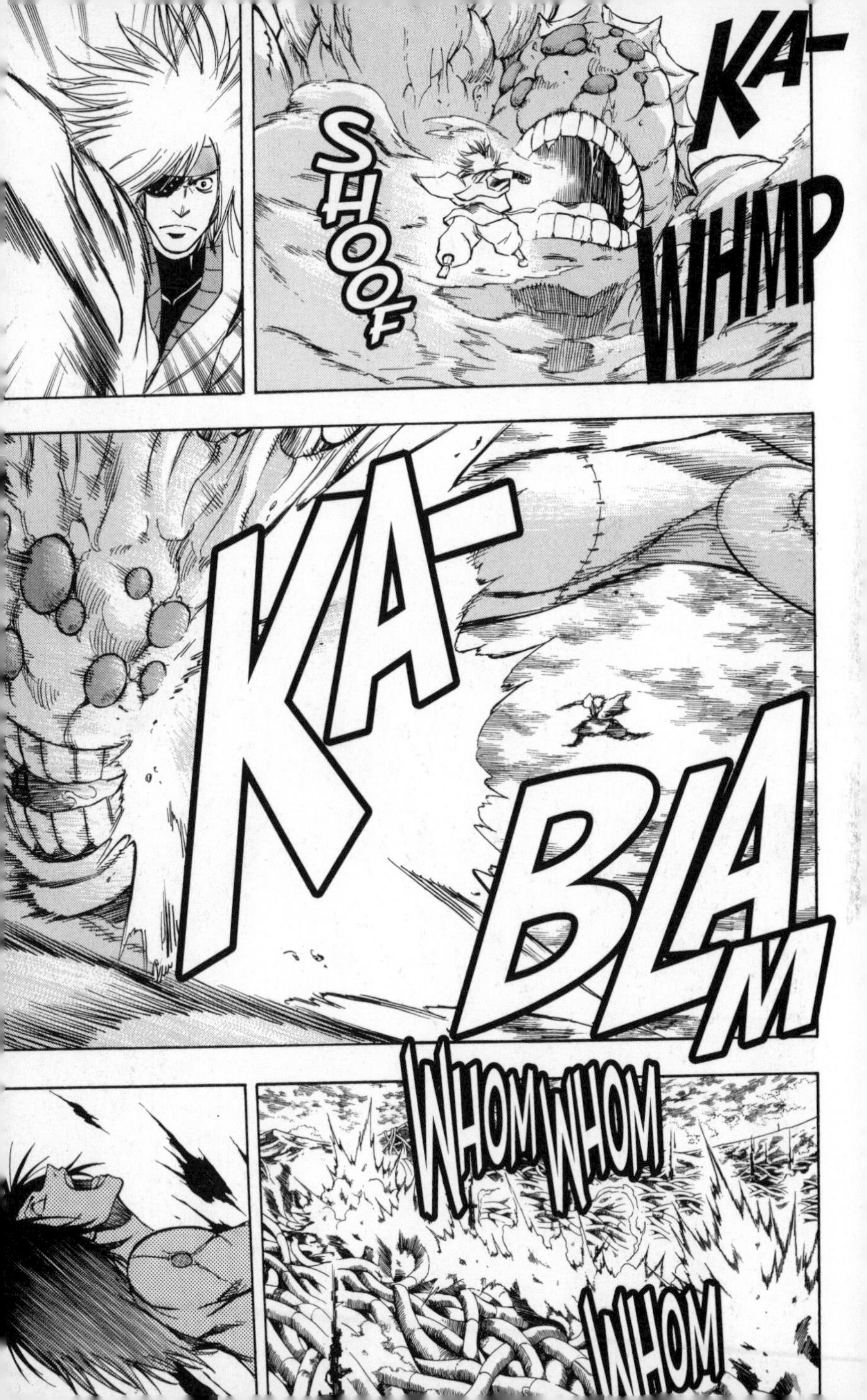
KA-WHMP
SHOOF
KA-BLAM
WHOM WHOM
WHOM

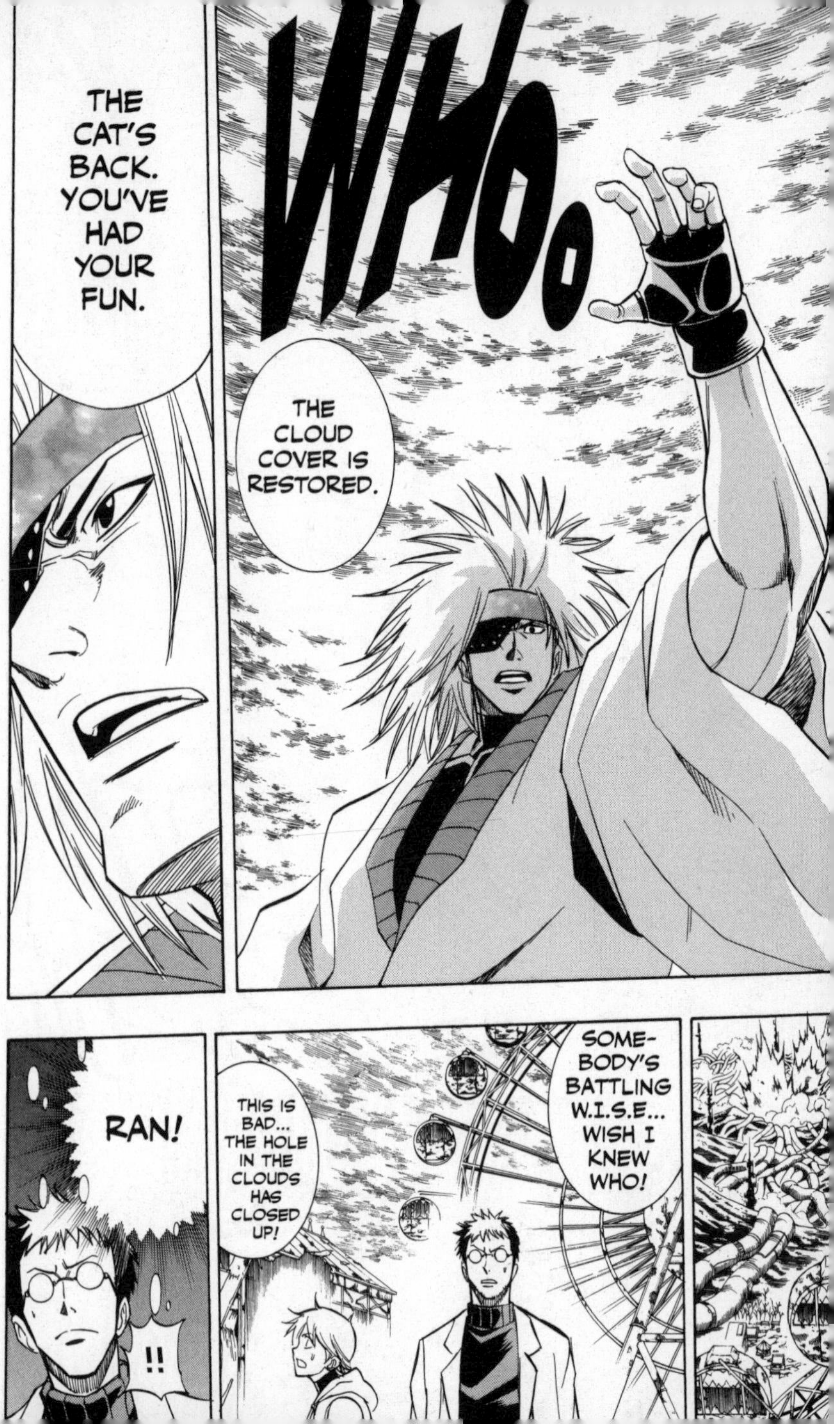
WHOO
THE CLOUD COVER IS RESTORED.
THE CAT'S BACK. YOU'VE HAD YOUR FUN.
SOME-BODY'S BATTLING W.I.S.E... WISH I KNEW WHO!
THIS IS BAD... THE HOLE IN THE CLOUDS HAS CLOSED UP!
RAN!
!!

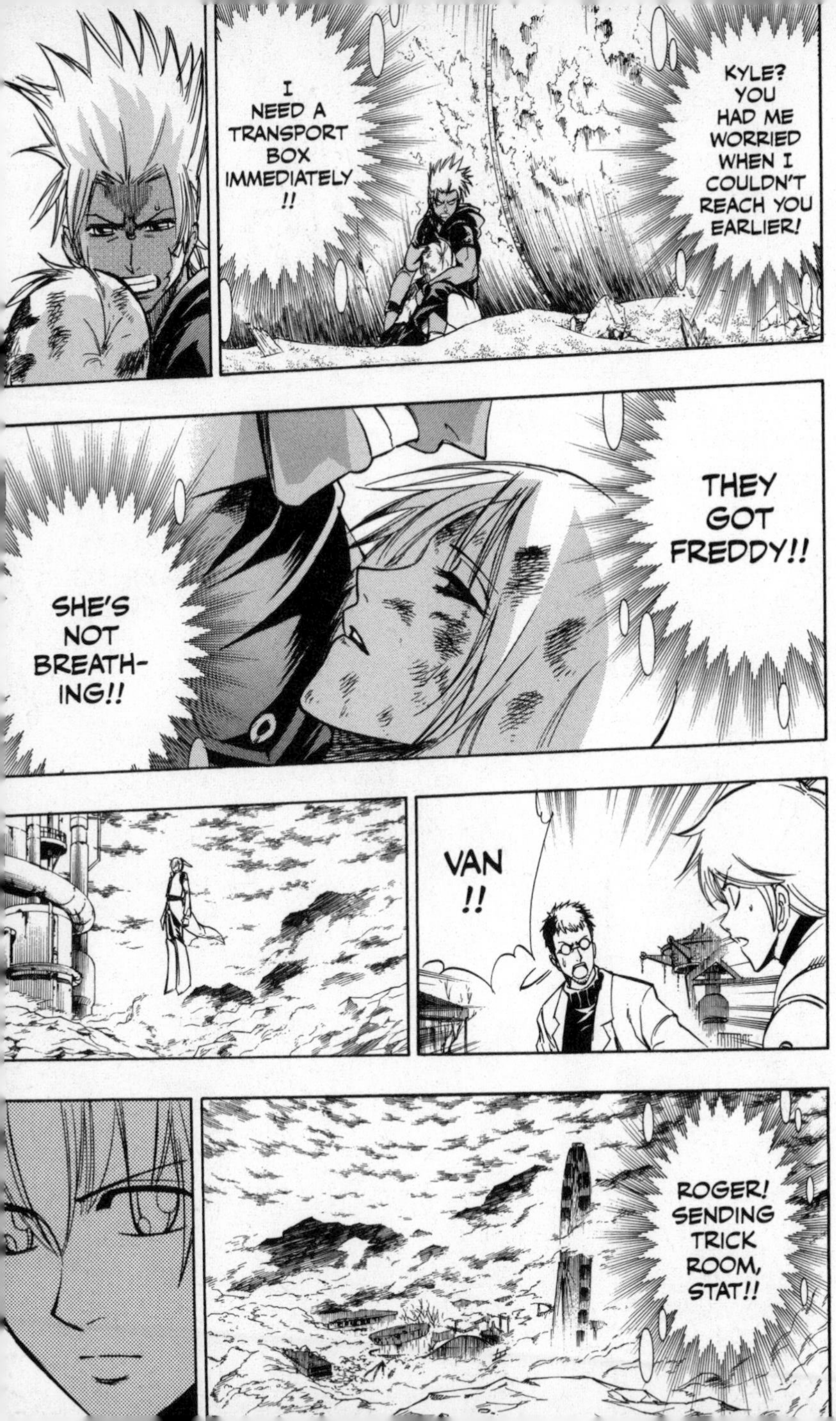
KYLE? YOU HAD ME WORRIED WHEN I COULDN'T REACH YOU EARLIER!
I NEED A TRANSPORT BOX IMMEDIATELY!!
THEY GOT FREDDY!!
SHE'S NOT BREATH-ING!!
VAN!!
ROGER! SENDING TRICK ROOM, STAT!!

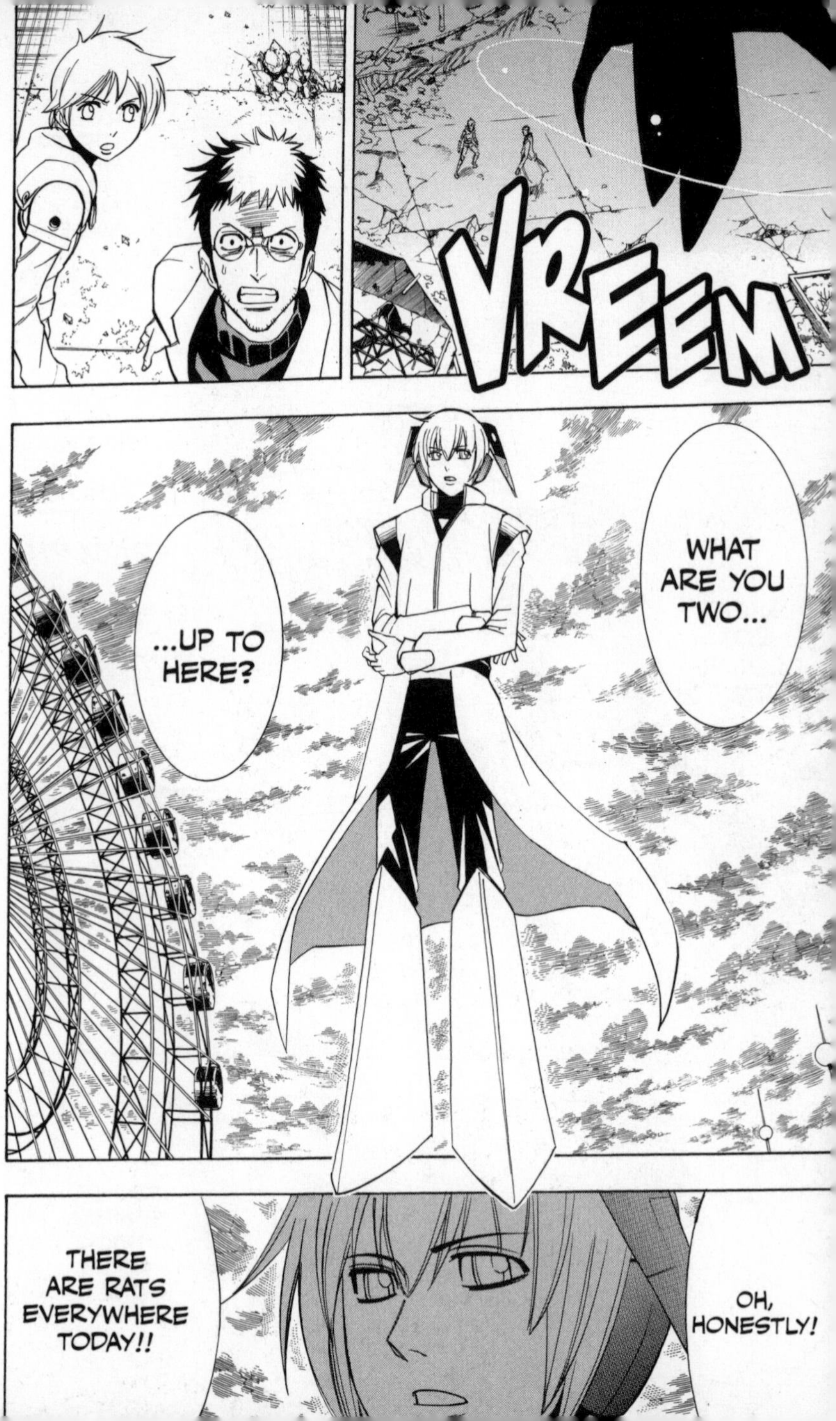
VREEM
WHAT ARE YOU TWO...
...UP TO HERE?
OH, HONESTLY!
THERE ARE RATS EVERYWHERE TODAY!!

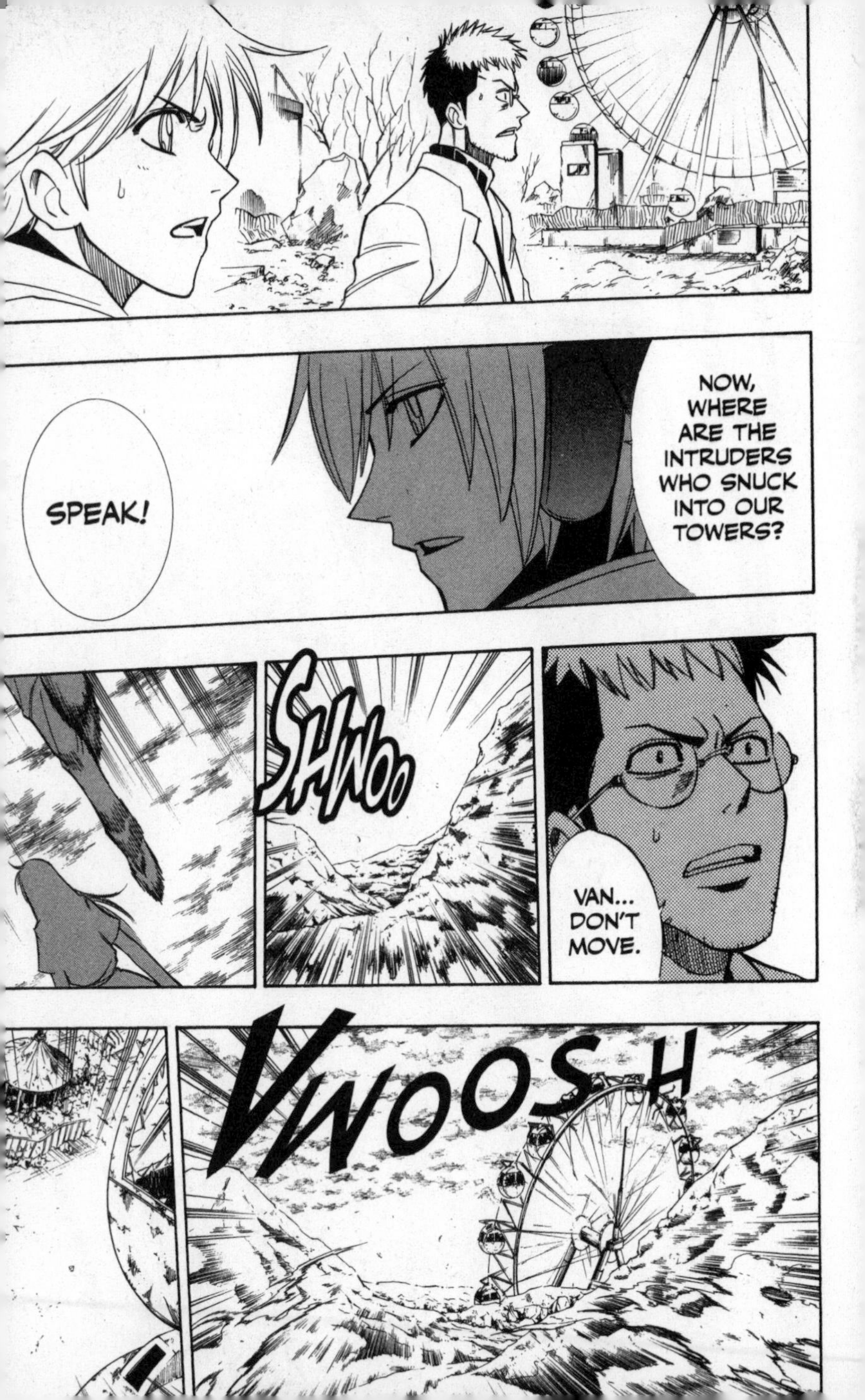
NOW, WHERE ARE THE INTRUDERS WHO SNUCK INTO OUR TOWERS?
SPEAK!
VAN... DON'T MOVE.
SHWOO
VWOOSH

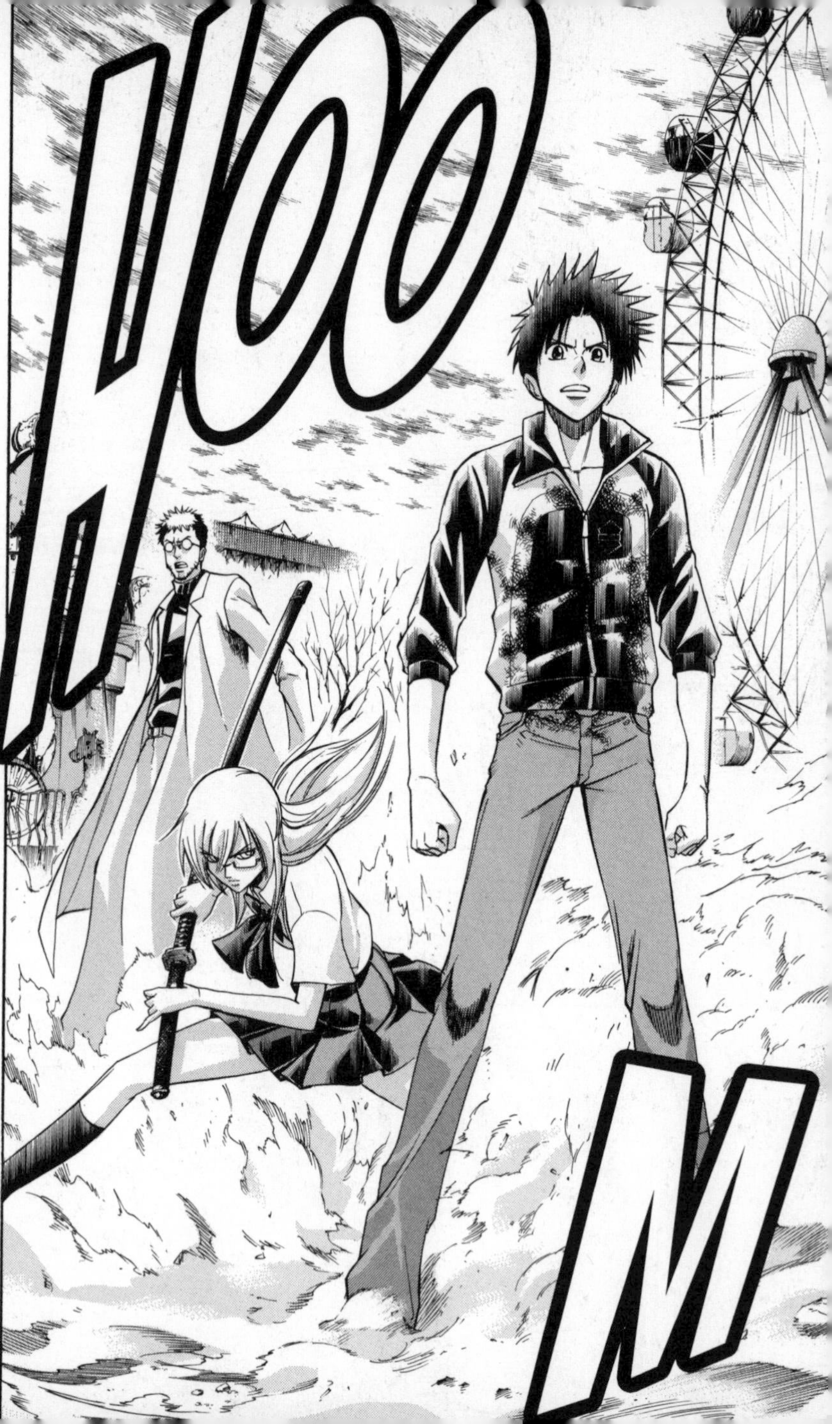
FOOM

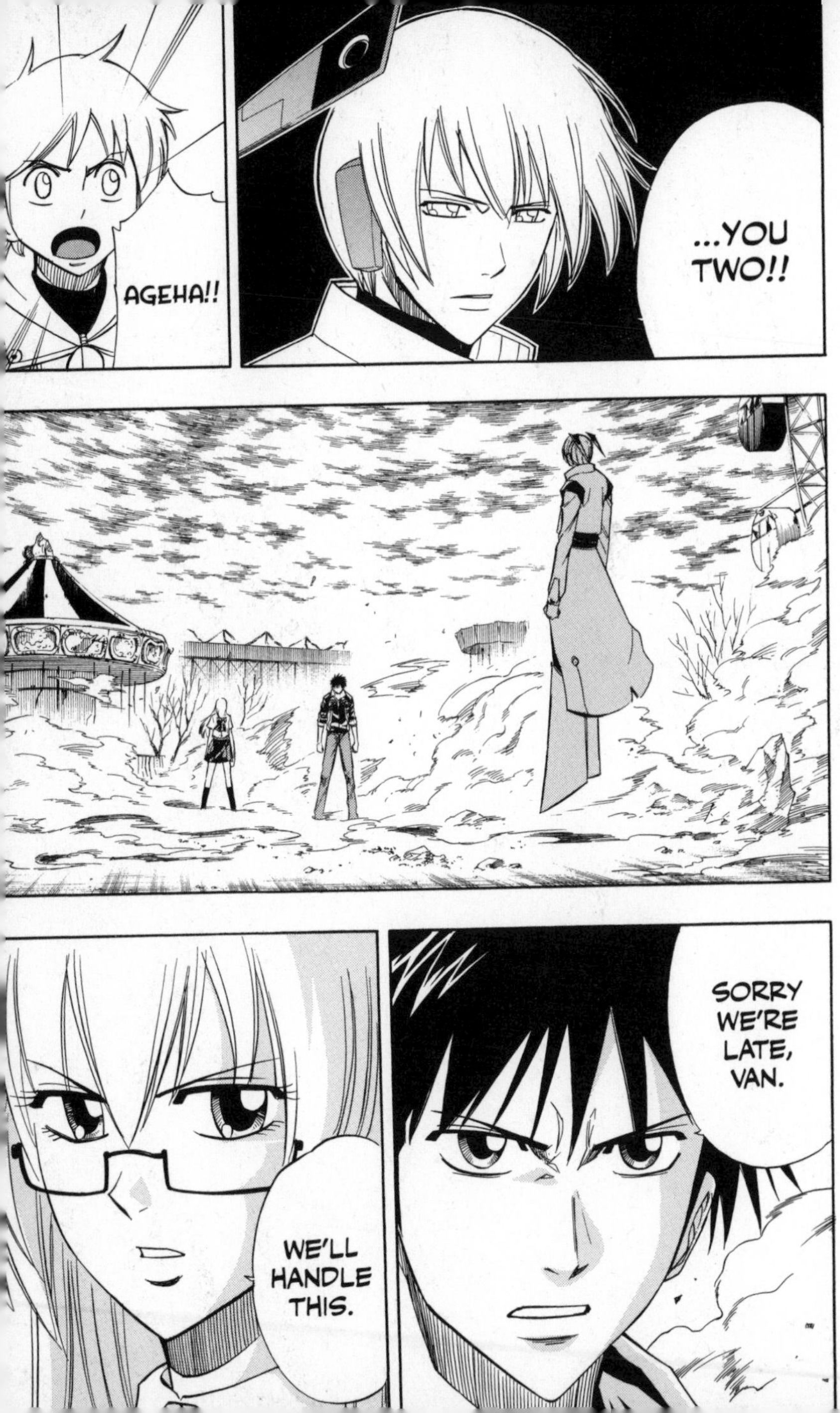
...YOU TWO!!
AGEHA!!
SORRY WE'RE LATE, VAN.
WE'LL HANDLE THIS.

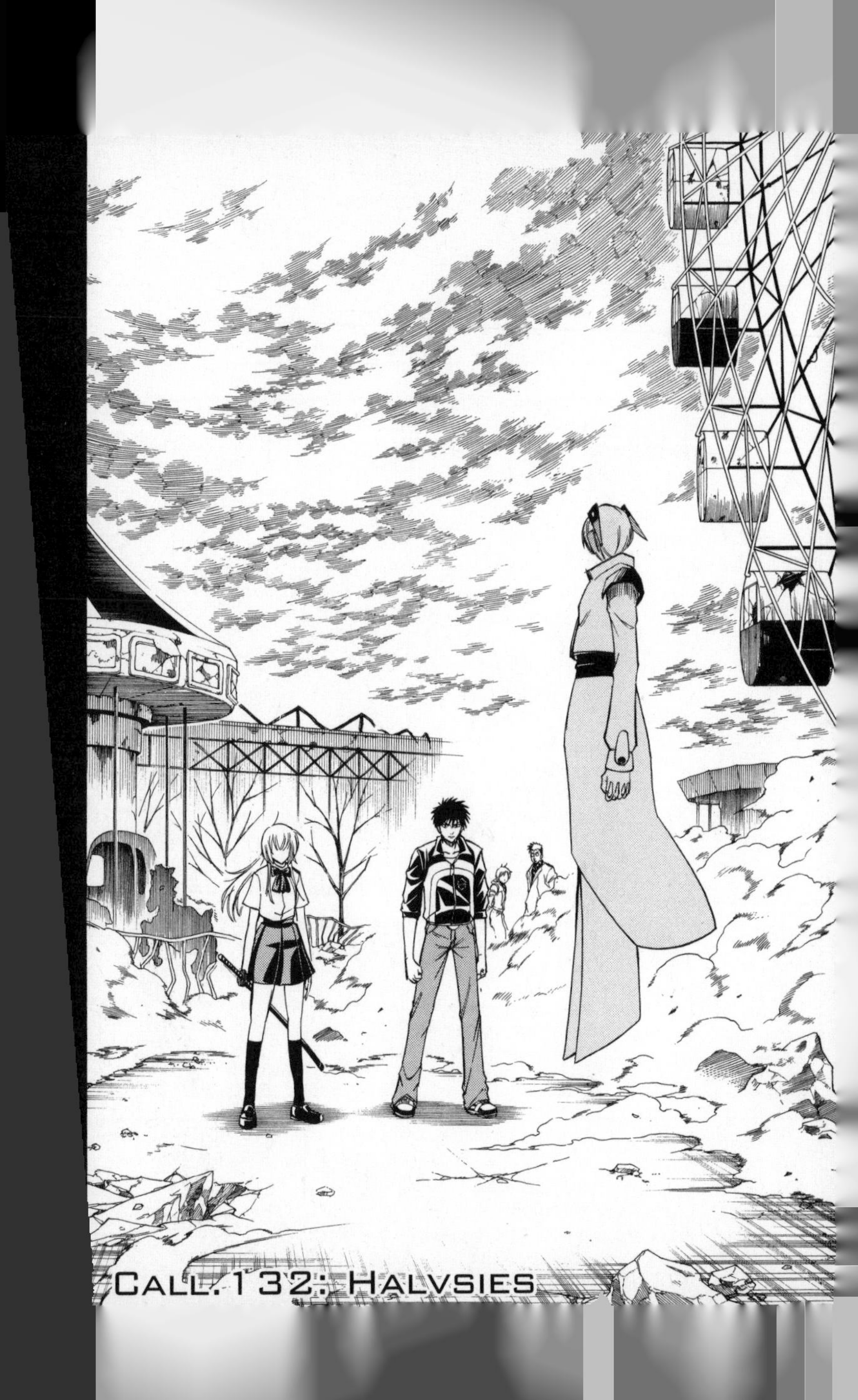
Call. 132: Halvsies

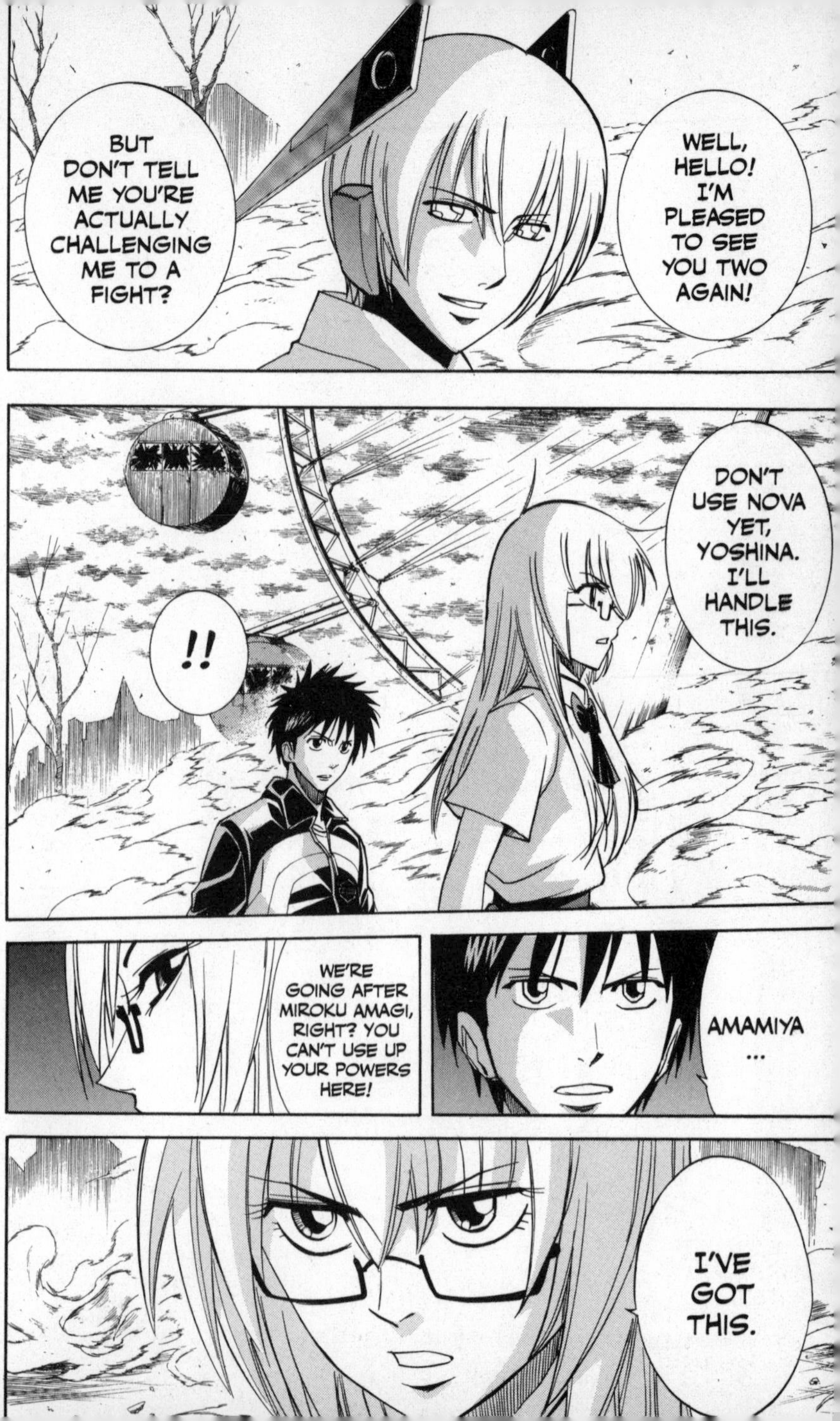
WELL, HELLO! I'M PLEASED TO SEE YOU TWO AGAIN!
BUT DON'T TELL ME YOU'RE ACTUALLY CHALLENGING ME TO A FIGHT?
DON'T USE NOVA YET, YOSHINA. I'LL HANDLE THIS.
!!
AMAMIYA ...
WE'RE GOING AFTER MIROKU AMAGI, RIGHT? YOU CAN'T USE UP YOUR POWERS HERE!
I'VE GOT THIS.

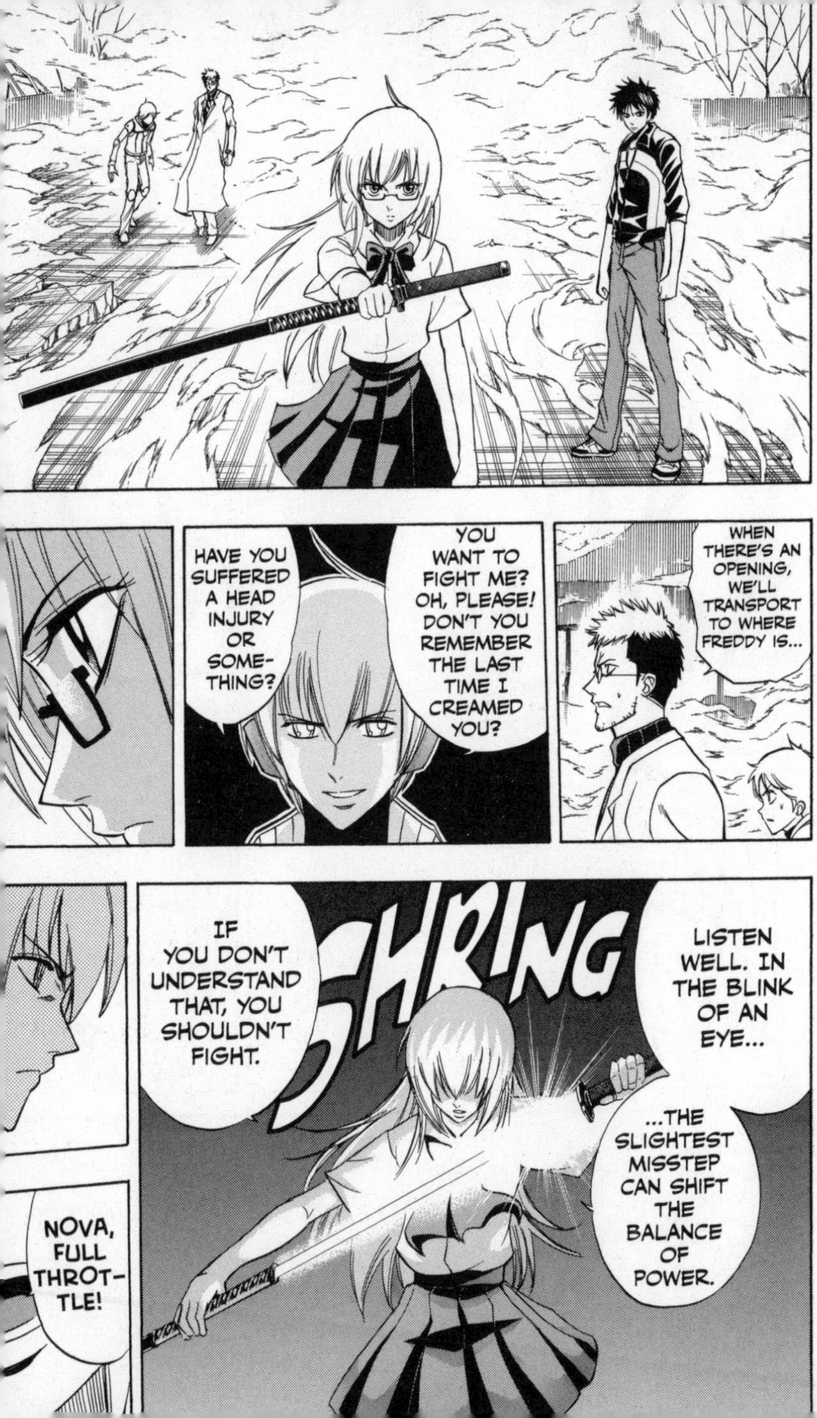
WHEN THERE'S AN OPENING, WE'LL TRANSPORT TO WHERE FREDDY IS...
YOU WANT TO FIGHT ME? OH, PLEASE! DON'T YOU REMEMBER THE LAST TIME I CREAMED YOU?
HAVE YOU SUFFERED A HEAD INJURY OR SOMETHING?
LISTEN WELL. IN THE BLINK OF AN EYE...
...THE SLIGHTEST MISSTEP CAN SHIFT THE BALANCE OF POWER.
SHRING
IF YOU DON'T UNDERSTAND THAT, YOU SHOULDN'T FIGHT.
NOVA, FULL THROTTLE!

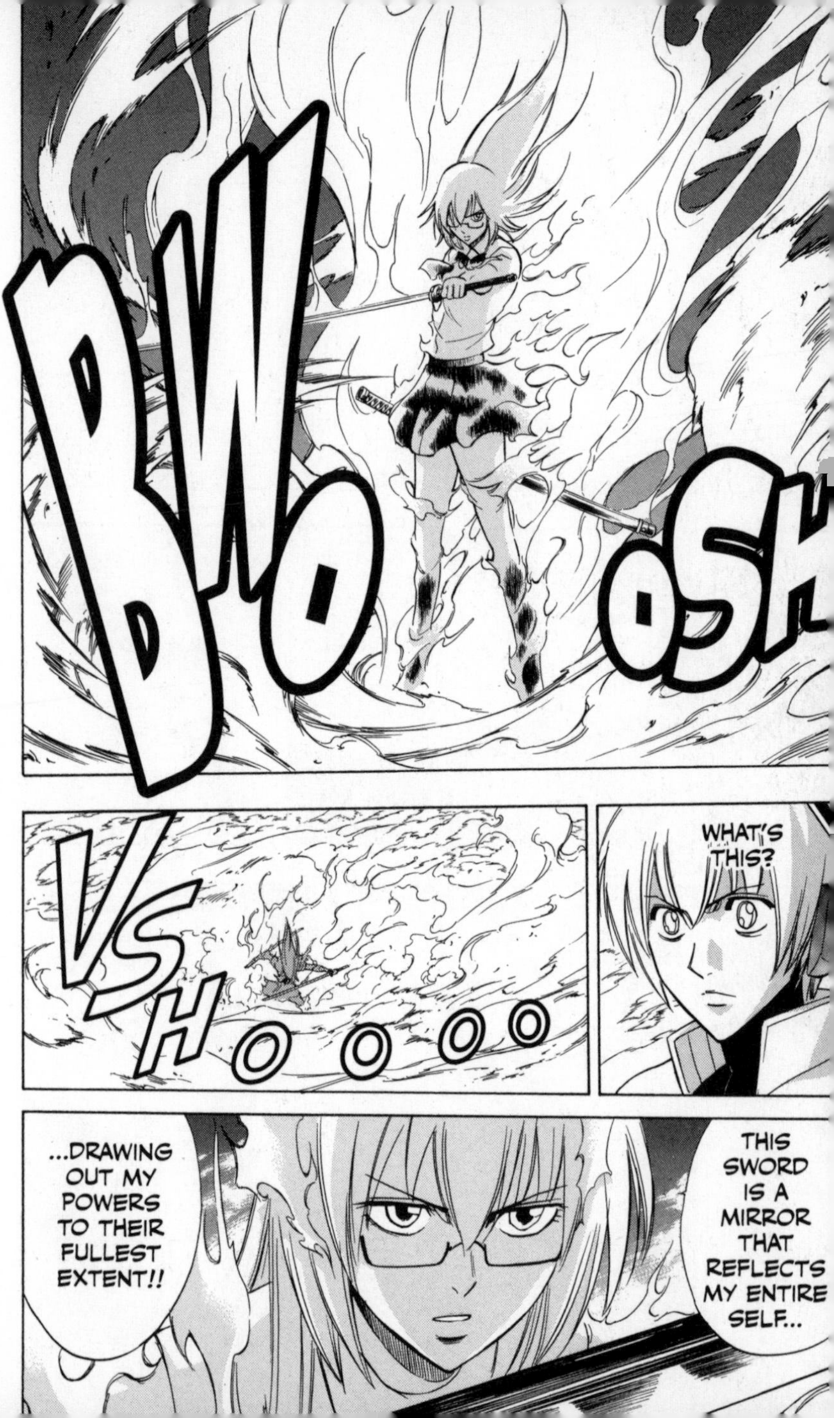
BWOOSH
WHAT'S THIS?
VSHOOOO
THIS SWORD IS A MIRROR THAT REFLECTS MY ENTIRE SELF...
...DRAWING OUT MY POWERS TO THEIR FULLEST EXTENT!!

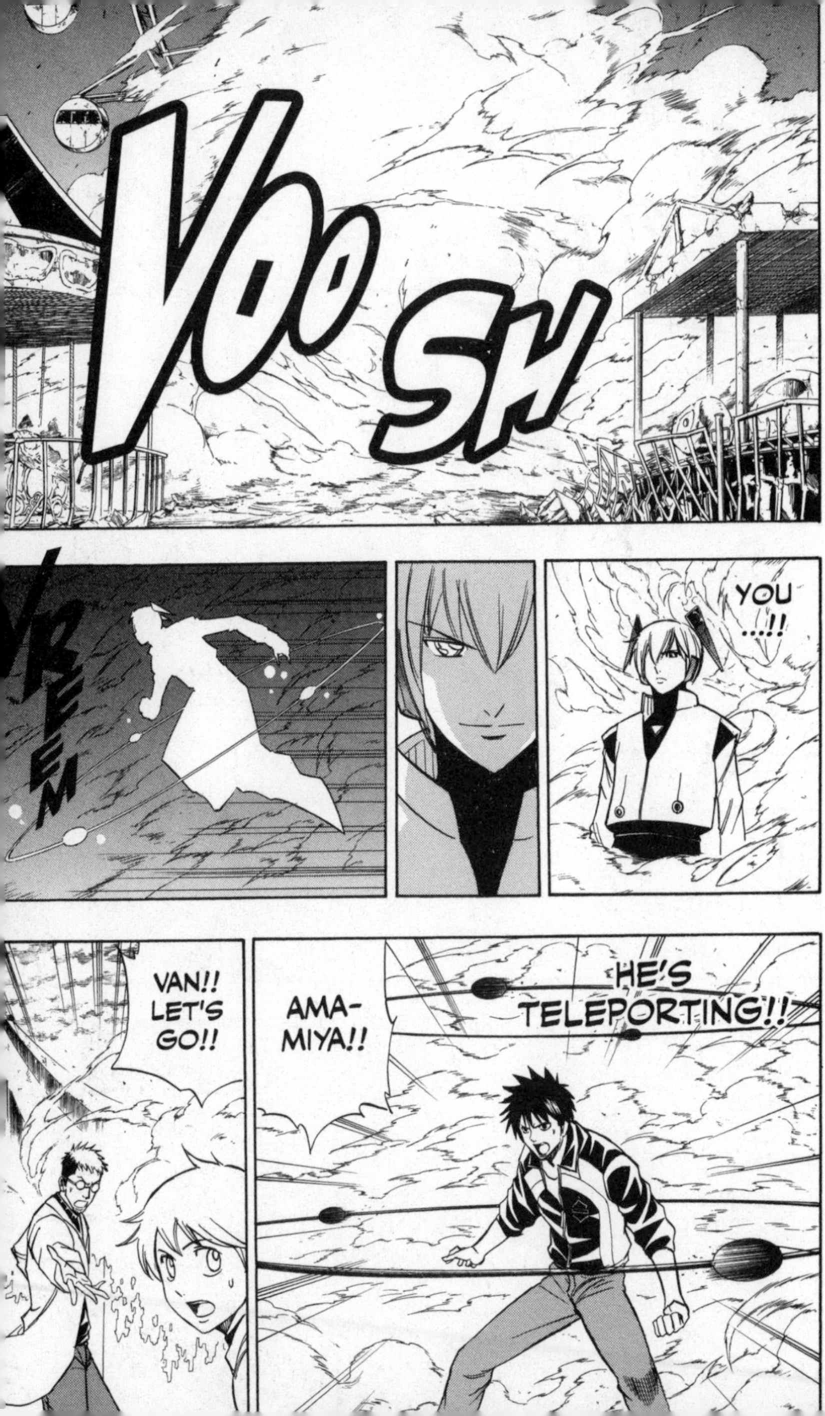
YOOSH
YOU ...!!
VREEM
HE'S TELEPORTING!!
AMA-MIYA!!
VAN!! LET'S GO!!

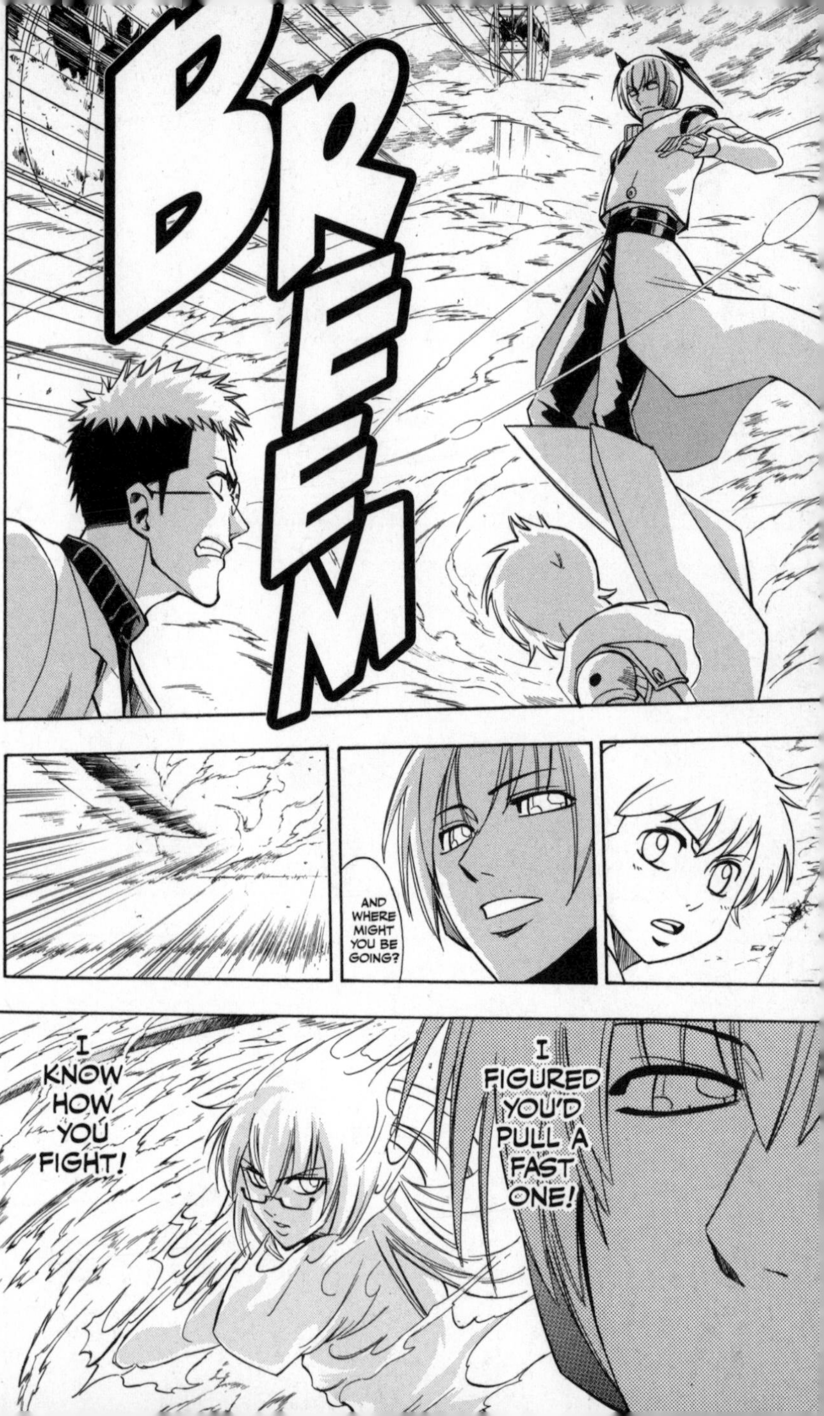
DREEM
AND WHERE MIGHT YOU BE GOING?
I FIGURED YOU'D PULL A FAST ONE!
I KNOW HOW YOU FIGHT!

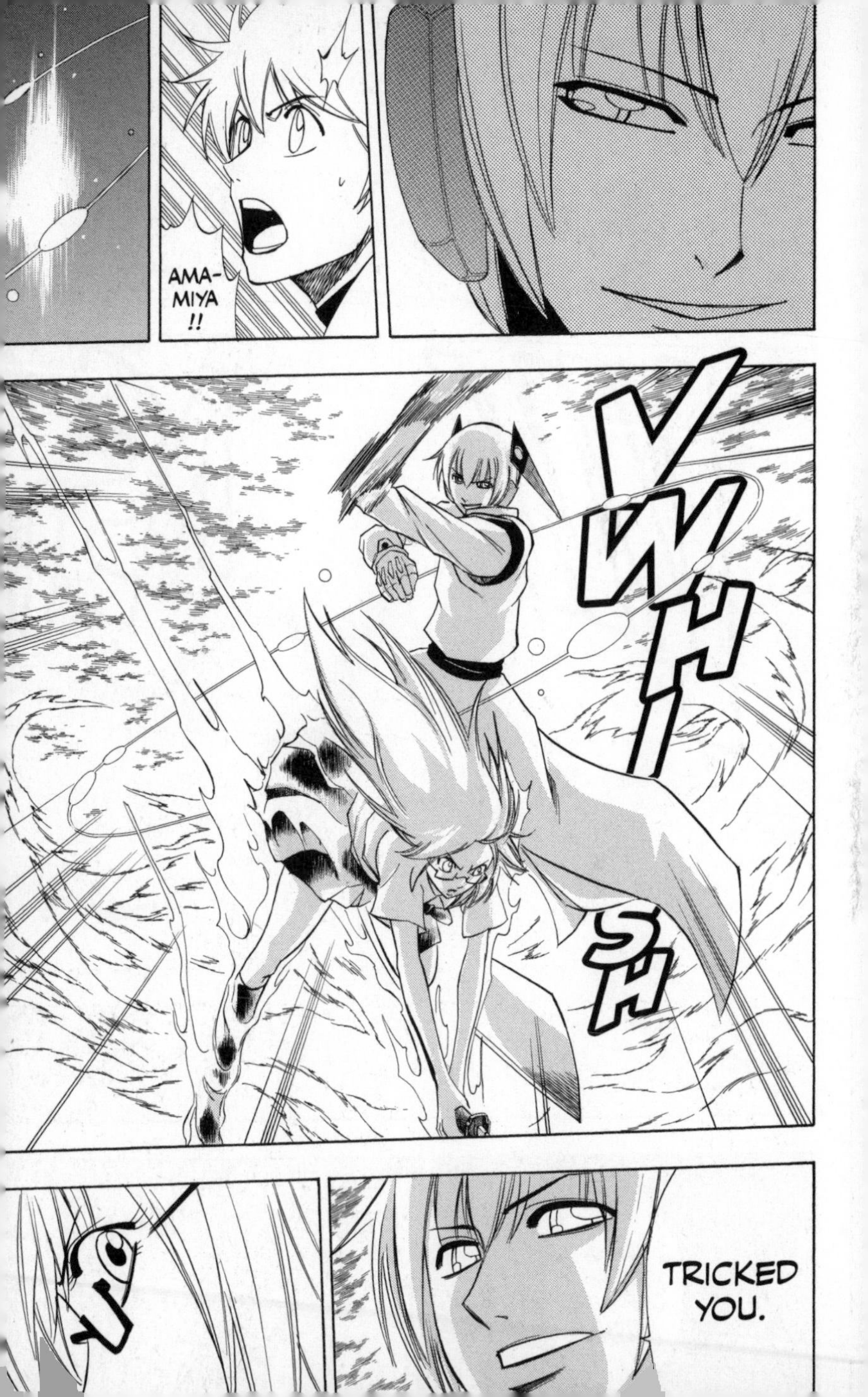
AMA-
MIYA
!!
VWHISH
TRICKED
YOU.

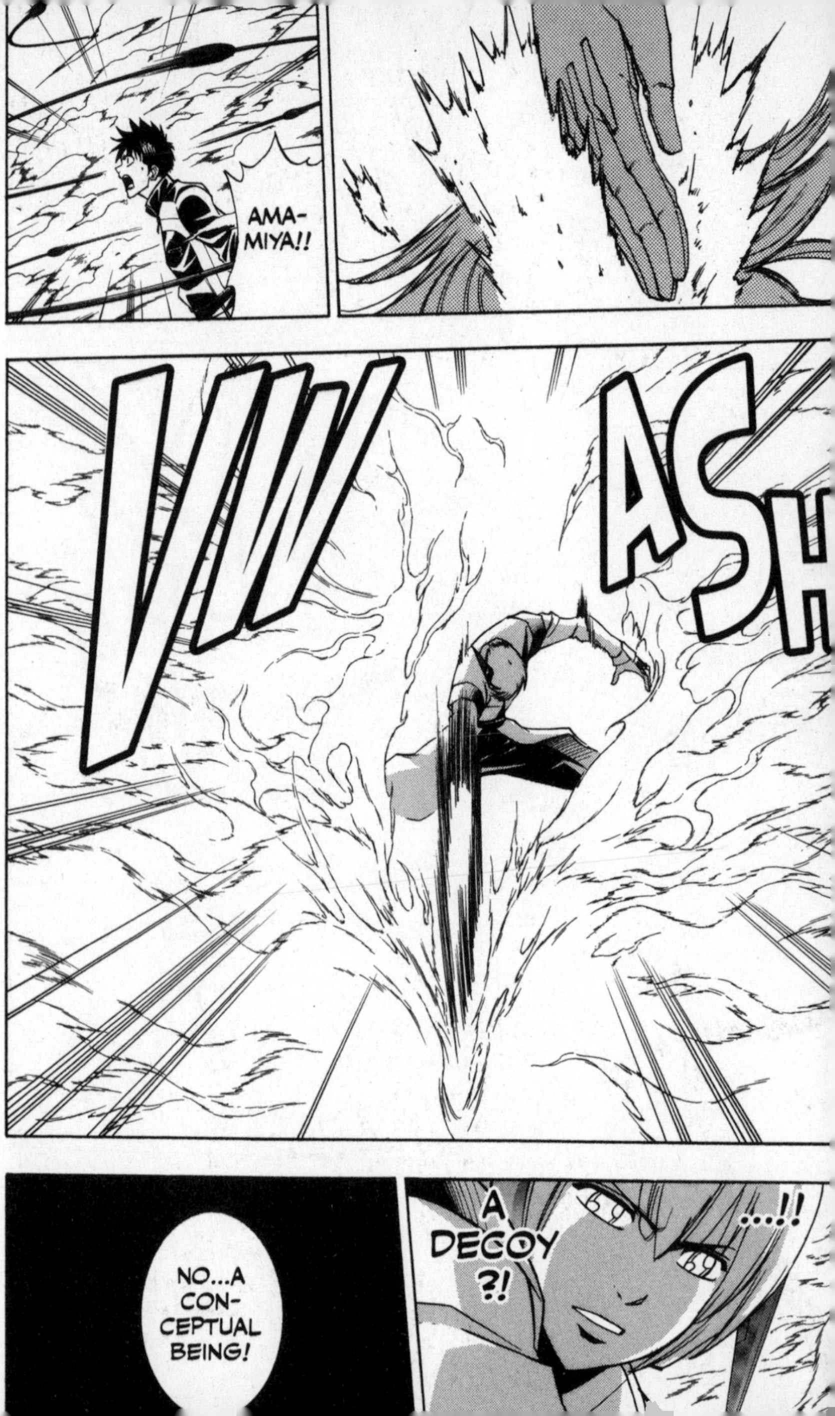
AMA-
MIYA!!
VWASH
...!!
A DECOY ?!
NO...A CON-
CEPTUAL
BEING!

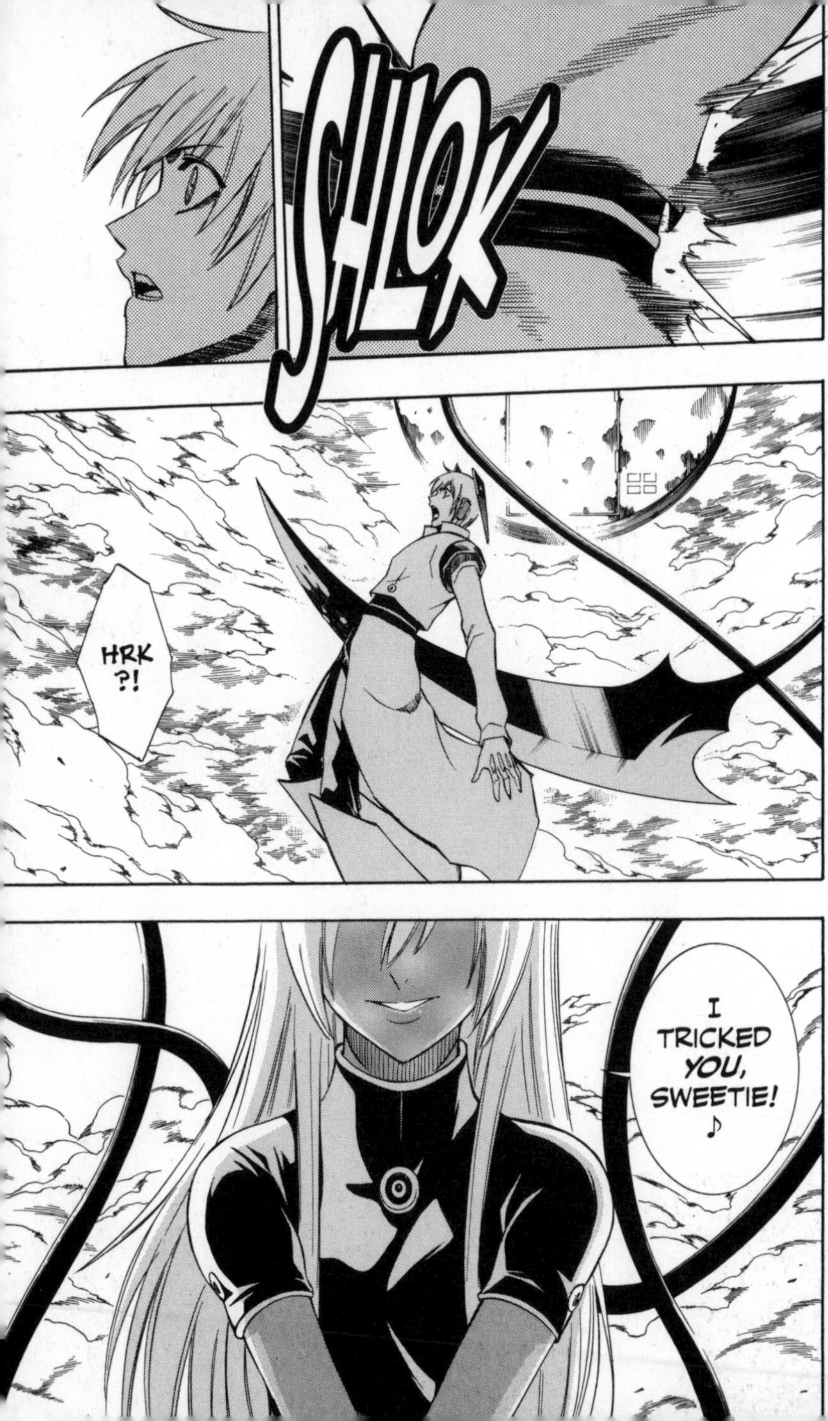
SHLOK
HRK ?!
I TRICKED YOU, SWEETIE! ♪

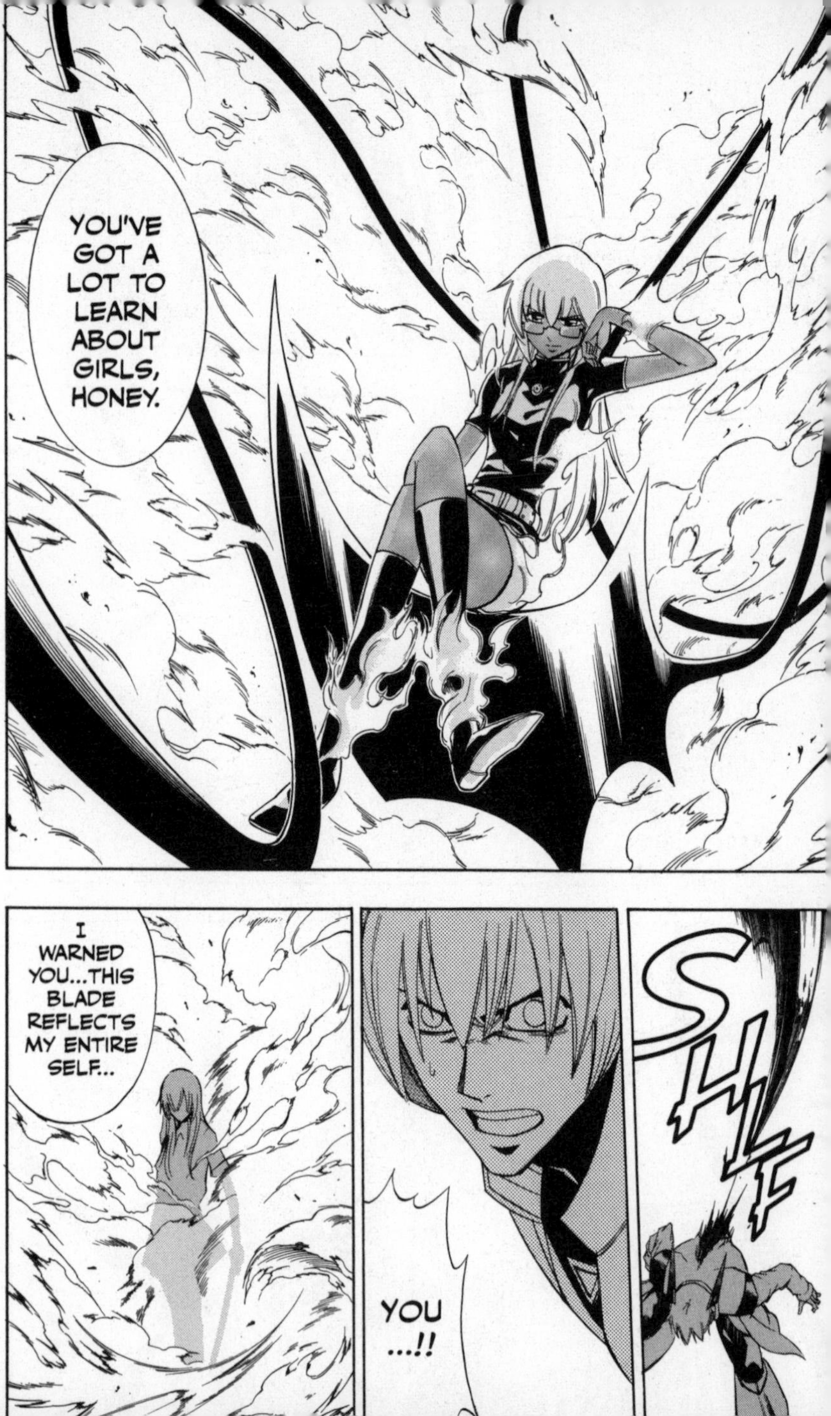
YOU'VE GOT A LOT TO LEARN ABOUT GIRLS, HONEY.
SHF
YOU ...!!
I WARNED YOU...THIS BLADE REFLECTS MY ENTIRE SELF...

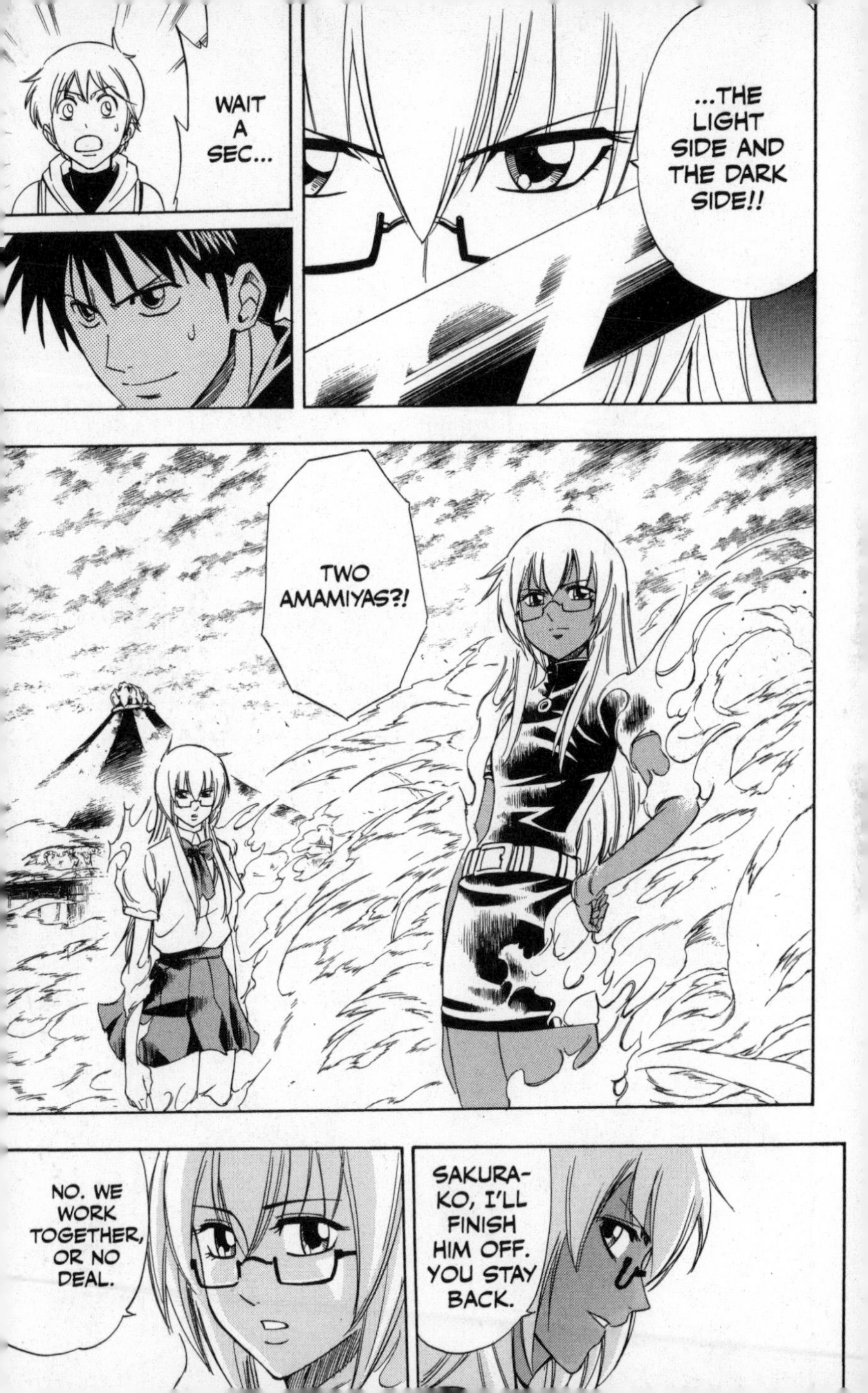
...THE LIGHT SIDE AND THE DARK SIDE!!
WAIT A SEC...
TWO AMAMIYAS?!
SAKURA-KO, I'LL FINISH HIM OFF. YOU STAY BACK.
NO. WE WORK TOGETHER, OR NO DEAL.

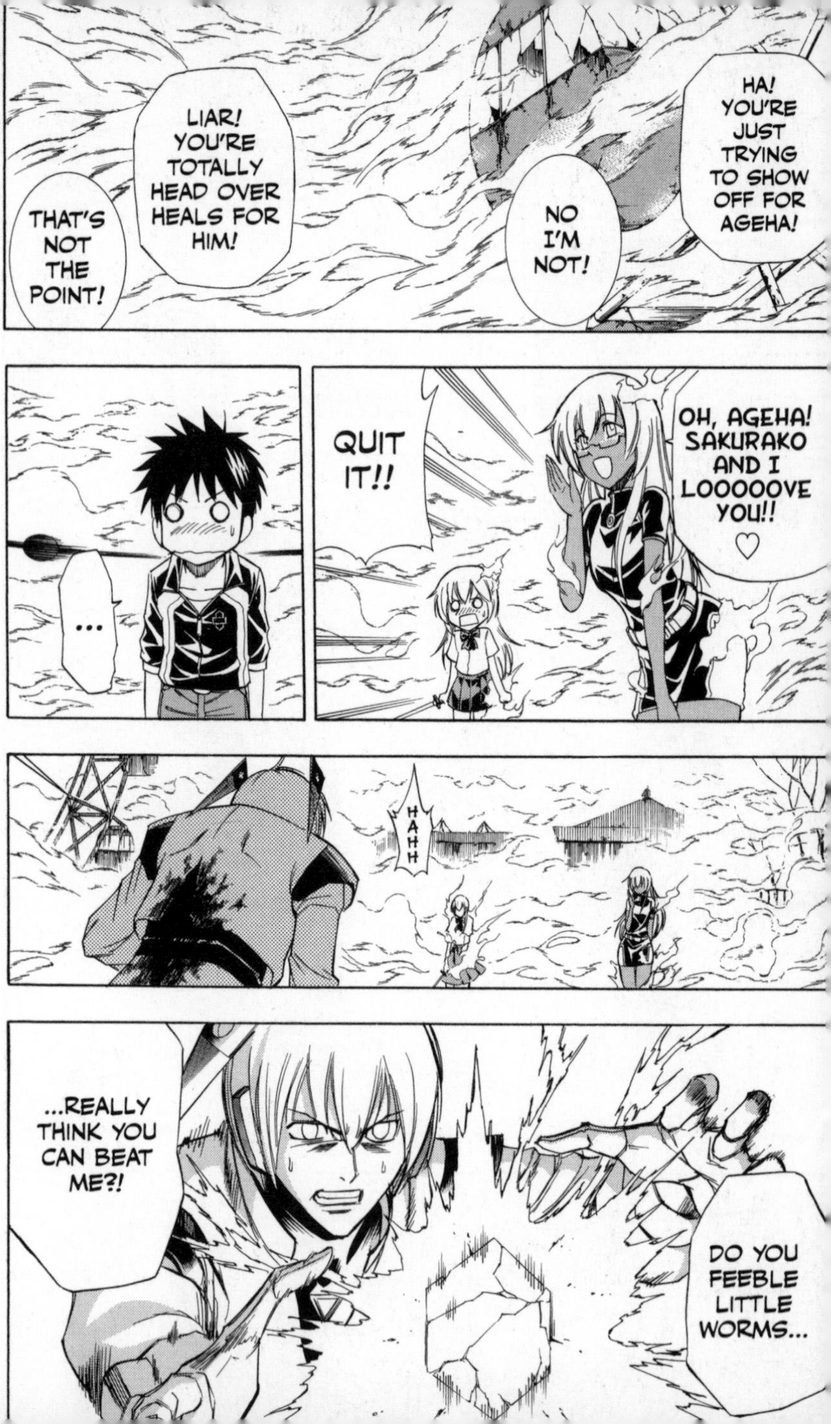
HA! YOU'RE JUST TRYING TO SHOW OFF FOR AGEHA!
NO I'M NOT!
LIAR! YOU'RE TOTALLY HEAD OVER HEALS FOR HIM!
THAT'S NOT THE POINT!
OH, AGEHA! SAKURAKO AND I LOOOOOVE YOU!! ♡
QUIT IT!!
...
HAHH
DO YOU FEEBLE LITTLE WORMS...
...REALLY THINK YOU CAN BEAT ME?!

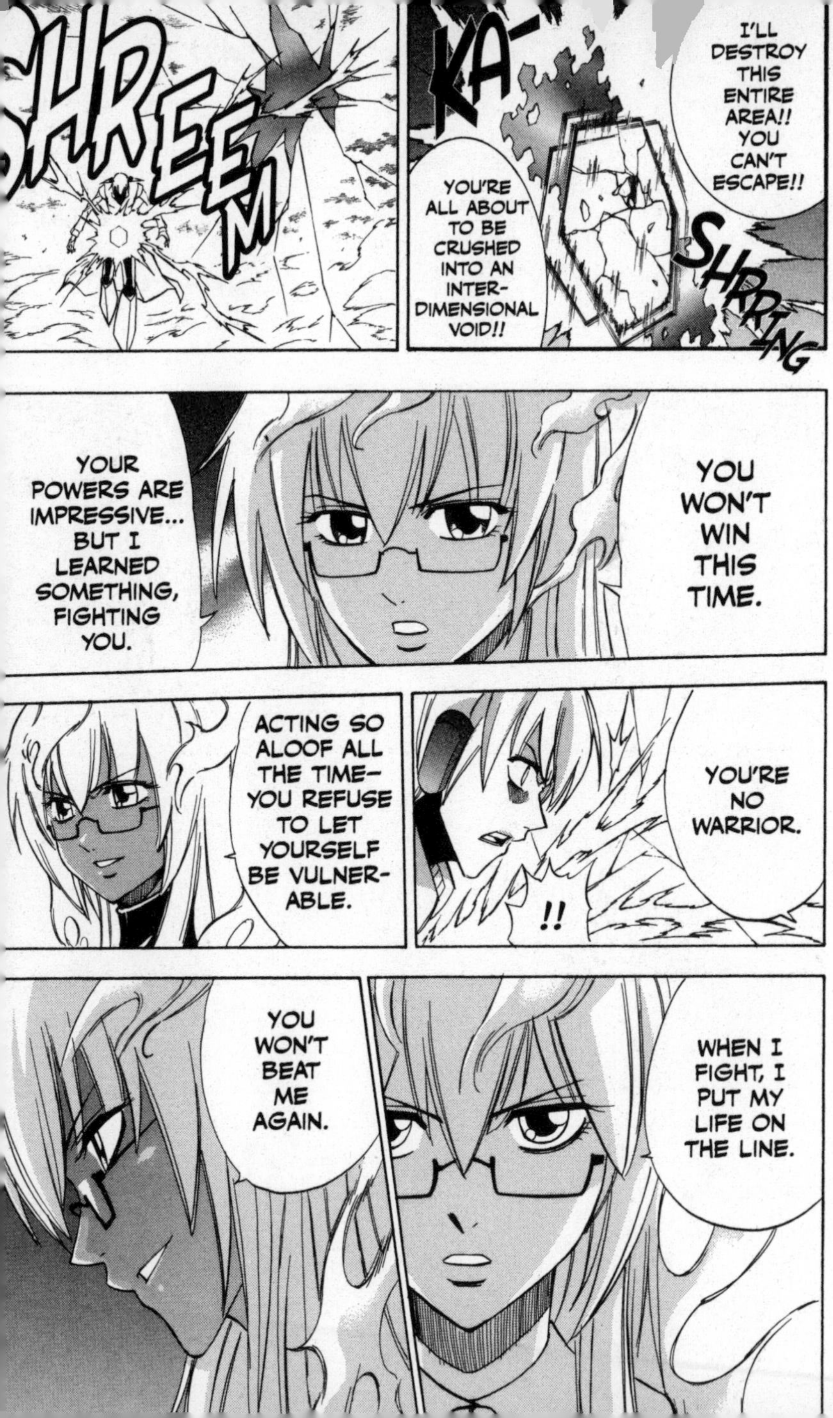
I'LL DESTROY THIS ENTIRE AREA!! YOU CAN'T ESCAPE!!
KA-
YOU'RE ALL ABOUT TO BE CRUSHED INTO AN INTER-DIMENSIONAL VOID!!
SHRRING
SHREEM
YOU WON'T WIN THIS TIME.
YOUR POWERS ARE IMPRESSIVE... BUT I LEARNED SOMETHING, FIGHTING YOU.
YOU'RE NO WARRIOR.
!!
ACTING SO ALOOF ALL THE TIME— YOU REFUSE TO LET YOURSELF BE VULNER-ABLE.
WHEN I FIGHT, I PUT MY LIFE ON THE LINE.
YOU WON'T BEAT ME AGAIN.

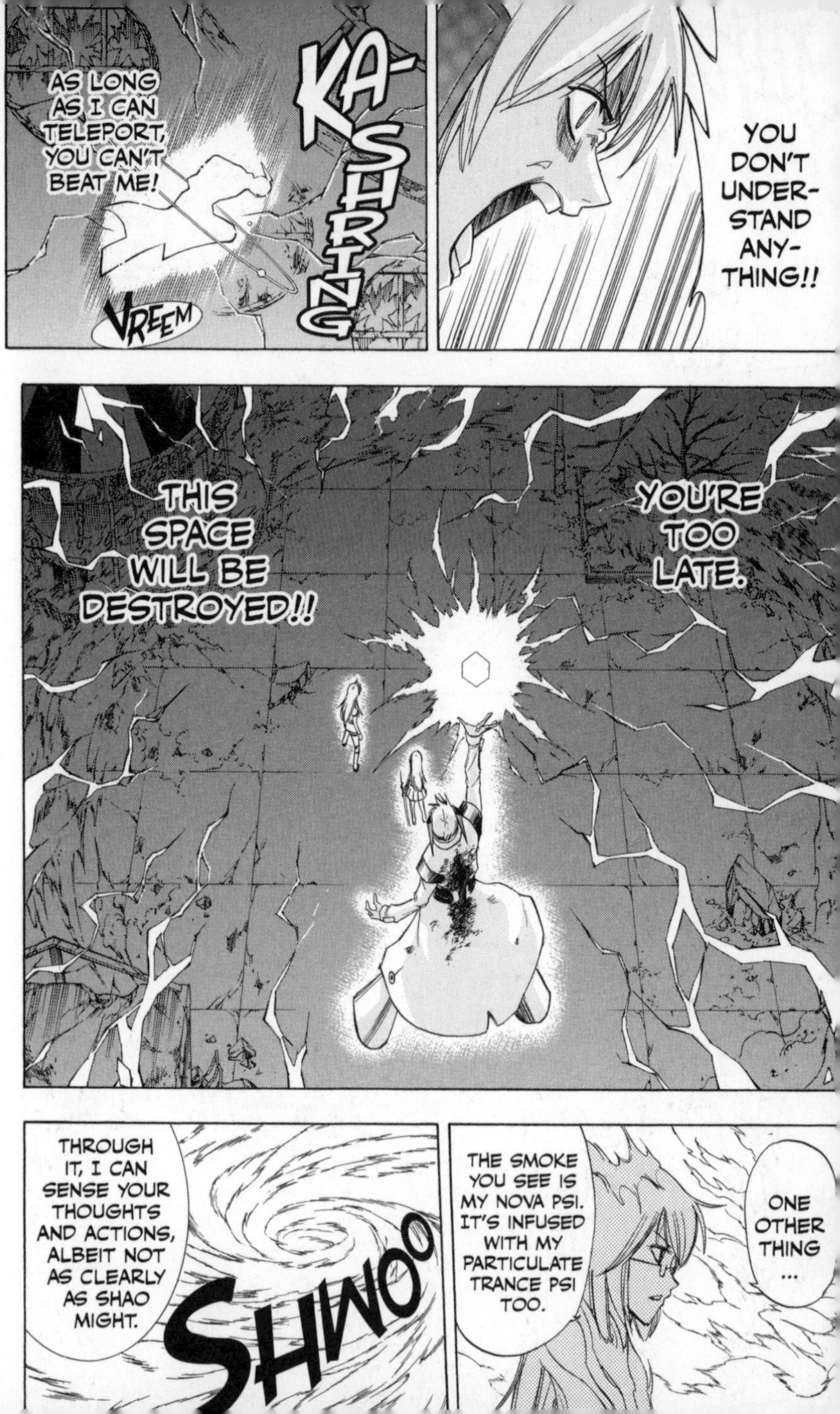
YOU DON'T UNDER-STAND ANY-THING!!
AS LONG AS I CAN TELEPORT, YOU CAN'T BEAT ME!
KA-SHRING
VREEM
YOU'RE TOO LATE.
THIS SPACE WILL BE DESTROYED!!
ONE OTHER THING ...
THE SMOKE YOU SEE IS MY NOVA PSI. IT'S INFUSED WITH MY PARTICULATE TRANCE PSI TOO.
THROUGH IT, I CAN SENSE YOUR THOUGHTS AND ACTIONS, ALBEIT NOT AS CLEARLY AS SHAO MIGHT.
SHWOO

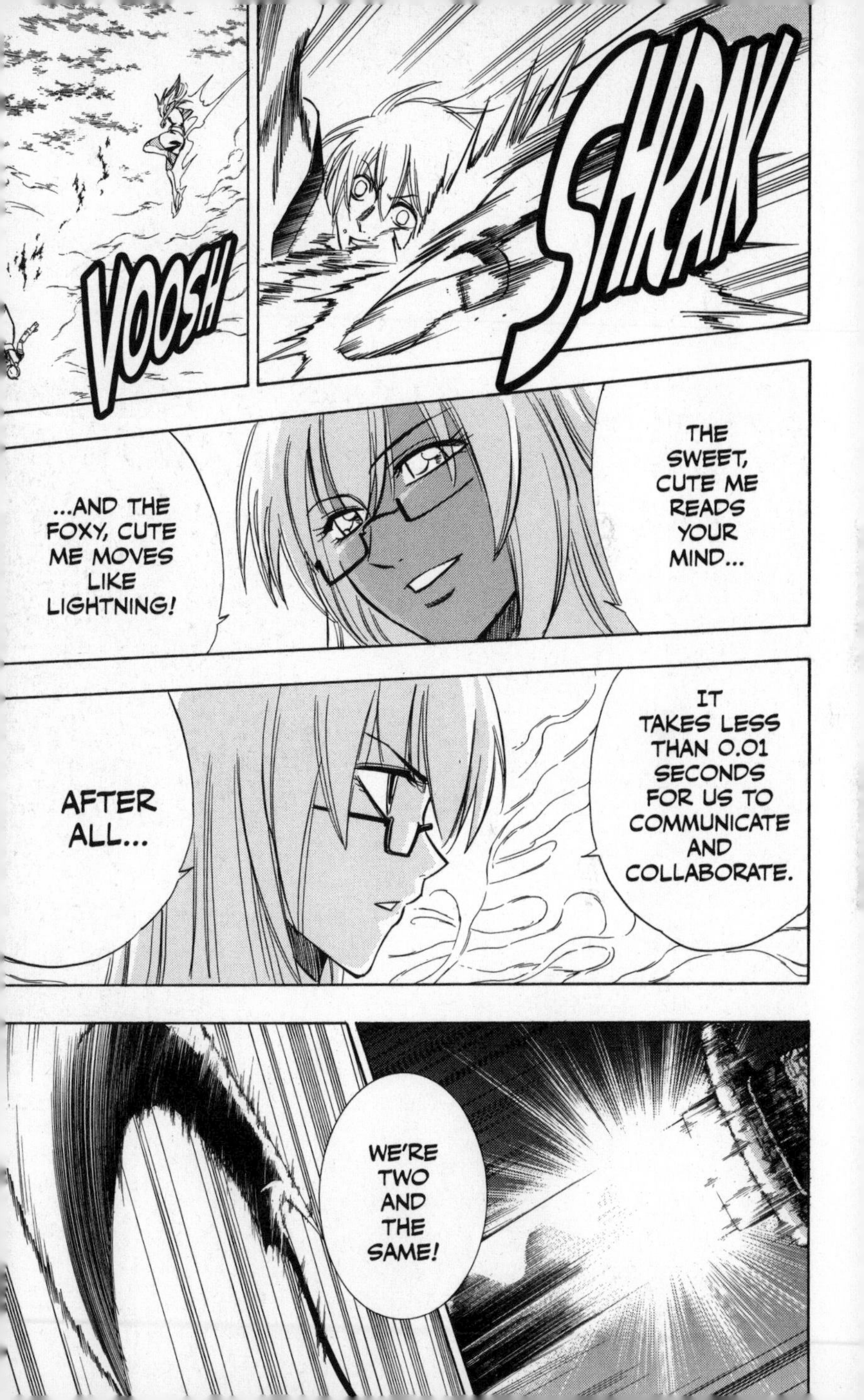
SHPAK
VOOSH
THE SWEET, CUTE ME READS YOUR MIND...
...AND THE FOXY, CUTE ME MOVES LIKE LIGHTNING!
IT TAKES LESS THAN 0.01 SECONDS FOR US TO COMMUNICATE AND COLLABORATE.
AFTER ALL...
WE'RE TWO AND THE SAME!

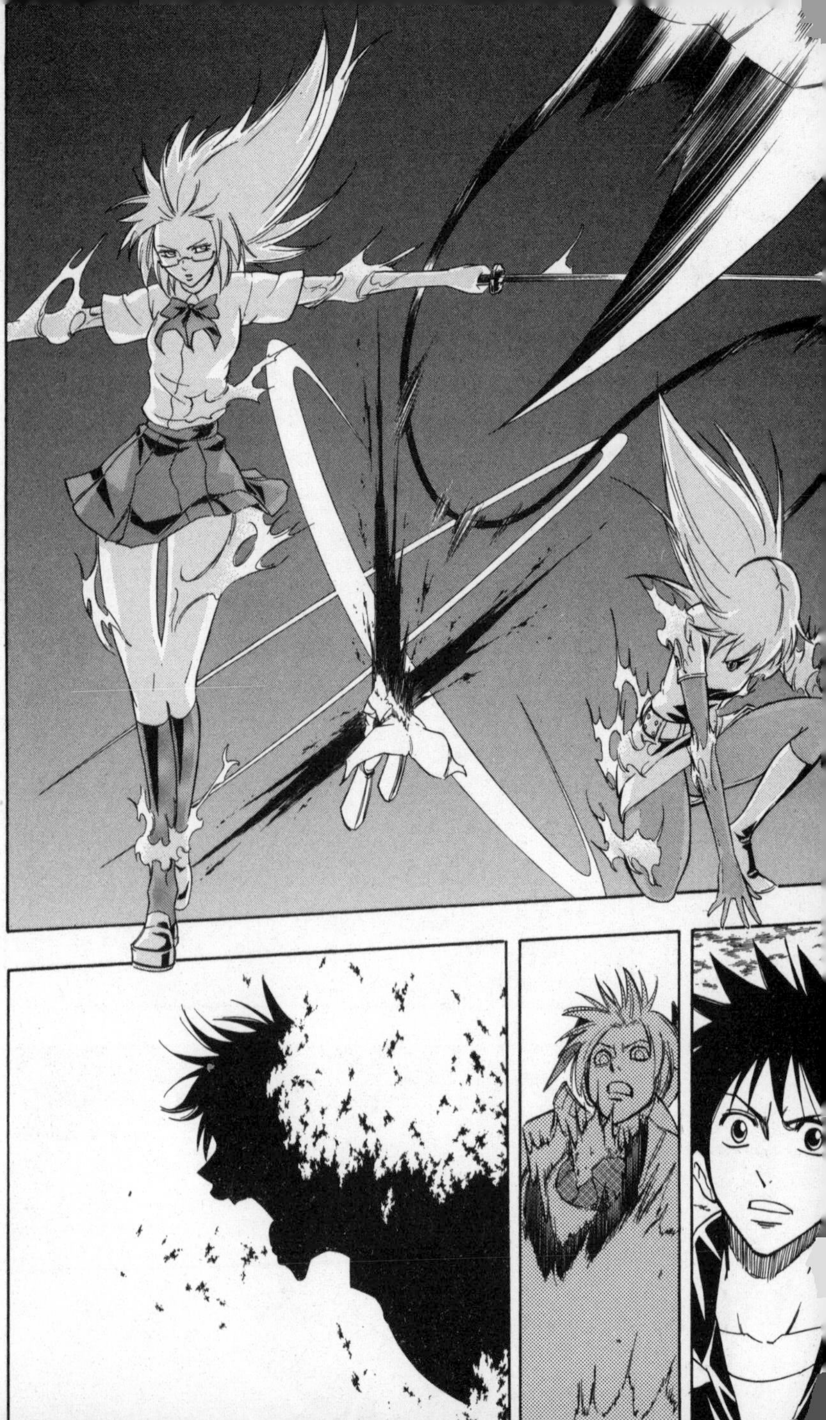

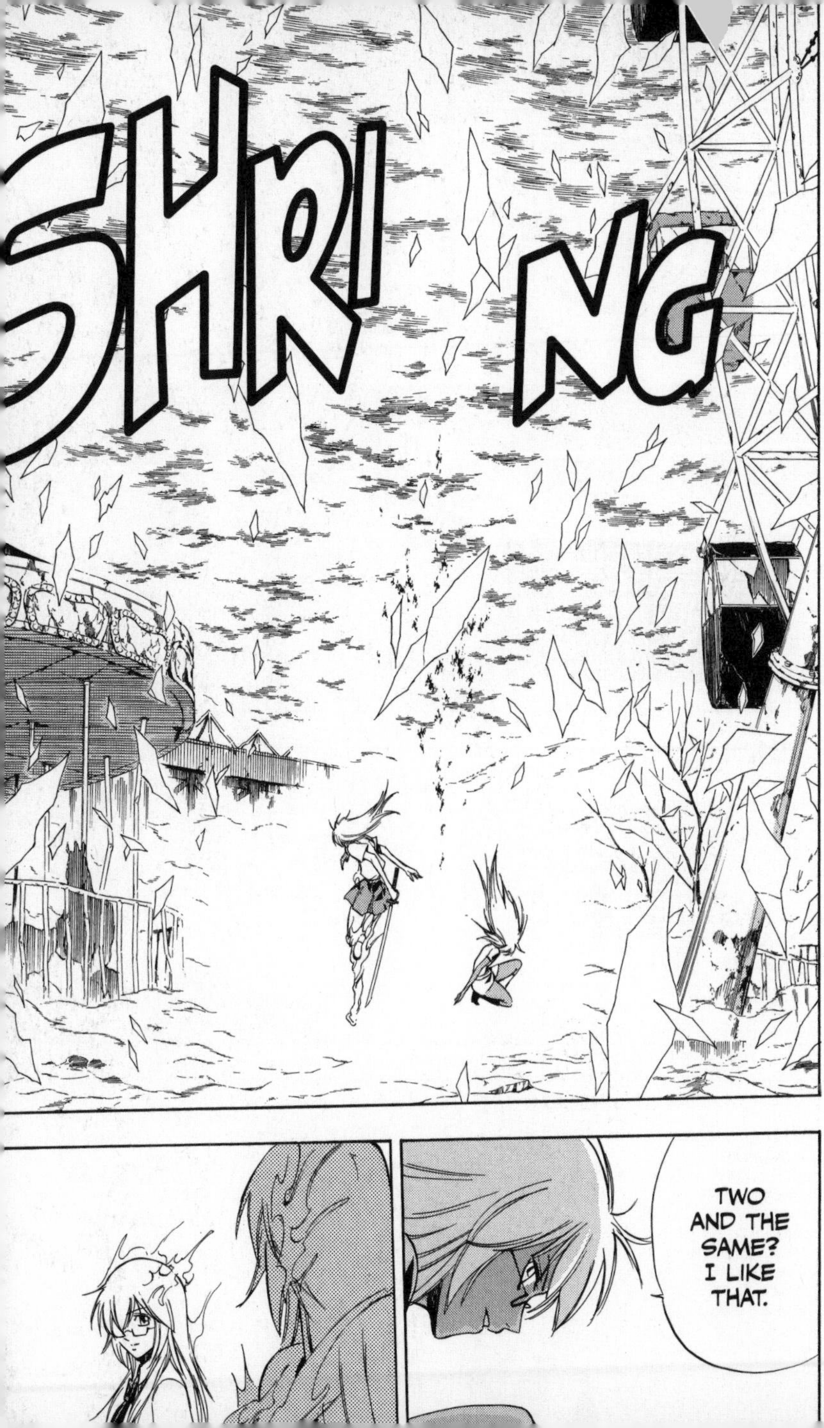
SHRI NG
TWO AND THE SAME? I LIKE THAT.

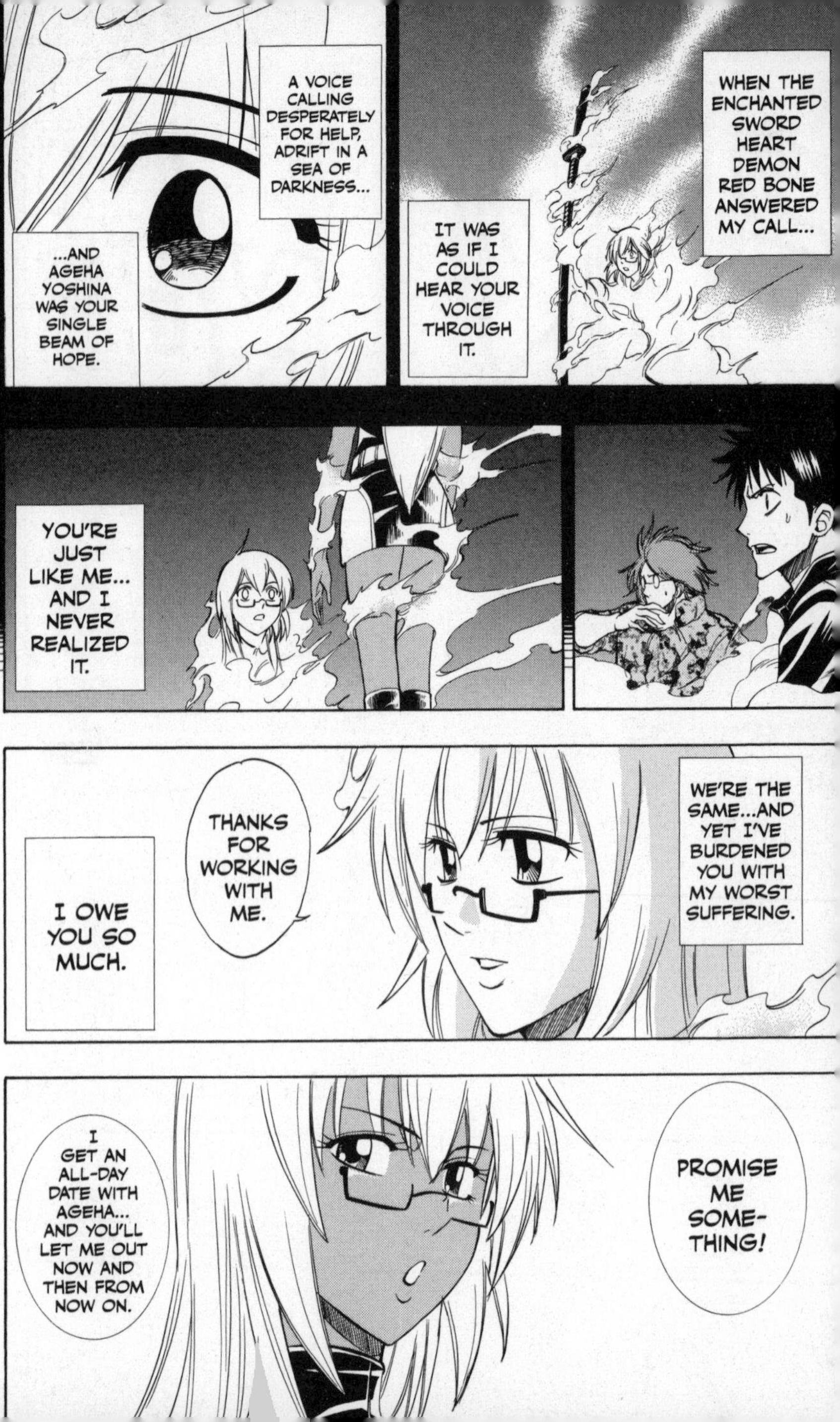
WHEN THE ENCHANTED SWORD HEART DEMON RED BONE ANSWERED MY CALL...
IT WAS AS IF I COULD HEAR YOUR VOICE THROUGH IT.
A VOICE CALLING DESPERATELY FOR HELP, ADRIFT IN A SEA OF DARKNESS...
...AND AGEHA YOSHINA WAS YOUR SINGLE BEAM OF HOPE.
YOU'RE JUST LIKE ME... AND I NEVER REALIZED IT.
WE'RE THE SAME...AND YET I'VE BURDENED YOU WITH MY WORST SUFFERING.
THANKS FOR WORKING WITH ME.
I OWE YOU SO MUCH.
PROMISE ME SOME-THING!
I GET AN ALL-DAY DATE WITH AGEHA... AND YOU'LL LET ME OUT NOW AND THEN FROM NOW ON.

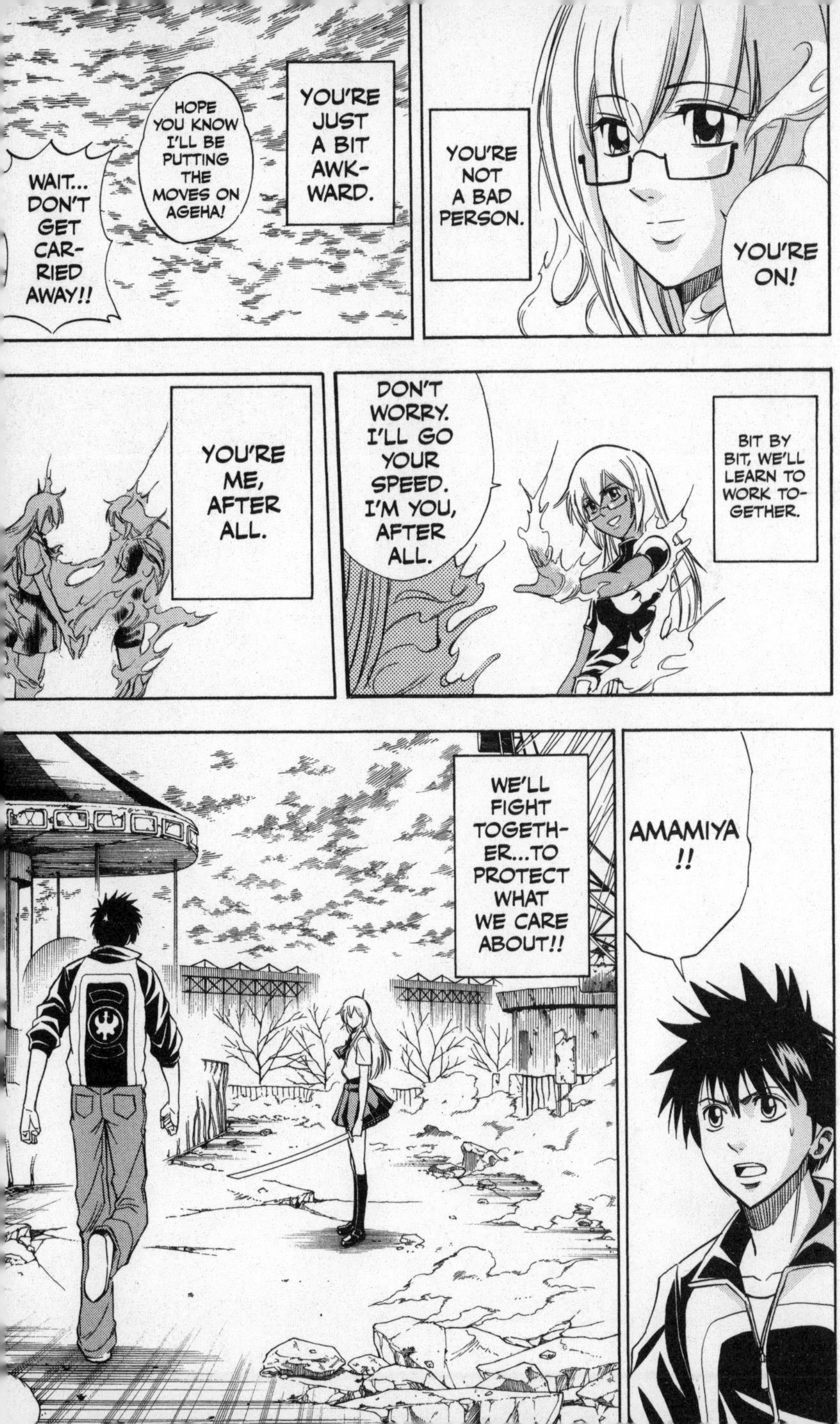
YOU'RE NOT A BAD PERSON.
YOU'RE ON!
YOU'RE JUST A BIT AWK-WARD.
HOPE YOU KNOW I'LL BE PUTTING THE MOVES ON AGEHA!
WAIT... DON'T GET CAR-RIED AWAY!!
BIT BY BIT, WE'LL LEARN TO WORK TO-GETHER.
DON'T WORRY. I'LL GO YOUR SPEED. I'M YOU, AFTER ALL.
YOU'RE ME, AFTER ALL.
AMAMIYA!!
WE'LL FIGHT TOGETH-ER...TO PROTECT WHAT WE CARE ABOUT!!

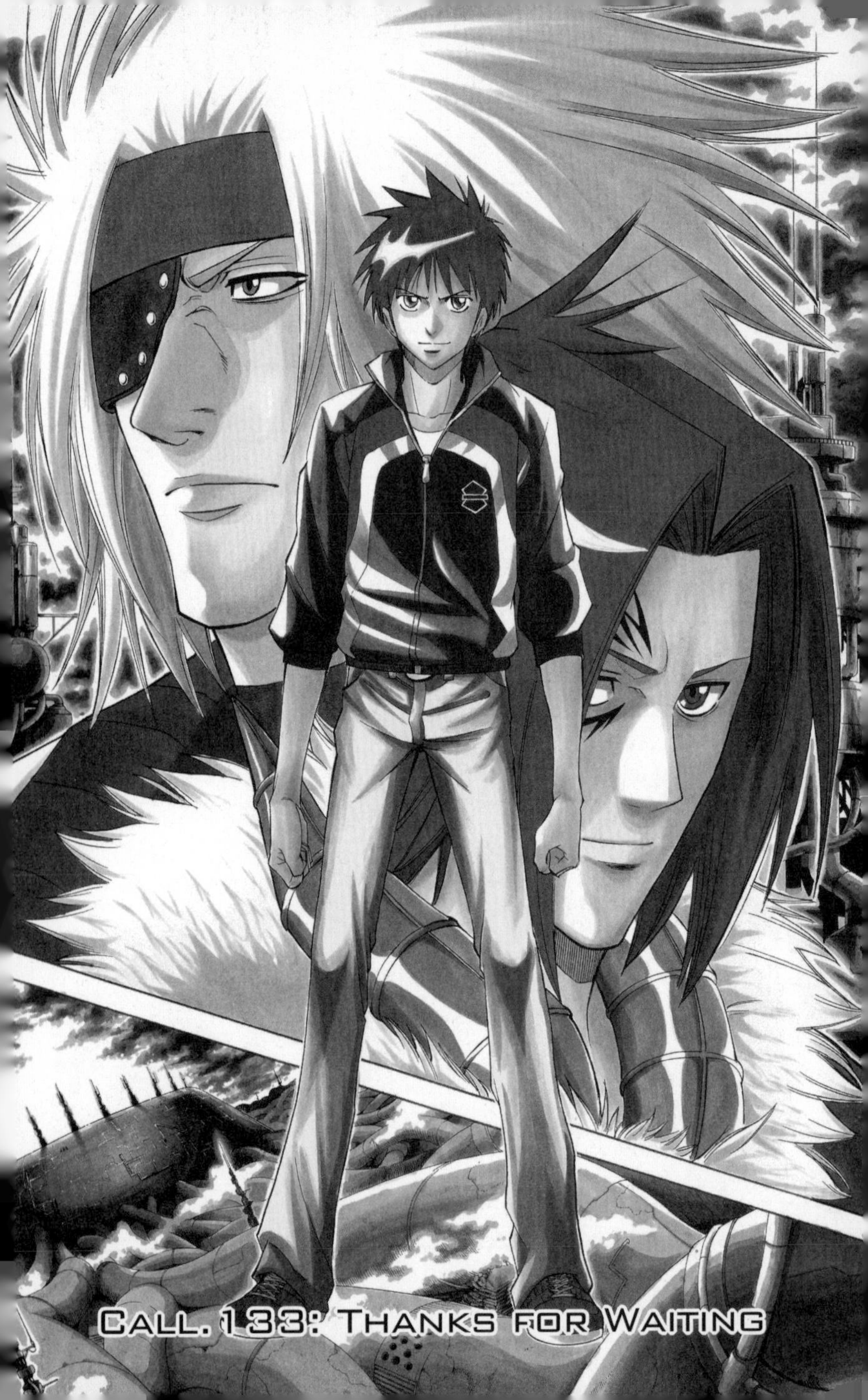
CALL. 133: THANKS FOR WAITING

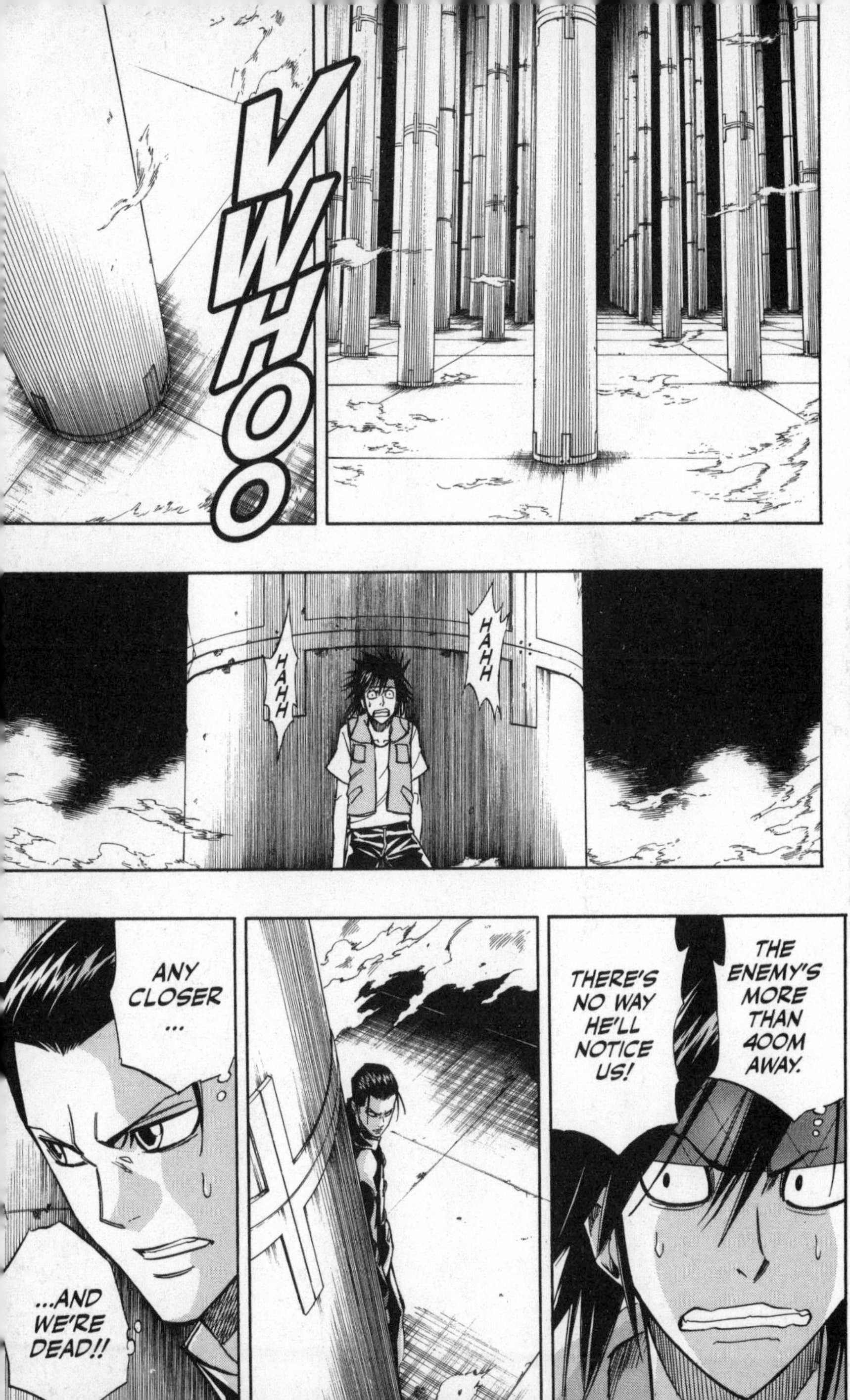
VWHOO
HAHH
HAHH
THE ENEMY'S MORE THAN 400M AWAY.
THERE'S NO WAY HE'LL NOTICE US!
ANY CLOSER ...
...AND WE'RE DEAD!!

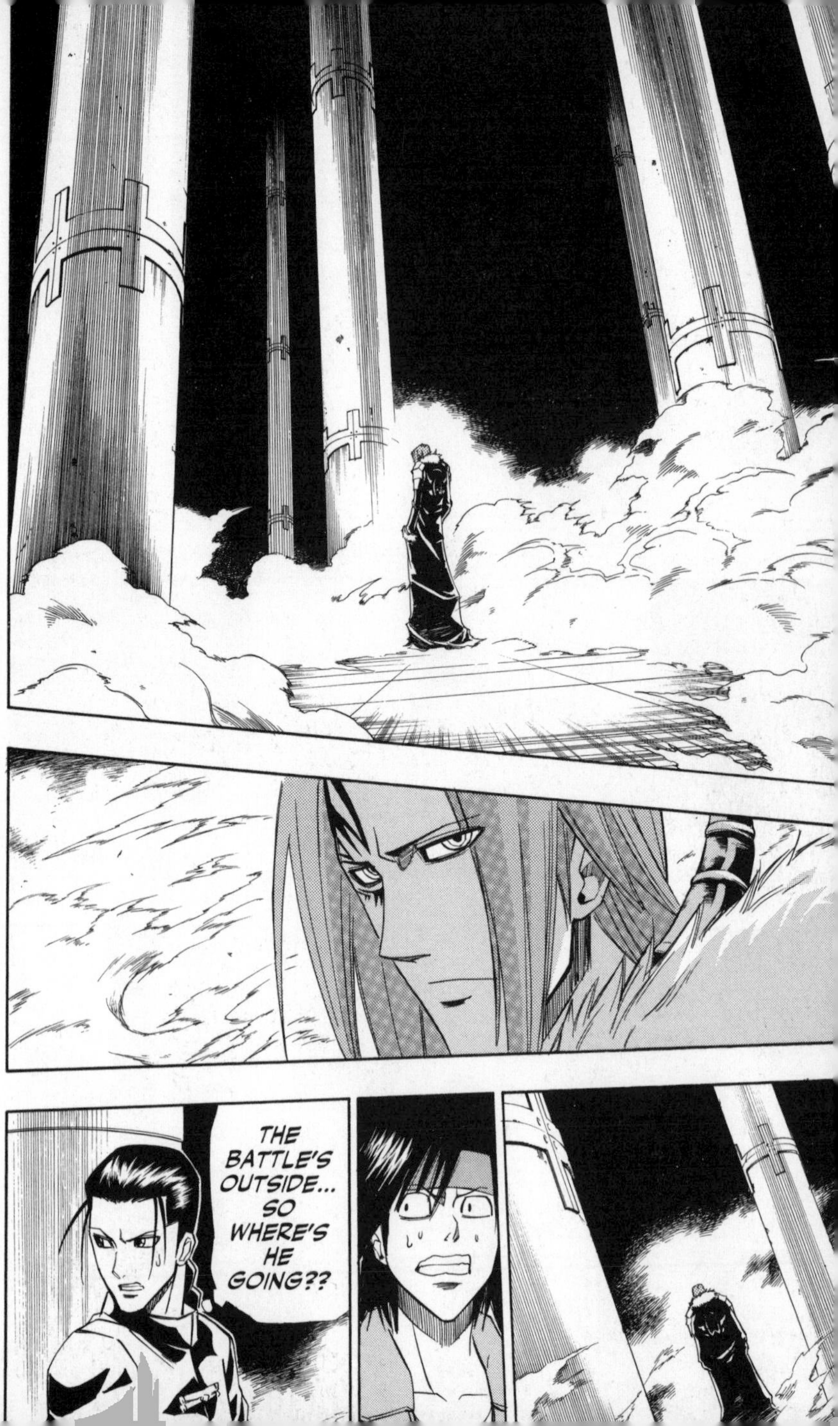
THE BATTLE'S OUTSIDE... SO WHERE'S HE GOING??

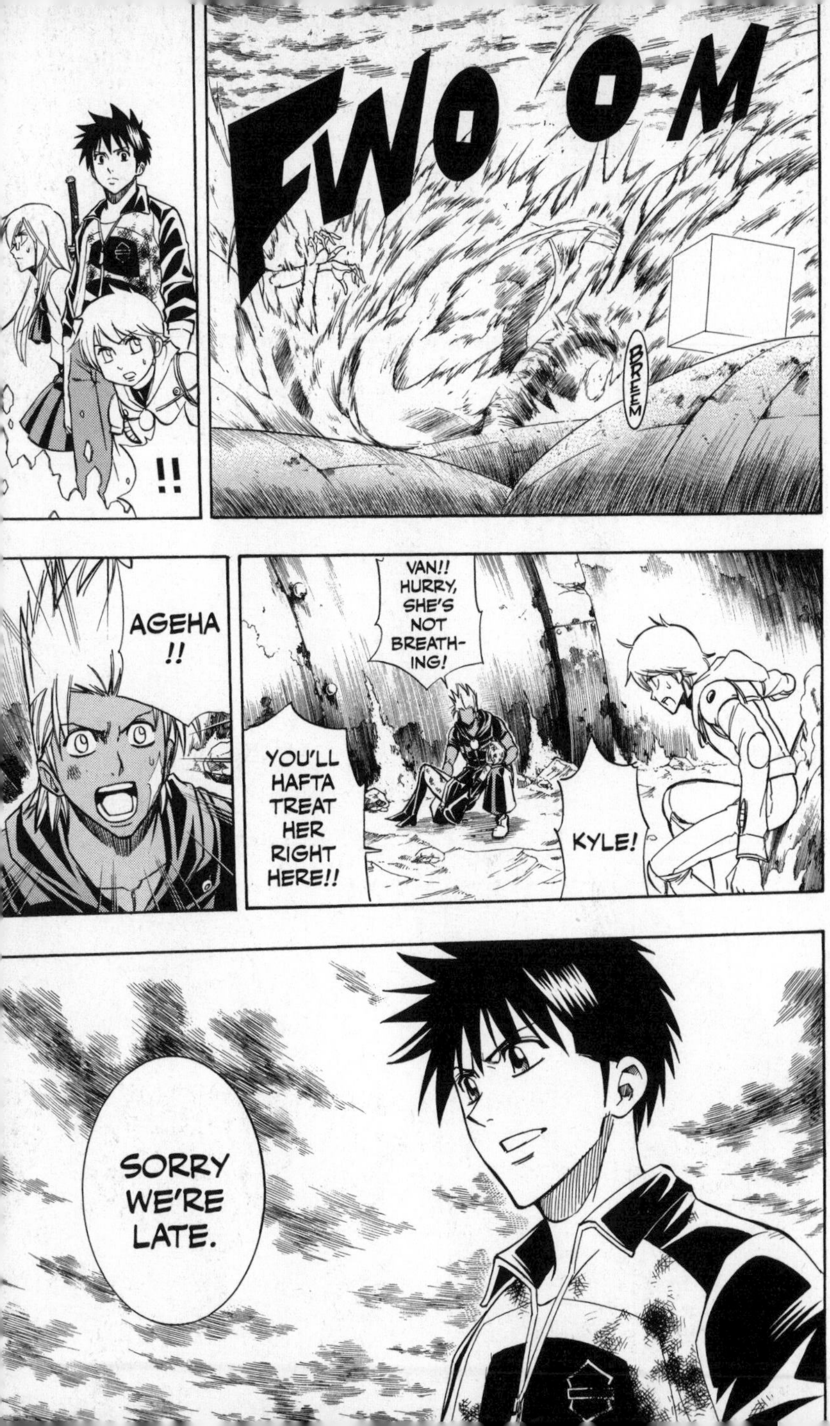
FWOOM
BREEM
!!
VAN!! HURRY, SHE'S NOT BREATHING!
KYLE!
YOU'LL HAFTA TREAT HER RIGHT HERE!!
AGEHA !!
SORRY WE'RE LATE.

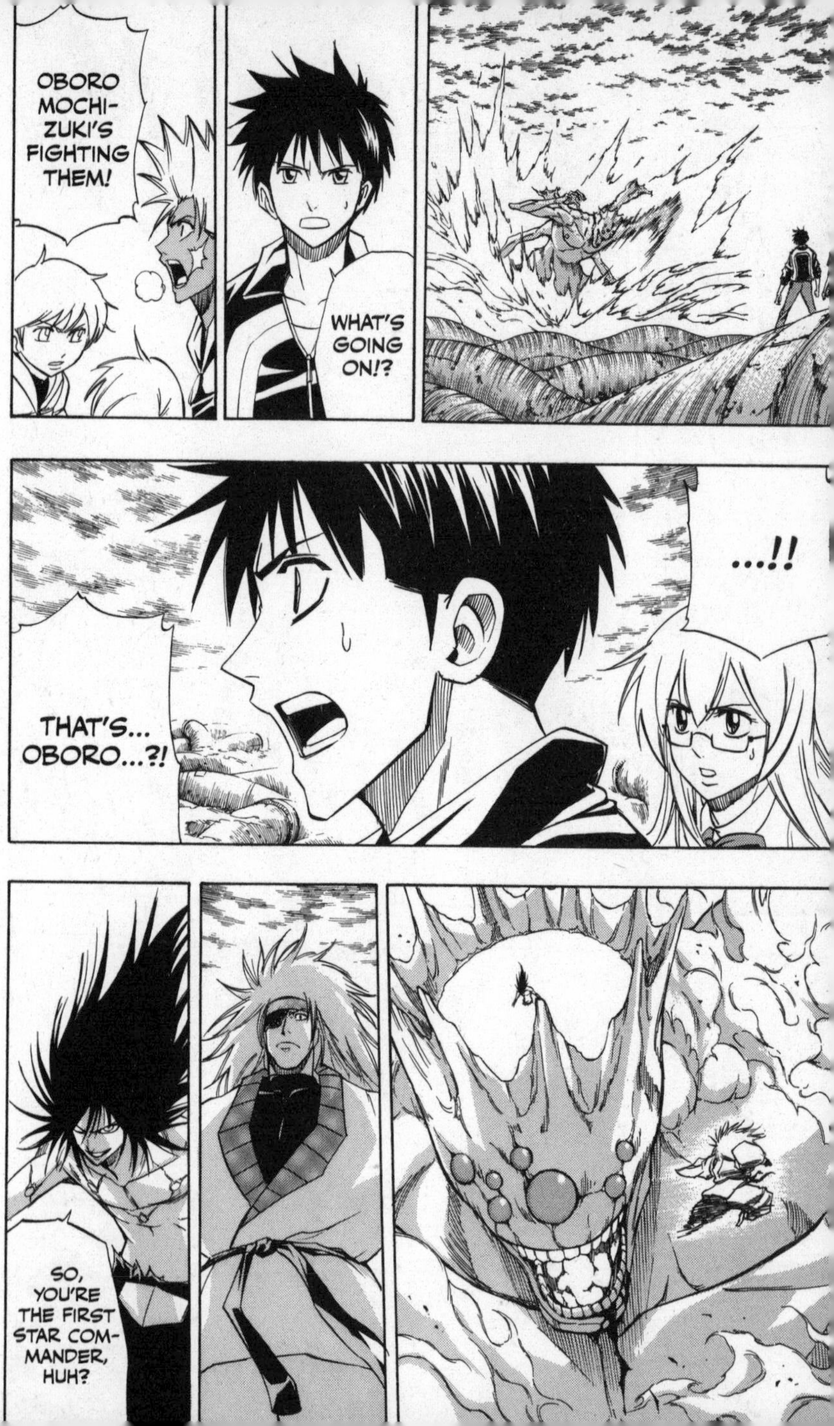
WHAT'S GOING ON!?
OBORO MOCHI-ZUKI'S FIGHTING THEM!
...!!
THAT'S... OBORO...?!
SO, YOU'RE THE FIRST STAR COM-MANDER, HUH?

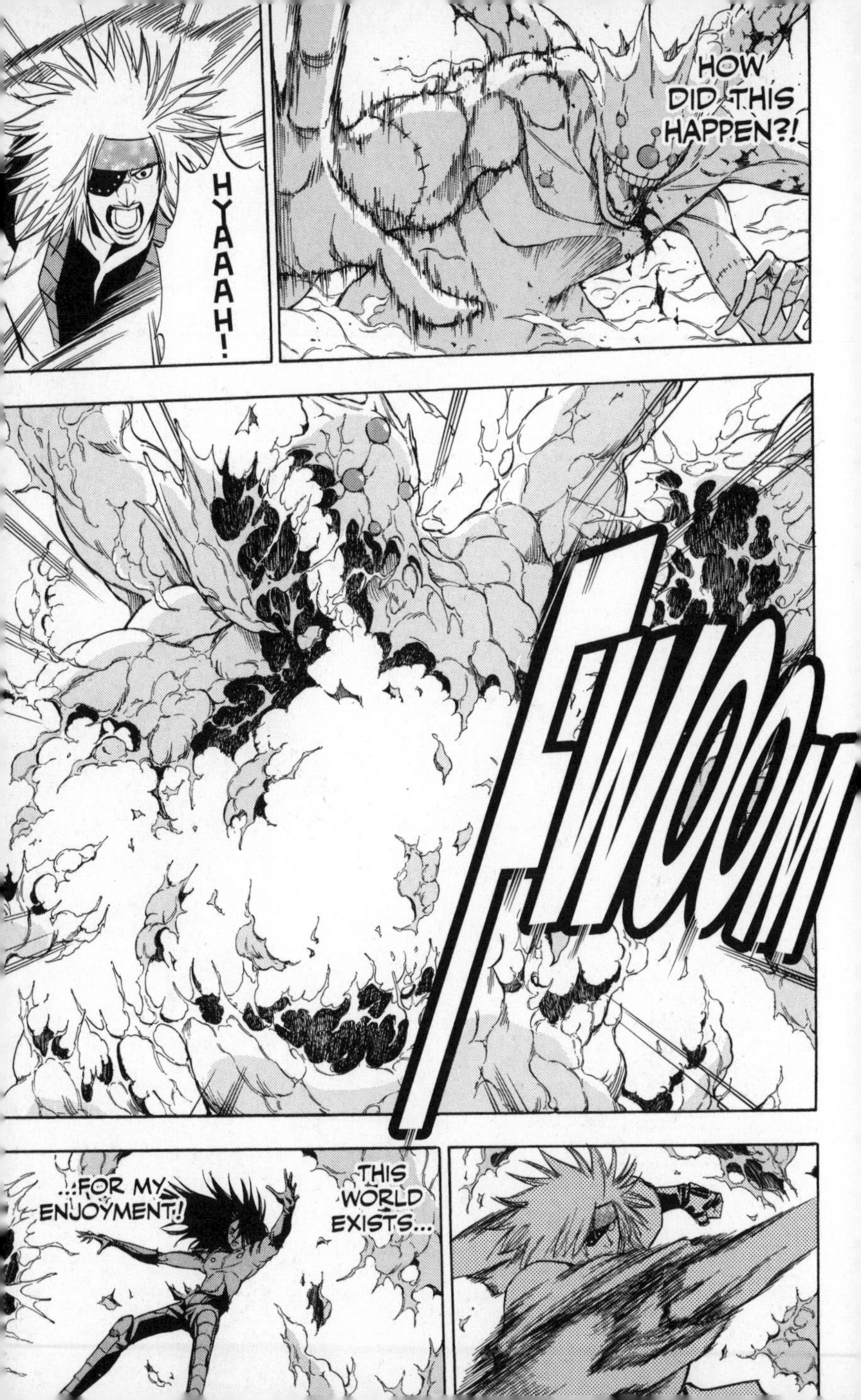
HOW DID THIS HAPPEN?!
HYAAAH!
THIS WORLD EXISTS...
...FOR MY ENJOYMENT!

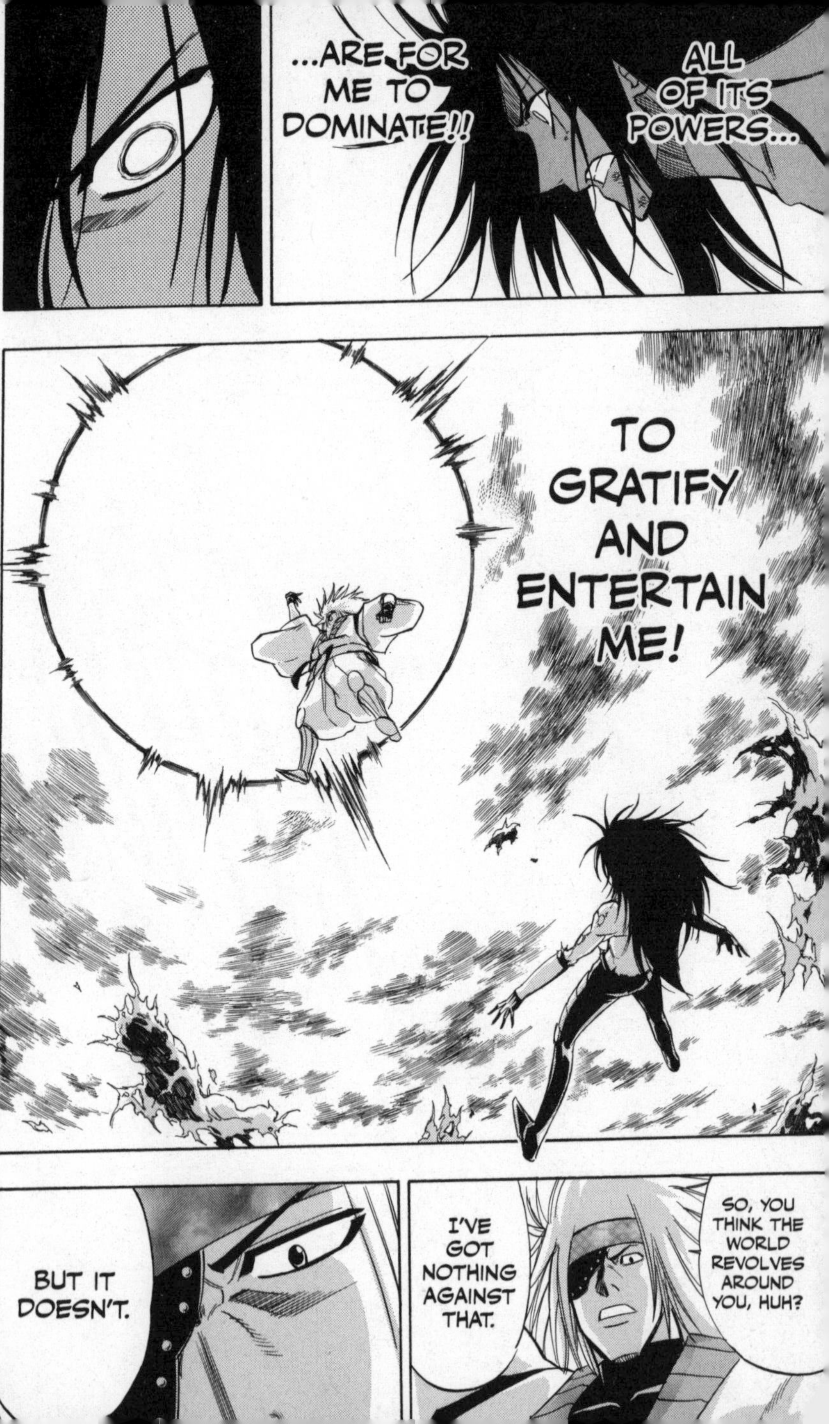
ALL OF ITS POWERS...
...ARE FOR ME TO DOMINATE!!
TO GRATIFY AND ENTERTAIN ME!
SO, YOU THINK THE WORLD REVOLVES AROUND YOU, HUH?
I'VE GOT NOTHING AGAINST THAT.
BUT IT DOESN'T.

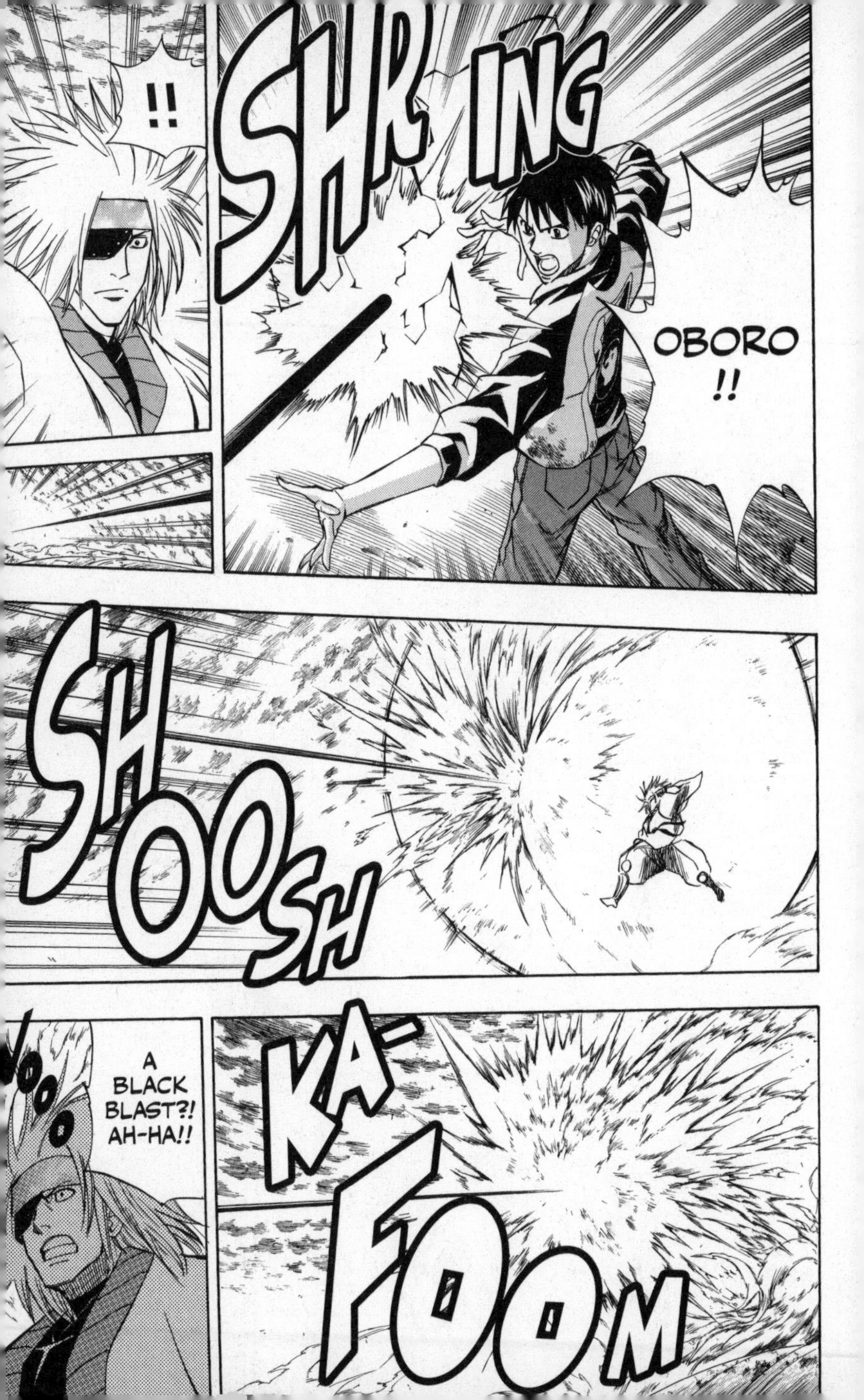
SHRING
OBORO !!
!!
SHOOSH
KA-FOOM
A BLACK BLAST?! AH-HA!!

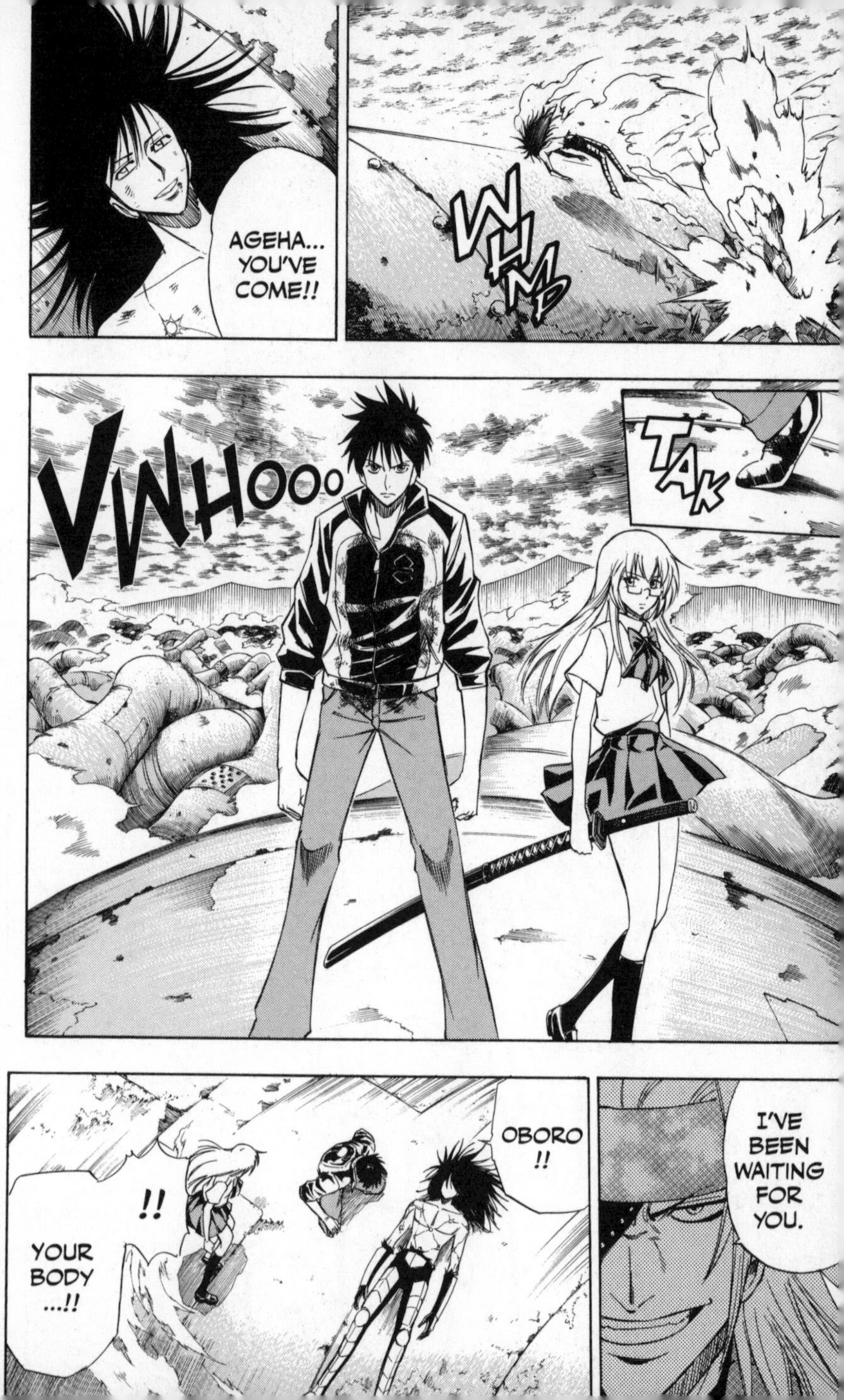
WHMP
AGEHA... YOU'VE COME!!
TAK
VWHOOO
I'VE BEEN WAITING FOR YOU.
OBORO!!
!!
YOUR BODY ...!!

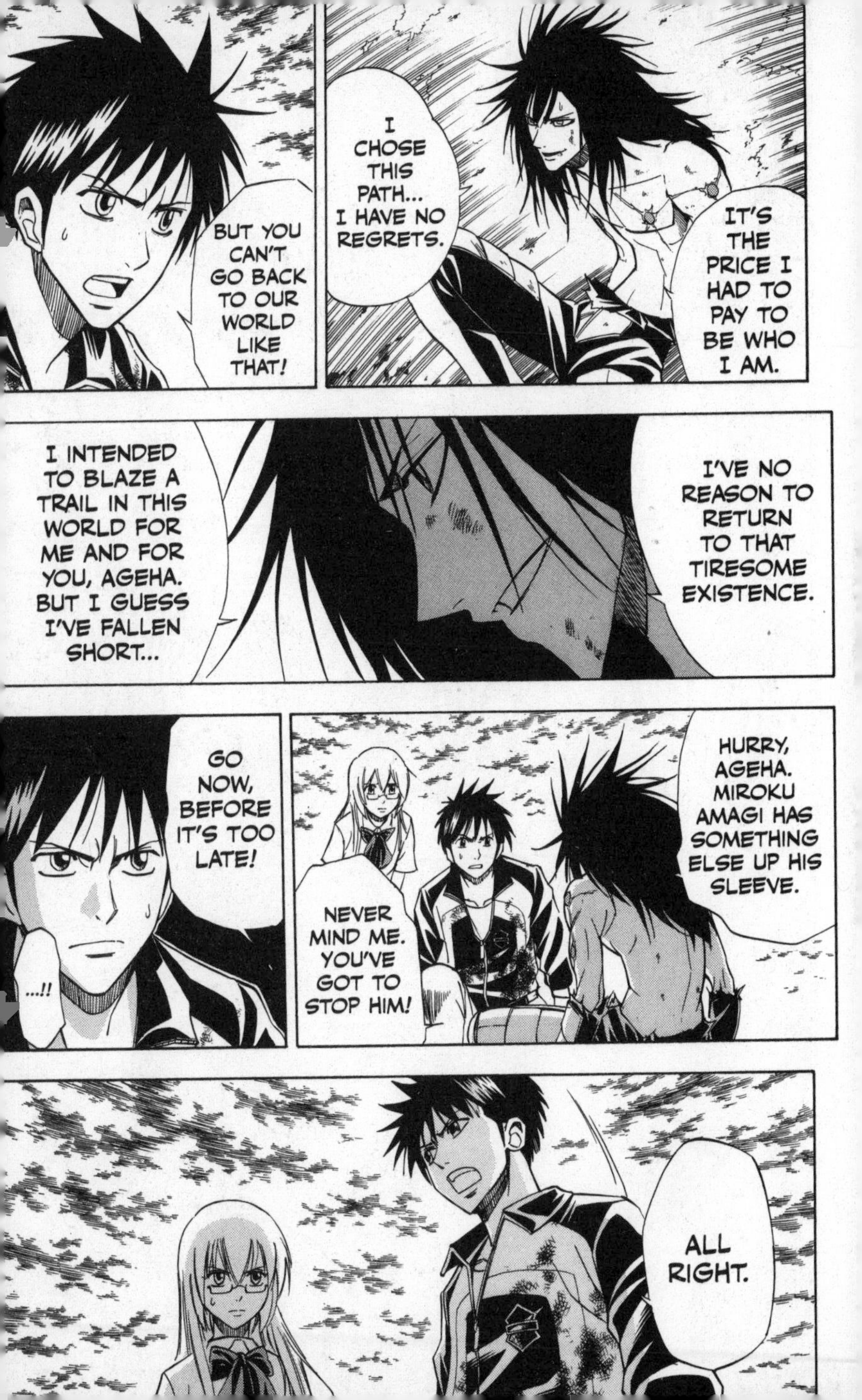
I CHOSE THIS PATH... I HAVE NO REGRETS.
IT'S THE PRICE I HAD TO PAY TO BE WHO I AM.
BUT YOU CAN'T GO BACK TO OUR WORLD LIKE THAT!
I'VE NO REASON TO RETURN TO THAT TIRESOME EXISTENCE.
I INTENDED TO BLAZE A TRAIL IN THIS WORLD FOR ME AND FOR YOU, AGEHA. BUT I GUESS I'VE FALLEN SHORT...
HURRY, AGEHA. MIROKU AMAGI HAS SOMETHING ELSE UP HIS SLEEVE.
NEVER MIND ME. YOU'VE GOT TO STOP HIM!
GO NOW, BEFORE IT'S TOO LATE!
...!!
ALL RIGHT.

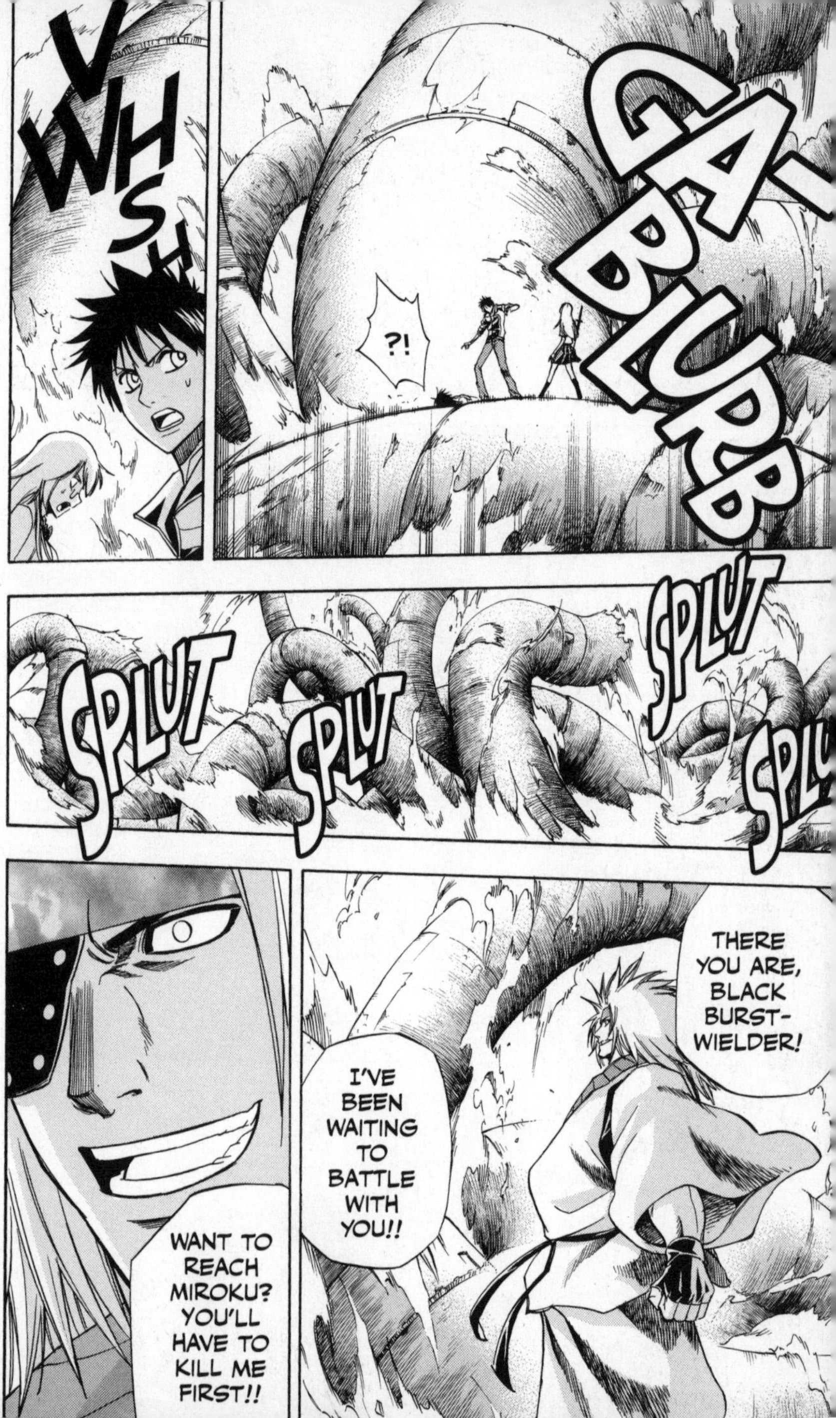
GA-BLURRB
?!
VWHSH
SPLUT
SPLUT
SPLUT
SPLU
THERE YOU ARE, BLACK BURST-WIELDER!
I'VE BEEN WAITING TO BATTLE WITH YOU!!
WANT TO REACH MIROKU? YOU'LL HAVE TO KILL ME FIRST!!

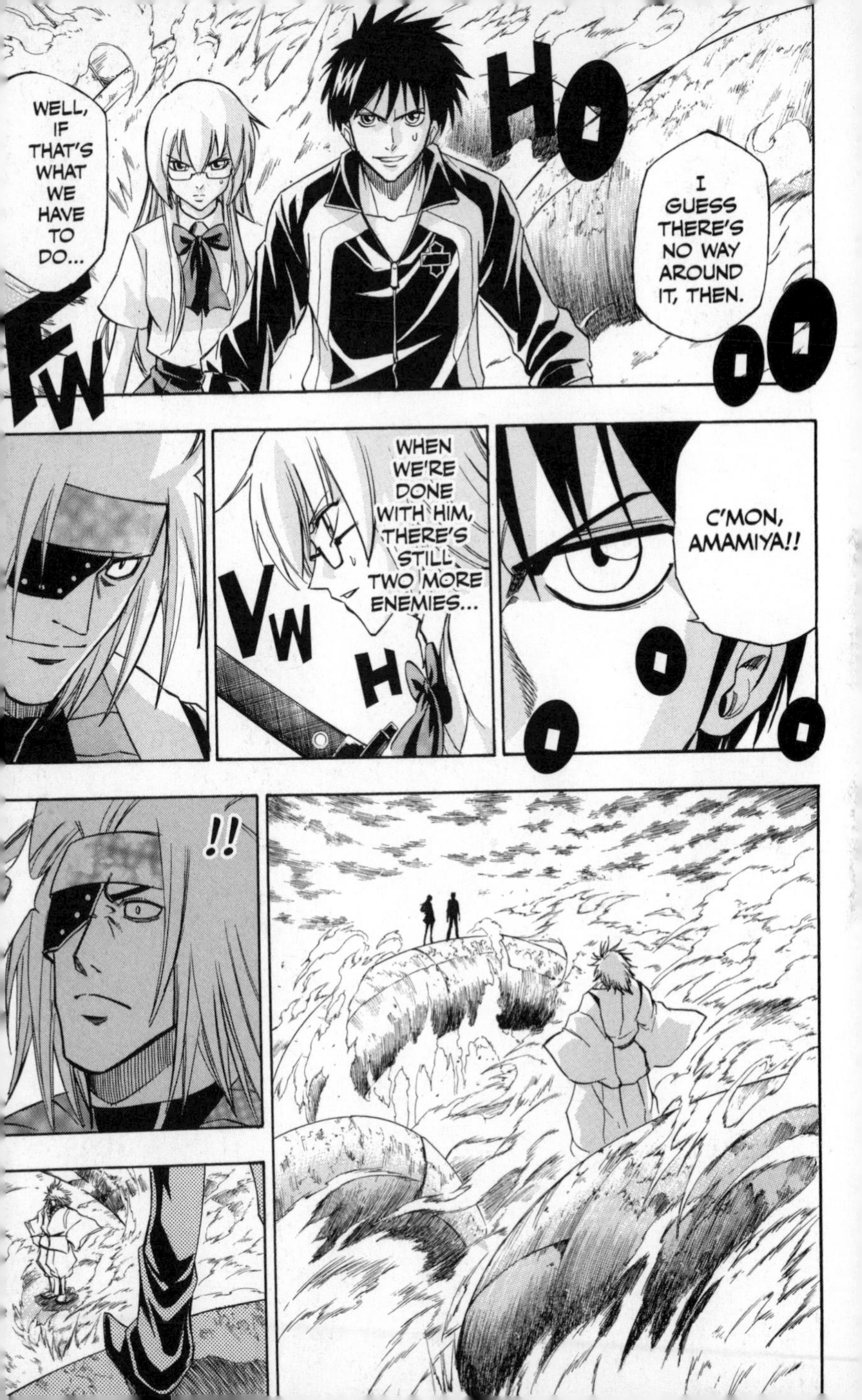
HO
I GUESS THERE'S NO WAY AROUND IT, THEN.
OO
WELL, IF THAT'S WHAT WE HAVE TO DO...
FW
C'MON, AMAMIYA!!
OOO
WHEN WE'RE DONE WITH HIM, THERE'S STILL TWO MORE ENEMIES...
VWH
!!

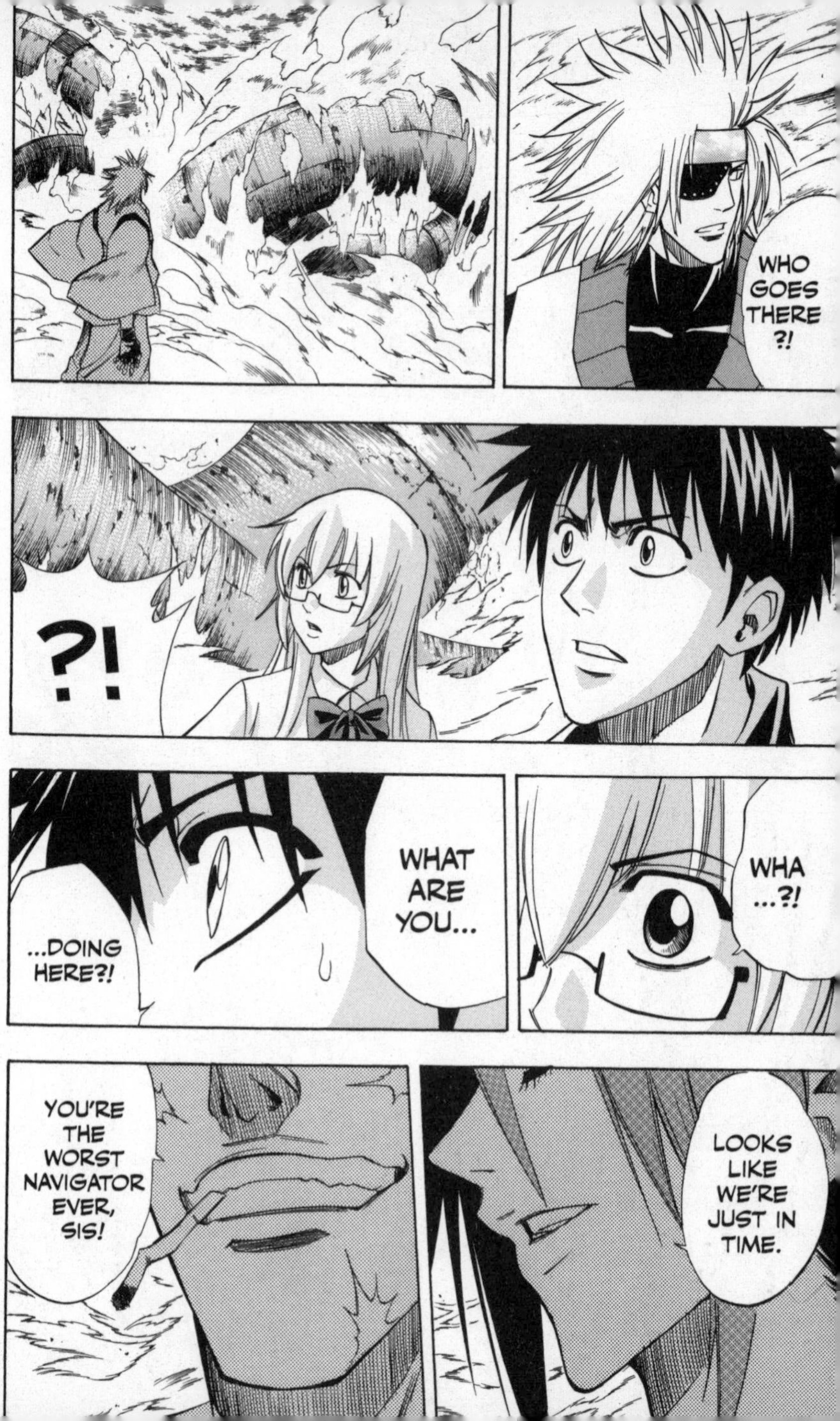
WHO GOES THERE?!
?!
WHA ...?!
WHAT ARE YOU...
...DOING HERE?!
LOOKS LIKE WE'RE JUST IN TIME.
YOU'RE THE WORST NAVIGATOR EVER, SIS!

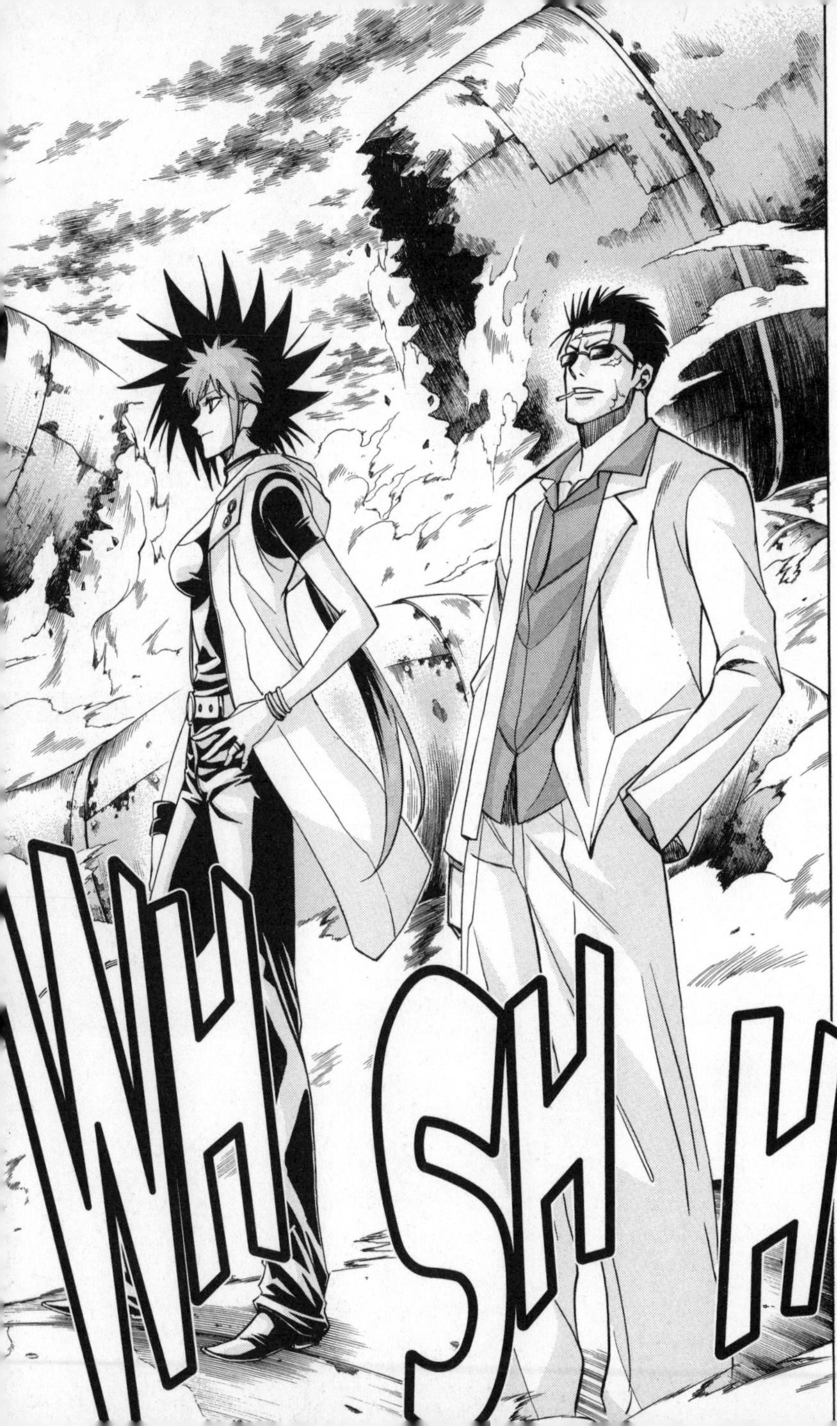
WHSHH

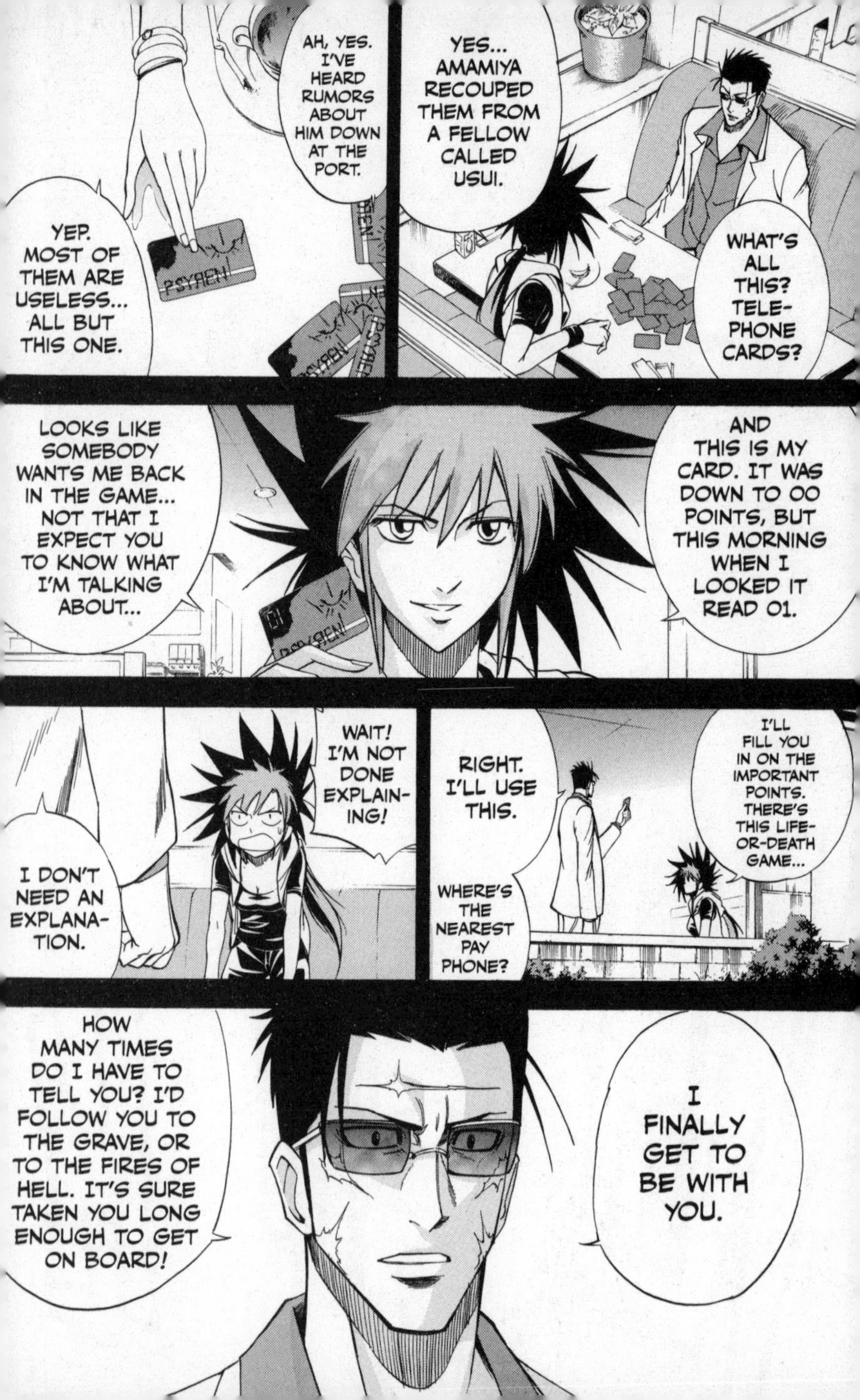
WHAT'S ALL THIS? TELEPHONE CARDS?
YES... AMAMIYA RECOUPED THEM FROM A FELLOW CALLED USUI.
AH, YES. I'VE HEARD RUMORS ABOUT HIM DOWN AT THE PORT.
YEP. MOST OF THEM ARE USELESS... ALL BUT THIS ONE.
AND THIS IS MY CARD. IT WAS DOWN TO 00 POINTS, BUT THIS MORNING WHEN I LOOKED IT READ 01.
LOOKS LIKE SOMEBODY WANTS ME BACK IN THE GAME... NOT THAT I EXPECT YOU TO KNOW WHAT I'M TALKING ABOUT...
I'LL FILL YOU IN ON THE IMPORTANT POINTS. THERE'S THIS LIFE-OR-DEATH GAME...
RIGHT. I'LL USE THIS.
WHERE'S THE NEAREST PAY PHONE?
WAIT! I'M NOT DONE EXPLAINING!
I DON'T NEED AN EXPLANATION.
I FINALLY GET TO BE WITH YOU.
HOW MANY TIMES DO I HAVE TO TELL YOU? I'D FOLLOW YOU TO THE GRAVE, OR TO THE FIRES OF HELL. IT'S SURE TAKEN YOU LONG ENOUGH TO GET ON BOARD!

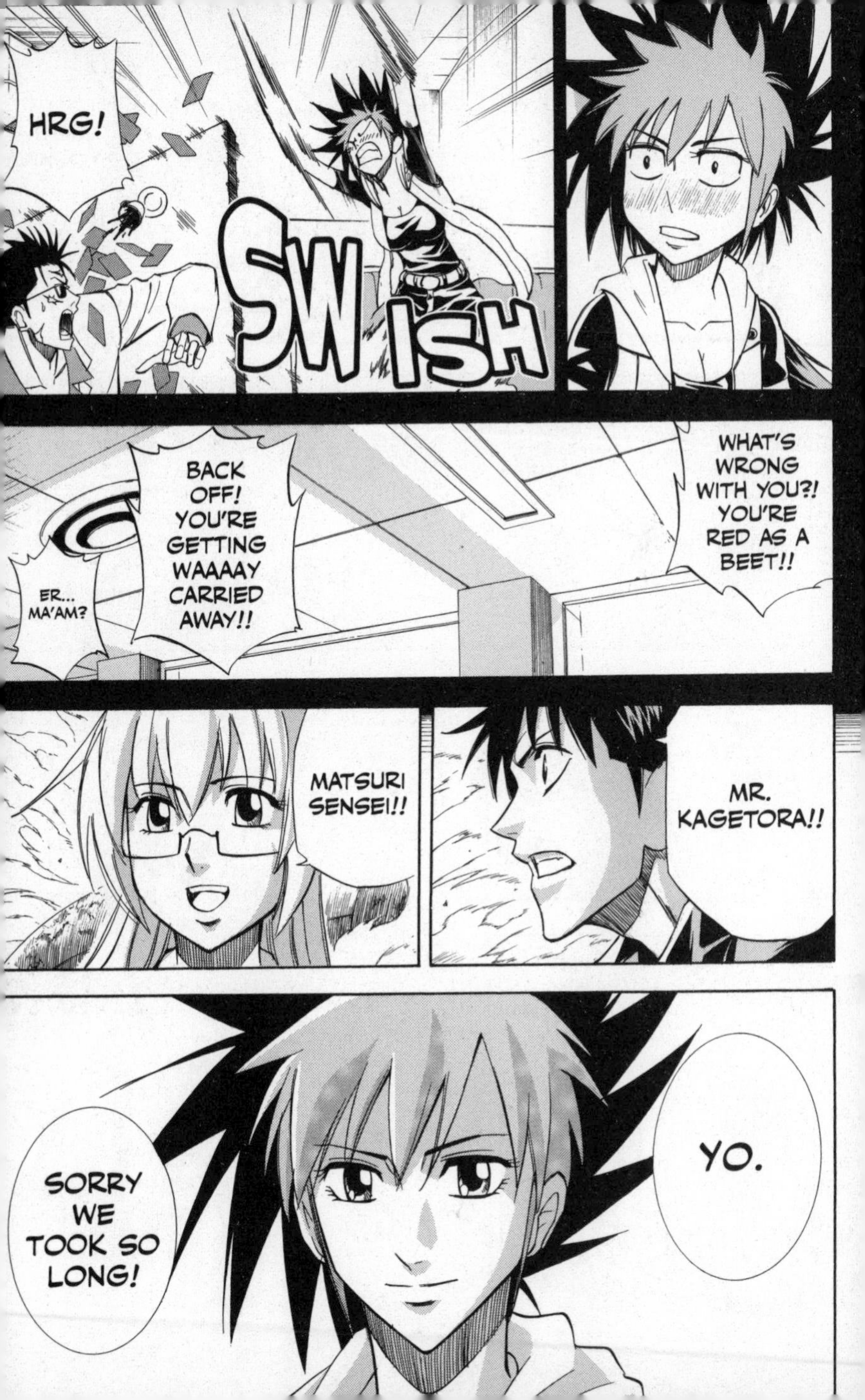
HRG!
SWISH
WHAT'S WRONG WITH YOU?! YOU'RE RED AS A BEET!!
BACK OFF! YOU'RE GETTING WAAAAY CARRIED AWAY!!
ER... MA'AM?
MR. KAGETORA!!
MATSURI SENSEI!!
YO.
SORRY WE TOOK SO LONG!

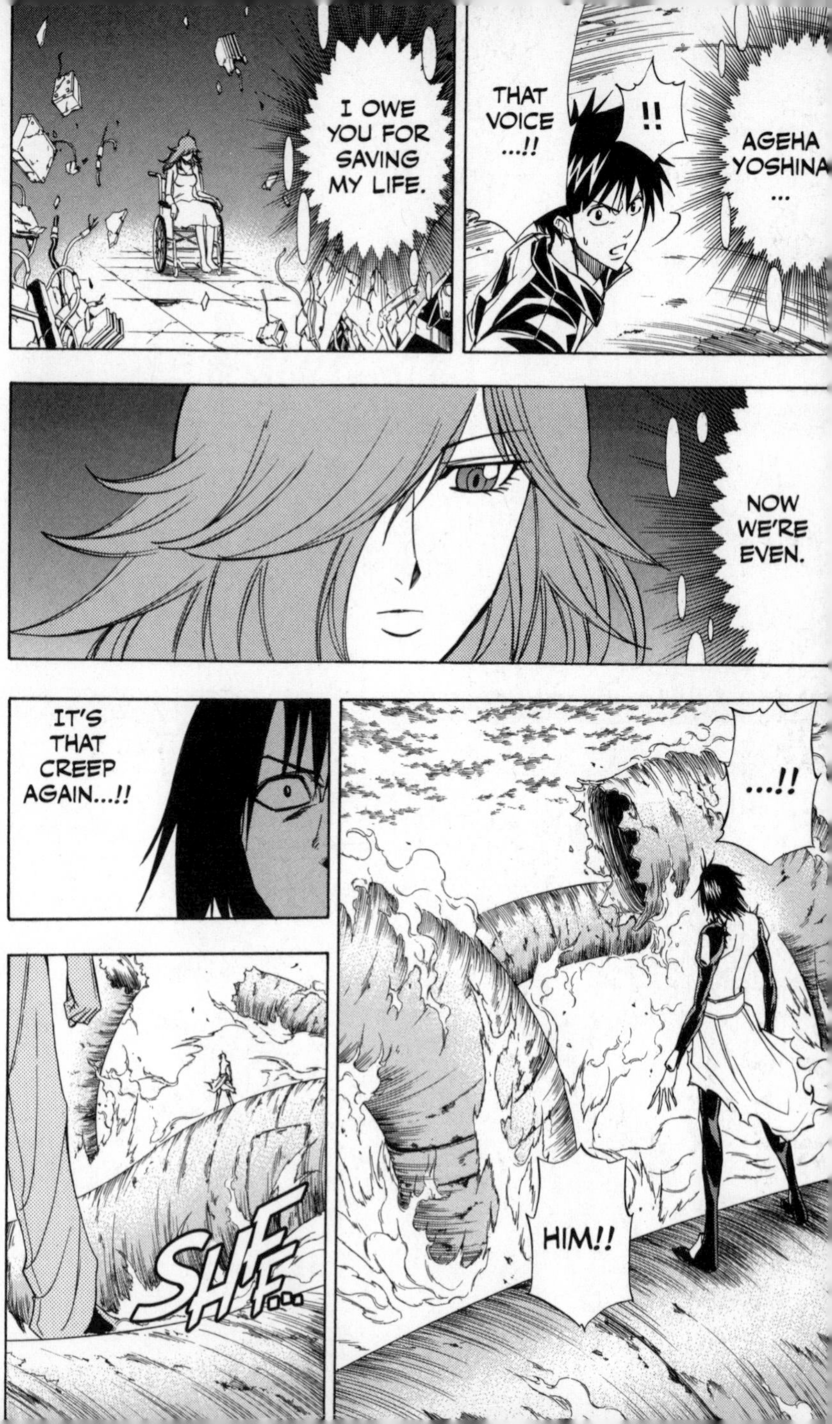
AGEHA YOSHINA...
!!
THAT VOICE ...!!
I OWE YOU FOR SAVING MY LIFE.
NOW WE'RE EVEN.
...!!
IT'S THAT CREEP AGAIN...!!
HIM!!
SHF...

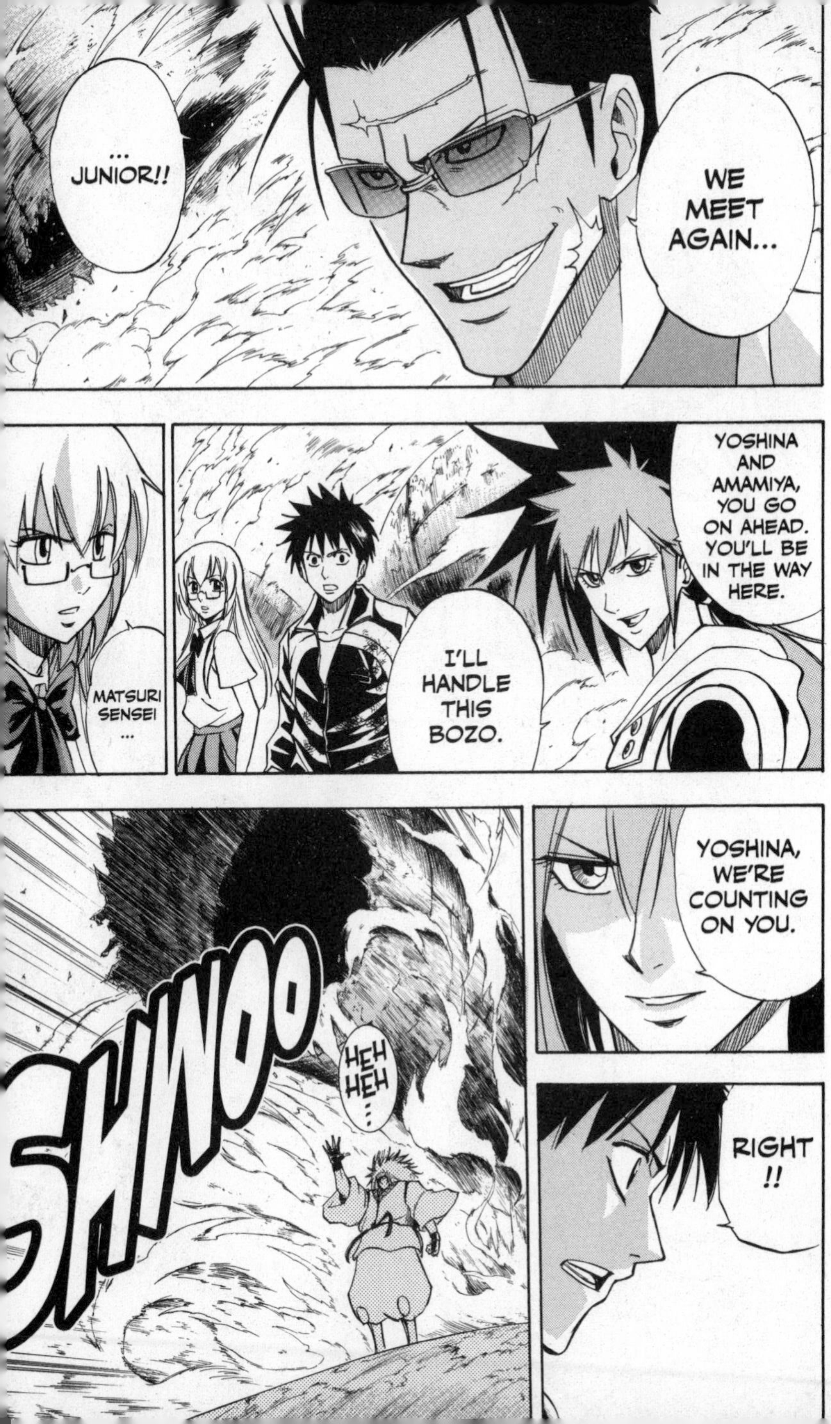
WE MEET AGAIN...
... JUNIOR!!
YOSHINA AND AMAMIYA, YOU GO ON AHEAD. YOU'LL BE IN THE WAY HERE.
I'LL HANDLE THIS BOZO.
MATSURI SENSEI ...
YOSHINA, WE'RE COUNTING ON YOU.
RIGHT !!
HEH HEH ...
SHWOOO

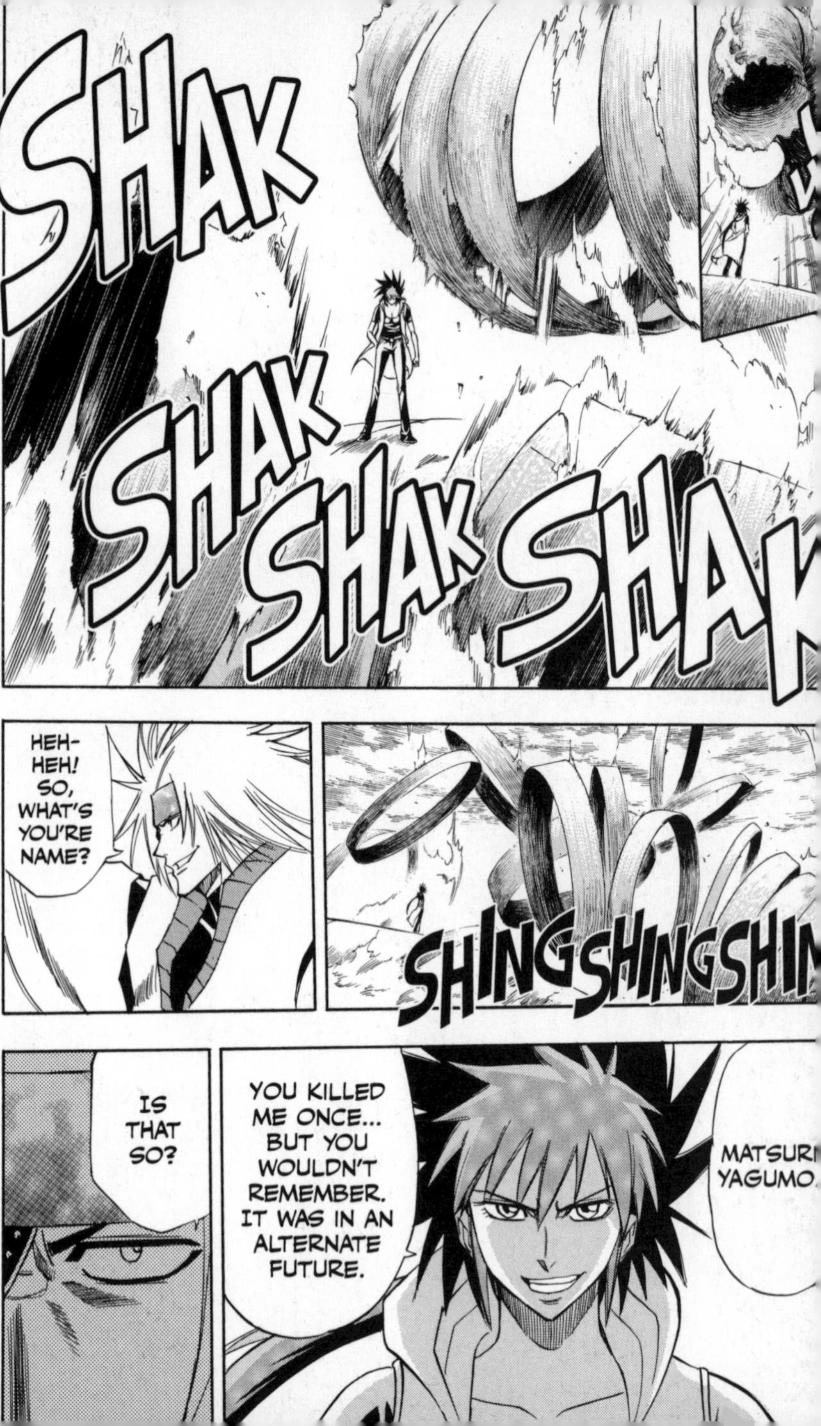
SHAK
SHAK
SHAK
SHA
SHINGSHINGSHIN
HEH-HEH! SO, WHAT'S YOU'RE NAME?
MATSURI YAGUMO.
YOU KILLED ME ONCE... BUT YOU WOULDN'T REMEMBER. IT WAS IN AN ALTERNATE FUTURE.
IS THAT SO?

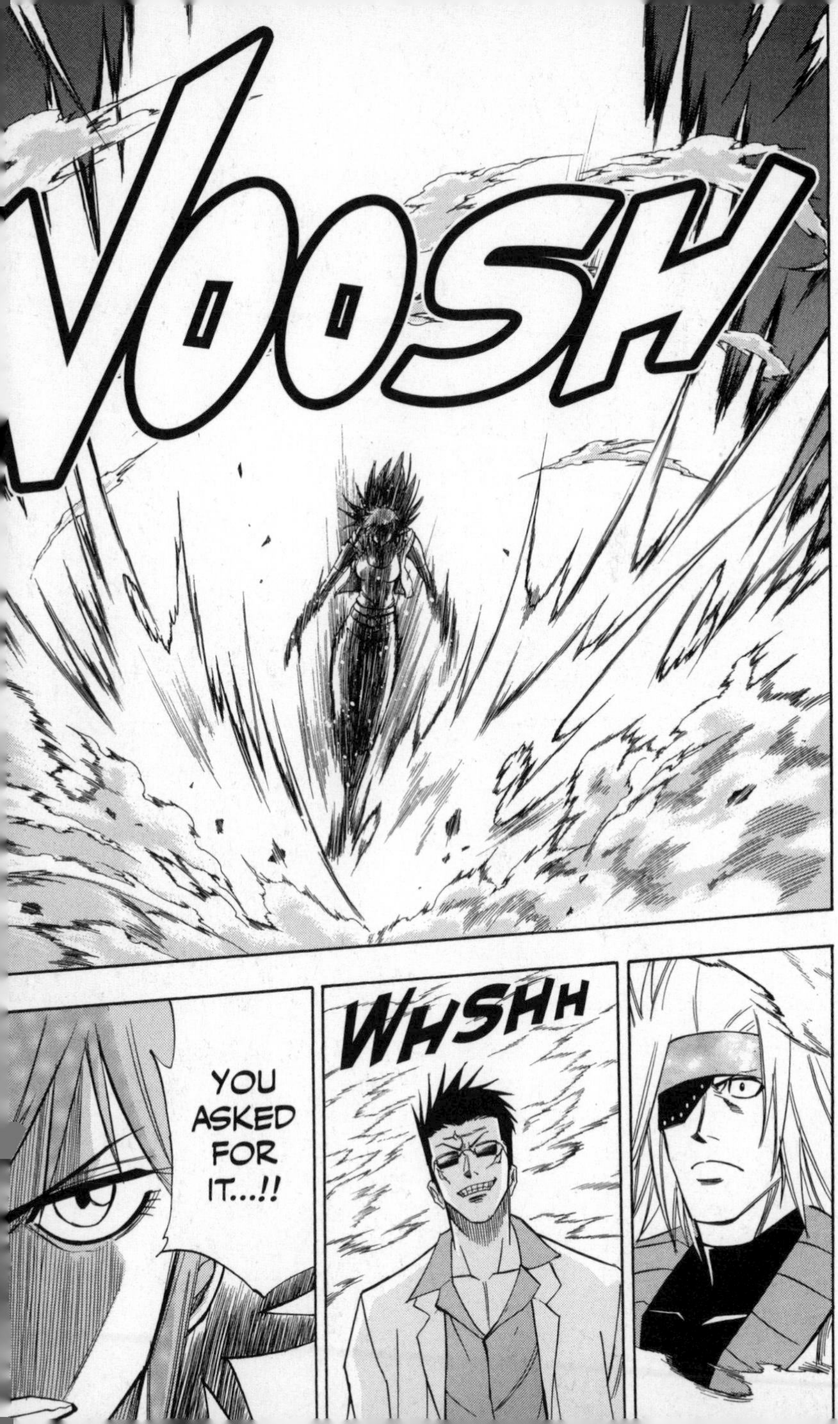
VOOSH
WHSHH
YOU ASKED FOR IT...!!

Mutters and mumblings...

PERSONALLY, I THINK CALL. 132: HALVSIES WENT PRETTY WELL.

I MANAGED TO PORTRAY SHINER'S WHOLE BATTLE IN ONE CHAPTER, AND RECONCILE SAKURAKO WITH AVIS, HER DARK SIDE.

BEFORE I STARTED STORYBOARDING, JUST THINKING ABOUT THE PAGE COMPOSITIONS MADE ME FEEL FAINT... BUT ANYWAY, I'M REALLY GLAD I WAS ABLE TO WORK THINGS OUT FOR AMAMIYA.

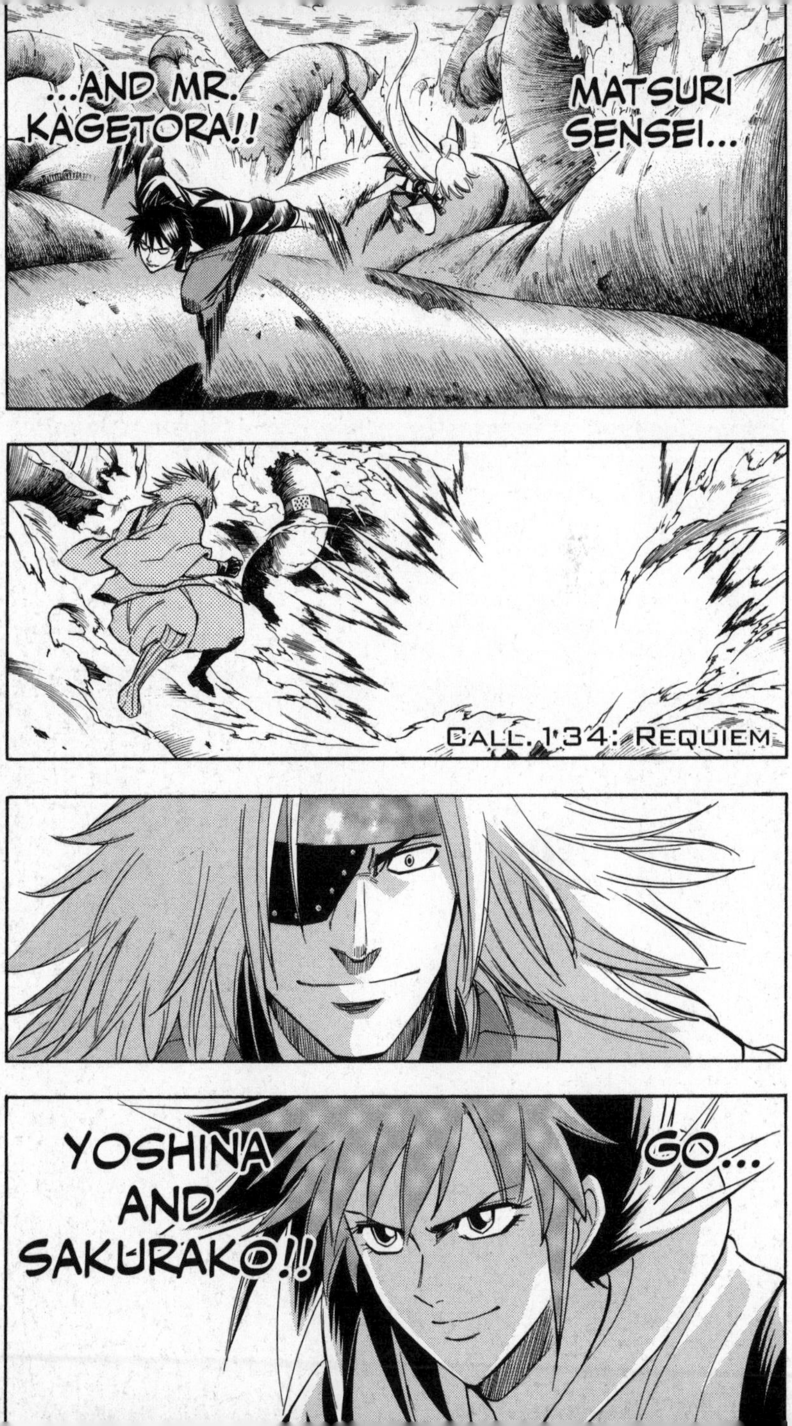
MATSURI SENSEI...
...AND MR. KAGETORA!!
CALL. 134: REQUIEM
GO...
YOSHINA AND SAKURAKO!!

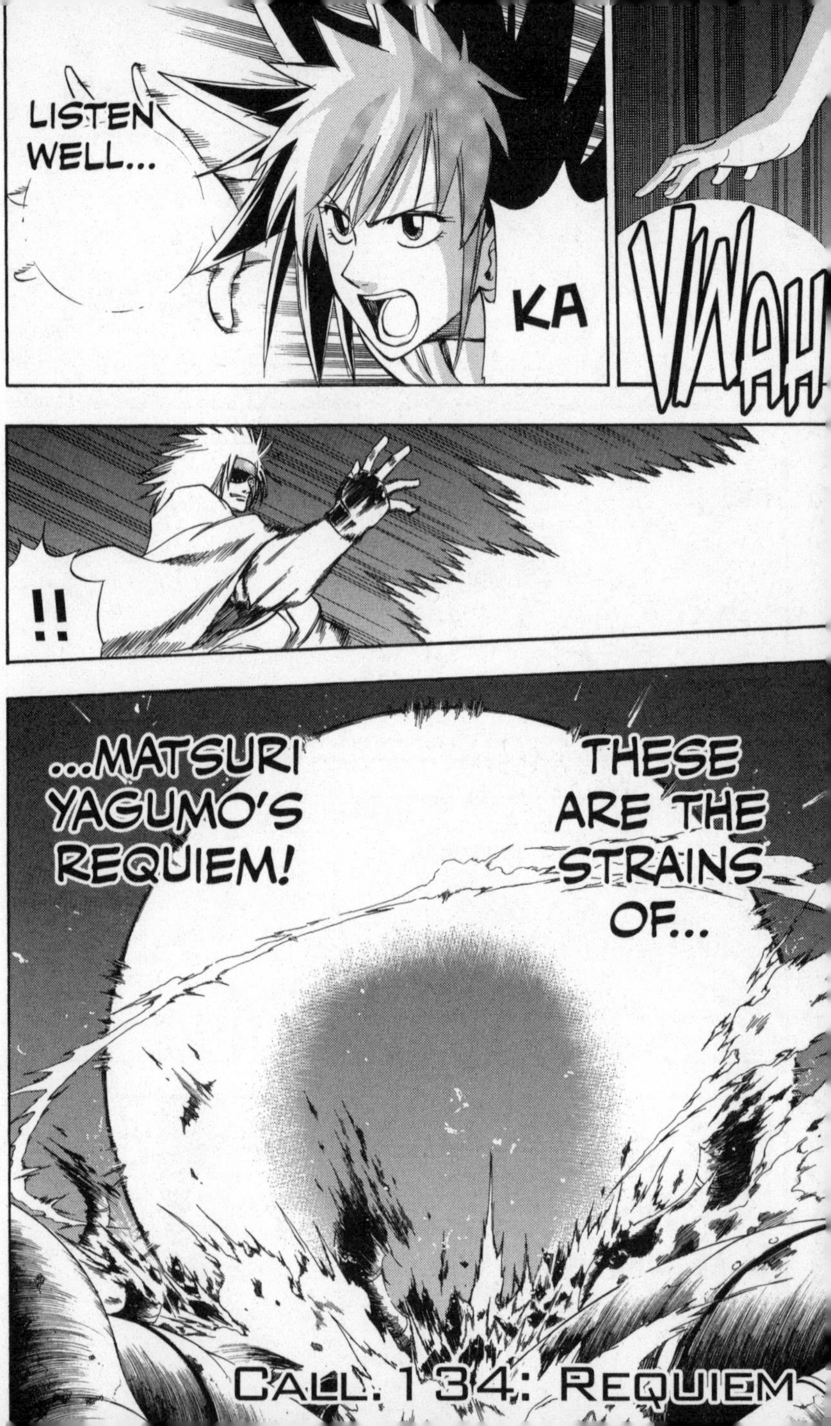
VWAH
LISTEN WELL...
KA
!!
THESE ARE THE STRAINS OF...
...MATSURI YAGUMO'S REQUIEM!
CALL 134: REQUIEM

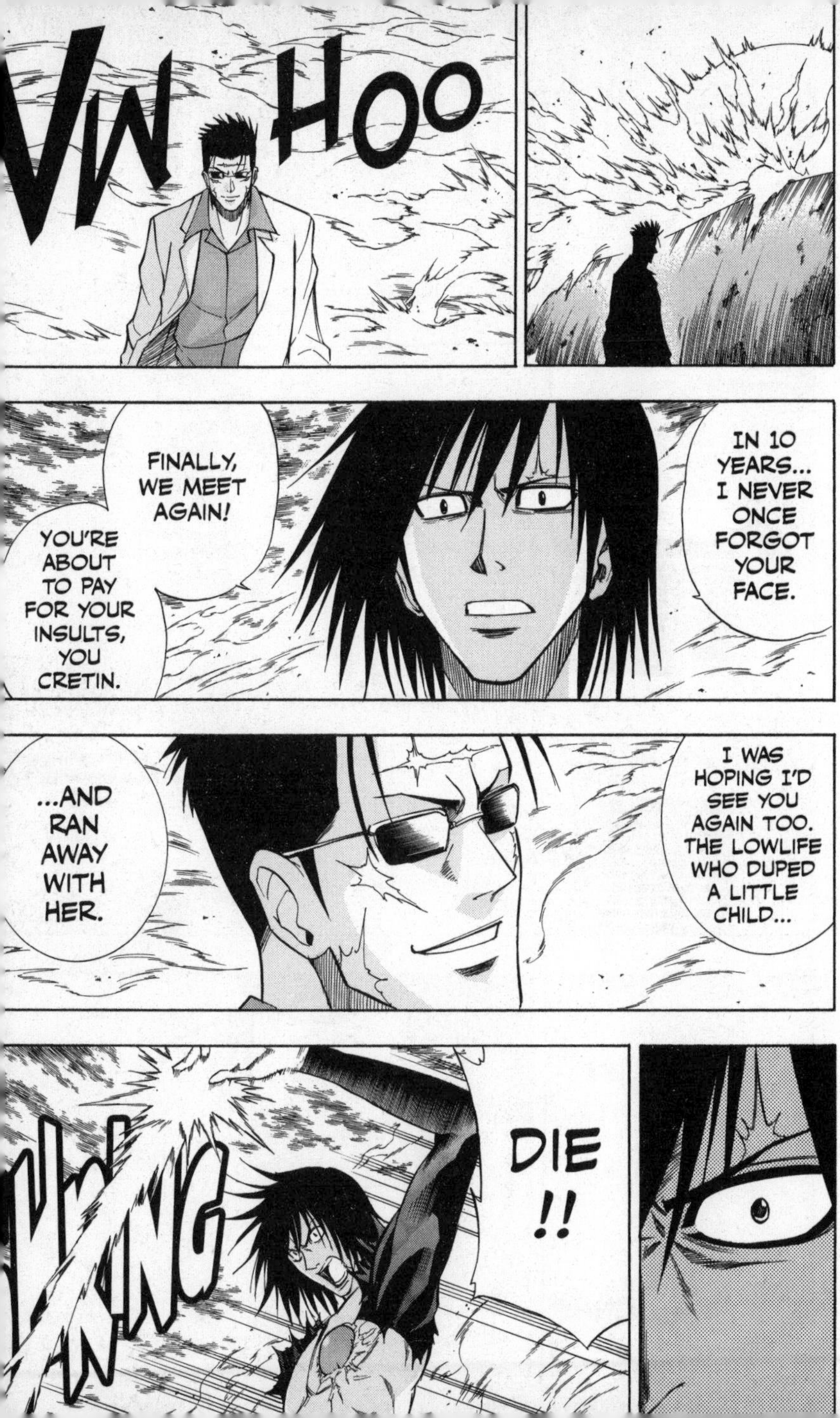

VW HOO
IN 10 YEARS... I NEVER ONCE FORGOT YOUR FACE.
FINALLY, WE MEET AGAIN!
YOU'RE ABOUT TO PAY FOR YOUR INSULTS, YOU CRETIN.
I WAS HOPING I'D SEE YOU AGAIN TOO. THE LOWLIFE WHO DUPED A LITTLE CHILD...
...AND RAN AWAY WITH HER.
DIE !!

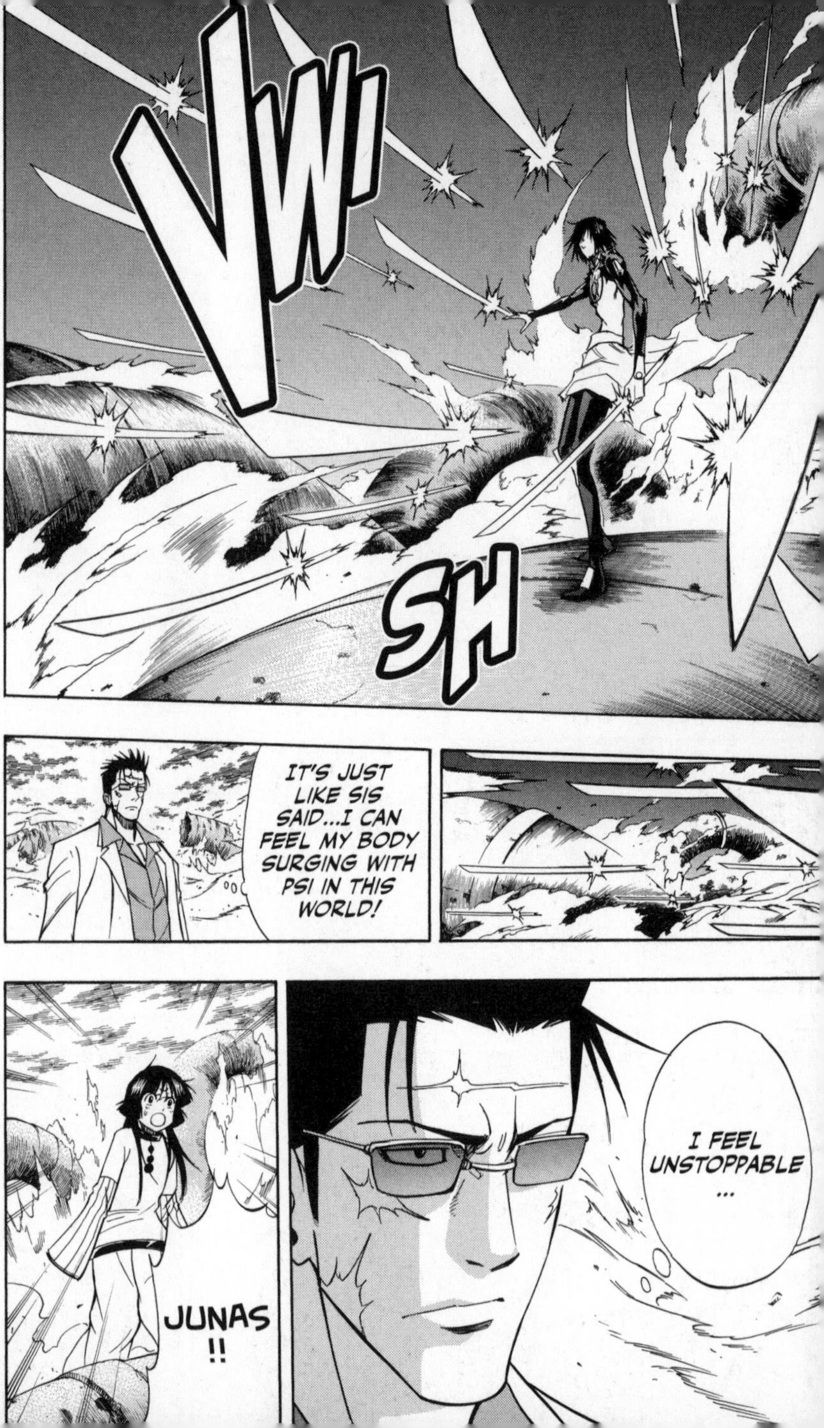
VWI
SH
IT'S JUST LIKE SIS SAID...I CAN FEEL MY BODY SURGING WITH PSI IN THIS WORLD!
I FEEL UNSTOPPABLE ...
JUNAS !!

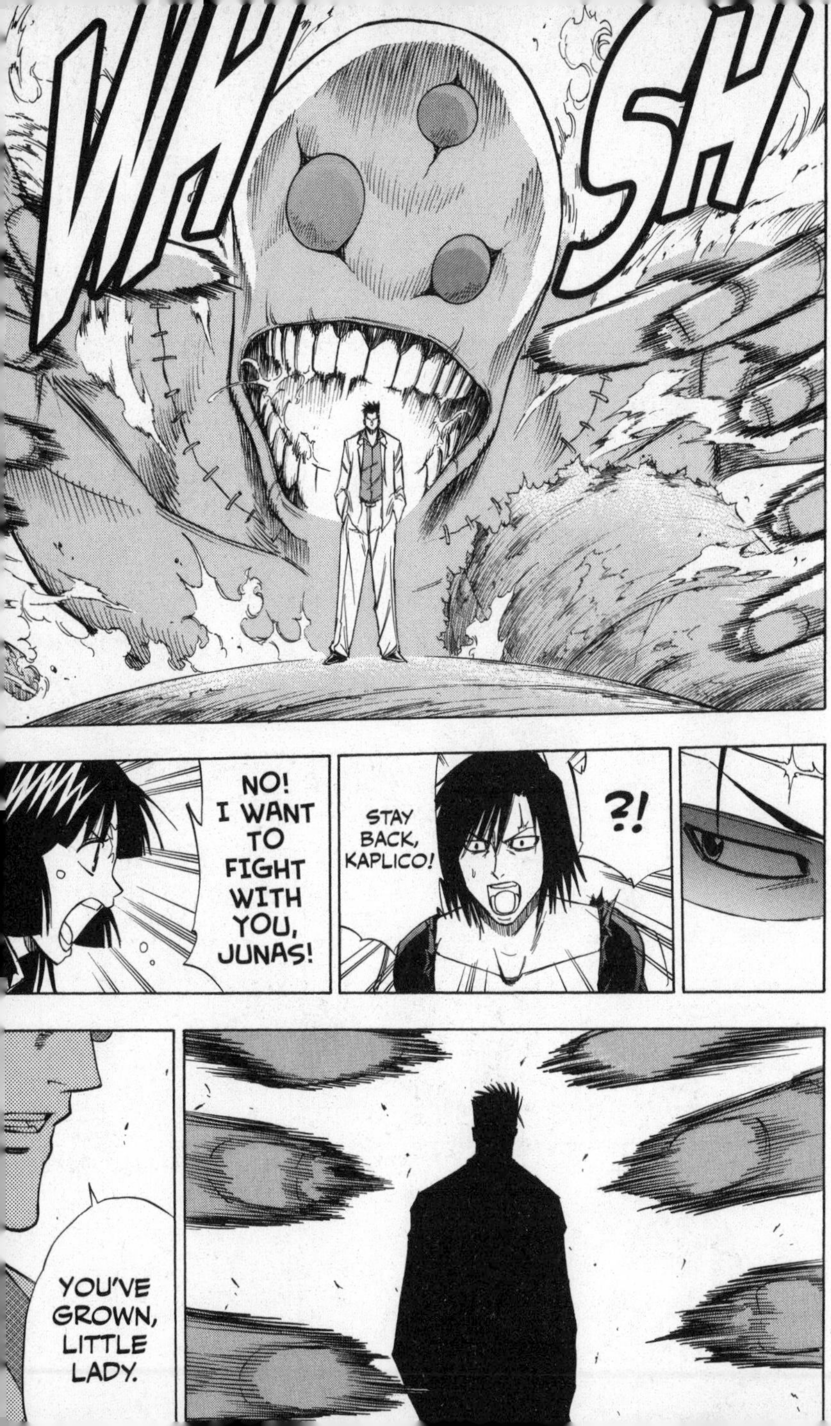
WH SH
?!
STAY BACK, KAPLICO!
NO! I WANT TO FIGHT WITH YOU, JUNAS!
YOU'VE GROWN, LITTLE LADY.

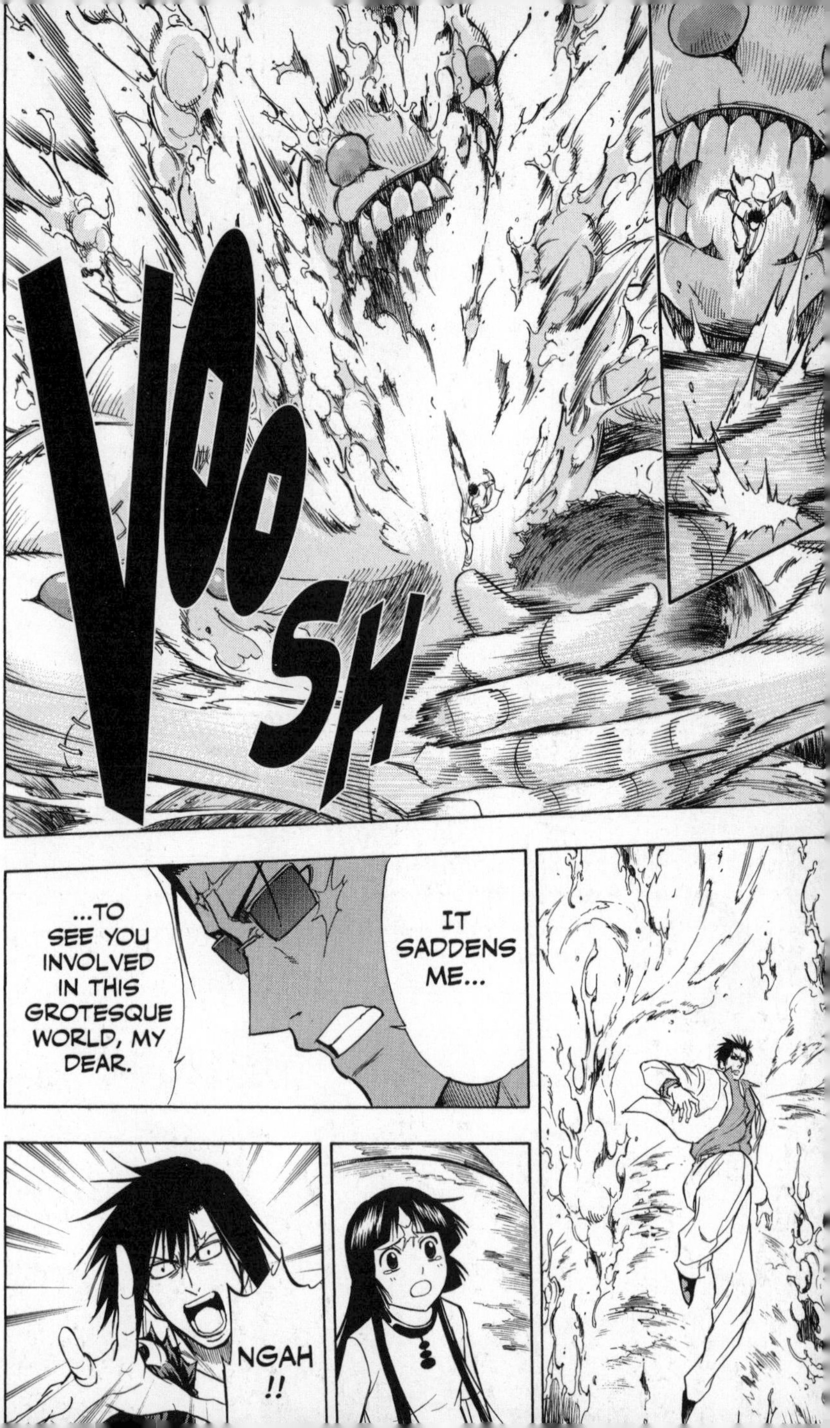
VOOSH
IT SADDENS ME...
...TO SEE YOU INVOLVED IN THIS GROTESQUE WORLD, MY DEAR.
NGAH!!

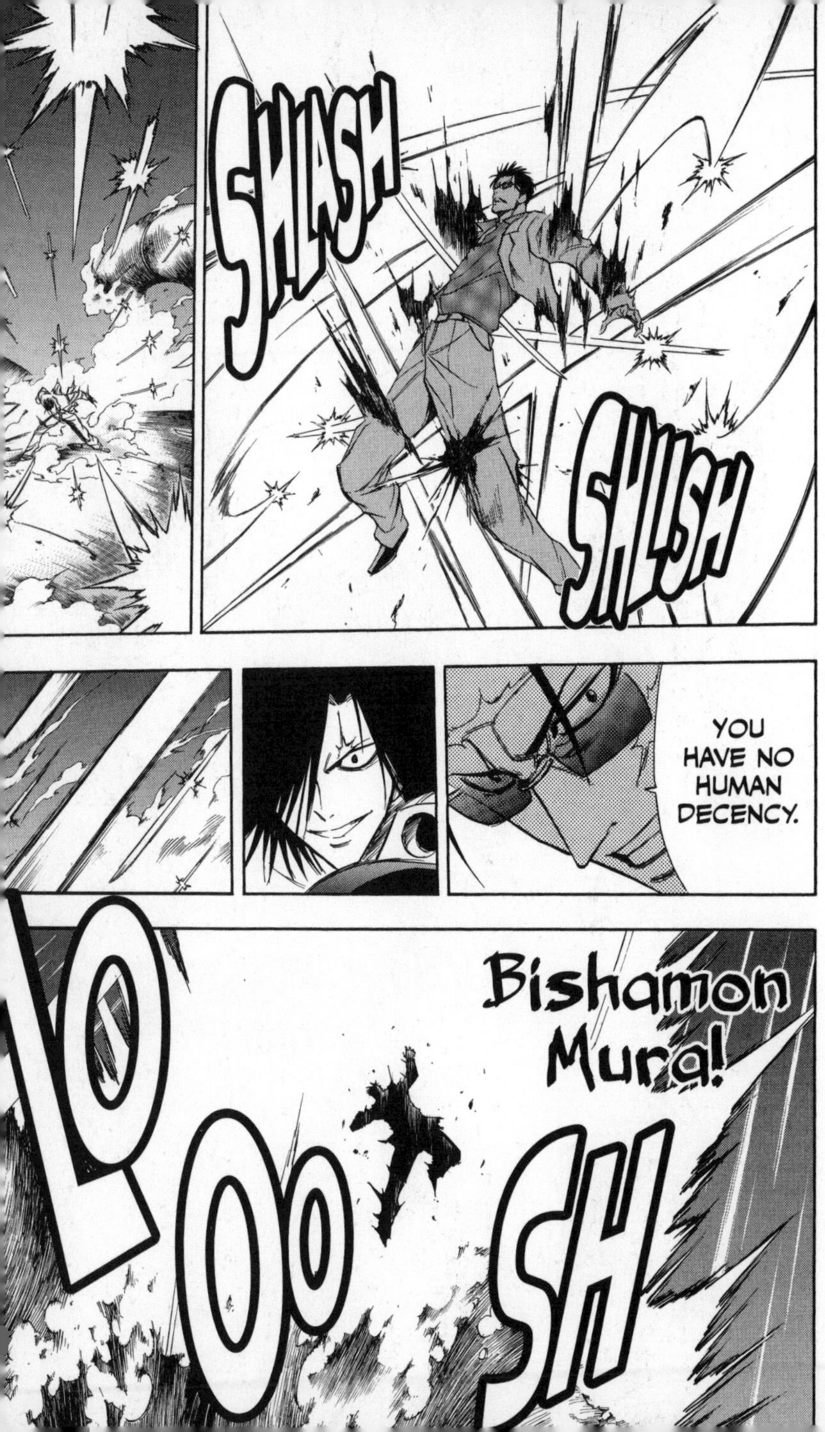
SHASH
SHASH
YOU HAVE NO HUMAN DECENCY.
Bishamon Mura!
LOOOOSH

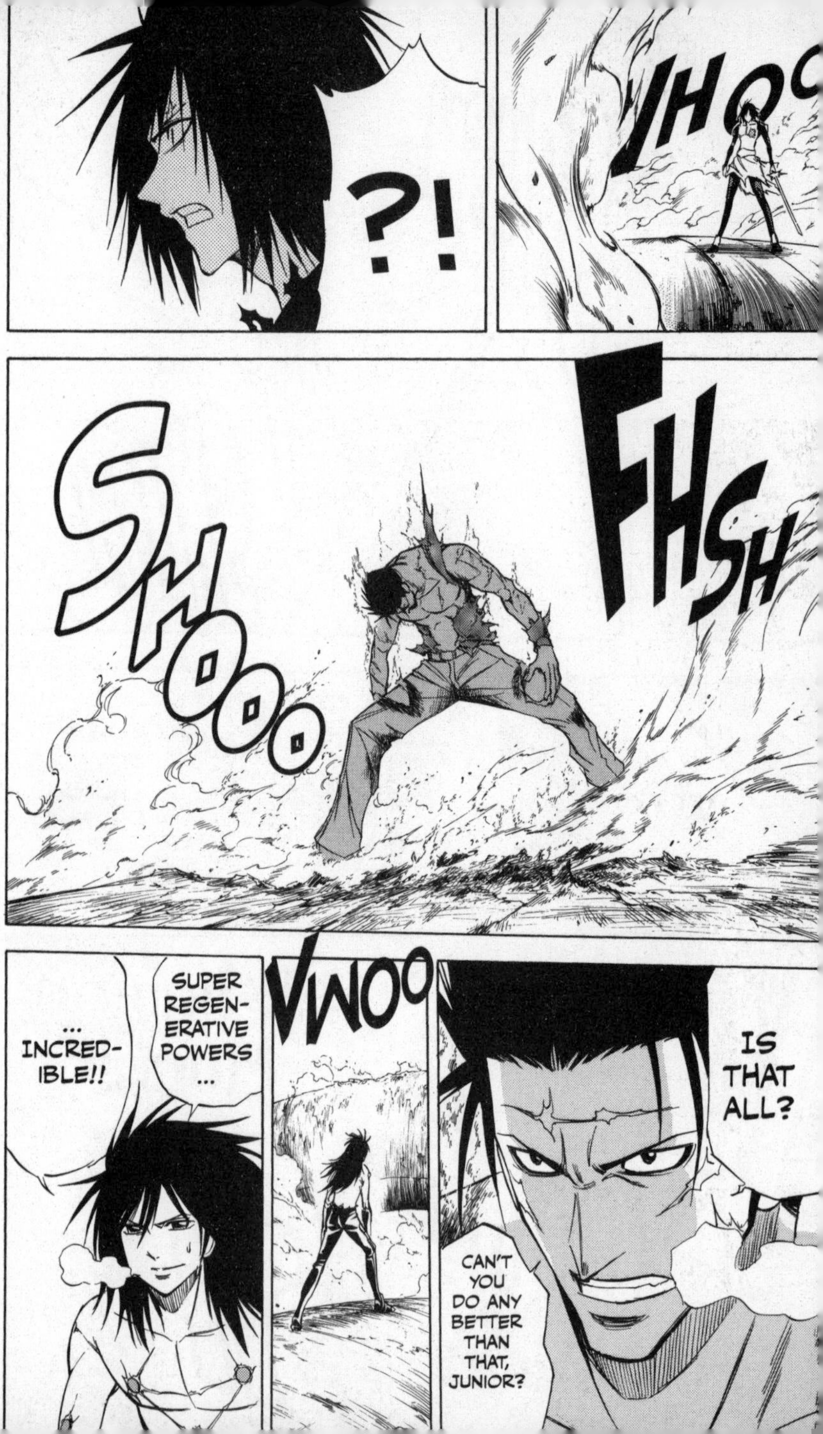

VHO
?!
FHSH
SHOOO
IS THAT ALL?
CAN'T YOU DO ANY BETTER THAN THAT, JUNIOR?
VWOO
SUPER REGENERATIVE POWERS ...
... INCREDIBLE!!

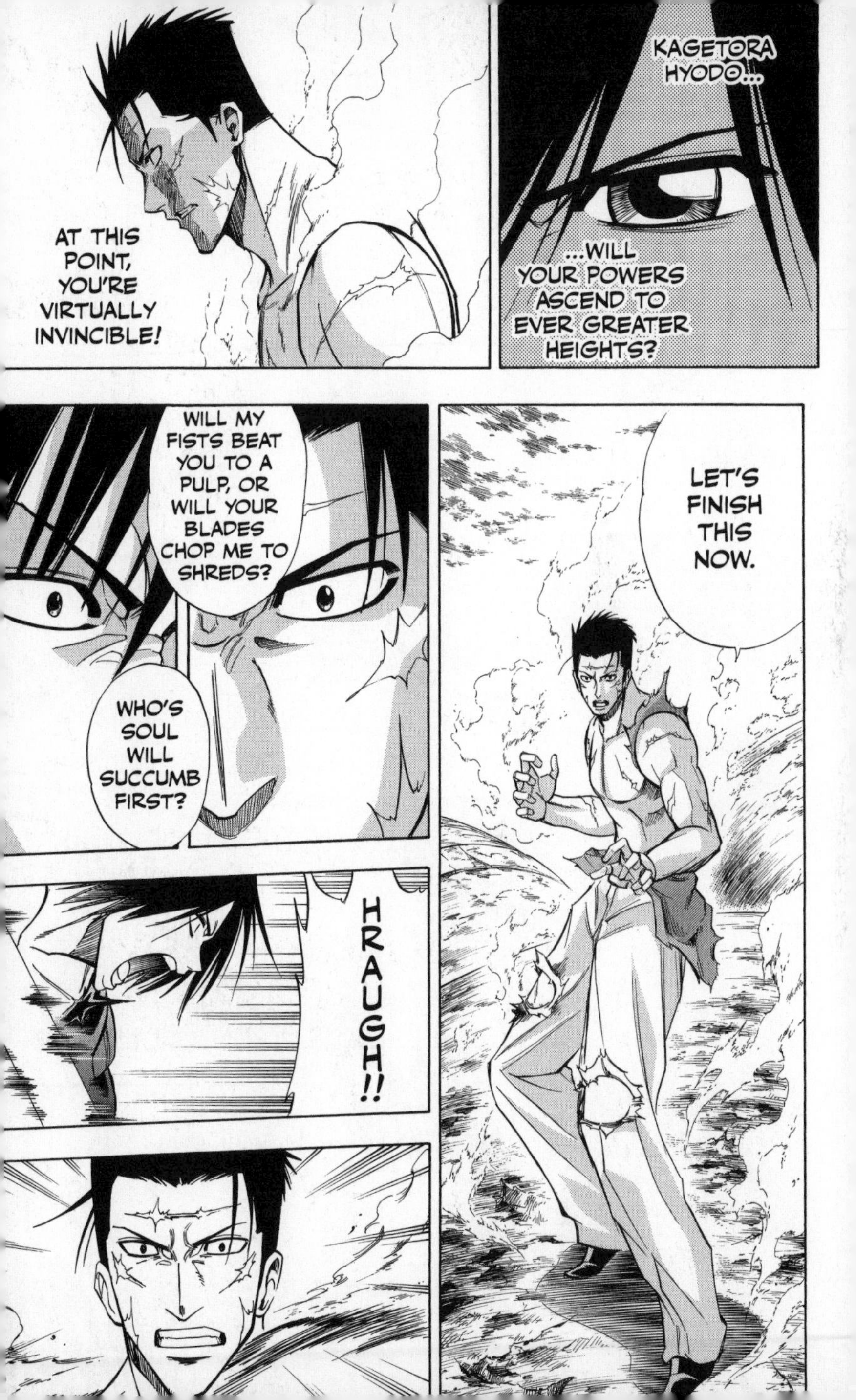
KAGETORA HYODO...
...WILL YOUR POWERS ASCEND TO EVER GREATER HEIGHTS?
AT THIS POINT, YOU'RE VIRTUALLY INVINCIBLE!
LET'S FINISH THIS NOW.
WILL MY FISTS BEAT YOU TO A PULP, OR WILL YOUR BLADES CHOP ME TO SHREDS?
WHO'S SOUL WILL SUCCUMB FIRST?
HRAUGH!!

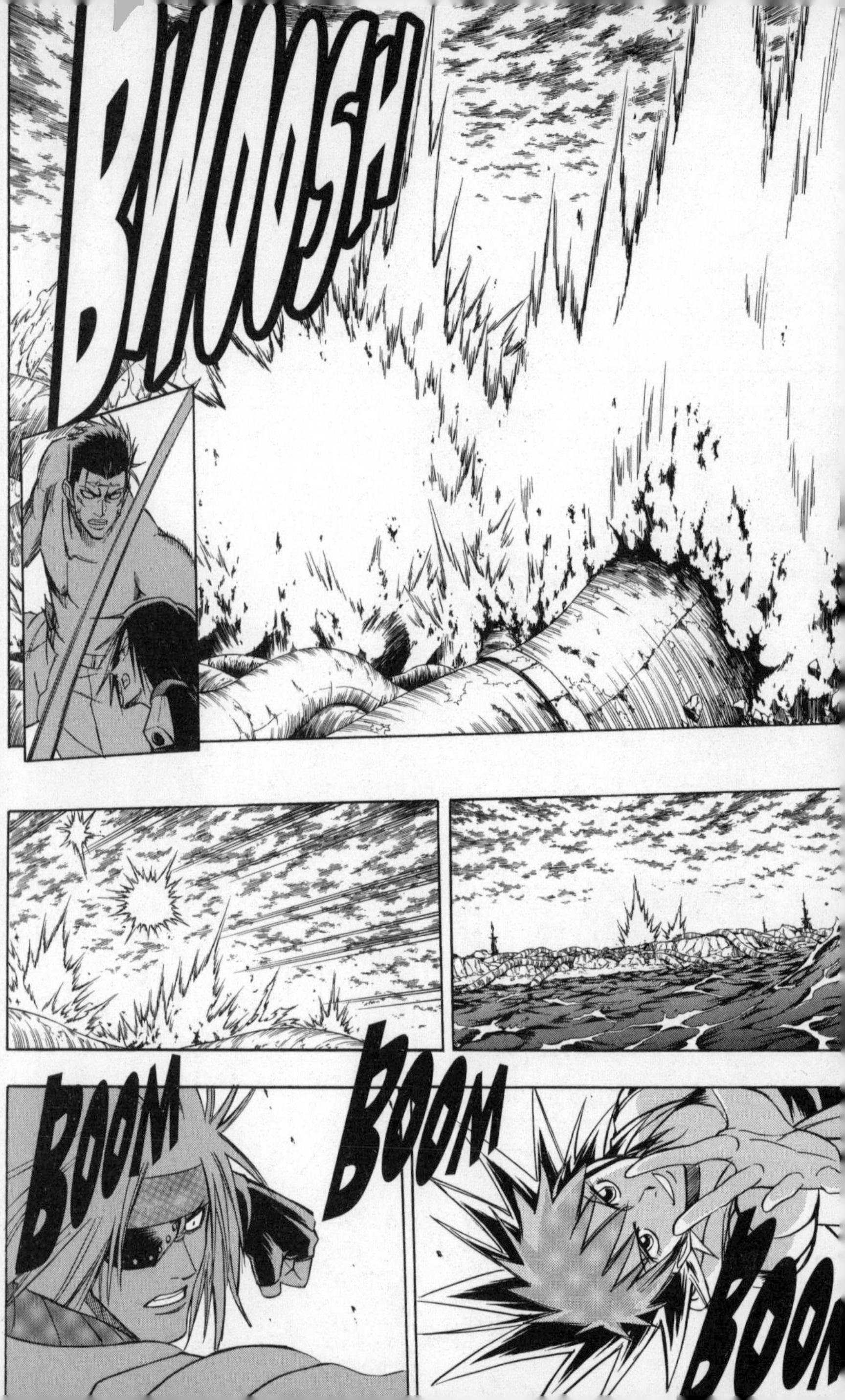
BWOOSH
BOO
BOOM
BOOM

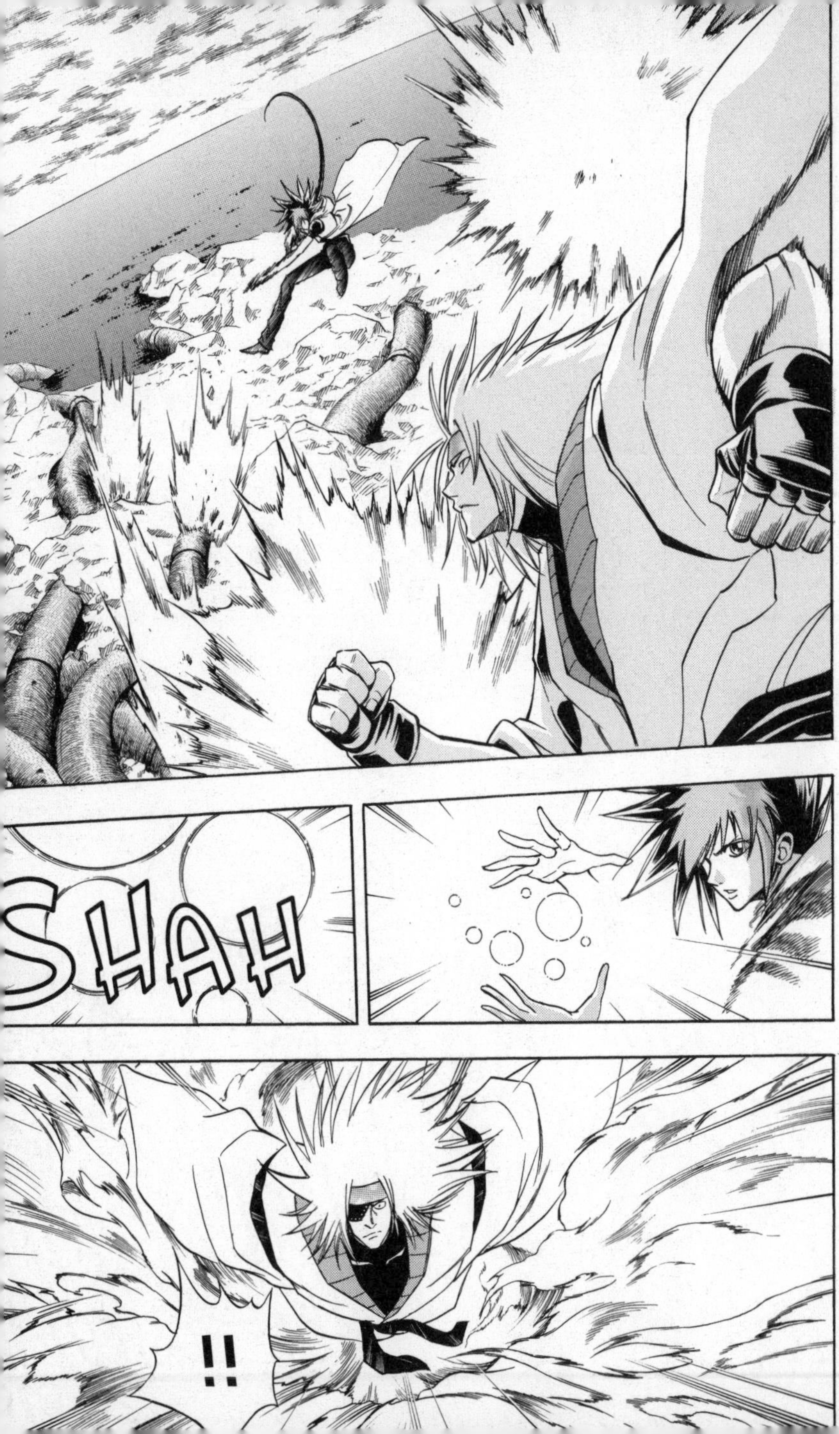
SHAH
!!

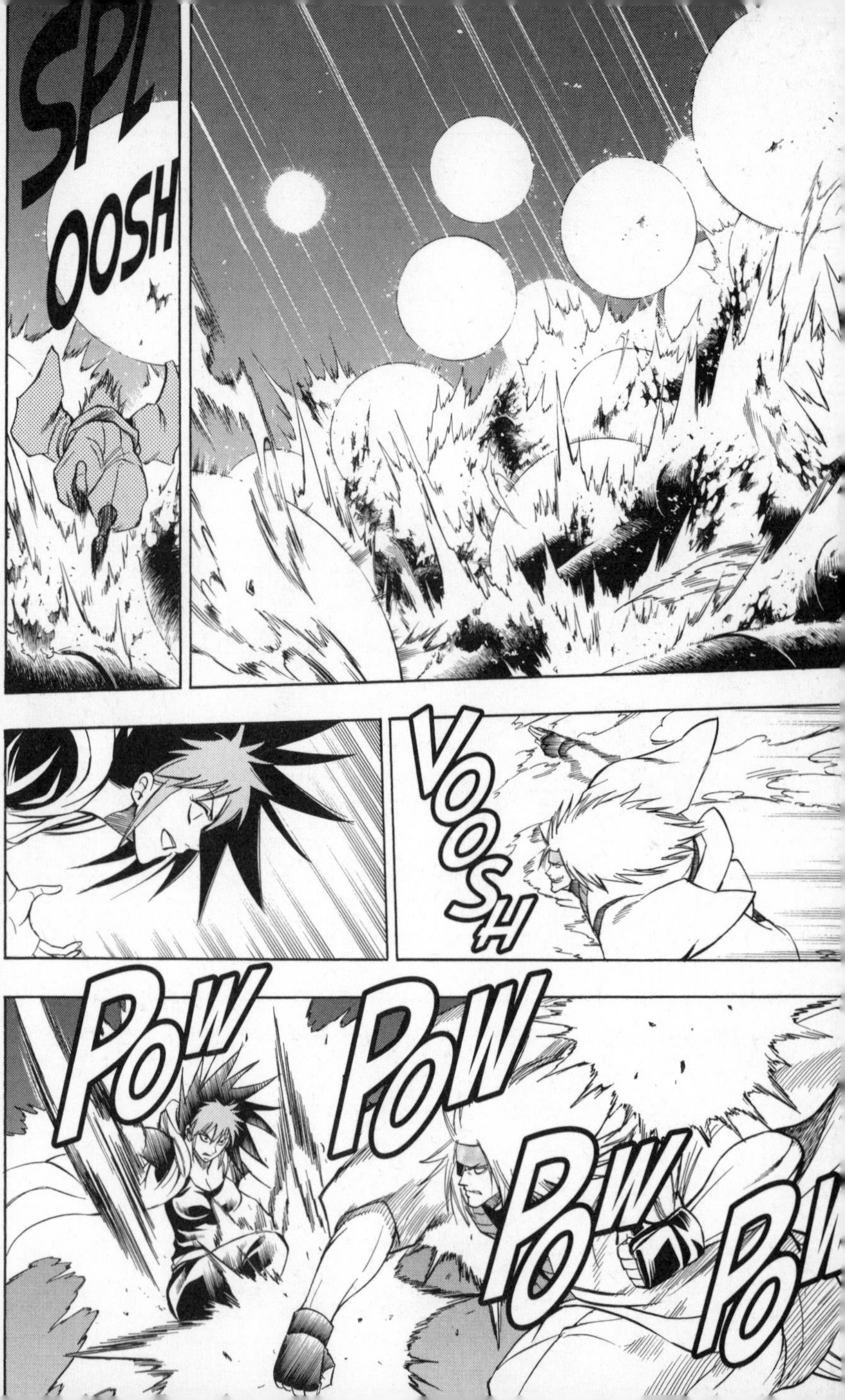
SPLOOSH
VOOSH
POW
POW
POW-PO

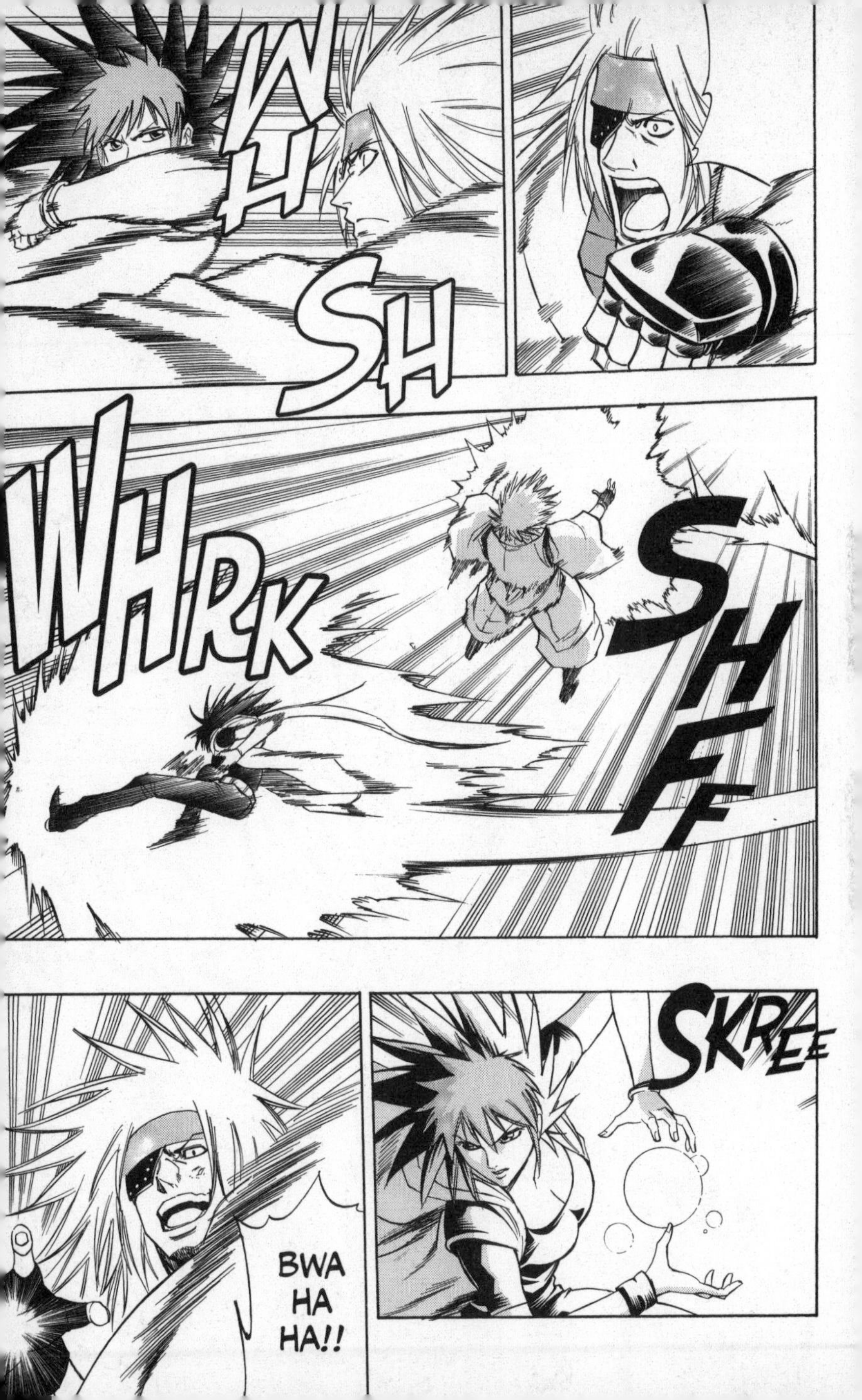
WH
SH
SHFF
WHRK
SKREE
BWA HA HA!!

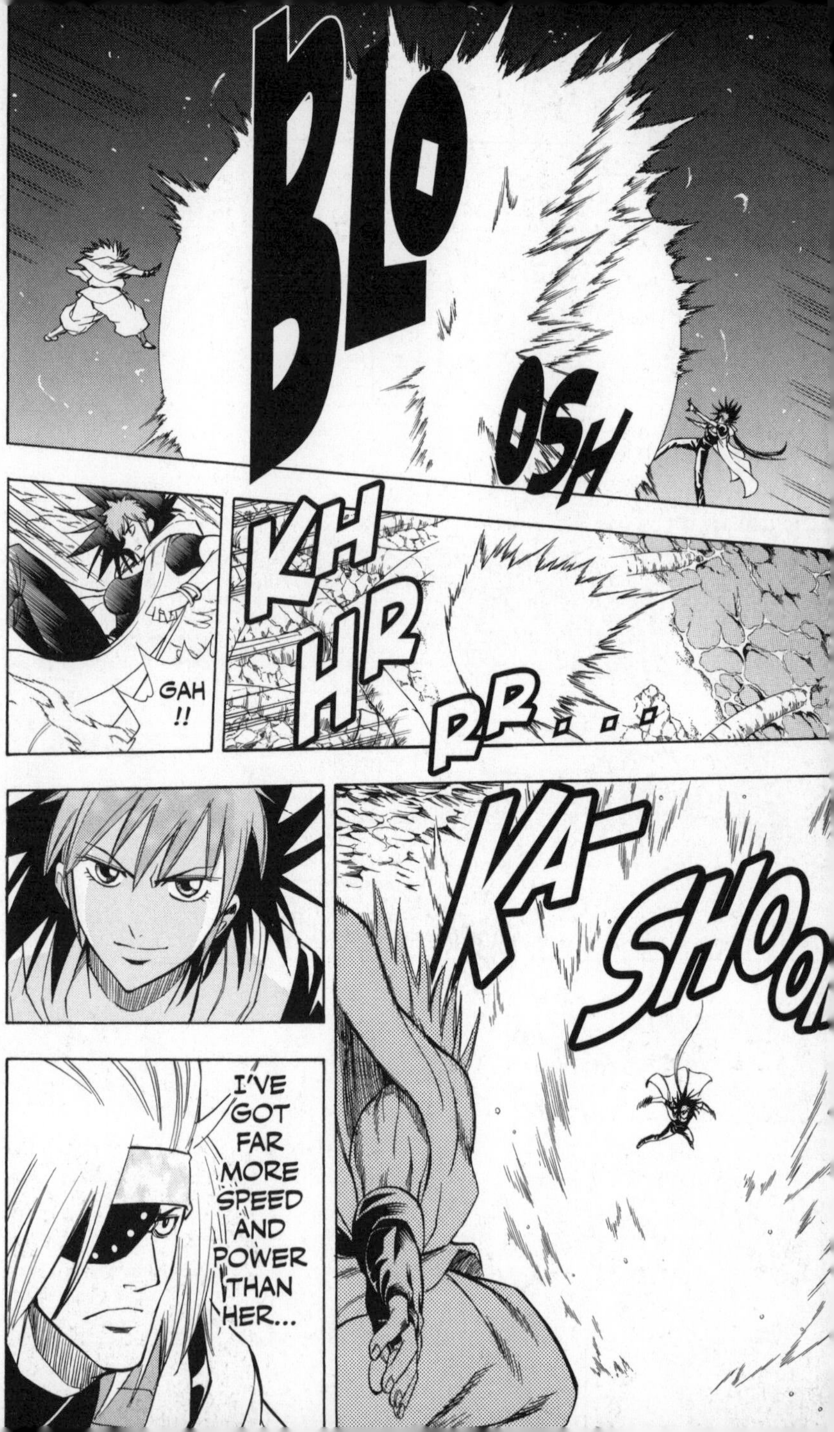
BLOOSH
KHHRRR...
GAH!!
KA-SHOOM
I'VE GOT FAR MORE SPEED AND POWER THAN HER...

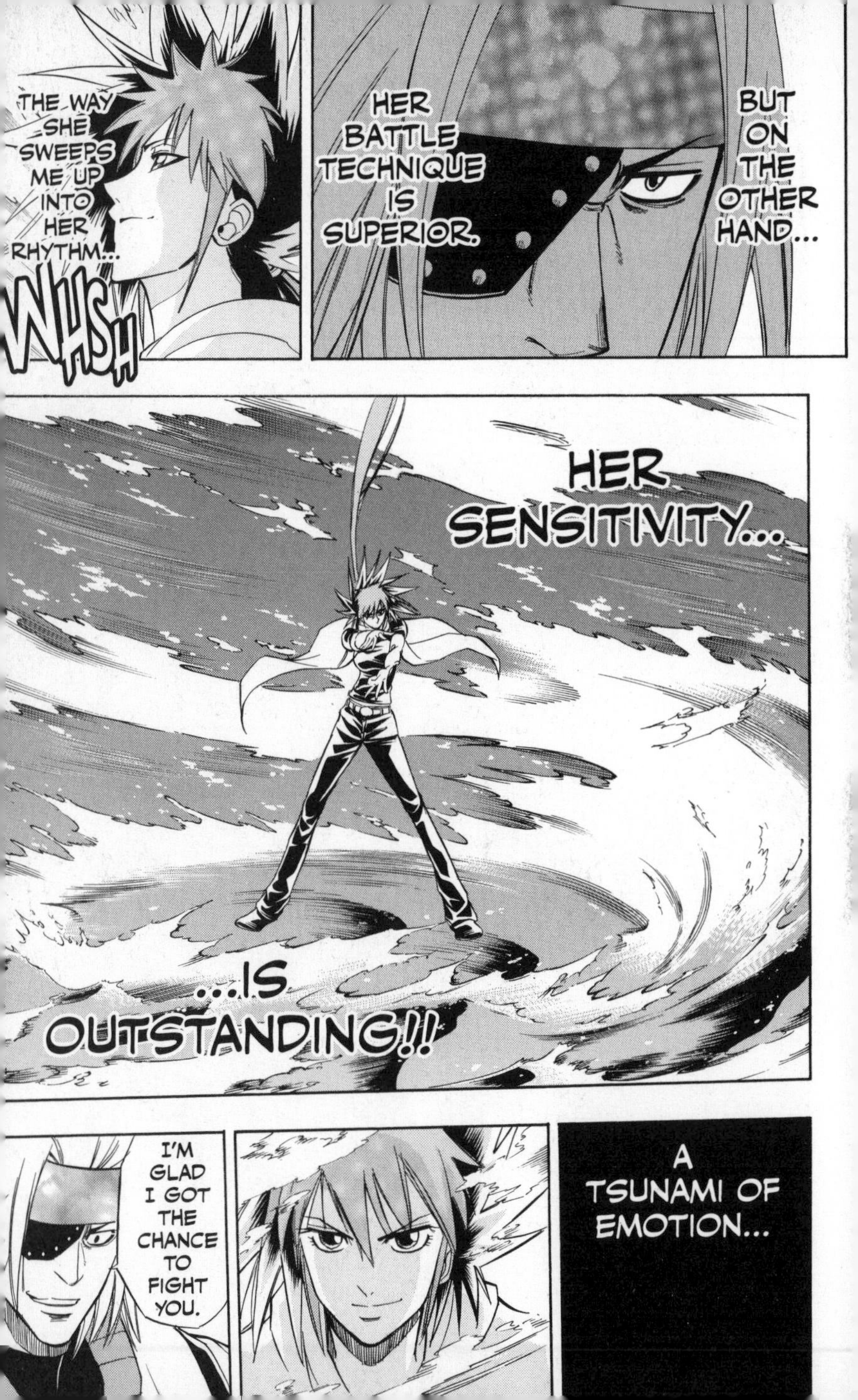
HER BATTLE TECHNIQUE IS SUPERIOR.
BUT ON THE OTHER HAND...
THE WAY SHE SWEEPS ME UP INTO HER RHYTHM...
WHSH
HER SENSITIVITY...
...IS OUTSTANDING!!
A TSUNAMI OF EMOTION...
I'M GLAD I GOT THE CHANCE TO FIGHT YOU.

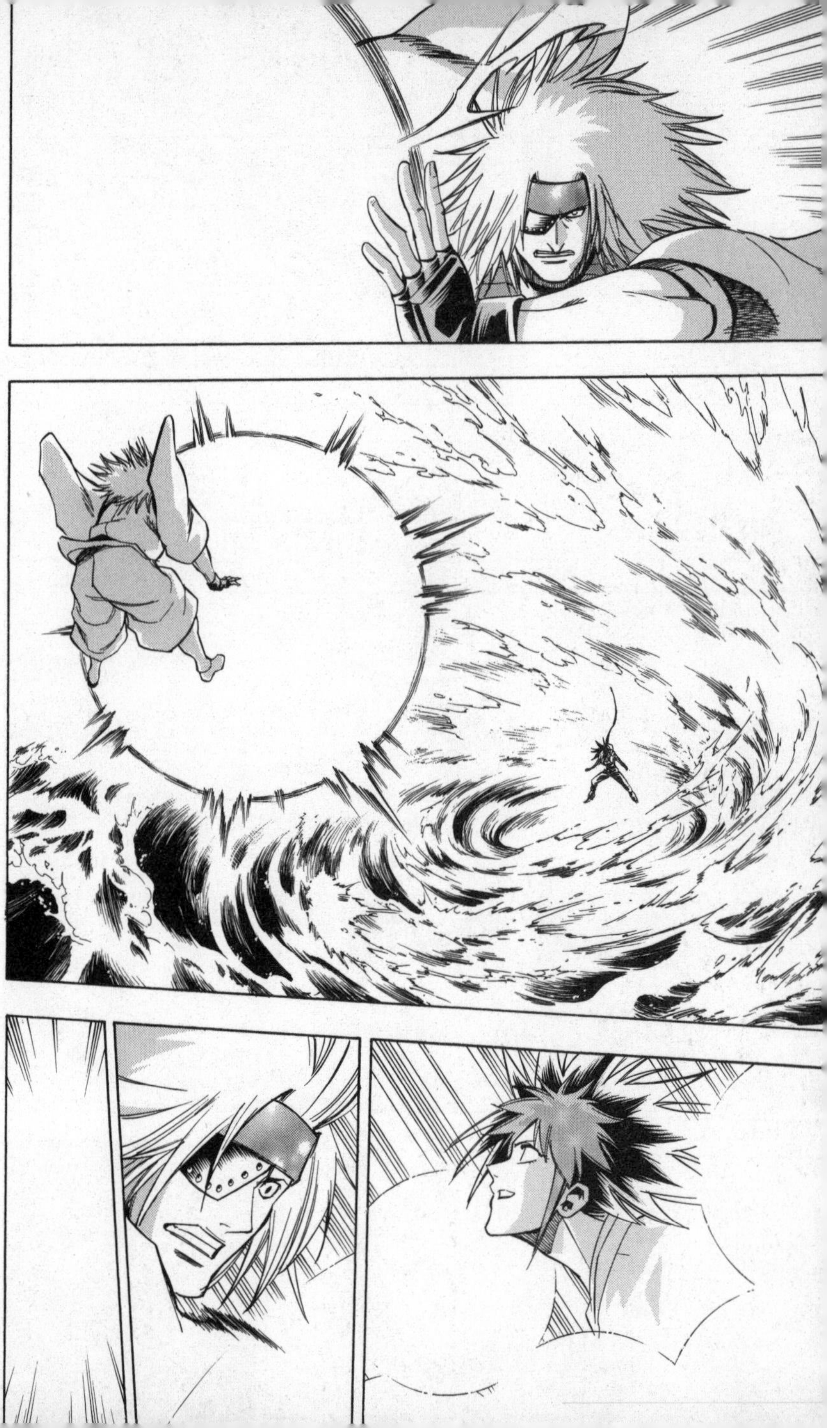

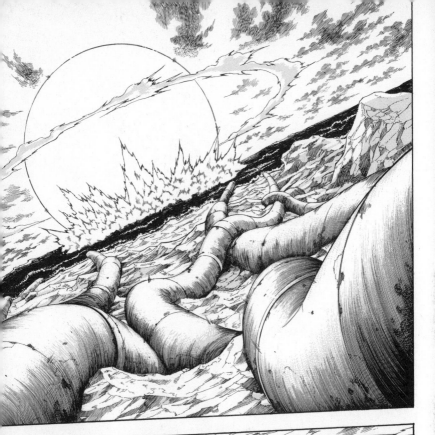

VWHO OO

HOW STUNNING!

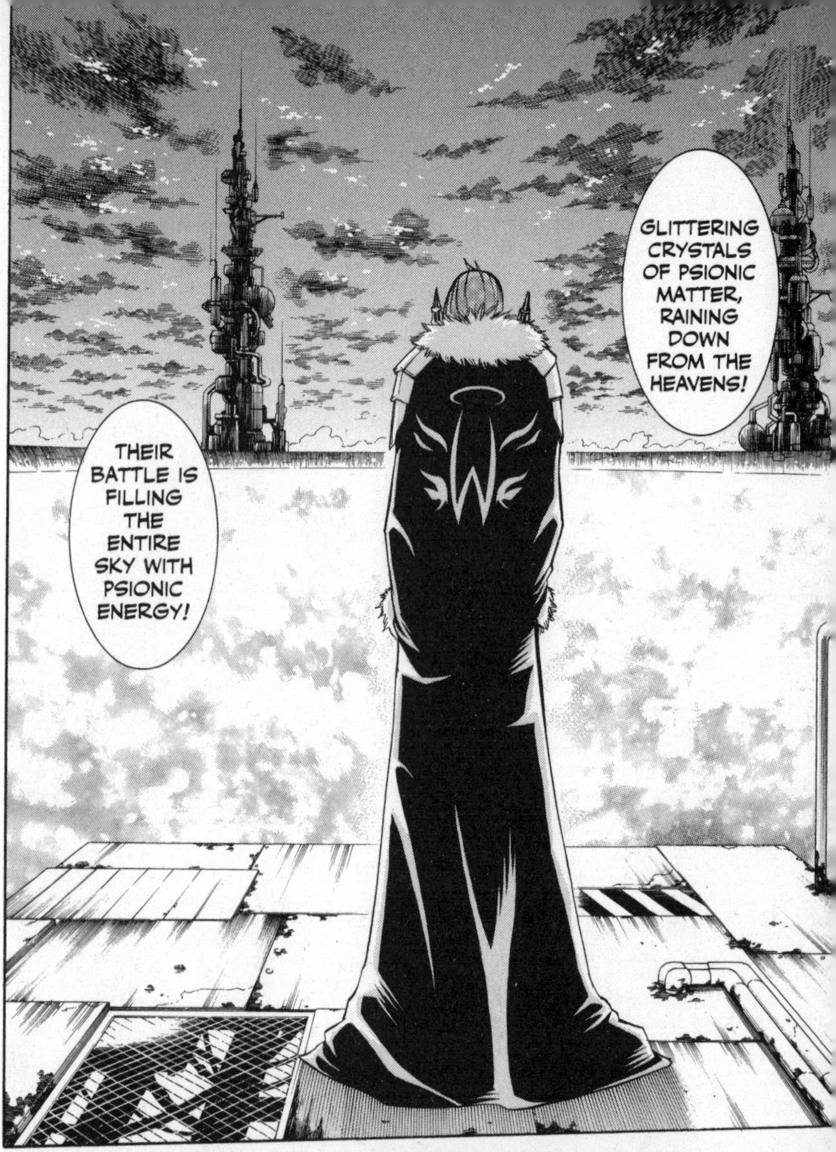
GLITTERING CRYSTALS OF PSIONIC MATTER, RAINING DOWN FROM THE HEAVENS!
THEIR BATTLE IS FILLING THE ENTIRE SKY WITH PSIONIC ENERGY!

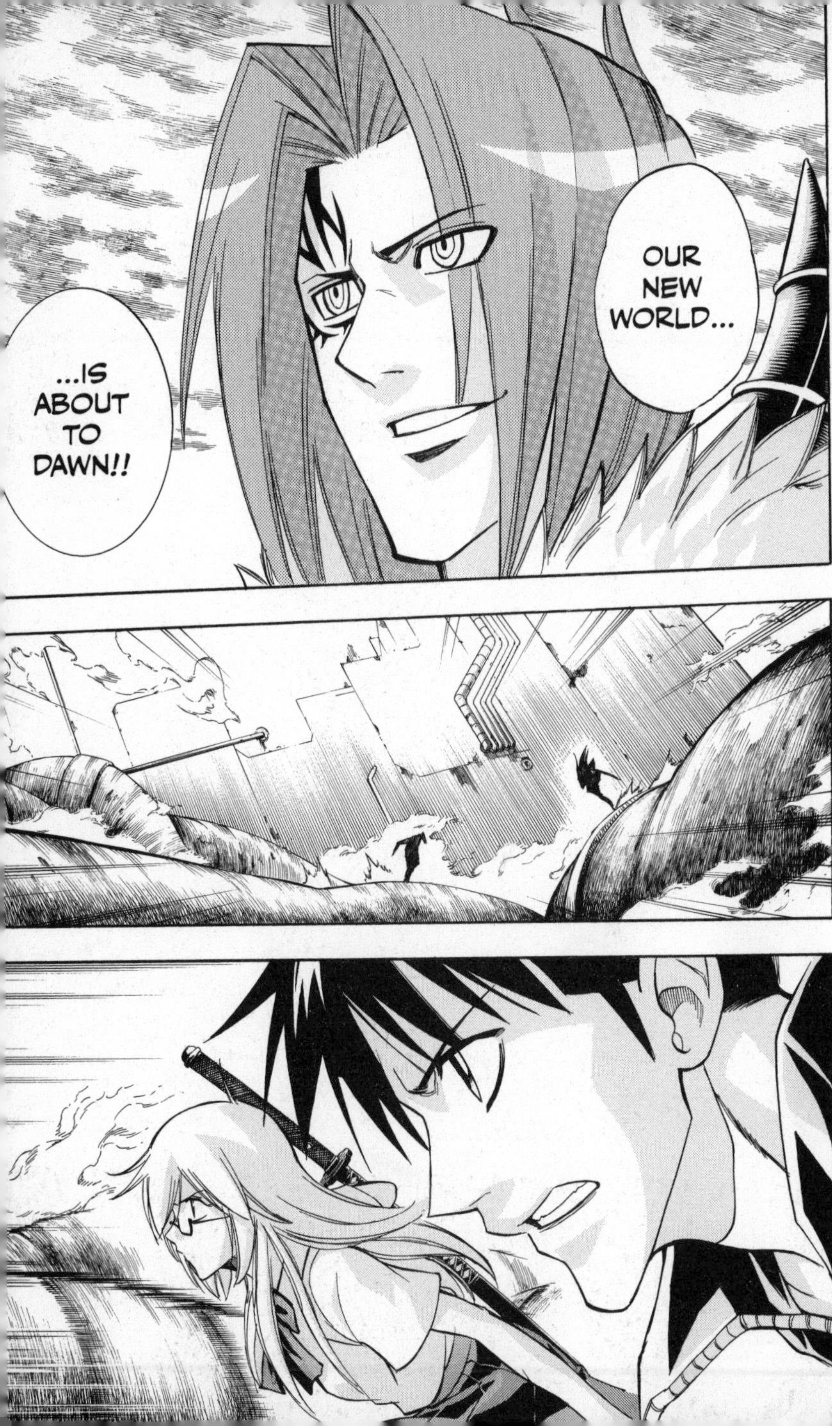
OUR NEW WORLD...
...IS ABOUT TO DAWN!!

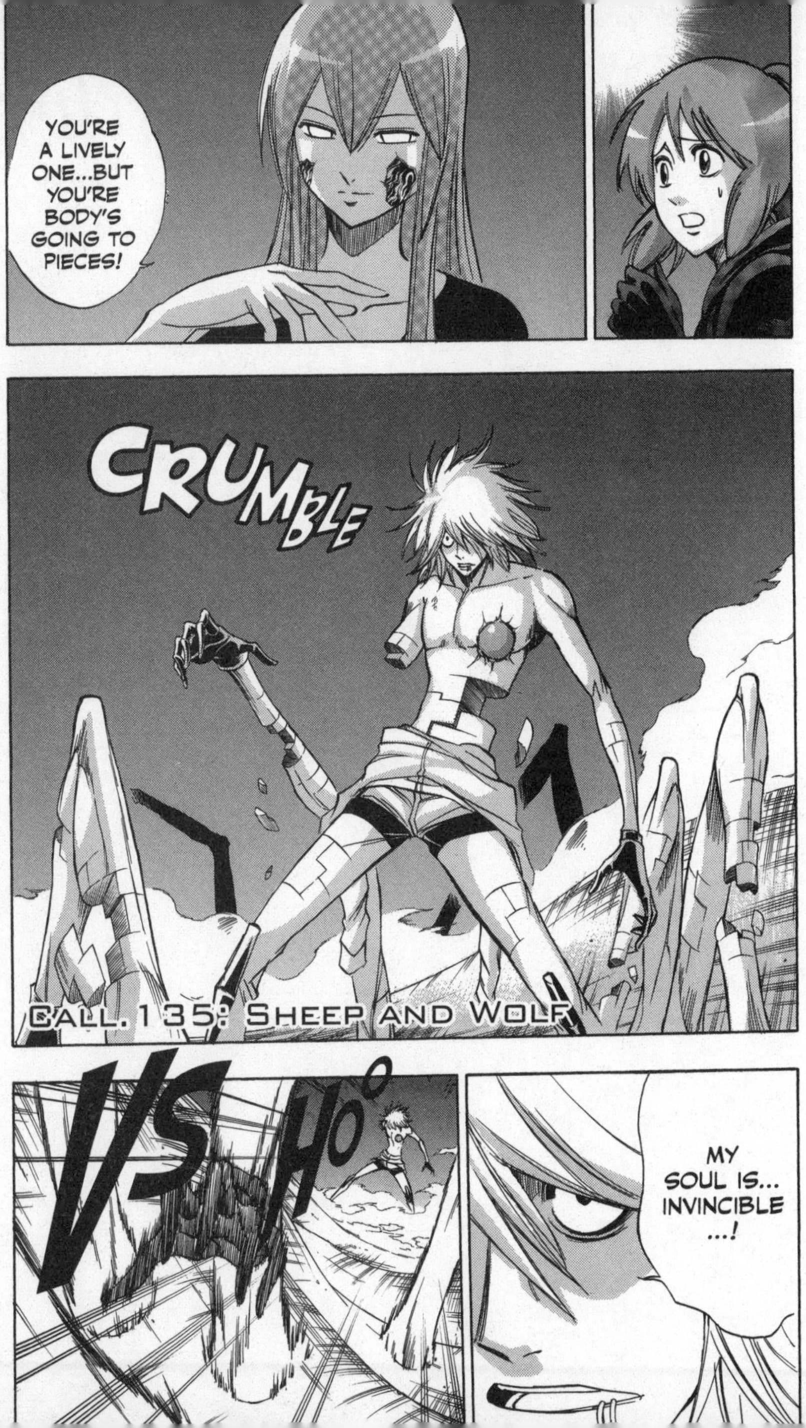
YOU'RE A LIVELY ONE...BUT YOU'RE BODY'S GOING TO PIECES!
CRUMBLE
CALL. 135: SHEEP AND WOLF
MY SOUL IS... INVINCIBLE ...!
VSHOO

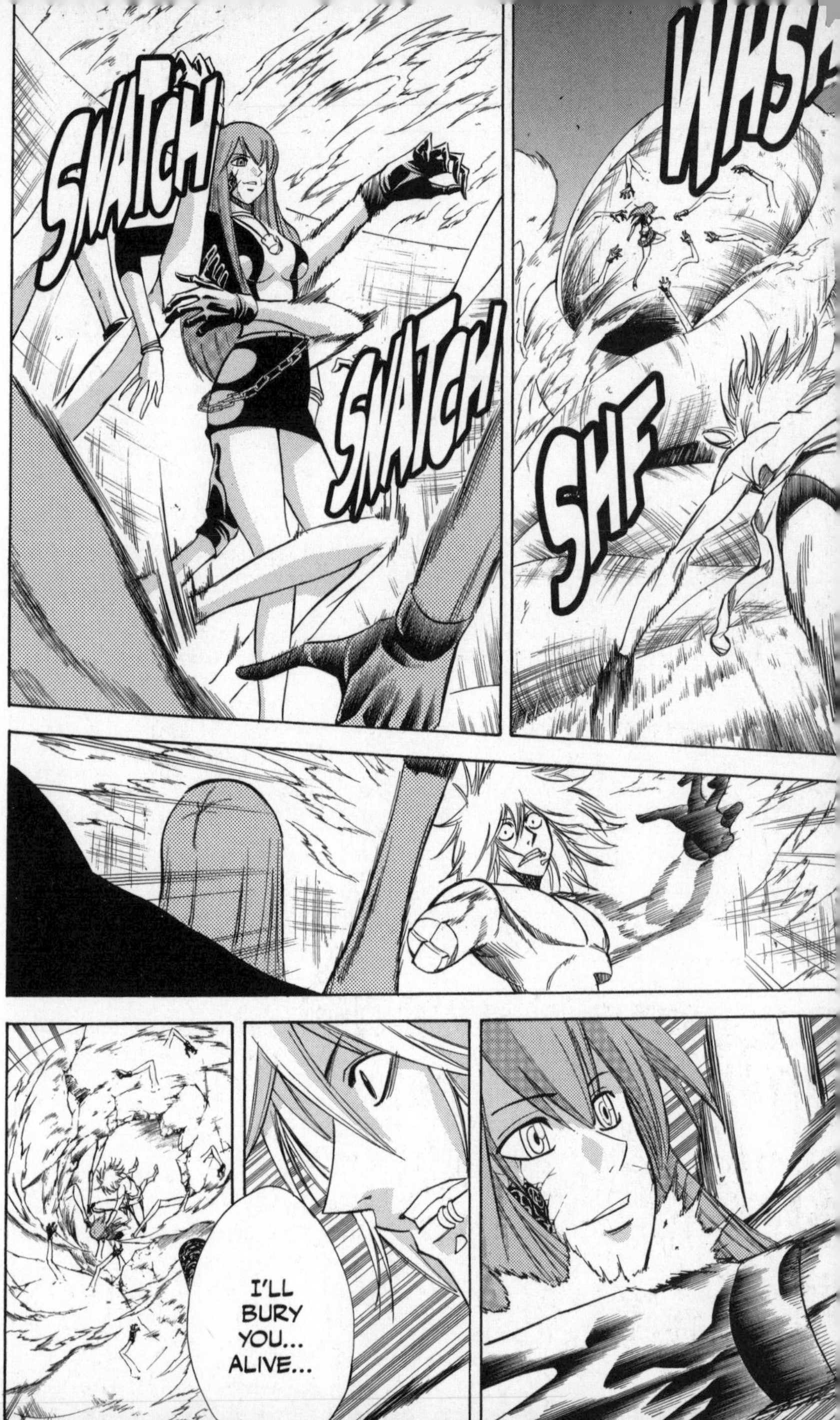
WHS
SHF
SNATCH
SNATCH
I'LL BURY YOU... ALIVE...

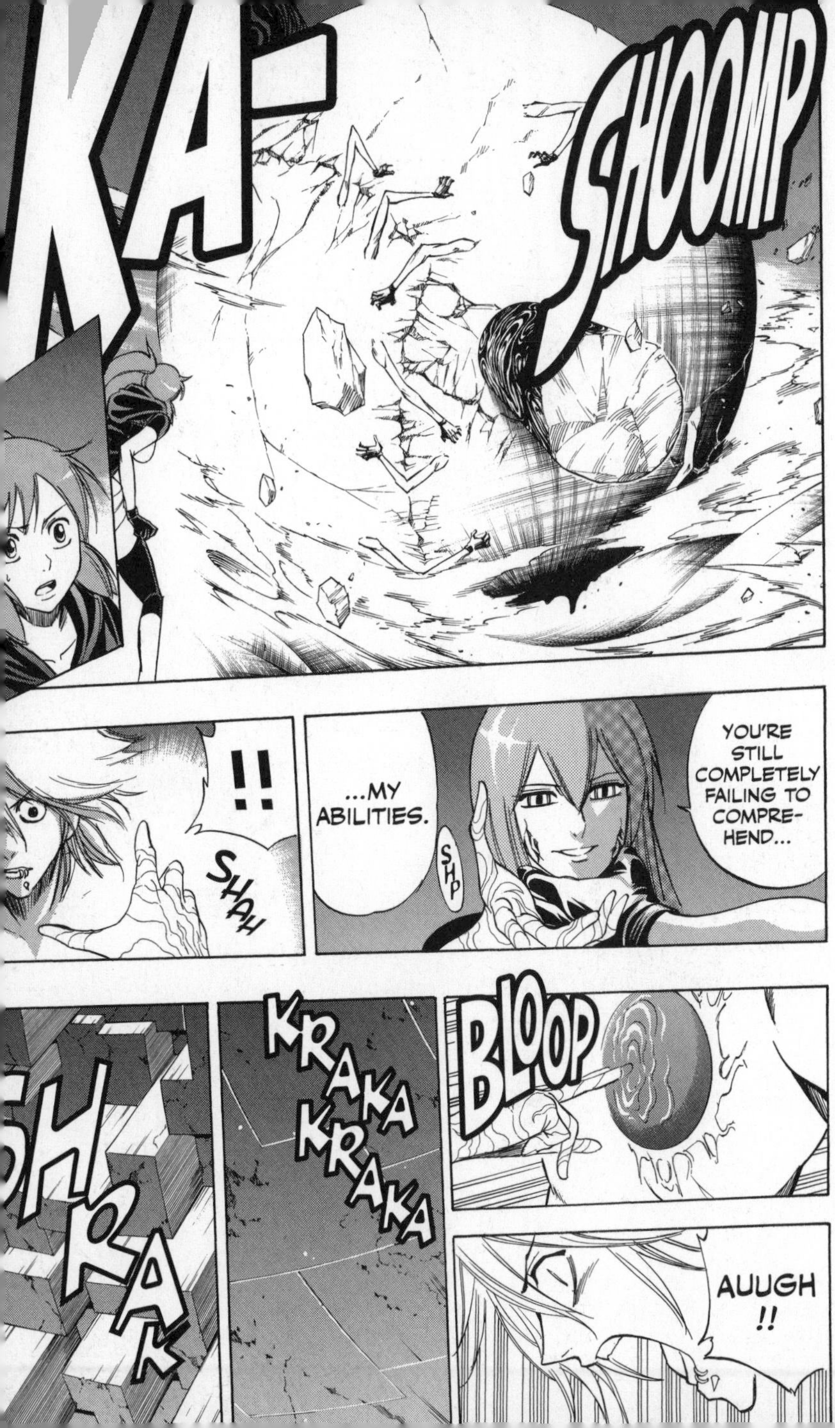
SHOOMP
KA-
YOU'RE STILL COMPLETELY FAILING TO COMPRE-HEND...
SHP
...MY ABILITIES.
!!
SHAH
BLOOP
AUUGH !!
KRAKA KRAKA
SHKLAK

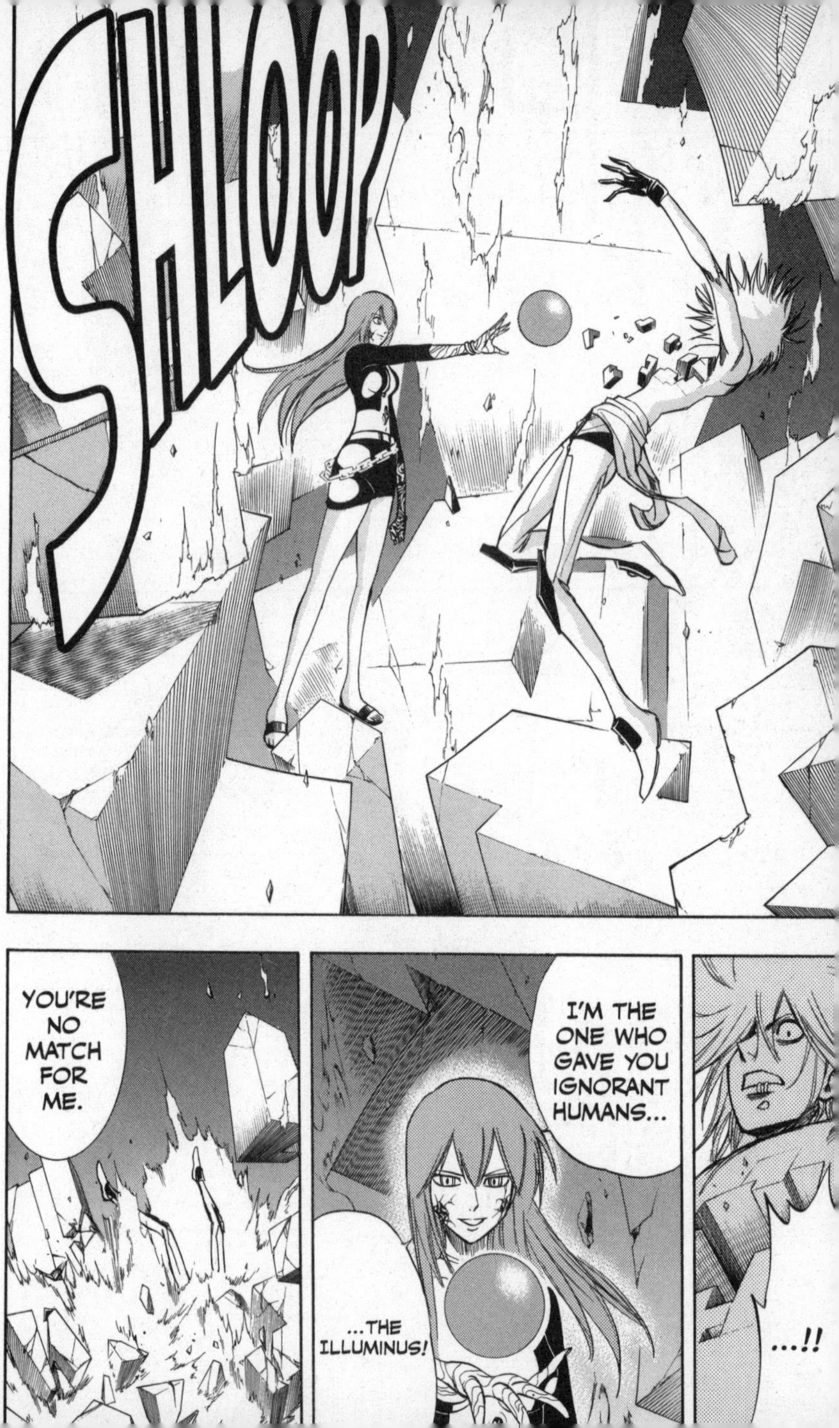
SHLOOP
...!!
I'M THE ONE WHO GAVE YOU IGNORANT HUMANS...
...THE ILLUMINUS!
YOU'RE NO MATCH FOR ME.

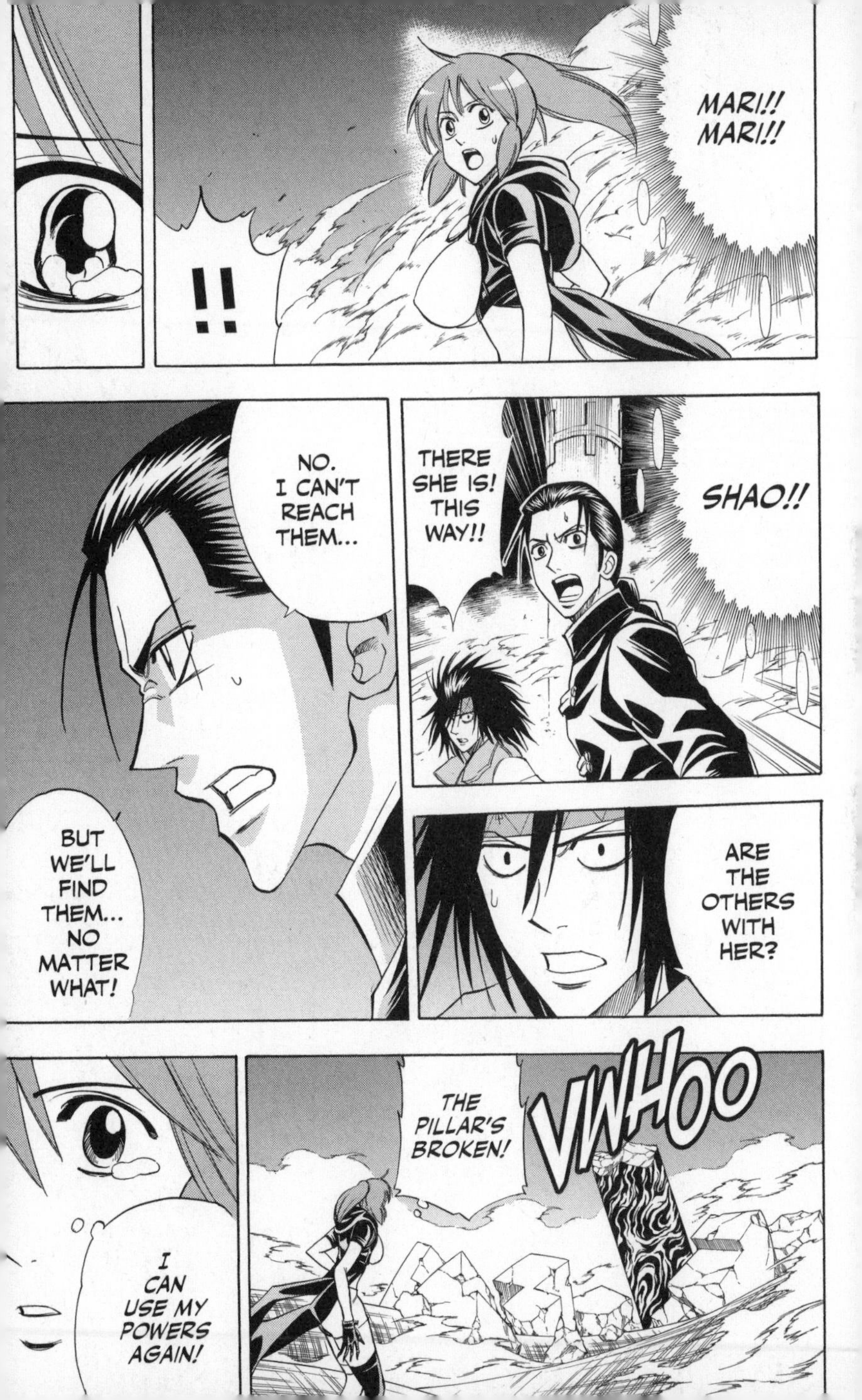
MARI!! MARI!!
!!
SHAO!!
THERE SHE IS! THIS WAY!!
ARE THE OTHERS WITH HER?
NO. I CAN'T REACH THEM...
BUT WE'LL FIND THEM... NO MATTER WHAT!
VWHOO
THE PILLAR'S BROKEN!
I CAN USE MY POWERS AGAIN!

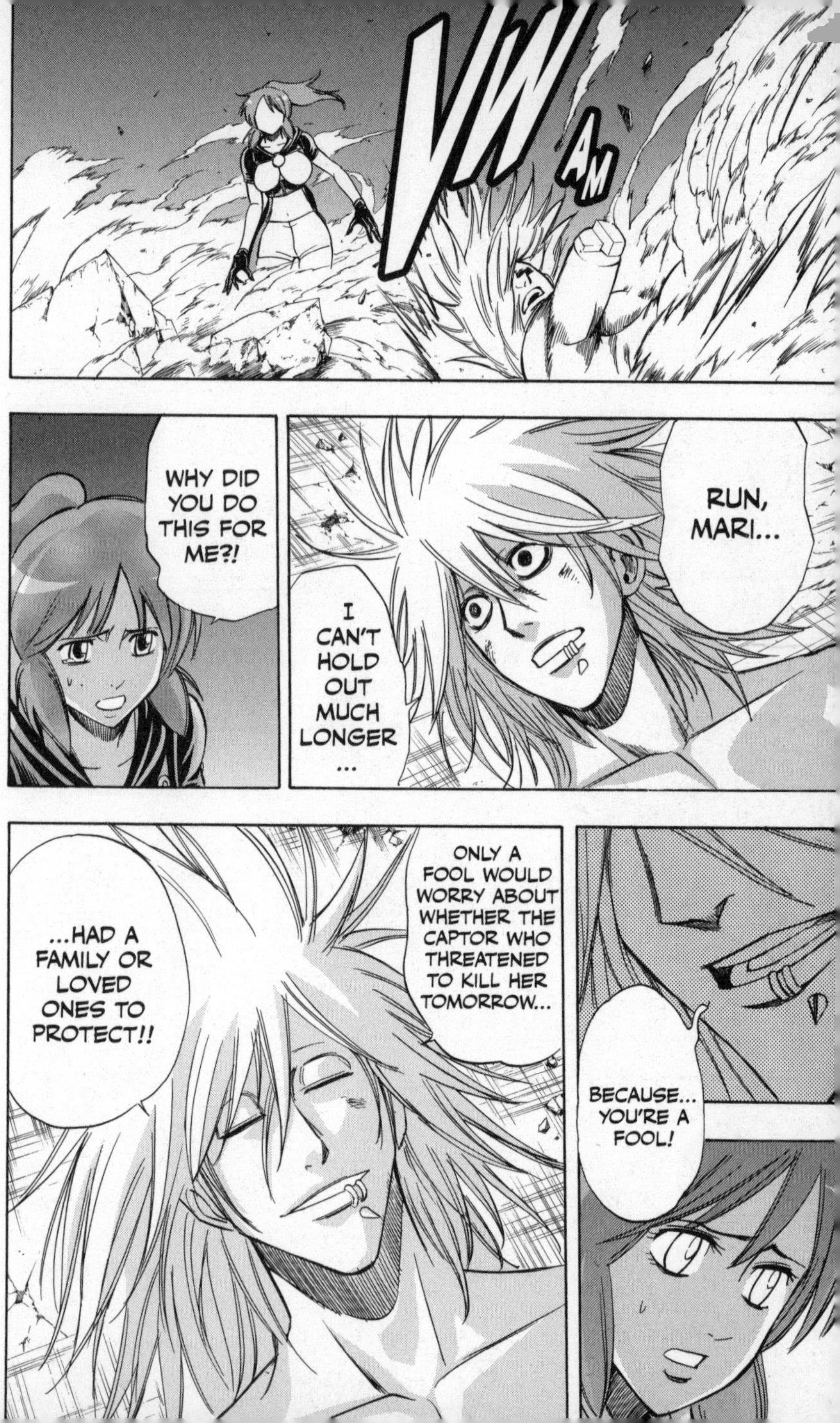
VWAM
RUN, MARI...
I CAN'T HOLD OUT MUCH LONGER...
WHY DID YOU DO THIS FOR ME?!
BECAUSE... YOU'RE A FOOL!
ONLY A FOOL WOULD WORRY ABOUT WHETHER THE CAPTOR WHO THREATENED TO KILL HER TOMORROW...
...HAD A FAMILY OR LOVED ONES TO PROTECT!!

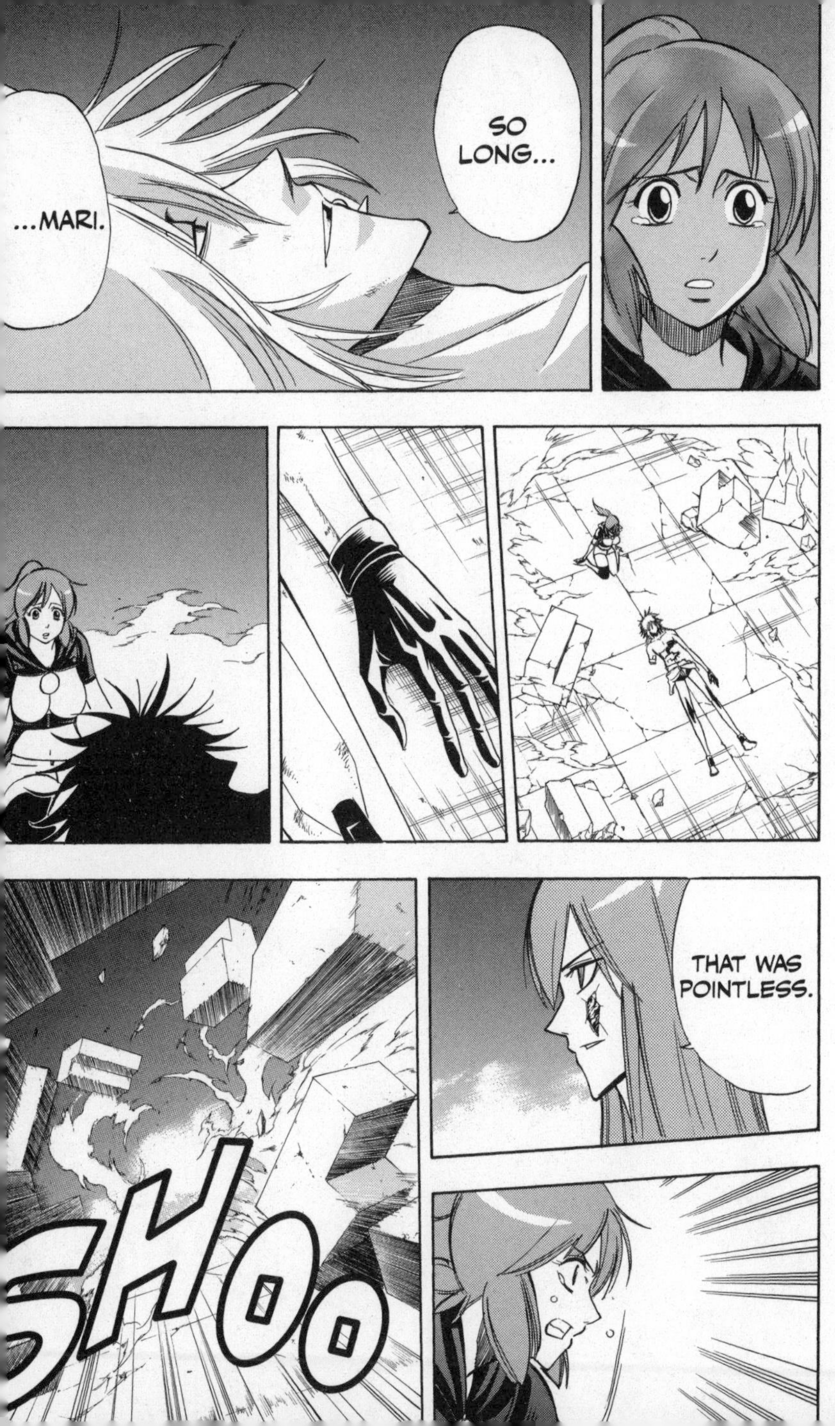
SO LONG...
...MARI.
THAT WAS POINTLESS.
SHOO

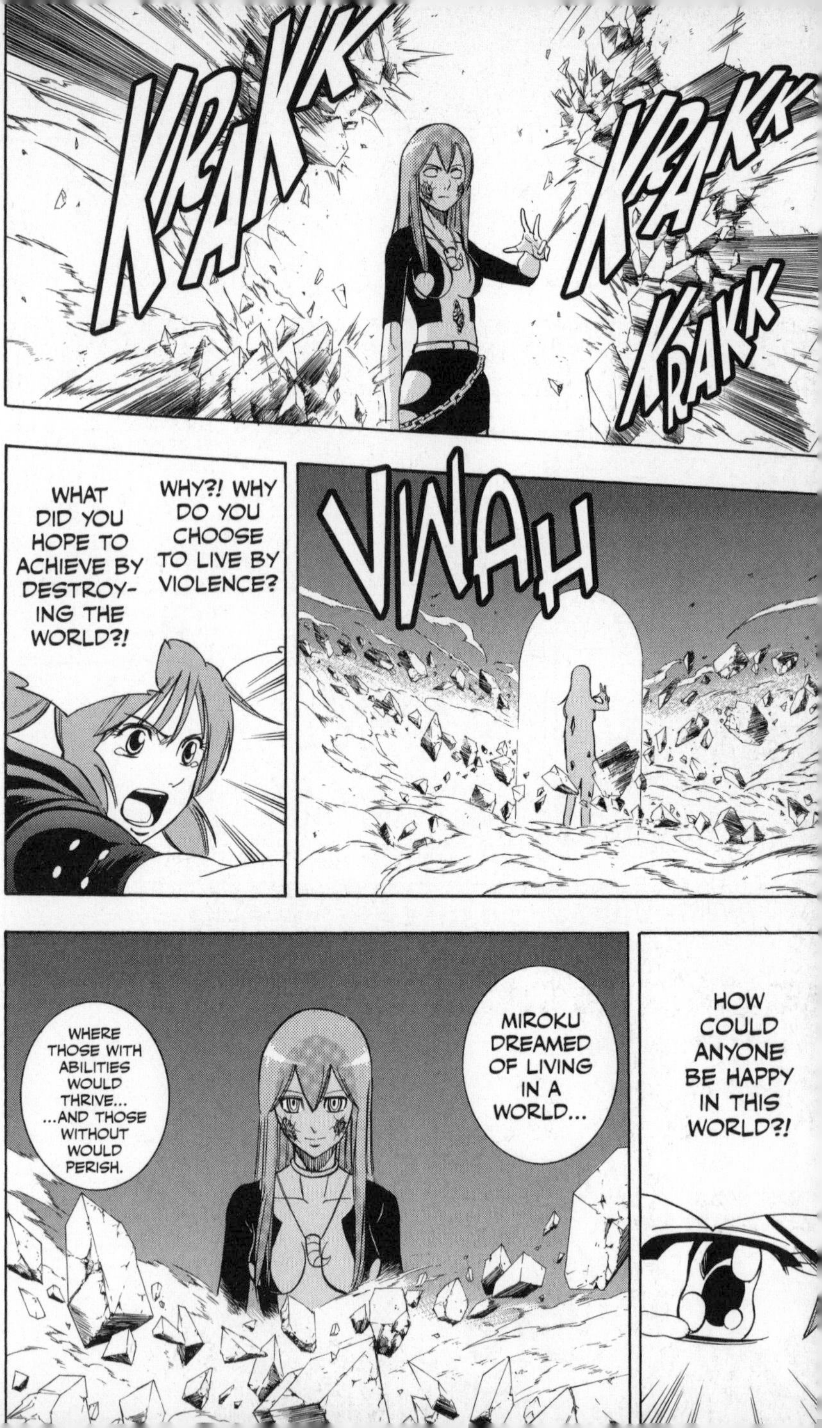
KRAKK
KRAKK
KRAKK
VWAH
WHY?! WHY DO YOU CHOOSE TO LIVE BY VIOLENCE?
WHAT DID YOU HOPE TO ACHIEVE BY DESTROY-ING THE WORLD?!
HOW COULD ANYONE BE HAPPY IN THIS WORLD?!
MIROKU DREAMED OF LIVING IN A WORLD...
WHERE THOSE WITH ABILITIES WOULD THRIVE... ...AND THOSE WITHOUT WOULD PERISH.

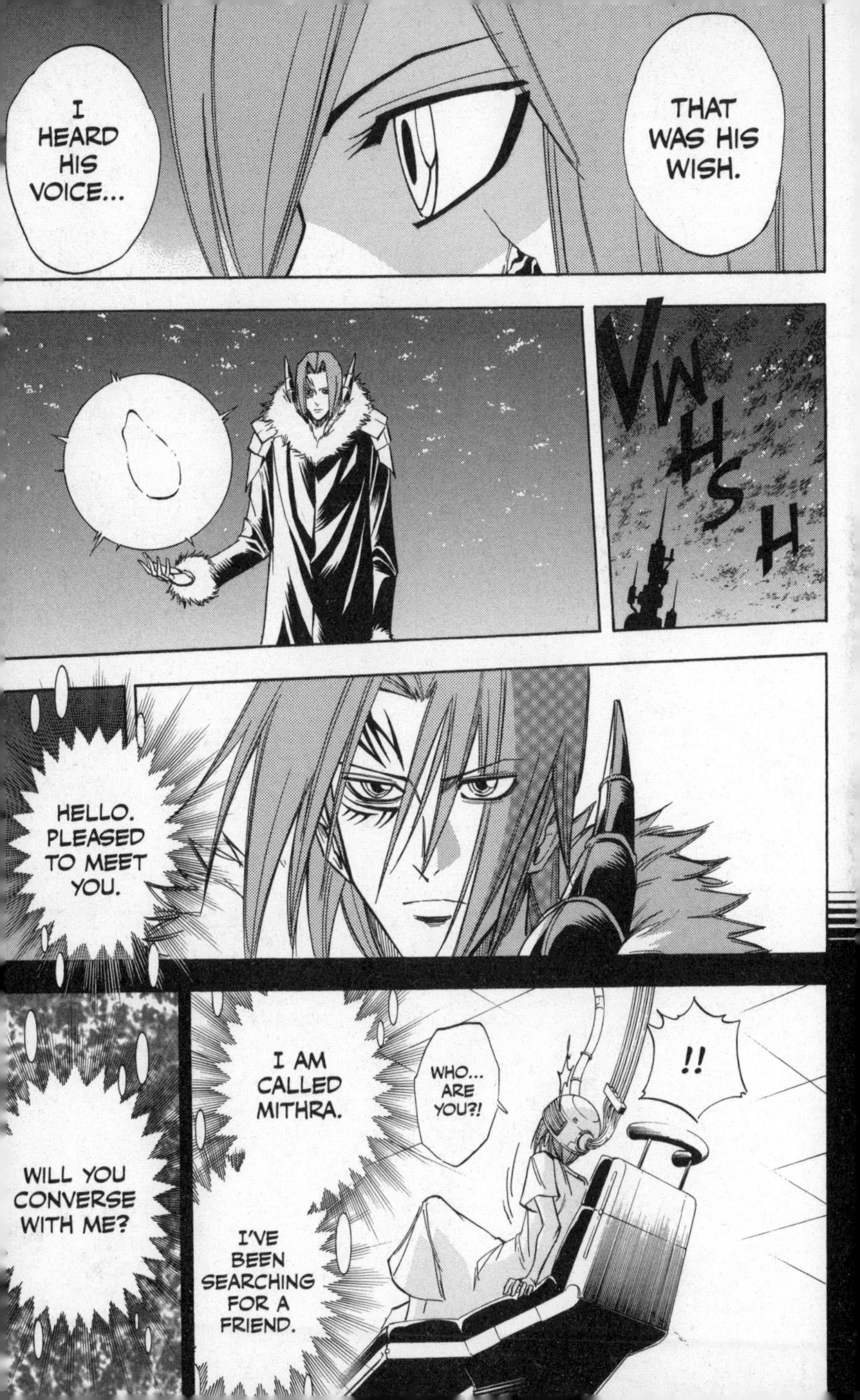
THAT WAS HIS WISH.
I HEARD HIS VOICE...
VWHSH
HELLO. PLEASED TO MEET YOU.
!!
WHO... ARE YOU?!
I AM CALLED MITHRA.
I'VE BEEN SEARCHING FOR A FRIEND.
WILL YOU CONVERSE WITH ME?

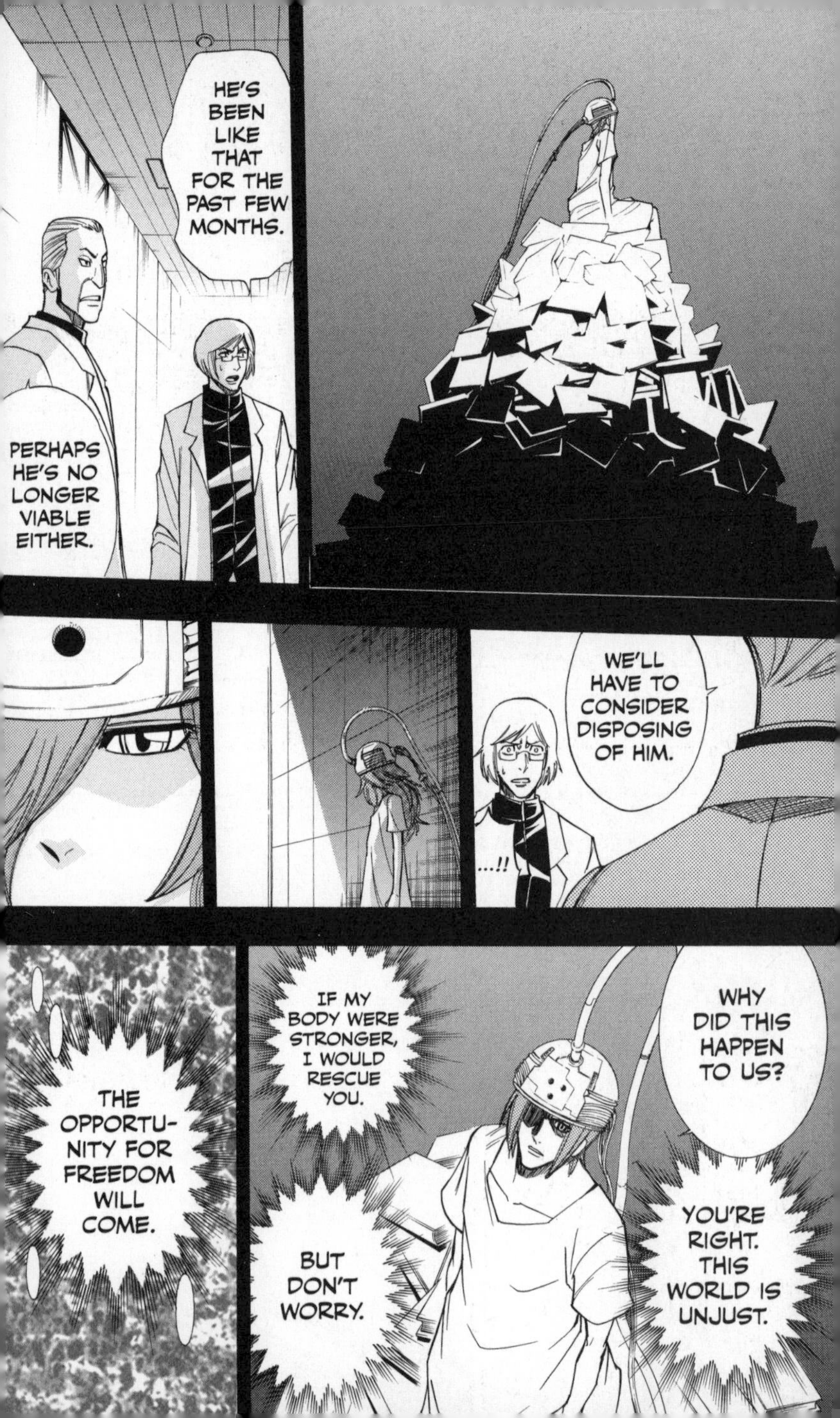
HE'S BEEN LIKE THAT FOR THE PAST FEW MONTHS.
PERHAPS HE'S NO LONGER VIABLE EITHER.
WE'LL HAVE TO CONSIDER DISPOSING OF HIM.
...!!
WHY DID THIS HAPPEN TO US?
YOU'RE RIGHT. THIS WORLD IS UNJUST.
IF MY BODY WERE STRONGER, I WOULD RESCUE YOU.
BUT DON'T WORRY.
THE OPPORTU-NITY FOR FREEDOM WILL COME.

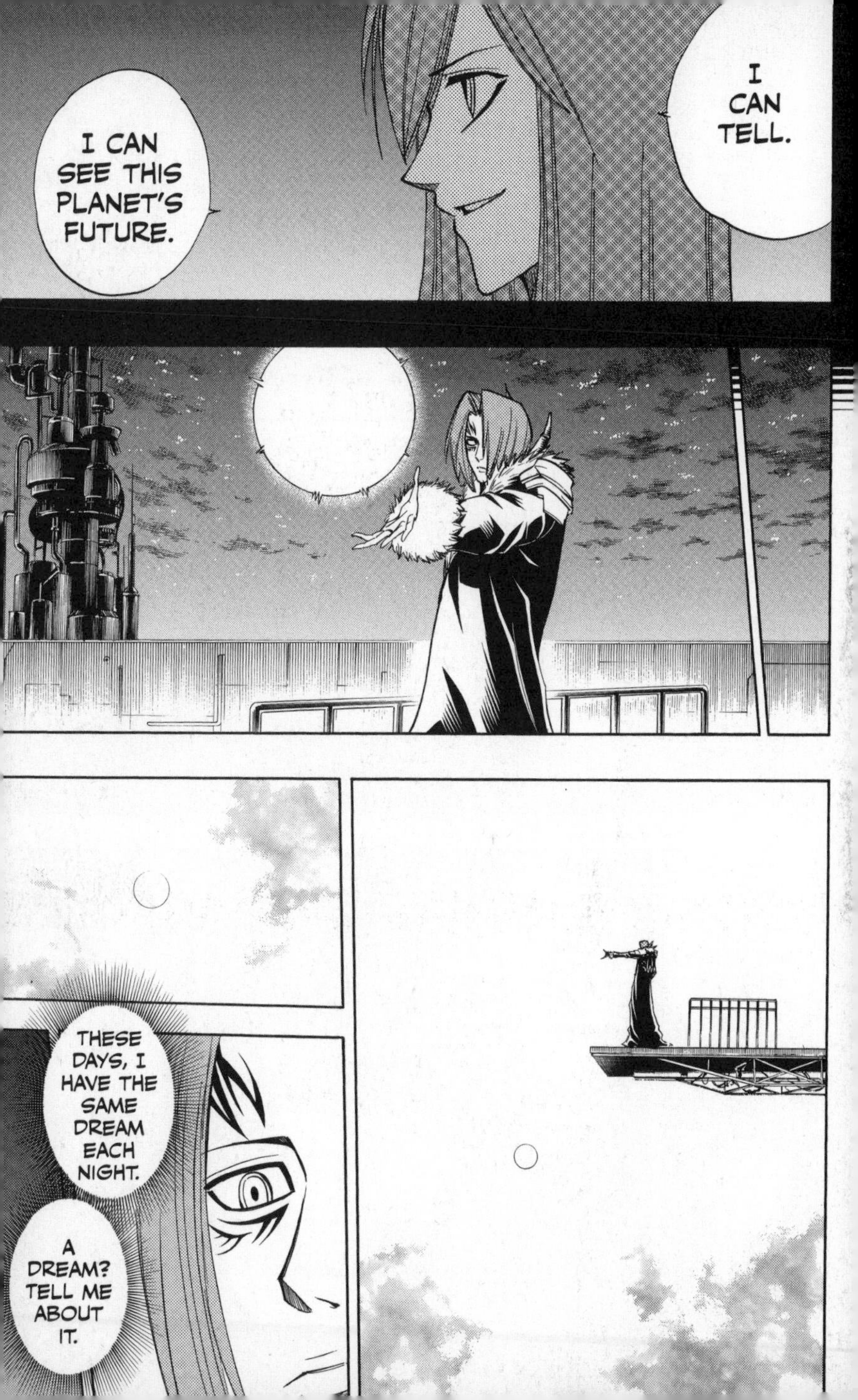
I CAN TELL.
I CAN SEE THIS PLANET'S FUTURE.
THESE DAYS, I HAVE THE SAME DREAM EACH NIGHT.
A DREAM? TELL ME ABOUT IT.

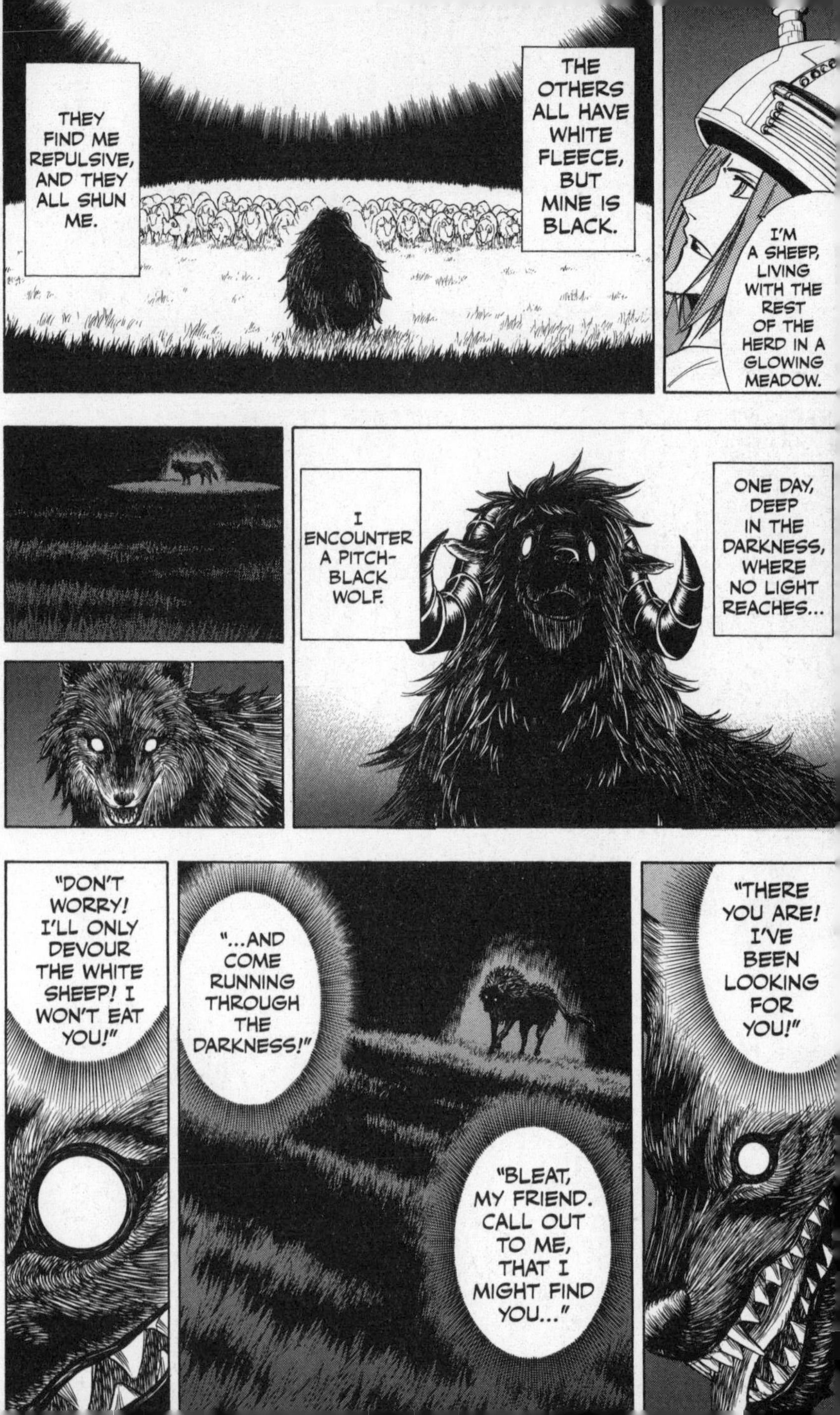
I'M A SHEEP, LIVING WITH THE REST OF THE HERD IN A GLOWING MEADOW.
THE OTHERS ALL HAVE WHITE FLEECE, BUT MINE IS BLACK.
THEY FIND ME REPULSIVE, AND THEY ALL SHUN ME.
ONE DAY, DEEP IN THE DARKNESS, WHERE NO LIGHT REACHES...
I ENCOUNTER A PITCH-BLACK WOLF.
"THERE YOU ARE! I'VE BEEN LOOKING FOR YOU!"
"BLEAT, MY FRIEND. CALL OUT TO ME, THAT I MIGHT FIND YOU..."
"...AND COME RUNNING THROUGH THE DARKNESS!"
"DON'T WORRY! I'LL ONLY DEVOUR THE WHITE SHEEP! I WON'T EAT YOU!"

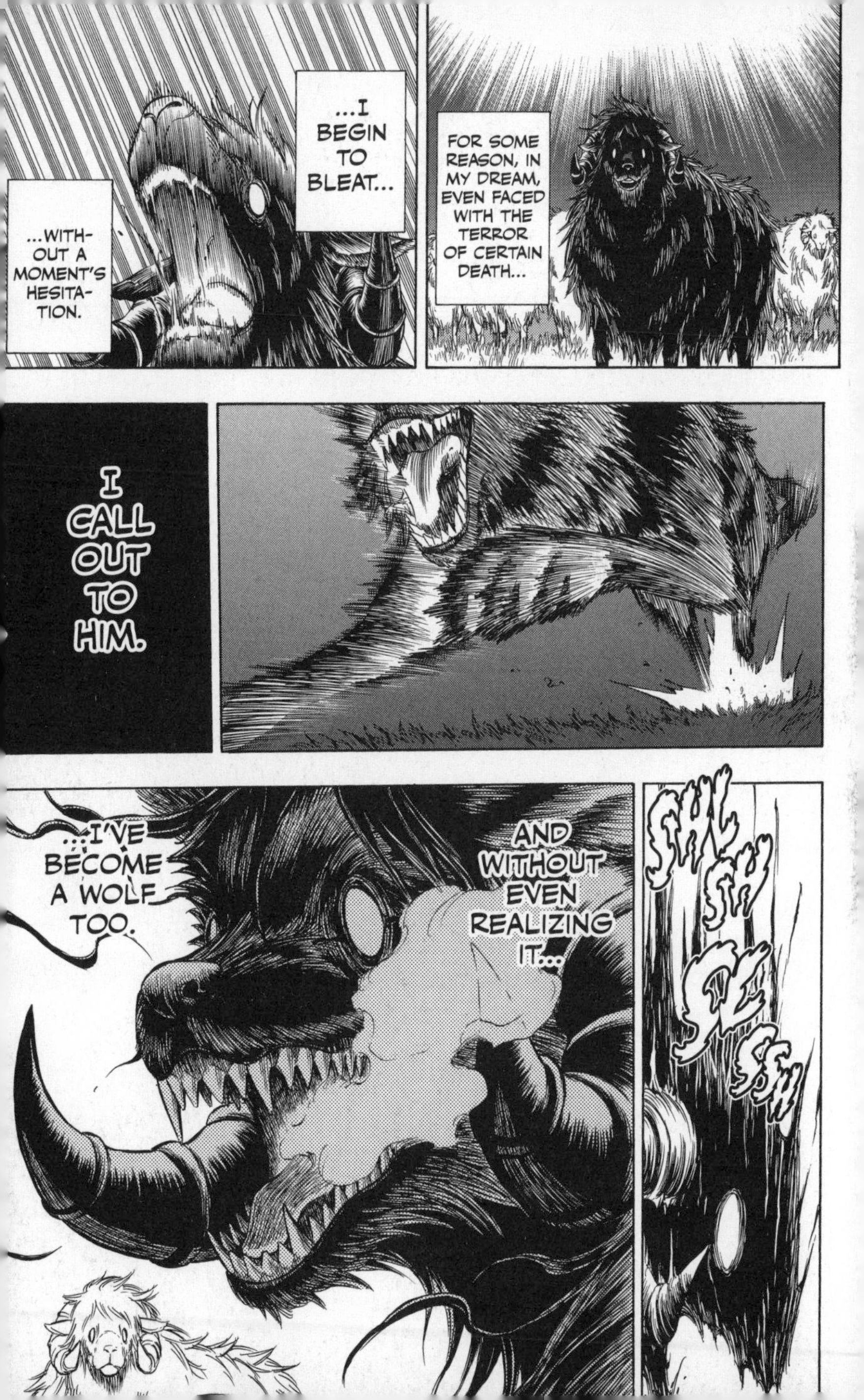
FOR SOME REASON, IN MY DREAM, EVEN FACED WITH THE TERROR OF CERTAIN DEATH...
...I BEGIN TO BLEAT...
...WITH-OUT A MOMENT'S HESITA-TION.
I CALL OUT TO HIM.
AND WITHOUT EVEN REALIZING IT...
...I'VE BECOME A WOLF TOO.

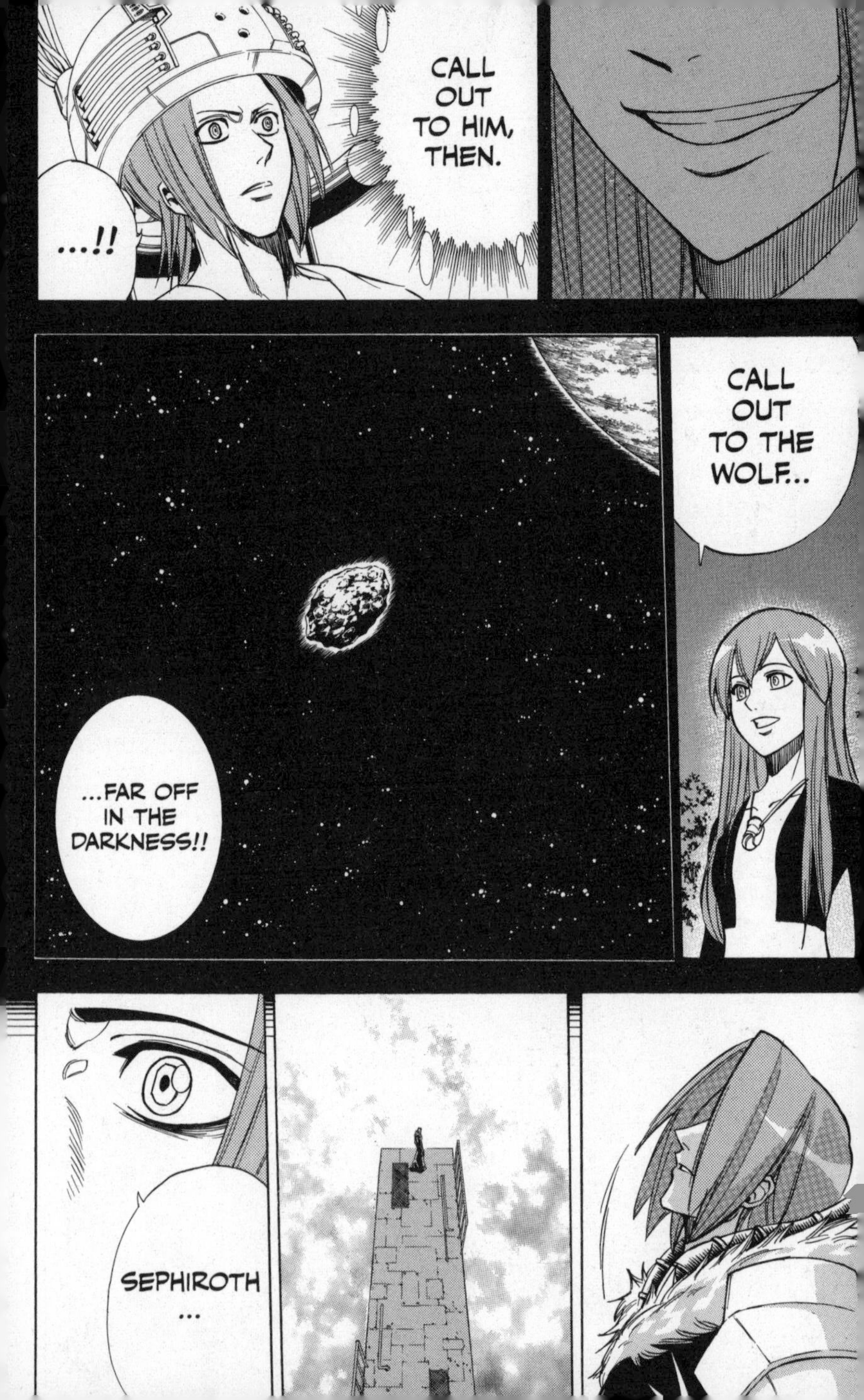
CALL OUT TO HIM, THEN.
...!!
CALL OUT TO THE WOLF...
...FAR OFF IN THE DARKNESS!!
SEPHIROTH ...

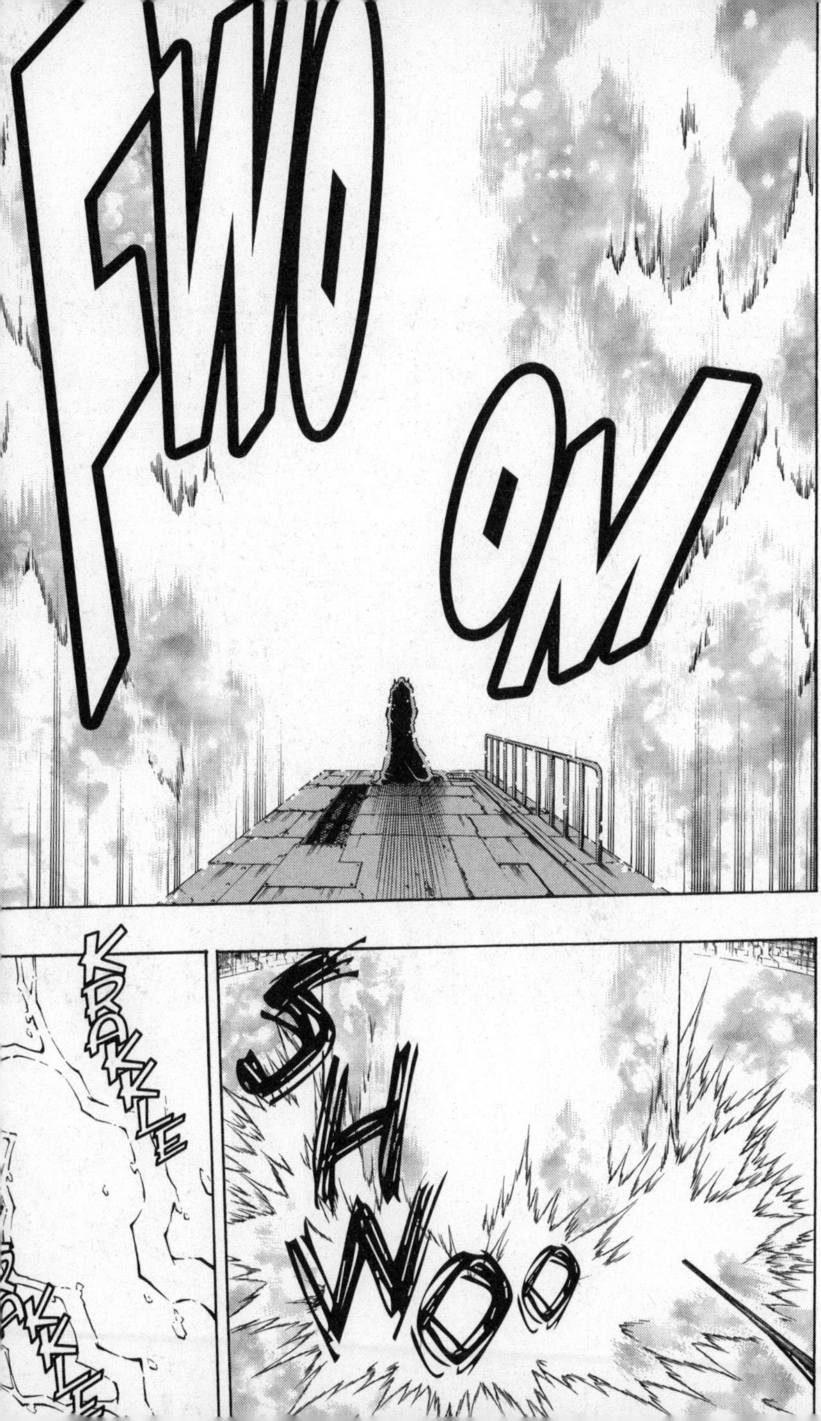
FWOOM
SHWOO
KRKKLE

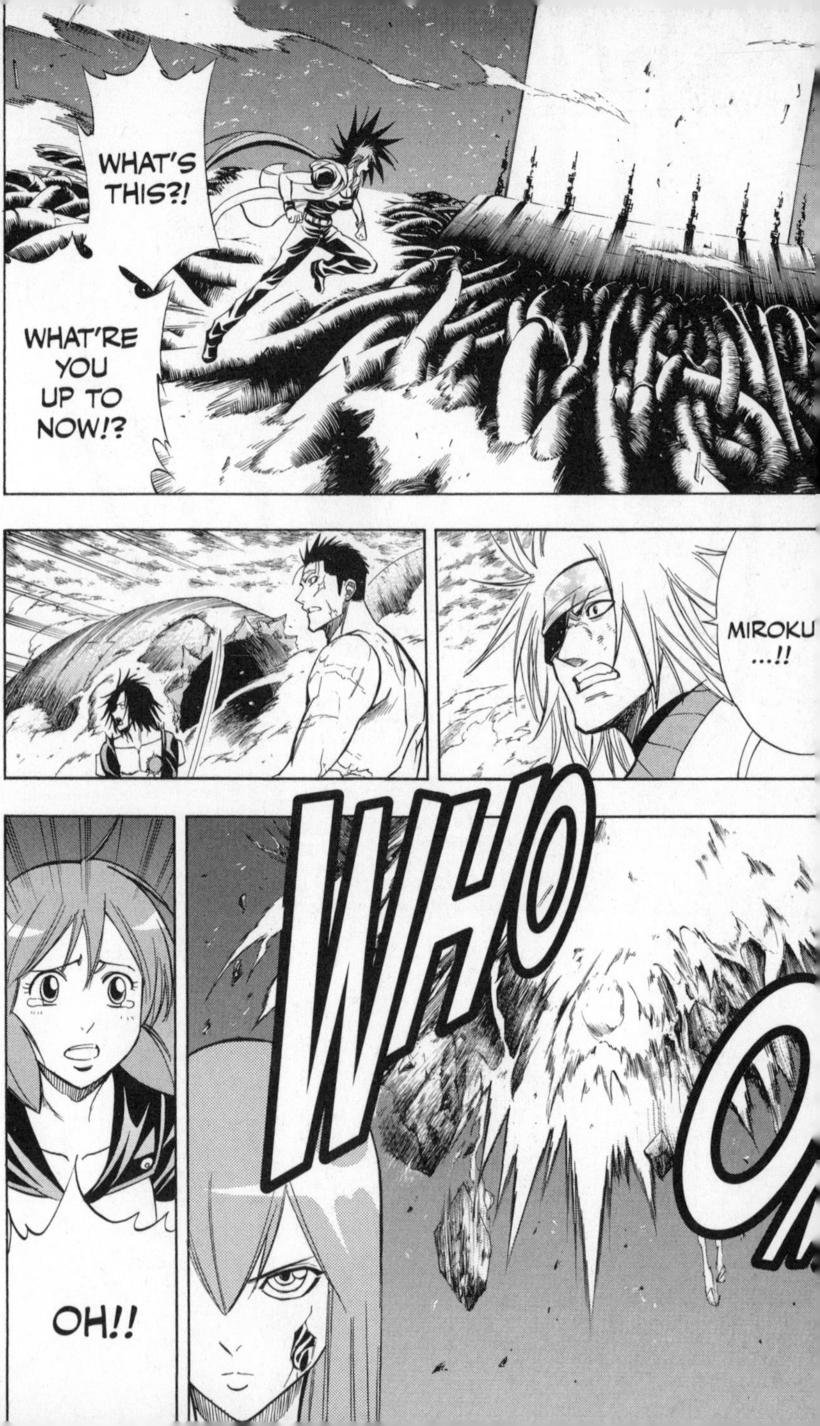
WHAT'S THIS?!
WHAT'RE YOU UP TO NOW!?
MIROKU ...!!
WHOOOH!!

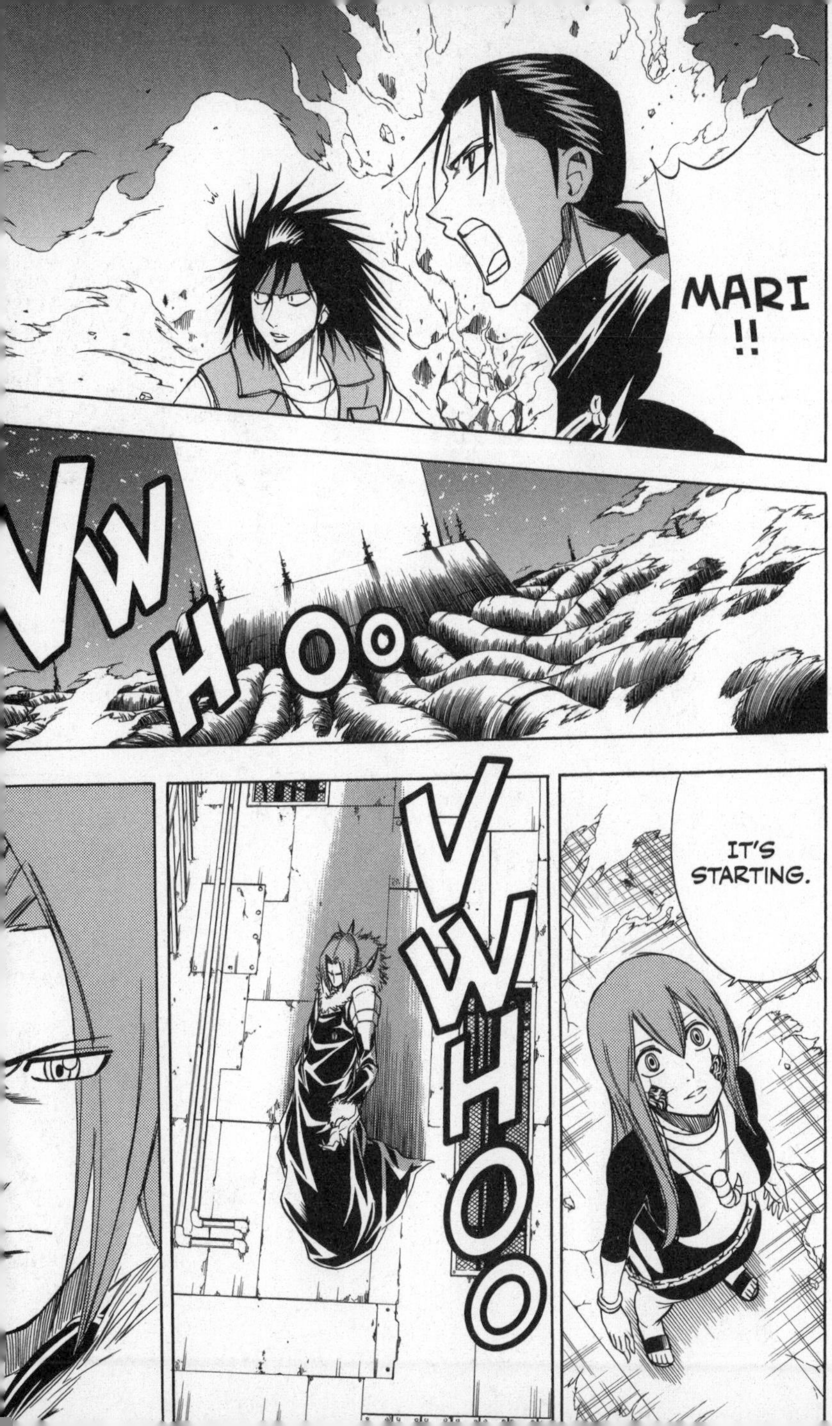
MARI !!
VWHOO
IT'S STARTING.
VWHOOO

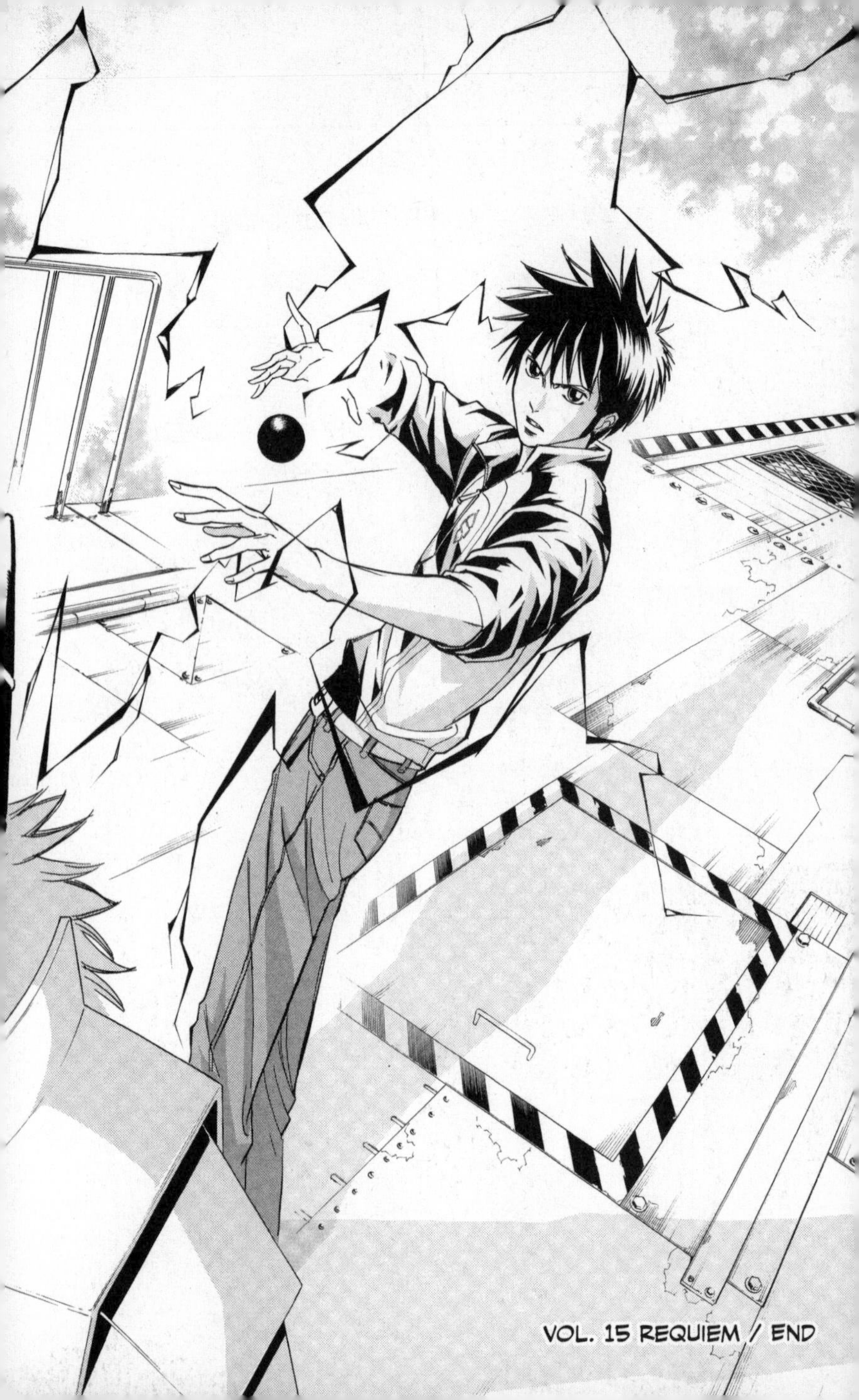
VOL. 15 REQUIEM / END